WHY WRITE WHEN YOU CAN

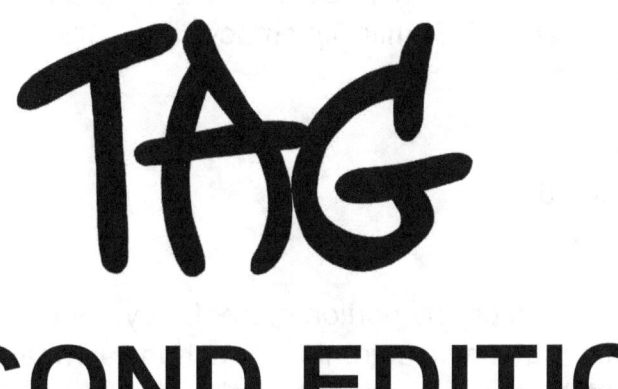

SECOND EDITION

LEARN TO DRAW THE BEST GRAFFITI TAGS EVER!

By Graffiti Diplomacy
Brooklyn, New York

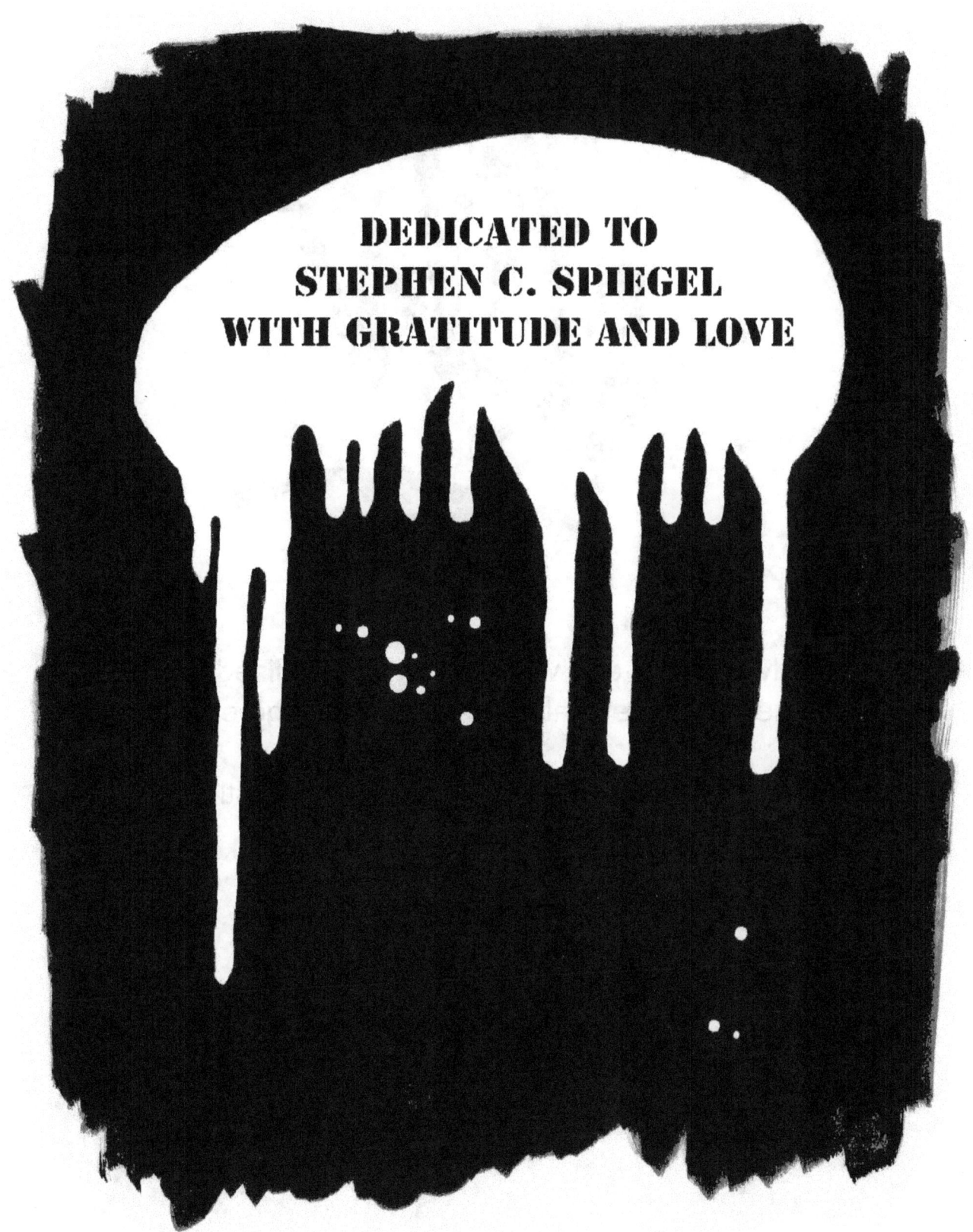

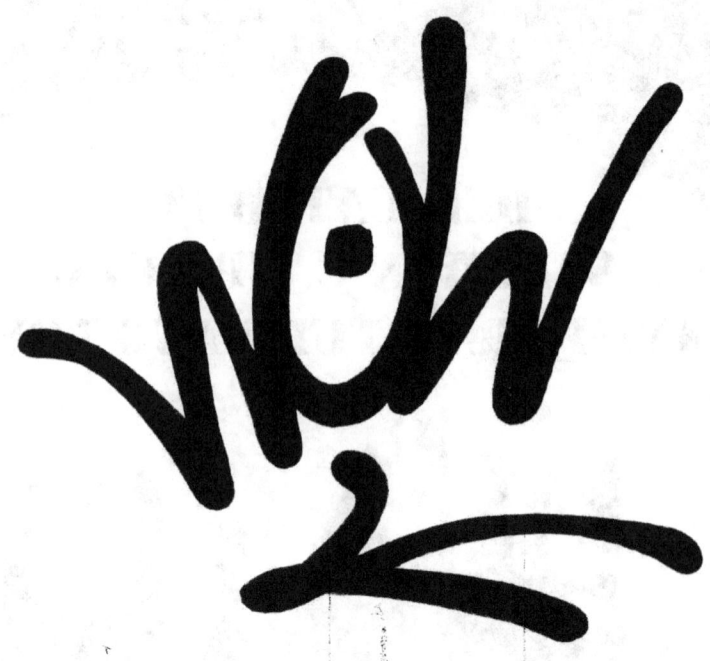

"A tag generally consists of a writer's name in stylized letters that are gathered together somewhat in the style of a logo or monogram."

- From the book "Getting Up" by Craig Castleman

TABLE OF CONTENTS

ABOUT THIS BOOK

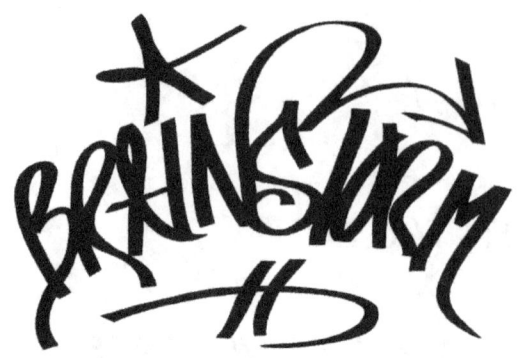

I've always been fascinated with the term urban jungle. But it wasn't until I attended the High School of Music and Art in upper Manhattan that I understood what the term really meant. It took a bus and three trains to get me and my best friend from our quiet neighborhood in southern Brooklyn all the way uptown to the base of the stairs in the park at 135th Street and St. Nicholas avenue. At the top of those crazy, steep stairs stood our school, an imposing, Gothic-style stone structure, complete with towers and gargoyles. The only way to get there was to climb up those stairs, and so, up we trudged every morning. I must admit the park was beautiful in winter, so cold and stark. There were lots of big, gray boulders to sit on and procrastinate on the way up. We always tried to come up with excuses for why we should turn around and go home, but of course there weren't any good ones, and so up we went. I can still see my smoky breath hanging in the crisp, frosty air.

What burned that trip to Harlem in my mind so indelibly were the gazillions of graffiti tags. They were everywhere. On the insides of trains, on the outsides, on the stations, on the street lights, on buildings, in doorways, in notebooks, and on jackets. Just about everywhere I looked, they were there, a tangled mass of scribbles, like vines in a jungle. At that time I didn't understand tags at all. I thought they were kind of weird and ugly. But I didn't mind them either. They were wild and untamed, an extraordinary feature of the colorful yet unfamiliar terrain of upper Manhattan. It was exotic. I liked it a lot to tell you the truth. Sometimes those tags reminded me of primitive cave drawings or Egyptian hieroglyphics. Eventually, I got so used to seeing them that I began to ignore them completely. But I never quite got them out of my head.

Fast forward to the year 2000. One day I was standing on a subway platform waiting for a D train and staring absentmindedly at a tag scribbled on a station pole. I turned my head sideways and suddenly realized to my amazement that I could read what it said. I could make out letters. And a name of sorts. It was like a bolt of lightening hit me. My mind flashed back to all those crazy tags I'd seen on my way to school all those years ago. I finally understood what it all meant. The tags were names. Nicknames mostly. Or aliases. How could I have missed it? They were logos, identifying markers, messages to anyone who saw them, a statement, a visual record of someone's having passed through that spot if only for a second or two at some point in the past. It made perfect sense now. What a revelation. It was epic!

From that point on I set out to learn everything I could about graffiti tagging. I bought books. I researched everything I could find on the subject which wasn't much at that time. I studied the tags I saw around the city and took thousands of photographs. Eventually, I taught myself to draw graffiti lettering and tags. I didn't know any graffiti artists back then, so it took a long time to learn. Graffiti was and still is kind of a secret art form. My best friend was fascinated by what I was doing and wanted to learn, so I taught him and he got hooked, too. Together we built our website, Graffiti Diplomacy, and wrote our first book "Learn To Draw a Graffiti Master-Piece" which has sold many thousands of copies worldwide. Go Figure!

This is our second book. The focus of this book is on graffiti tagging only. This book will teach you how to tag. It demonstrates in detail the techniques that we use to design our tags. It's not the be-all and end-all of graffiti tagging books, it's just the methods that work for us. If you follow the instructions in this book, you will learn to create a respectable graffiti tag. Through the repeated process of drawing tag letters and alphabets, you will learn to read graffiti tags, too. That's important. Reading a tag is kind of like unraveling a secret code or solving a puzzle. My sister Jill refers to deciphering a tag as "visually unwrapping it". That's a great metaphor. There are still some tags I just can't read even after all this time. I print them out, hang them up in my studio, and stare at them endlessly. They are hypnotic, dense, captivating.

The ultimate goal of a graffiti artist or writer (more on that later) is to design a tag that has style. Style is that magic something or other that makes a tag flow. It's like rhythm in a piece of great music. Style is not something we can teach you. It is a quality you will have to develop yourself over time with lots of practice and patience. And just so you know, we are only interested in legal tagging here. That means only writing tags where you have permission. We want to be really clear about that. This book was created to present graffiti tagging as an art form only.

And it really is a great art form, full of expression and creativity. I totally love designing new tags, even if I feel like pulling my hair out sometimes. Tags are a real challenge. I never know where I am going to end up and the finished tag is always a surprise. Obviously not every tag is a great work of art just like not every painting is a masterpiece. But a well-designed graffiti tag becomes a kind of glyph, an ornament, a symbol or character that identifies and distinguishes you. It's like a logo or a brand. It's brand "YOU".

I have come to appreciate and view graffiti tagging as a high art form, just like Calligraphy. Not everyone gets it right away. Some people never get it at all and that's okay, too. But if you love graffiti tagging and want to learn to design your own tags, this book will show you the way. I often hear people argue about whether or not graffiti, especially tagging, can ever be considered art at all. I believe it is as much an art as drawing, painting or sculpture. A well-designed graffiti tag evolves over time. As you modify it, refine it, apply it, and live with it, you ultimately come to cherish it, like a precious gemstone. A well-designed graffiti tag is just that special! Yup!

Essentially a graffiti tag is a signature. It is a nickname or alias that you pick for yourself. Your tag becomes your identity and your logo. A graffiti tag is written or drawn in a similar way that you sign your name. Therefore traditional graffiti taggers call themselves writers.

What sets graffiti tagging apart from other types of writing is a unique form of lettering style known as Tag Style. Tag style letters are drawn freehand and have lots of movement and energy. A graffiti writer's personal style of writing is referred to as his or her handstyle. Handstyle communicates not only the name of a writer, but also the writer's individual style. Just as all people differ in their appearances and personalities, so too their handstyles vary and are unique.

This is a photograph of a great "BASH" tag seen on a wall near 5 Pointz, the outdoor graffiti museum that <u>was</u> located in Queens, New York. We really love the style of the tag letters used here: the exclamation marks, the curlicue extension on the "B" and the oval or halo over the "A". This tag demonstrates great handstyle.

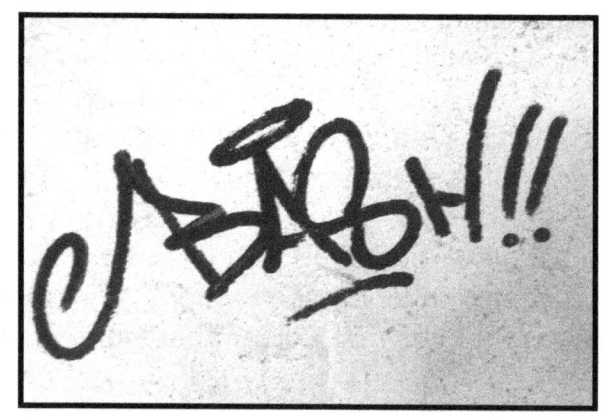

Many different styles of tag letters and alphabets were invented by graffiti writers in the 1960's and 1970's with different regions of the United States becoming known for their own particular styles. Christian Acker's book "Flip The Script" is an excellent place for you to get educated on tagging history and letter development from different time periods and regions of the country. We will refer back to "Flip the Script" frequently, as it is very informative and the best resource on graffiti tagging available. It is an amazing book and we highly recommend it.

Here is another great tag from the sidewalk at 5 Pointz. Graffiti tags are always challenging to decipher. This one appears to say "WISE 2", but unless you know the writer it's always a guessing game. That's one of the best things about a graffiti tag - it's a puzzle you just have to solve. We will take this tag apart and examine it further in Chapter Seven.

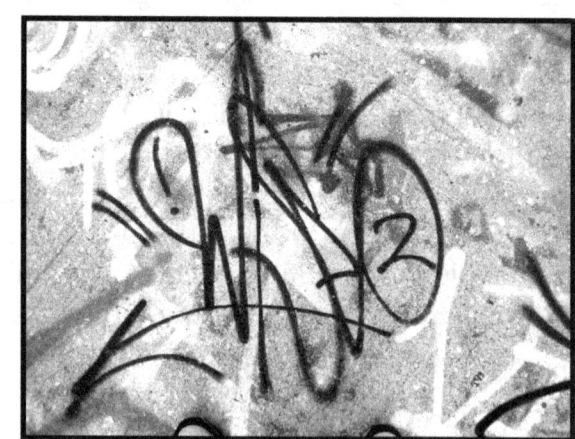

Because tag letters are drawn free-hand, a finished tag has a living quality. Tags don't contain stiff lines drawn with a ruler. Movement and action are the foundations of tagging. Tags are expressive and communicate emotions just like any other type of art.

Here is a basic tag alphabet. Notice that the letters don't look uniform like a typeface because they are hand-drawn. Through the repetition of copying tag alphabets like this one, you will become familiar and comfortable with drawing tag letters of your own. Eventually, you will develop your own handstyle.

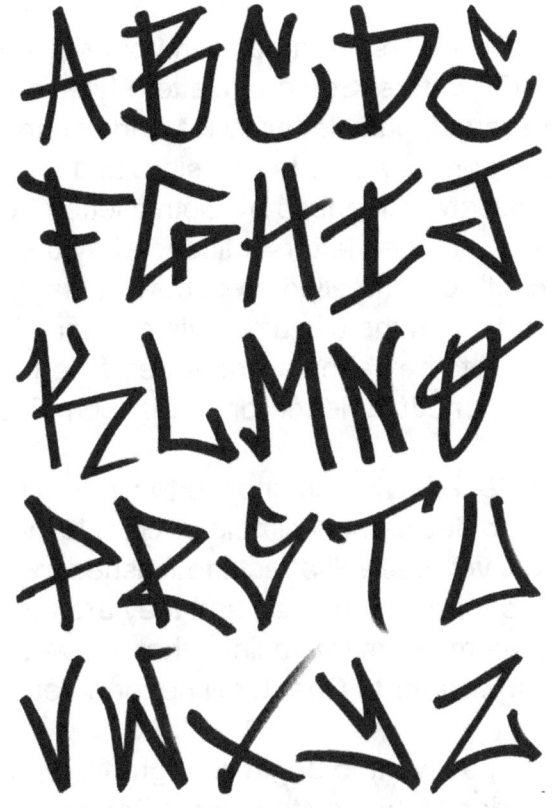

The tag letter handstyle in this "RESPECT" tag below is called Backslanting because the letters lean way back toward the left. You can also lean your letters over to the right.

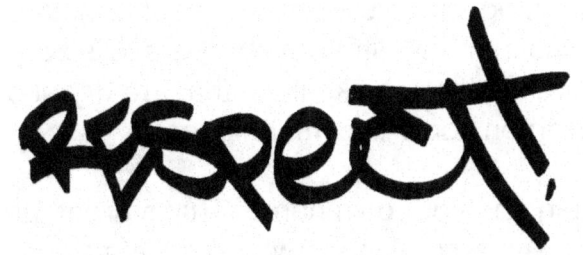

Some writers combine the letters in their tag name with a character of some type. One of the most famous examples of this style of tagging was created by graffiti writer "Stay High 149" who placed a stick figure in various poses alongside his letters. Other writers sometimes use a character to substitute for letters, such as the bear claw created by graffiti artist "Claw Money", or the evil bunny created by graffiti artist "Pure Evil".

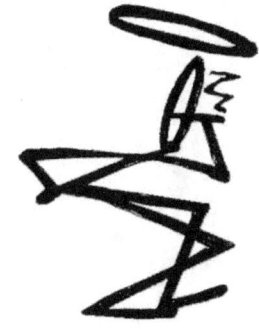
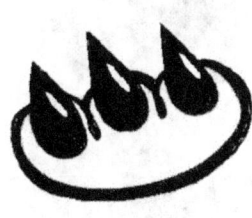
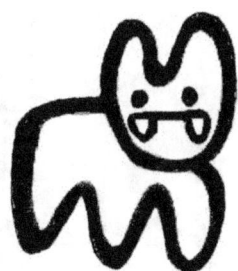

STAY HIGH 149   CLAW MONEY   PURE EVIL

In his introduction to "Flip the Script" Christian Acker writes "A decent handstyle is an essential skill in the arsenal of artists and designers". Even people who don't necessarily like graffiti are amazed and delighted by the handstyle displayed in a well-executed tag. Designing a graffiti tag offers you an excellent opportunity to sharpen your creative problem-solving skills and improve your drawing ability.

When you first start out with your tag letter training you will be imitating the styles of other graffiti writers. Some tag letter styles are easy to read and some are almost illegible. There are round, curly letter styles and square, boxy letter styles. There are very angular letters that lean way over to one side, and tall, skinny letters with rounded bottoms. Some letter styles are influenced by Gothic letters reminiscent of the Middle Ages. Others look like fancy, scripted letters influenced by the Renaissance. Once again you can refer to "Flip the Script" for a detailed breakdown of tagging styles by region. Christian Acker writes "Depending on the city and style of origin, intentions change. In some, tags are individual and meant to be seen as signatures or logos, while other cities have a much more regimented use of modular letter forms that combine for any number of words or phrases."

The letter style you choose to begin a tag design is simply a starting point. It will be up to you to decide how simple or complex you want your finished tag to be. Also, the writing tools you use will affect the finished look of your tag. Magic markers are the most popular tools for drawing a tag and they are available with tips in many different shapes and sizes. Some markers make lines that are wet and drippy while others make lines that are dry and sharp. Refer to Chapter Nine for a detailed discussion on Tools and Techniques.

You may want to begin your graffiti tag training by tagging your own name. That's great, but you don't have to stop there. Once you have gained some confidence why not try tagging different words and phrases. Try tagging in a foreign language. Some of the best tags out there are based on Arabic or Japanese lettering. You might even try adding a simple character like STAY HIGH 149's stick figure. The keys that unlock the door to successful graffiti tagging are practice, repetition, and time. You need to give your tag time to evolve.

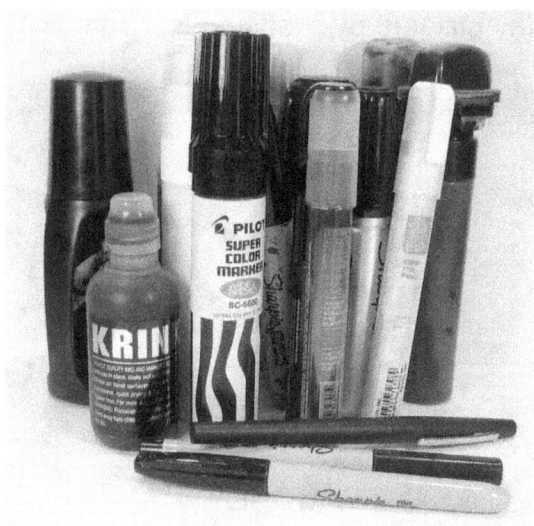

Assorted Marker Brands

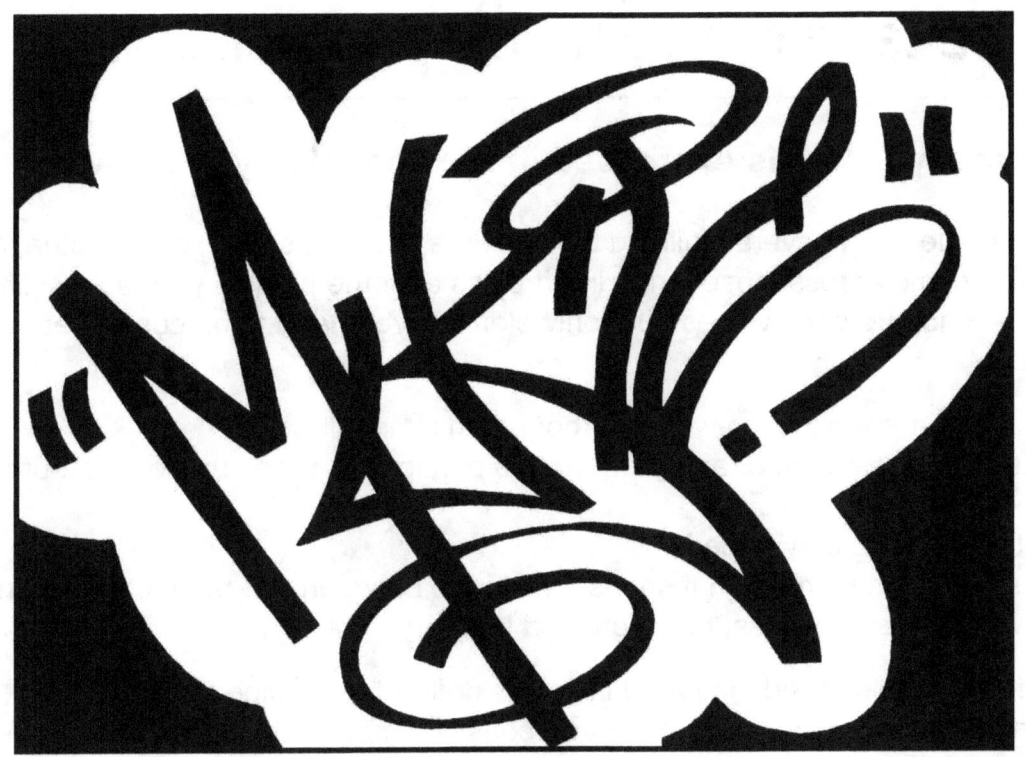

Can you read this tag? It says "M-U-S-I-C".
Each individual letter is shown below.

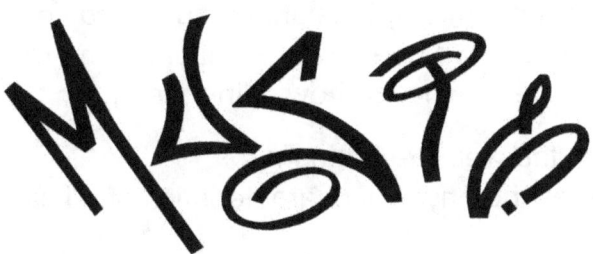

"For those who learn to read tags, a world of aesthetic expression and communication opens up. Tags are a universal language, the jazz of lettering".

-From the book "Tag Town" by Martha cooper

CHAPTER TWO
DESCRIPTIVE AND EXPRESSIVE LINES

The way that you feel is expressed in the lines that you draw

A picture is made up of several building blocks - line, texture, shape, color, value, and form. You probably came across those terms in art class at some point in your school life. But a graffiti tag is made up of only lines. The only element you need to be concerned with at this time is a line.

The definition of a line from the website About.com is as follows:
•   A line is a basic element of art, referring to a continuous mark, made on a surface, by a moving point.
The definition of a line on Wikipedia is:
•   A line is defined as a mark that spans a distance between two points, taking any form along the way. It has thickness, direction, and length.

Art made from lines is called Line art. Line art is defined on Wikipedia as:
•   Line art or line drawing is any image that consists of distinct straight and curved lines placed against a (usually plain) background.

Graffiti tagging would definitely fall into the category of line art because tags are made up of letters which are drawn with lines. But a graffiti tag is more than just the lines that are used to construct it. A tag contains momentum, tension, balance and communicates emotions. Therefore to fully understand tags, we need two definitions. One for descriptive lines (how a line looks) and another for expressive lines (how a line feels).

Here are the definitions from the website Ask.com:
•   A descriptive line describes the physical characteristics of a line, such as thin, thick, curvy or straight.
•   An expressive line is a kind of line that seems to directly spring from the artist's emotions or feelings - gestural, loose, and energetic.

Here are some terms that describe the expressive qualities of different kinds of lines. Lines that are BOLD and THICK appear AGGRESSIVE and STRONG. THIN lines are DELICATE and FRAGILE. STRAIGHT lines often create a sense of BALANCE. SPIRAL lines create the appearance of RHYTHM and MOTION. CURVING lines suggest GRACEFULNESS. JAGGED, ZIG-ZAGGING lines appear ENERGETIC, EXPLOSIVE, and DRAMATIC.

So tags are made up of letters that communicate emotions using descriptive and expressive lines. Pretty simple.

This little tag says FREE. It's a great example of expressive line drawing. The letters look like they are flying off the end of the word and escaping.

Here's a short story about line art. Several years ago we attended a retrospective of the Impressionist artist, Henri Mattisse at the Museum of Modern Art. Impressionism is a style of painting in which the artist uses loose, undefined brush strokes to capture the image of an object or person. The exhibit stretched out in an endless chain of galleries, overflowing with giant, colorful canvases. It recorded Matisse's life and work in chronological order. At the very end there was this strange looking picture. It was composed of a few black lines depicting a crudely drawn outline of a woman's body, surrounded by three orange circles and some green, leafy shapes. It was appropriately called "Nude with Oranges". The drawing of the woman's body was startling with its severe, black lines. We walked into that final room and - POW - there was that picture. It was amazing! We bought a postcard in the gift shop and it's been hanging up on the wall in our studio ever since.

How Henri Mattisse might have tagged his name.

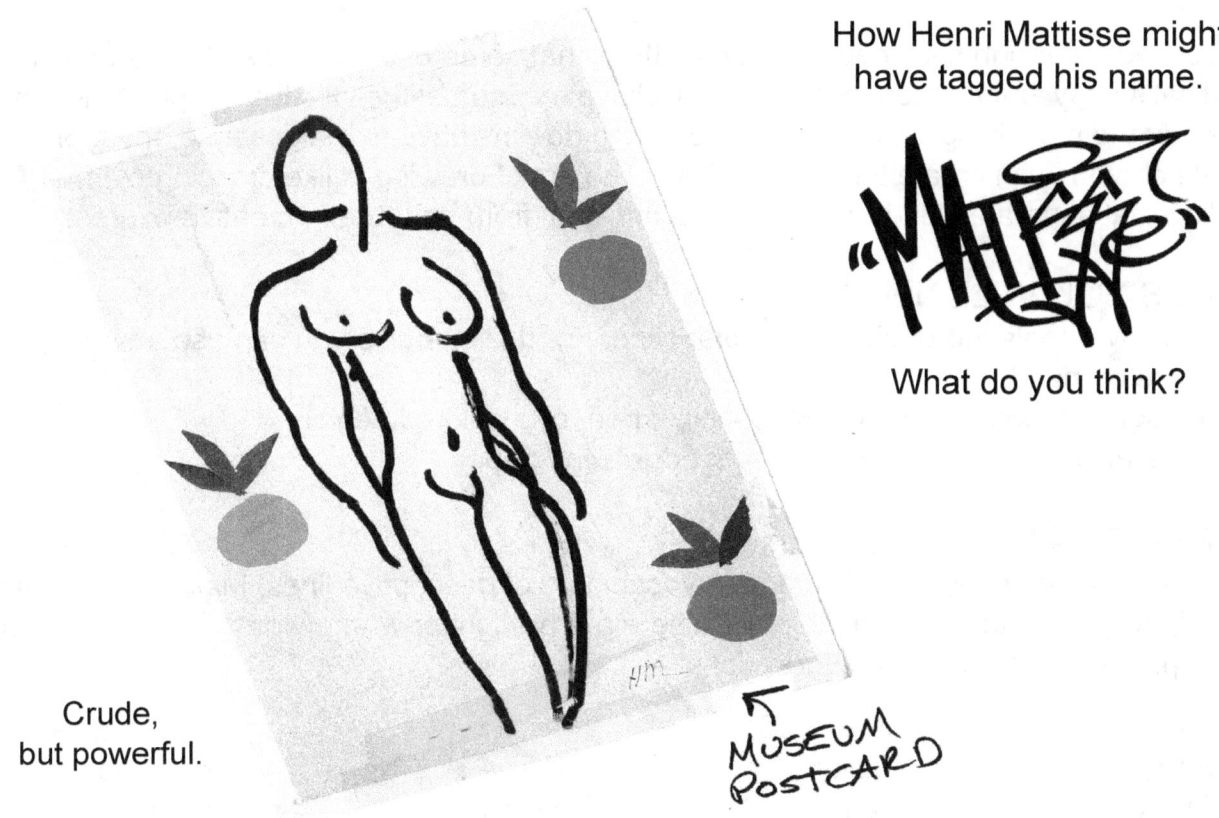

What do you think?

Crude,
but powerful.

MUSEUM
POSTCARD

Now that's a pretty simple drawing and we often wonder why it has such a strong impact. At the end of his life Matisse was confined to his bed where he still managed to create artwork by attaching his paintbrush to a really long pole and drawing on paper tacked up on the wall over his bed. That might explain why his final drawings were so minimal, just lines and simple shapes, but it doesn't explain why these art works held so much power.

We think the impact is in the simplicity of his lines. Lines are direct and expressive. Lines make a statement and are powerful. Clearly Matisse loved lines and understood how to use them in his art to communicate how he felt. So here's a rule for you to consider - the way that you feel is expressed in the lines that you draw.

DESCRIPTIVE AND EXPRESSIVE LINES

Imagination is the Key

Did you ever read the book "Harold and the Purple Crayon" when you were little? In a nutshell, armed with a giant, magic, purple crayon, Harold draws himself a whole world made from just some simple, purple lines. Basically, Harold draws a bunch of really fun stuff to play with and everything he draws comes to life. He has fantastic adventures, then he draws his bedroom, crawls into bed, draws up the covers (literally) and goes to sleep. The pictures are just lines without too much detail and there are large areas of white paper on most of the pages designed to emphasize Harold and everything he draws. The point of the story is that Harold's imagination is the key that unlocks the door to his creativity.

As you work through this chapter you may think that some of the exercises are a bit simplistic. That's okay, but try them out anyway. Believe me, sometimes it's the simple things that give you the most insight. And besides, drawing doesn't have to make sense any more than purple crayons can create things in real life. The act of drawing is like crossing over a magical line that separates left-brain, analytical thinking, from right-brain, creative expression.

TOOLS YOU WILL NEED
We will cover tools thoroughly in Chapter Nine. For this exercise you can use anything that you have on hand:
* a magic marker, a crayon, a #2 pencil, a pen, or a colored pencil
* Several sheets of cheap copy paper or drawing paper

EXERCISE #1: Descriptive Lines
The first thing we need to do is create a vocabulary of descriptive lines. Make a list of all the descriptive words that you can think of. There are no right or wrong words. Just think about descriptions. Here are some suggestions:

• Straight	• Fancy	• Furry	• Energetic
• Curvy	• Dark	• Spiral	• Broken
• Hard	• Horizontal	• Fast	• Tall
• Soft	• Vertical	• Slow	• Thin
• Thick	• Diagonal	• Explosive	• Radiating
• Branching	• Dotted	• Zig-Zag	• Quiet

Next, take a clean sheet of and draw some rows of boxes. They don't have to be perfect, just sketch them out freehand. Pick some of the words from your list and write them on top of the boxes. Think about the word and draw one or more lines in the box underneath that best fits the description of the word on top. This exercise is actually fun, especially for people who think they can't draw a straight line. This will get you started drawing.

Our Examples:

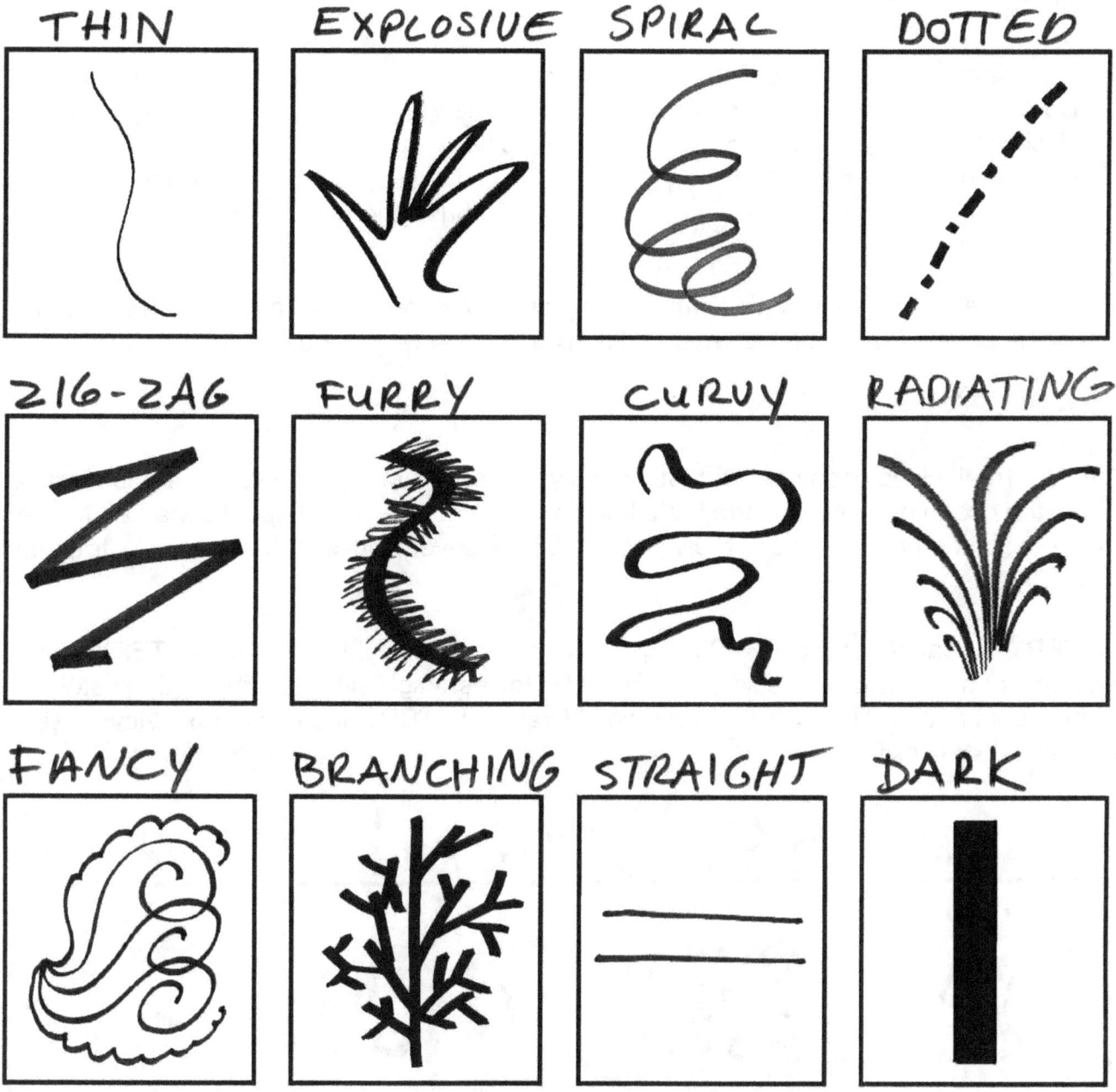

THIN · EXPLOSIVE · SPIRAL · DOTTED

ZIG-ZAG · FURRY · CURVY · RADIATING

FANCY · BRANCHING · STRAIGHT · DARK

Using a descriptive vocabulary to draw lines is a quick and easy way to distinguish between different types - thick, thin, hard, soft, zig-zag, curvy, straight, etc. You will see how this concept applies to graffiti tagging later on in this book.

You might try to experiment with different writing tools to see how the lines change. Magic marker lines look very different from pencil lines. You can also use any color, although black is our preference for drawing lines and tags. Practice with a few different tools, then lets move on.

EXERCISE #2: Expressive Lines

Now, make a list of expressive words. An expressive word is a word that describes how you might feel.

- Confident
- Bored
- Excited
- Confused
- Silly

- Tired
- Aggressive
- Scared
- Sad
- Decisive

- Calm
- Lonely
- Jittery
- Cold
- Enthusiastic

- Happy
- Angry
- Dizzy
- Annoyed
- Rattled

On a clean sheet of paper draw some boxes just like before and put a few of the words on top of the boxes. Start with one word and think about the word for a moment.

EXAMPLES

CALM - Try thinking of something that makes you feel CALM, like sitting on a beach listening to the ocean or taking a warm bath. Imagine that you are CALM and draw a CALM line in the box underneath. You can draw just one line or several lines in the box to illustrate the word CALM.

JITTERY - What about JITTERY? Imagine a situation that might make you JITTERY, like standing at a bus stop on a cold, dark, foggy Halloween night after reading a ghost story. Think about how a JITTERY line might look? Draw a JITTERY line in the box below or several JITTERY lines.

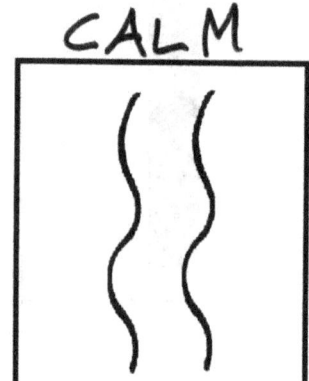
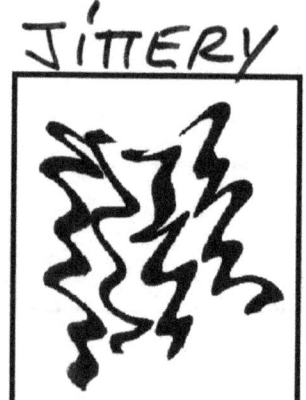
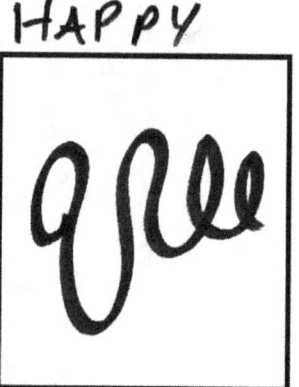
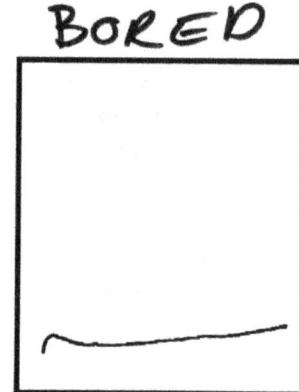

There are no right or wrong answers to this exercise. Just experiment with lines. Make a few more boxes and do a few more expressive lines until you get the hang of it.

As you draw expressive lines, think about descriptive words that best define the lines. A HAPPY line might be curvy. A BORED line maybe is flat. An AGGRESSIVE line could be dark and bold. A COLD line is probably a bit shaky or very trembly.

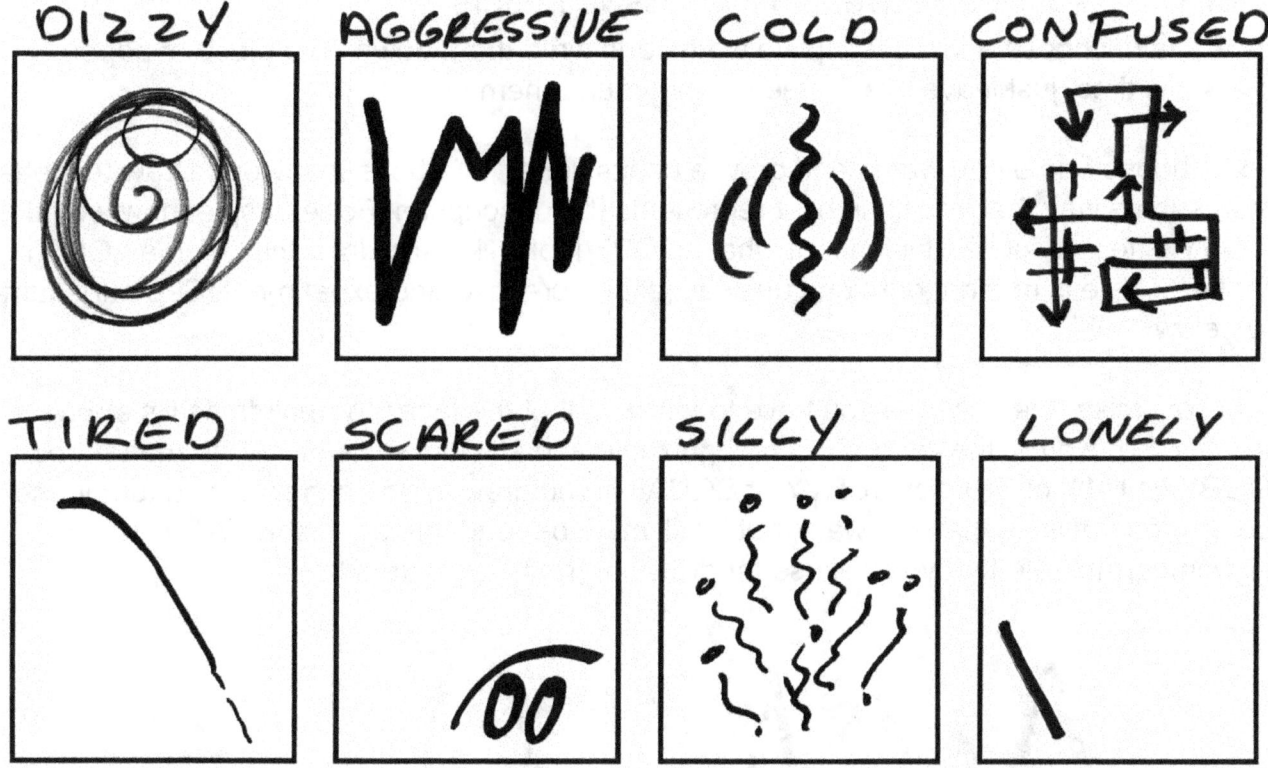

People who view your drawings will sense the emotions they contain

Here's the amazing part about drawing. When you draw a line that is calm, a person who views that drawing will experience a calm line. If you draw a line that is jittery, a person who views that drawing will experience a jittery line. It's not always apparent on a conscious level, but your emotions are contained within the lines that you draw. People who view your drawings will sense the emotions they contain.

Did you ever get really mad at somebody and tried to hide your anger from them? How did that go? Probably not very well. Or did you ever have a really great surprise gift to give someone and you felt like you were going to burst at the seams. You can't hide the emotions in your drawings anymore than you can hide your emotions in your body language.

But don't worry. This is actually a good thing. The reason art is such a powerful part of the human experience is that it is a form of expression that communicates emotions. For example, think of a great song that you like. How does it make you feel when you hear it? Happy? Sad? Well, drawing works in the same way.

Now we will apply these ideas to letter design and graffiti tagging. In graffiti, you don't want stiff, emotionless lines that are drawn with a ruler. Instead you want interesting, expressive lines that are exciting and vibrate with energy. You want a tag that communicates to your audience that you have something important to say!

EXERCISE #3: Descriptive and Expressive Letters

Once again, choose a few descriptive words and write them down on a piece of paper. No boxes this time, just leave lots of free space around them.

Next, choose one of the words and draw a capital letter "A" above that word. Draw the letter "A" in such a way that you think best represents the description. For example, how would a LOOPY letter "A" look? Think about what LOOPY looks like and draw the "A" in a LOOPY manner. There is no right or wrong answer, just be creative and experiment. See our example below.

In this exercise, the only rule you have to follow is that the letter "A" maintains it's structure. In other words, the letter "A" is recognizable and still looks like an "A" no matter how LOOPY or TALL or THIN or CURVY or SQUARE you draw it. You can twist and turn it and use any kind of lines that you want, but it still must be readable as a letter "A". This is a really important rule that you will use for drawing graffiti tag letters later on.

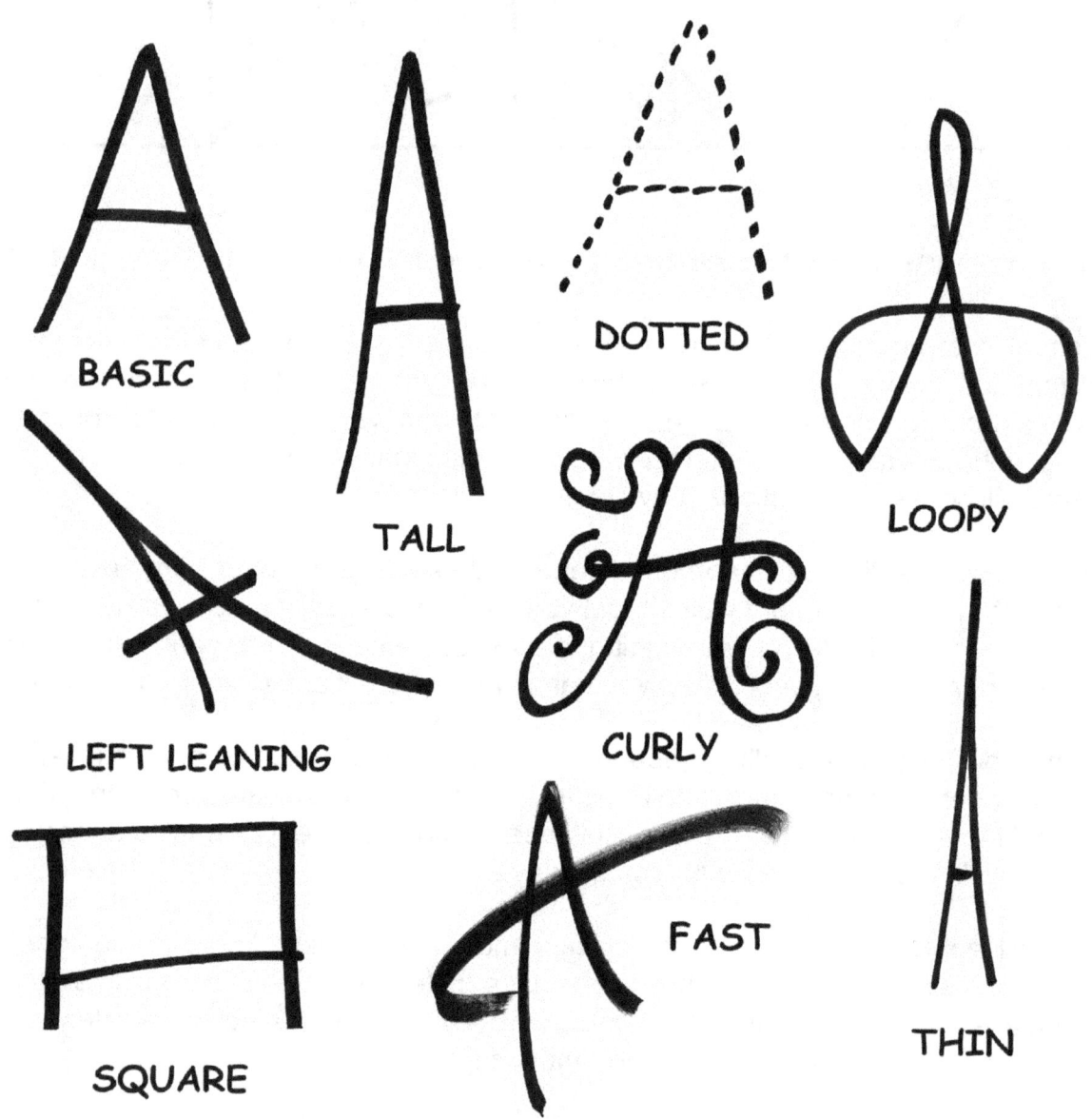

BASIC

DOTTED

TALL

LOOPY

LEFT LEANING

CURLY

SQUARE

FAST

THIN

WHY WRITE WHEN YOU CAN TAG

More....These descriptive letters are also known as "Illustrated Letters". You can get really creative with these.

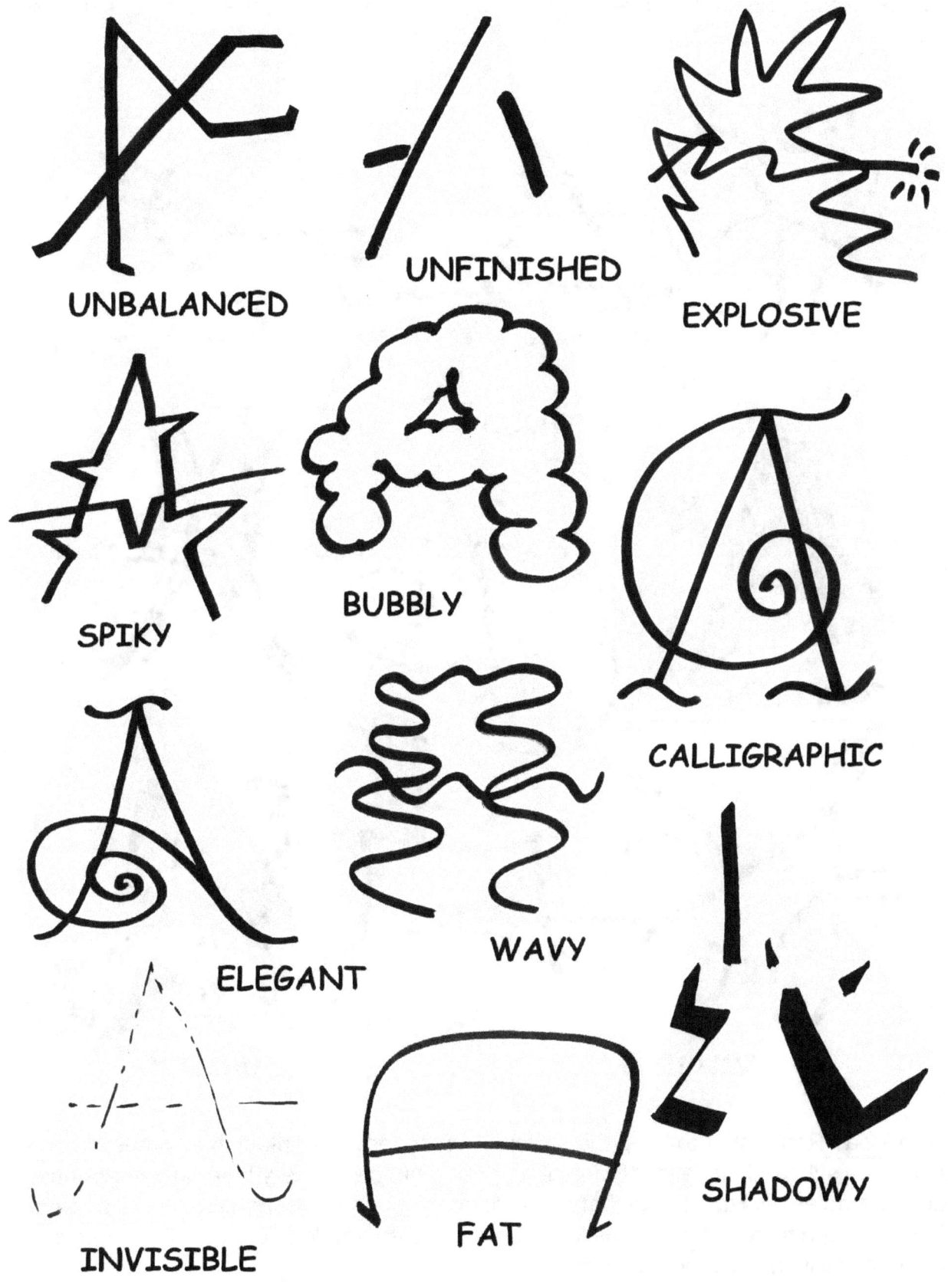

UNBALANCED

UNFINISHED

EXPLOSIVE

SPIKY

BUBBLY

CALLIGRAPHIC

ELEGANT

WAVY

INVISIBLE

FAT

SHADOWY

Now write down some expressive words. Draw a letter "A in a way that best captures that word. Try not to worry about how your drawing looks or you might get stuck. Just think about the word and try to interpret that feeling in your drawing. These are also "Illustrated Letters".

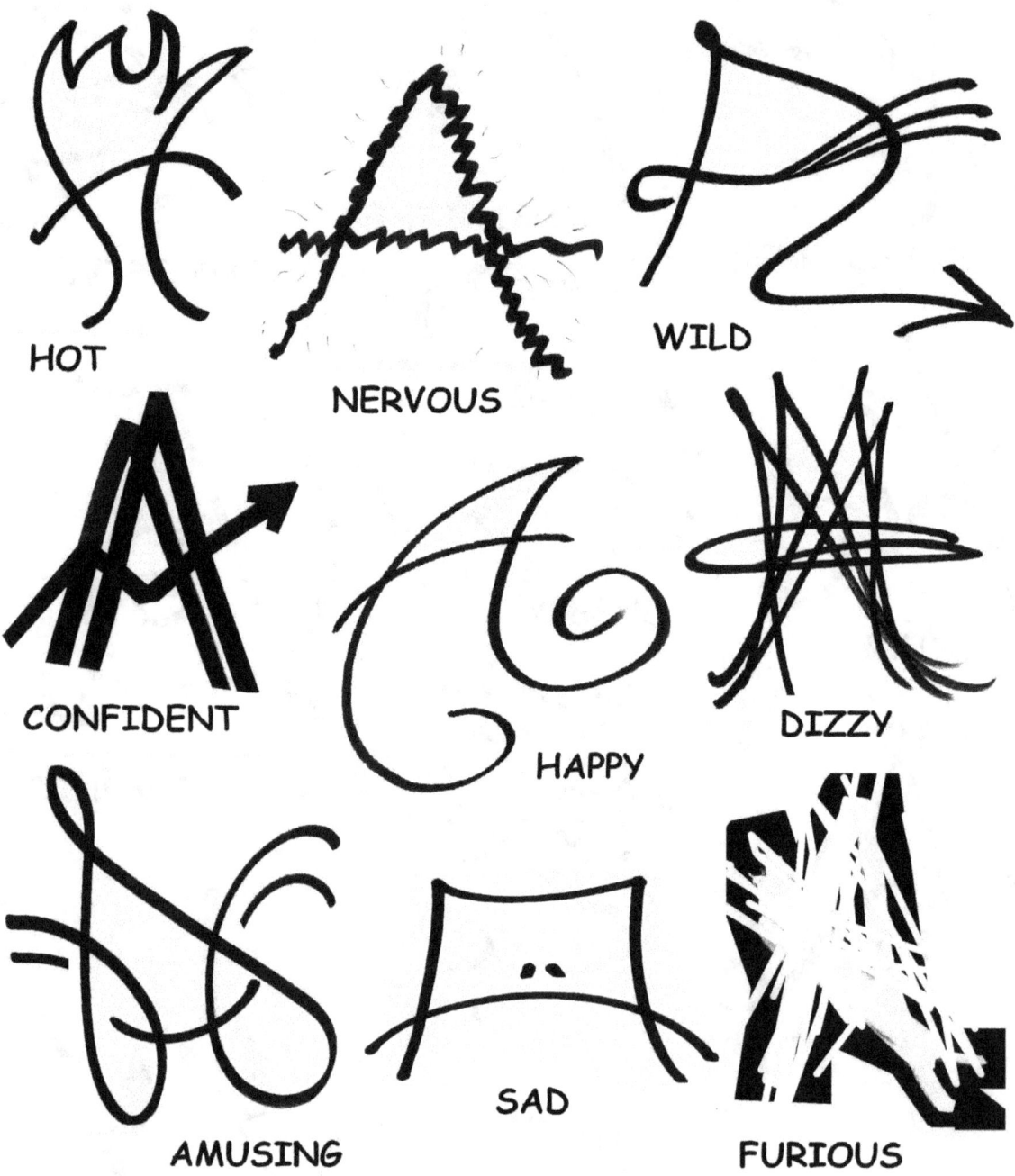

Get the idea? Remember to keep the structure of the letter "A" intact at all times. Notice that you can still read the letter "A" in each of our examples. Every letter in the alphabet has unique characteristics that make that letter recognizable and distinguishable from the other 25 letters. Learn to search for those key elements when you look at any letter. Maintaining letter structure is the essence of graffiti.

WHY WRITE WHEN YOU CAN TAG

CHARACTERISTICS OF TAG LETTERS

This seems like a really good place to introduce some of the characteristics of tag letters. There are an infinite number of ways that a tag letter can be constructed, but there are some general similarities that many tag letter styles have in common. We have divided them into a few simple categories. Think of these categories as descriptive and/or expressive. For example, a left-leaning letter leans way over to the left, and so on.....

LEFT-LEANING
tag letters lean way over to the left.

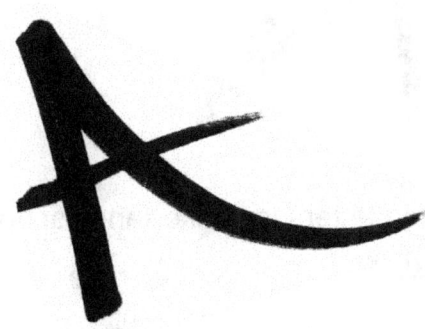

RIGHT-LEANING
tag letters lean way over to the right.

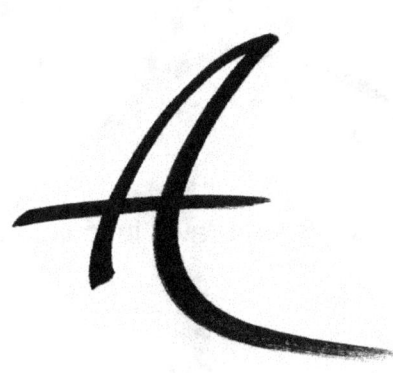

SQUARE
tag letters can be square and blocky.

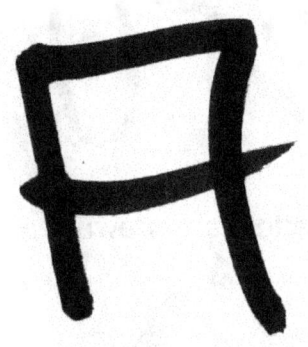

ANGULAR
tag letters can be angular and sharp.

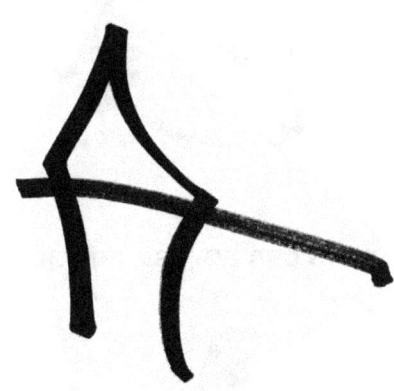

CURVY
tag letters can be curvy and round.

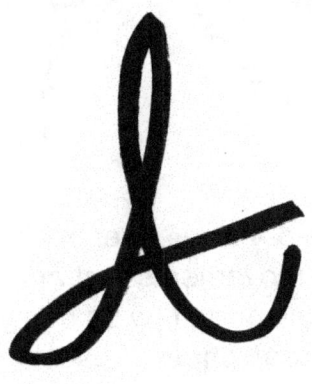

Another style of curvy and round tag letter.

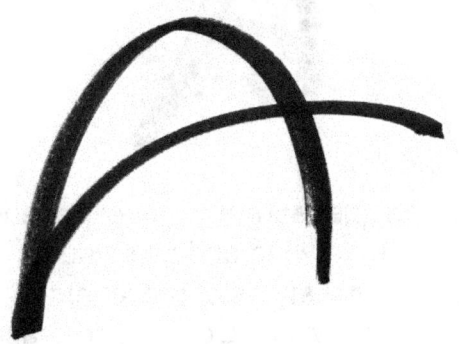

A few more characteristics of tag letters:

Some tag letters are draw with extra parts.

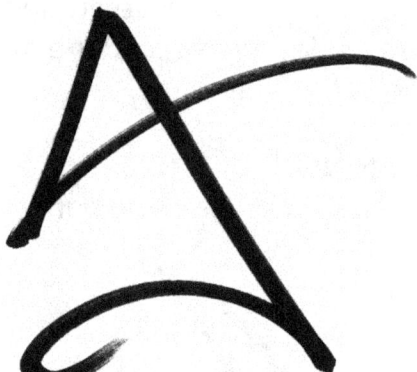

Tag letters can be drawn with arrows.

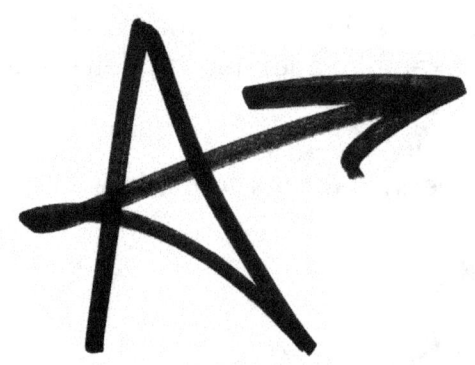

Tag letters can be drawn in lower case.

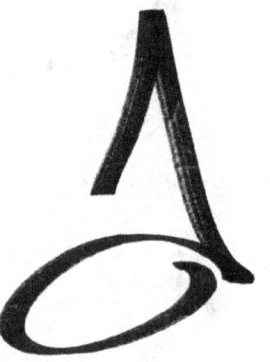

Some tag letters look like fancy script.

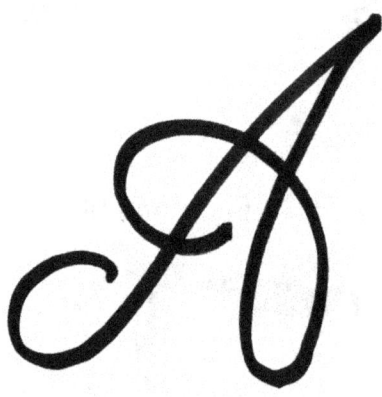

Tag letters can be just regular letters.

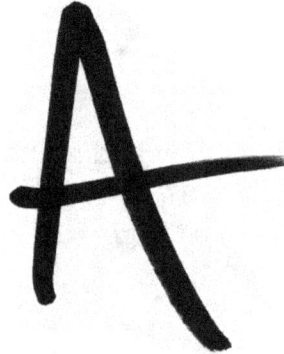

Most tag letters are drawn really fast.

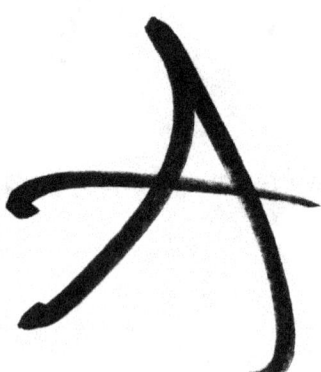

Since people learn best by experience, we have provided a practice sheet on the next page to get you drawing and give you an awareness of the hand movements that are used to form different styles of tag letters. Copy each letter on the line and draw as many copies of the letter as will fit. Continue to practice these letters on a clean sheet of paper.

EXERCISE: DRAW TAG LETTERS

Trace the grey letter with a pencil. Then draw your own copies of the letter on the line.

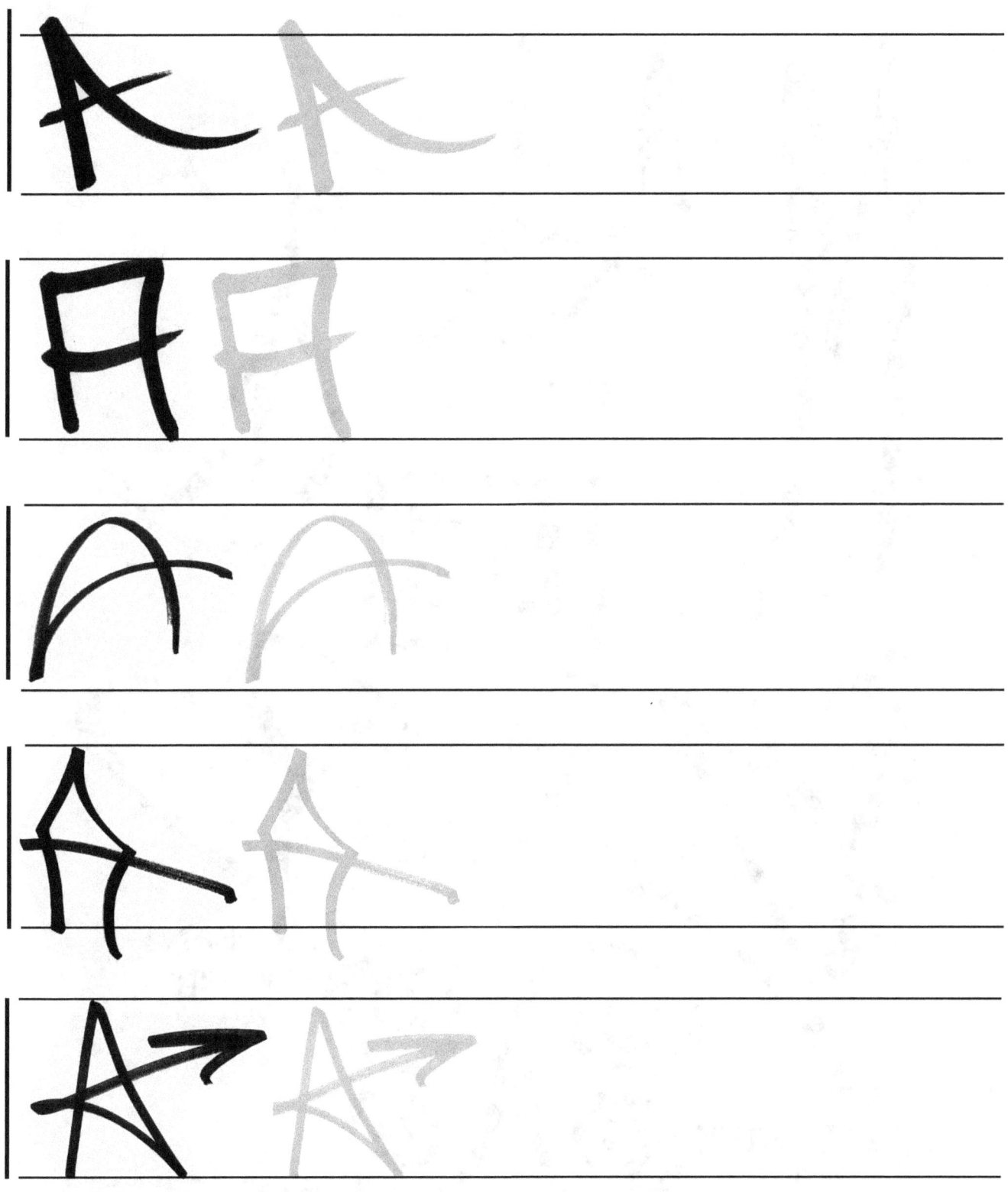

Congratulations!. You have just drawn your first tag letters. Simple but effective!

Here are some more descriptive and expressive letters we just made up. Copy some of these letters. You'll see they are actually fun to draw.

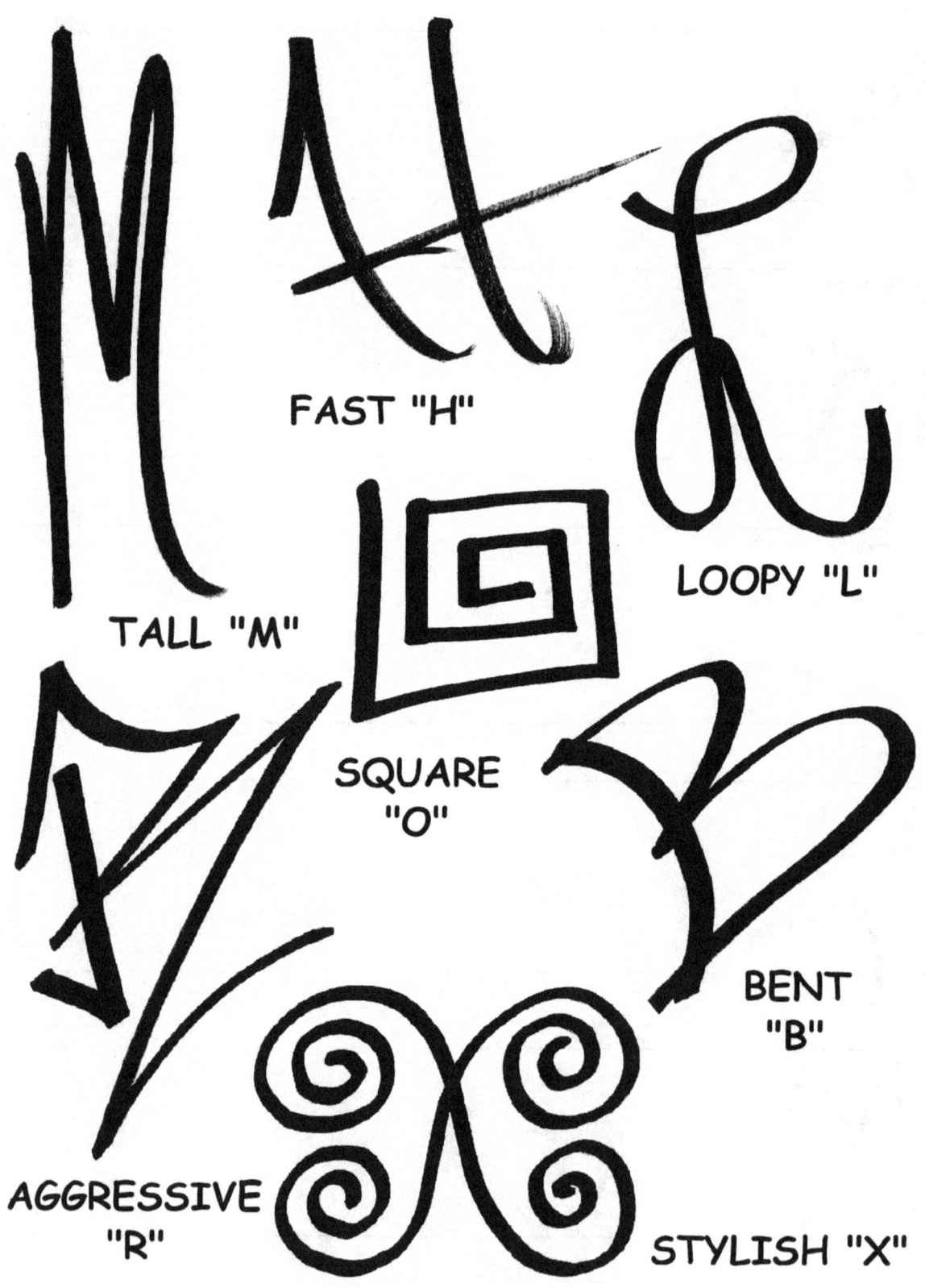

FAST "H"

LOOPY "L"

TALL "M"

SQUARE "O"

BENT "B"

AGGRESSIVE "R"

STYLISH "X"

And here are some more tag letters. Notice that these letters and the letters on the opposite page are basically the same. Tag letters can be anything you want them to be, as long as you draw them free-hand and make them expressive. The entire point of this chapter was to get you started drawing and to show you that tag letter drawing is easy with a few helpful tips and tricks.

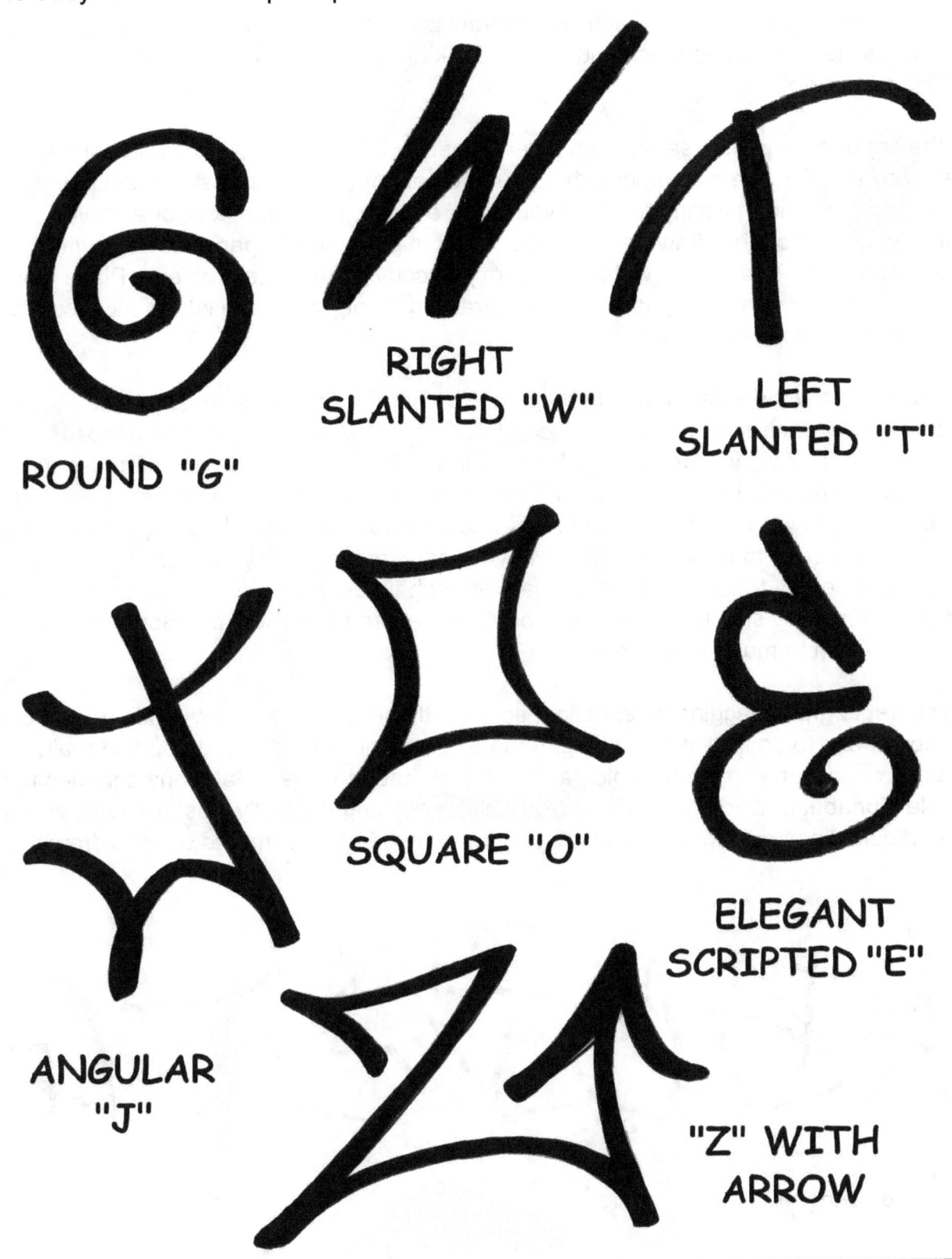

ROUND "G"

RIGHT SLANTED "W"

LEFT SLANTED "T"

SQUARE "O"

ELEGANT SCRIPTED "E"

ANGULAR "J"

"Z" WITH ARROW

The only way that we know to teach you to draw tag letters is to first get you used to drawing in tag style and then to teach you how to think in tag style. "Why write when you can tag?" is our motto.

On the opposite page is a sample tag letter alphabet. It leans slightly to the left and the letters are angular. We recommend that you trace or copy this alphabet at least four or five times. Use any kind of writing tool that you want: a magic marker, a pen, or a crayon. The easiest way to trace this drawing is to cover it with a piece of thin paper through which the letters are visible. You also have the option of just copying the letters by eye. Place this book to the left or right of the paper you are drawing on and copy the letters as accurately as possible. Either way will work fine.

Continue to draw the letters again and again. Number the pages as you go in the top left-hand corner of each page so you can keep track of your progress. Don't be concerned with how your letters look, just draw them. When you are finished spread your sketches out on a table and compare them. Your letters on Page 1 will probably look a little shaky. By Page 5, however, you will notice that your letters begin to look more steady and your lines are more confident. Try to relax the muscles in your hand and arm as you draw. The thing that is important here is that you draw the letters enough times that you begin to memorize how to draw them. They should start to flow from your pen and feel rhythmic. Some people say it helps to listen to music while drawing.

The secret to graffiti tagging is repetition, so draw these letters as many times as you can. You don't have to do it all in one sitting. If there is a particular letter that you find really interesting or challenging, do a whole page with just that one letter. Make any changes to our sample alphabet that you want. Don't worry about copying it exactly. Just get familiar with the particular lines and shapes of each letter and the hand movements used to draw them.

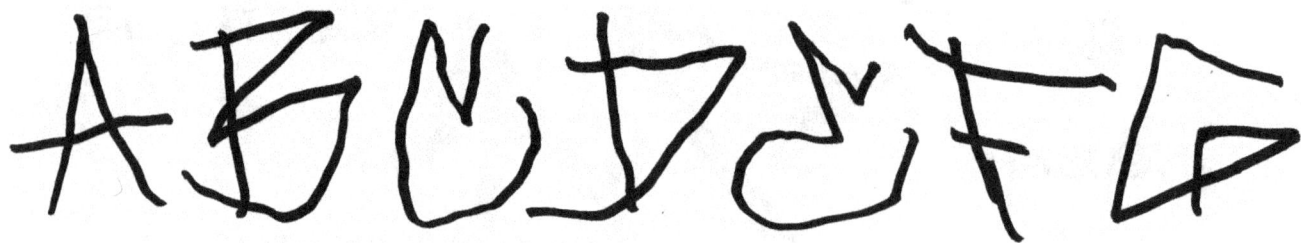

Student drawing - very shaky at first.

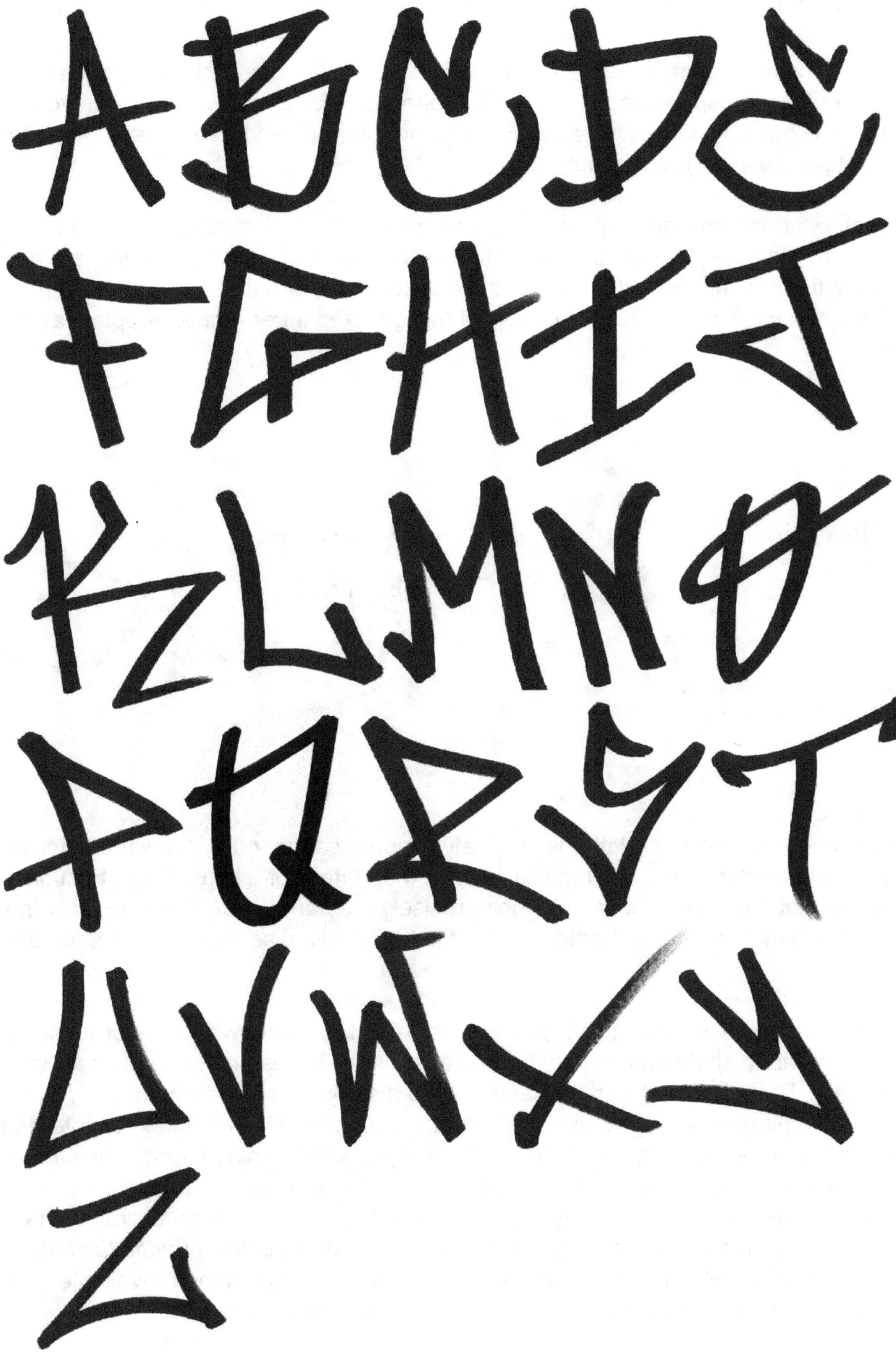
ABCDE
FGHIJ
KLMNO
PQRST
UVWXY
Z

YOU CAN TURN ANY LETTER INTO A TAG LETTER

Tag style writing is a natural extension of handwriting. That means that tag letters are formed by writing in a spontaneous, freestyle manner similar to the way you sign your name. But just because tag letters appear to be spontaneous and free doesn't mean they aren't carefully drawn or thought out.

The secret to turning any letter into a tag letter is repetition. An ordinary letter evolves into a tag letter through the process of drawing that letter over and over again - dozens, even hundreds of times - until the letter develops a distinctive pattern that has a flowing, rhythmic sensation when you write it. This is our way of design a tag letter - other people may do it differently.

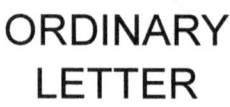 ORDINARY LETTER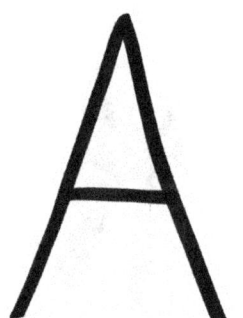

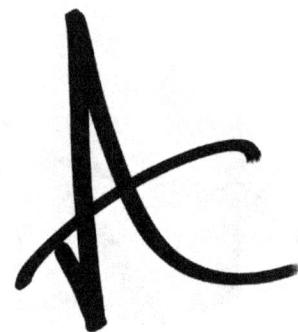 TAG STYLE LETTER

The process for creating a tag letter is relatively simple - continuously draw the letter until it develops a blueprint that you can replicate. The exact details of a letter's construction aren't all that important and it doesn't have to look precisely the same each time you draw the finished letter. What matters is that the finished letter follows a set pattern and should feel effortless.

There are no other rules we can give you for designing tag letters when you are first starting out other than to study and imitate the tag letter styles in this book and of accomplished graffiti writers. There is a long and well-established history of graffiti tagging that you can research for inspiration. We have provided several tag alphabets in the next chapter to get you started. Get used to studying graffiti tags when you see them and look at how the individual letters are formed. Trace them with your eyes or your finger. Look at the shape of the tags as a whole and for stylish details. You will notice that many tags have similar characteristics, such as stars or arrows added to the letters. Search the term *graffiti tag letters* on the Internet for ideas. Refer to graffiti books. There are hundreds of them available. Eventually, you will add your own nuances to existing, traditional letter styles.

LETTER MODIFICATION AND PROGRESSION

Graffiti tagging is essentially a balance between control and freedom. Control refers to drawing the letter in a set pattern. Freedom refers to memorizing that pattern and drawing the letter with fast, rhythmic, confident strokes. The more you draw the letter, the faster you will become, and the more skill you will gain.

You can transform an ordinary letter into a tag letter through a process known as **letter modification**. In letter modification, a letter changes from one form to the next in a series of small steps. These steps are called **progression**. It might sound complicated, but it's not. The only rule you need to follow is the finished tag letter should be structurally sound. That means that an "A" looks like an "A" no matter how much modification you apply to it.

Below is an example of modification of the letter "A" from the facing page. The letter slowly progresses from an ordinary, basic letter "A" into a finished tag letter "A" in small steps. Study each step and notice the small changes. The letter that you start with is called the STARTING POINT. The last step is the FINISHED TAG LETTER. There are no set number of steps that you should use to modify a letter. That's completely up to you. Use as many steps as you need until you think the letter looks done.

#1 - STARTING POINT

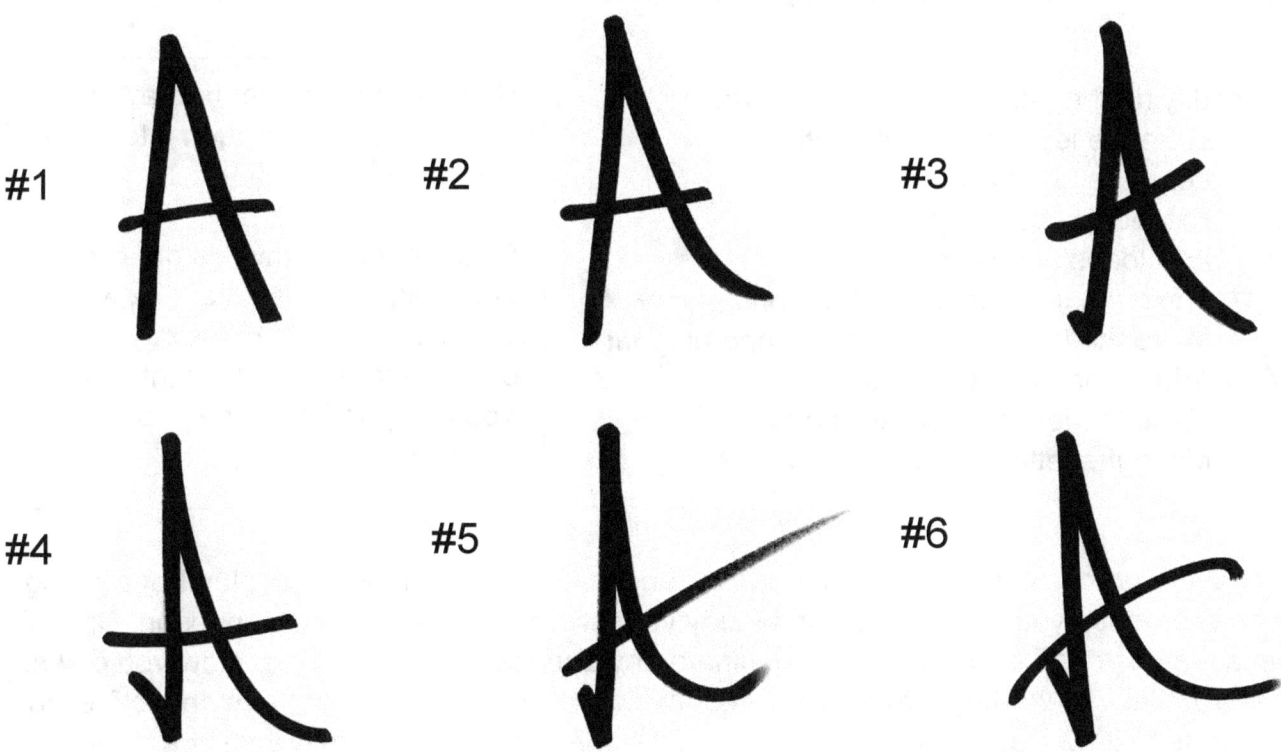

#6 - FINISHED TAG LETTER

You will be using letter modification and progression to design tags later on in this book so this page is important.

EXERCISE: MODIFYING AN ORDINARY LETTER INTO A TAG LETTER

The key to drawing a tag letter is repetition!

TOOLS YOU WILL NEED

- a stack of 8.5"x11" cheap copy paper - use thin paper that you can see through.
- you can use anything to draw with: a pen, crayon, or any kind of magic marker - use something dark, so it is visible through the paper.

INSTRUCTIONS

Choose any letter from A to Z. Just a plain, basic letter. Draw the letter on a sheet of paper. This letter will be your Starting Point. Next, put a clean piece of paper on top and trace the letter. Use thin paper that you can see through. NOTE: If you have a lightbox it will be much easier to trace. A light box is a flat box with a piece of frosted glass or plastic on top and an electric light inside. You also have the option to just copy the letter by eye. Redraw the letter. Put another piece of paper on top and draw it again. Do this several times. Each time you draw the letter change it slightly. Make small changes to different parts of the letter. Use each letter that you draw as a jumping off point to form the next letter. Draw quickly. Just let the letter evolve and think about how you want your finished tag letter to look. Use big, sweeping movements or sharp, pointed angles and be dramatic.

Try modifying the letter in the following ways:
1. Lean the letter over to the left
2. Lean the letter over to the right
3. Extend the bottom ends
4. Add loops and curls to the ends
5. Make the lines angular, sharp and pointy
6. Make the letter curvy, rounded and elegant
7. Add an arrow to one end
8. Make the letter really tall and thin
9. Make the letter square and boxy

Use thin copy paper to draw on so you can see through it to trace your drawings.

Or trace your drawings on a light box. A light box is a flat box with a piece of frosted glass or plastic on top and an electric light inside. You can purchase one at an art supply store.

Repeat the process and draw the letter over and over at least thirty times. Number the pages as you go, so you can go back and study your sketches later on for comparison. Draw it with as few strokes as possible and eliminate any unnecessary details that slow you down. After a while, you will begin to notice that drawing the letter has a smooth, rhythmic feeling and starts to flow. Keep going until you can draw the letter automatically with your eyes closed.

Our example on the opposite page (it wasn't necessary to include all 30 drawings) demonstrates the progression from an ordinary, basic letter "M" to a finished tag letter "M".

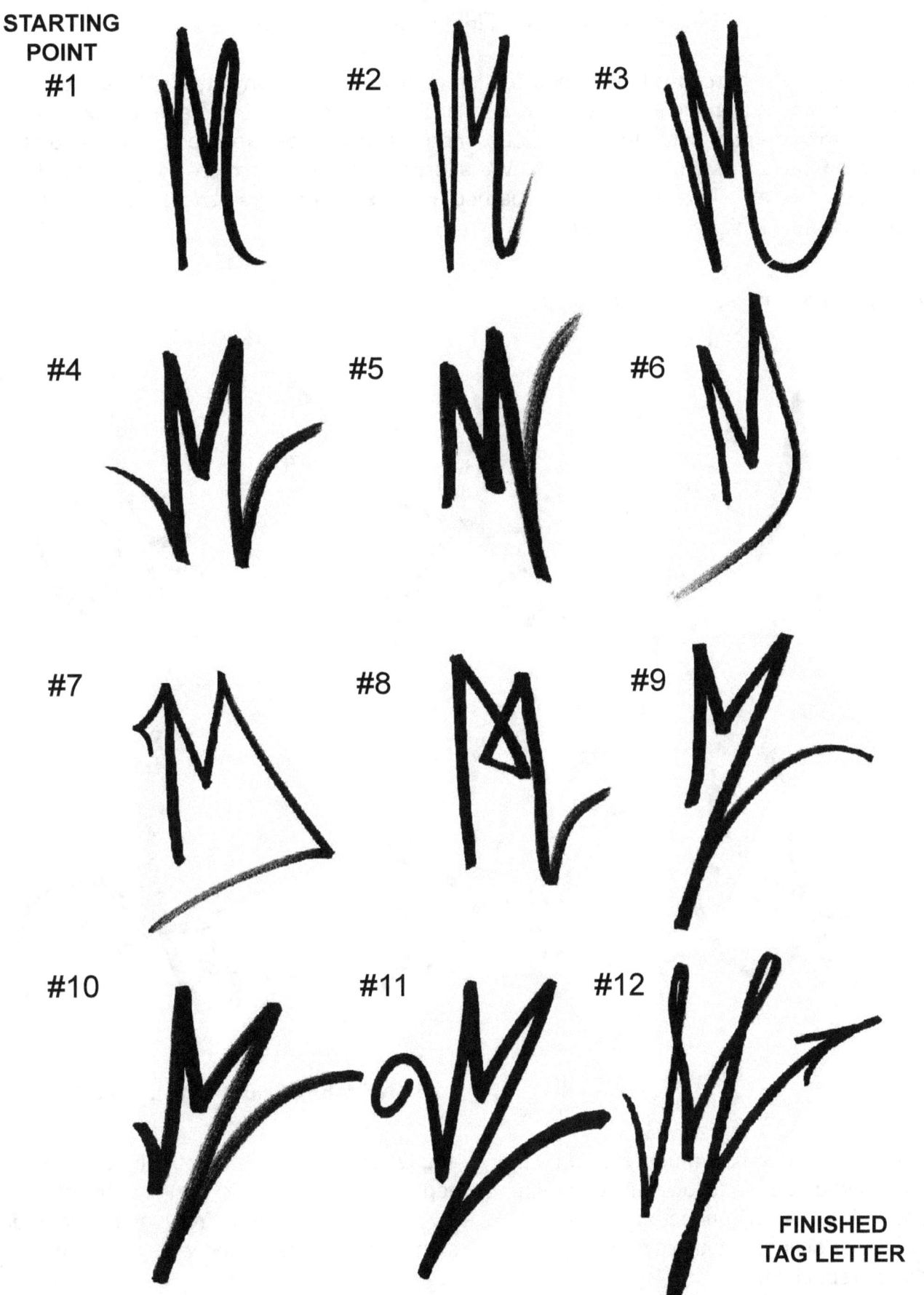

#2

#3

#4

#5

#6

#7

#8

#9

#10

#11

#12

**FINISHED
TAG LETTER**

MODIFYING A LETTER FROM ANOTHER TAG LETTER

You can begin the process of letter modification at any point with any style of letter. Any letter can act as a Starting Point. You can even build a tag letter from an already existing tag letter, following the same formula of letter modification. Below we used the finished tag letter from Page 25 as our Starting Point. We altered it into an even more exaggerated tag letter using the same letter modification method. Here is the progression from the Starting Point to the new Finished Tag Letter.

#1 - STARTING POINT (from Page 25)

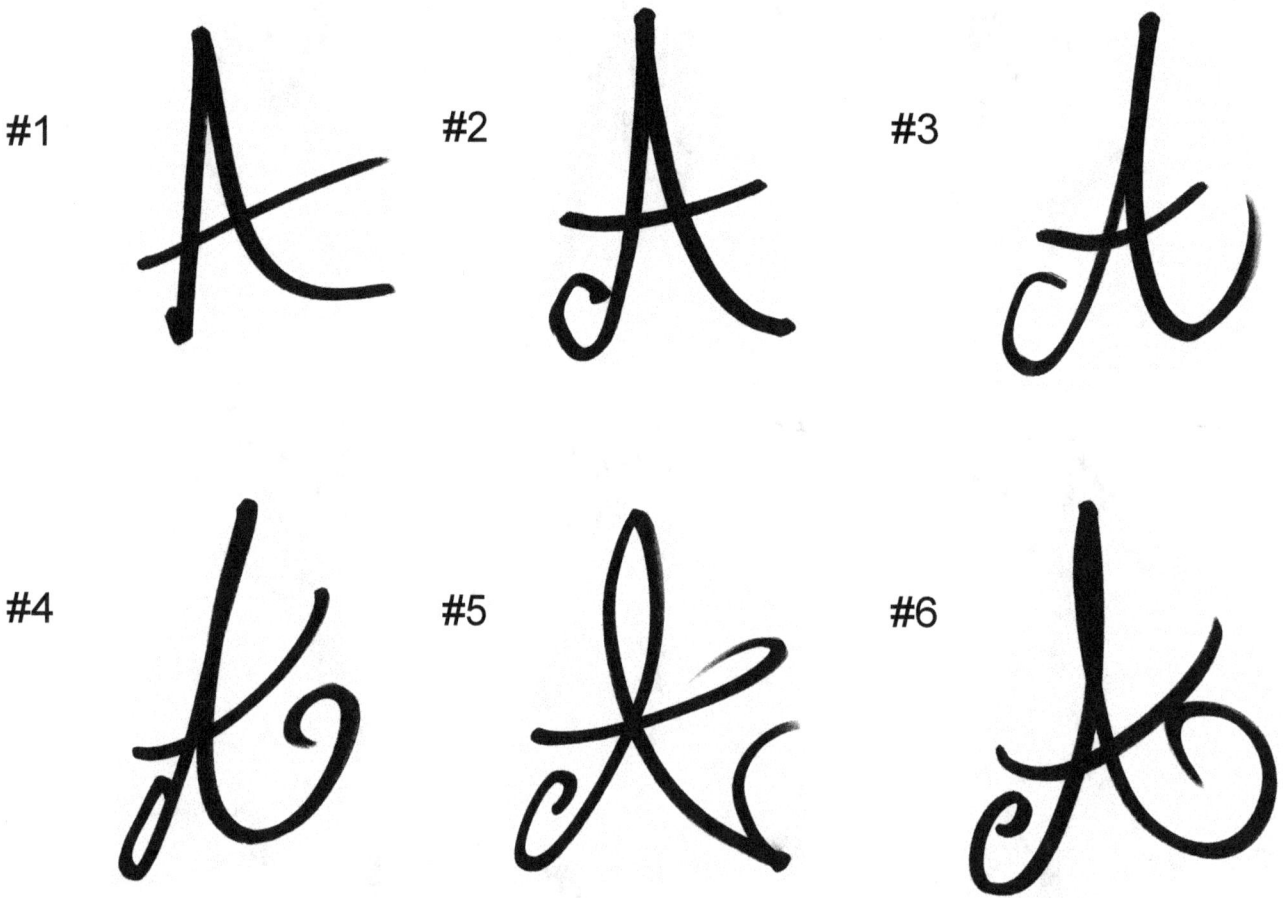

#1   #2   #3

#4   #5   #6

#6 - NEW FINISHED TAG LETTER

There is no end to how much you can modify a tag letter. There are no set number of steps, no rules you need to follow. Just use as many steps as you need until you think the letter is done. Eliminate any unnecessary details that slow your drawing down. You don't have to do it all in one sitting. If you get tired or frustrated, come back to it later and work on it with a fresh perspective.

MODIFYING A LETTER INTO DIFFERENT LETTERS

Wait, it gets better. You can use your finished tag letter as a blueprint to build the rest of the alphabet.

Try this exercise: Draw the finished tag letter "A" (#6) from the opposite page on a fresh sheet of paper. Look at the letter. Turn it sidewards. Turn it upside down. Draw it on tracing paper and flip it over so it is backward. Squint at it a little. See what other letters you can form using parts of the letter. Turn it up-side-down and it becomes a letter "V". Maybe the curved bottoms can be part of a "C" or an "M". Place a clean sheet of paper on top and draw a different letter using parts of the "A".

The letters below were all constructed from the finished tag letter "A" on the opposite page. Notice that all the letters are drawn in a similar style and seem to match. You can use this technique to build a whole alphabet from just one existing letter.

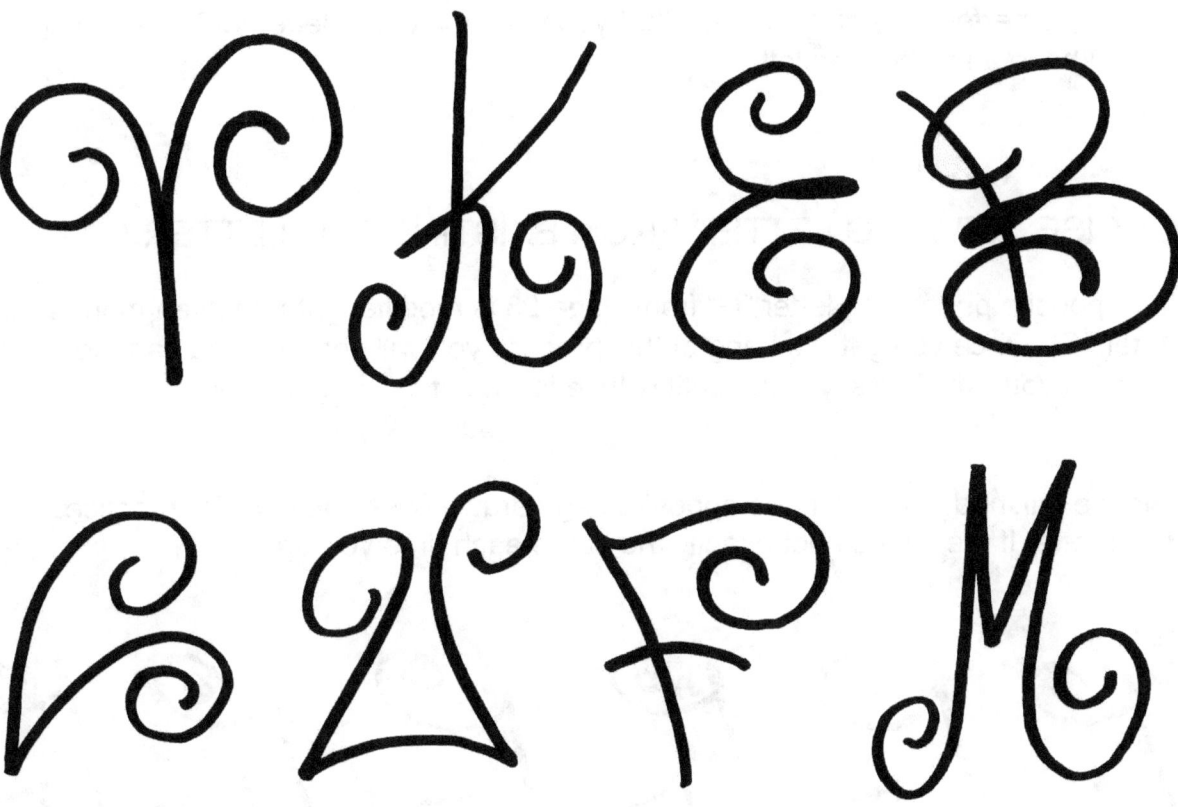

To summarize, any letter can act as a Starting Point to build a tag letter. What makes the Finished Letter a tag letter? It's a tag letter because you say it is. Draw it fast and loose and think about the feeling you want it to express as you draw it over and over in a set pattern and it's a tag letter. In the next chapter, we will group tag letters into some basic descriptive and expressive categories that you can use to act as a guide when drawing your own letters.

REVIEW: OUR BASIC FORMULA FOR DESIGNING A TAG LETTER

STEP 1) Draw a letter. This is your Starting Point.

STEP 2) Redraw the letter over and over again, adding and changing elements as you go.

STEP 3) Continue to change the letter as much as you want. Eventually, you will get to a point where it starts to flow and feel automatic when you draw it. That's when the pattern or blueprint is set.

STEP 4) Redraw the tag letter. Take out any details that interrupt the movement of your pen or slow it down when you draw the letter. Memorize the letter's essential features so that you can draw it the same way over and over very quickly. Don't worry if the letter is not exactly the same each time you draw it.

STEP 5) Redraw the finished letter several more times until it just flows from your pen. Enhance and perfect any of the details that you think make the letter look interesting. At this point, you have a finished tag letter.

EXERCISE: NEW TAG LETTER FROM EXISTING TAG LETTER

On the opposite page a tag letter "G" from Page 23 is modified into an even more stylized tag letter "G". Once you get the hang of this process you will see that you can modify letters as much as you like. The sky is the limit with letter modification and progression.

Here is the finished letter from the opposite page drawn over and over for practice. It doesn't matter if the letter is not exactly the same each time you draw it.

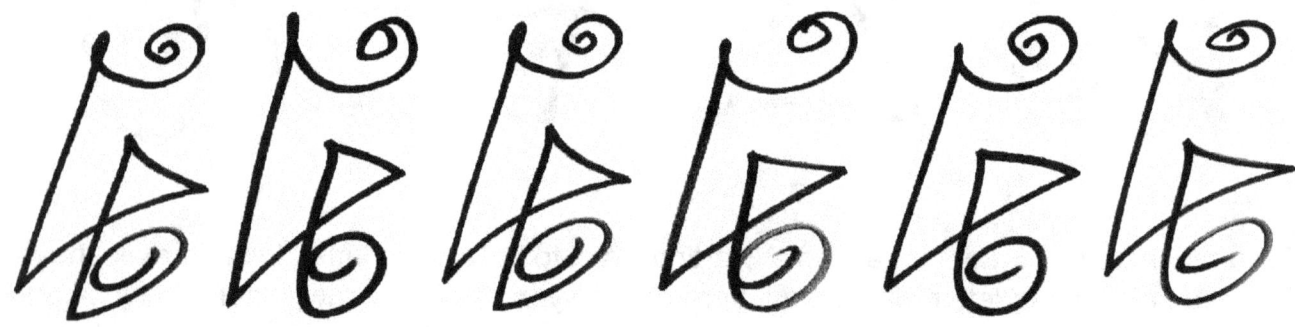

BONUS EXERCISE: Try to form a different letter using parts of the finished tag letter "G".

WHY WRITE WHEN YOU CAN TAG

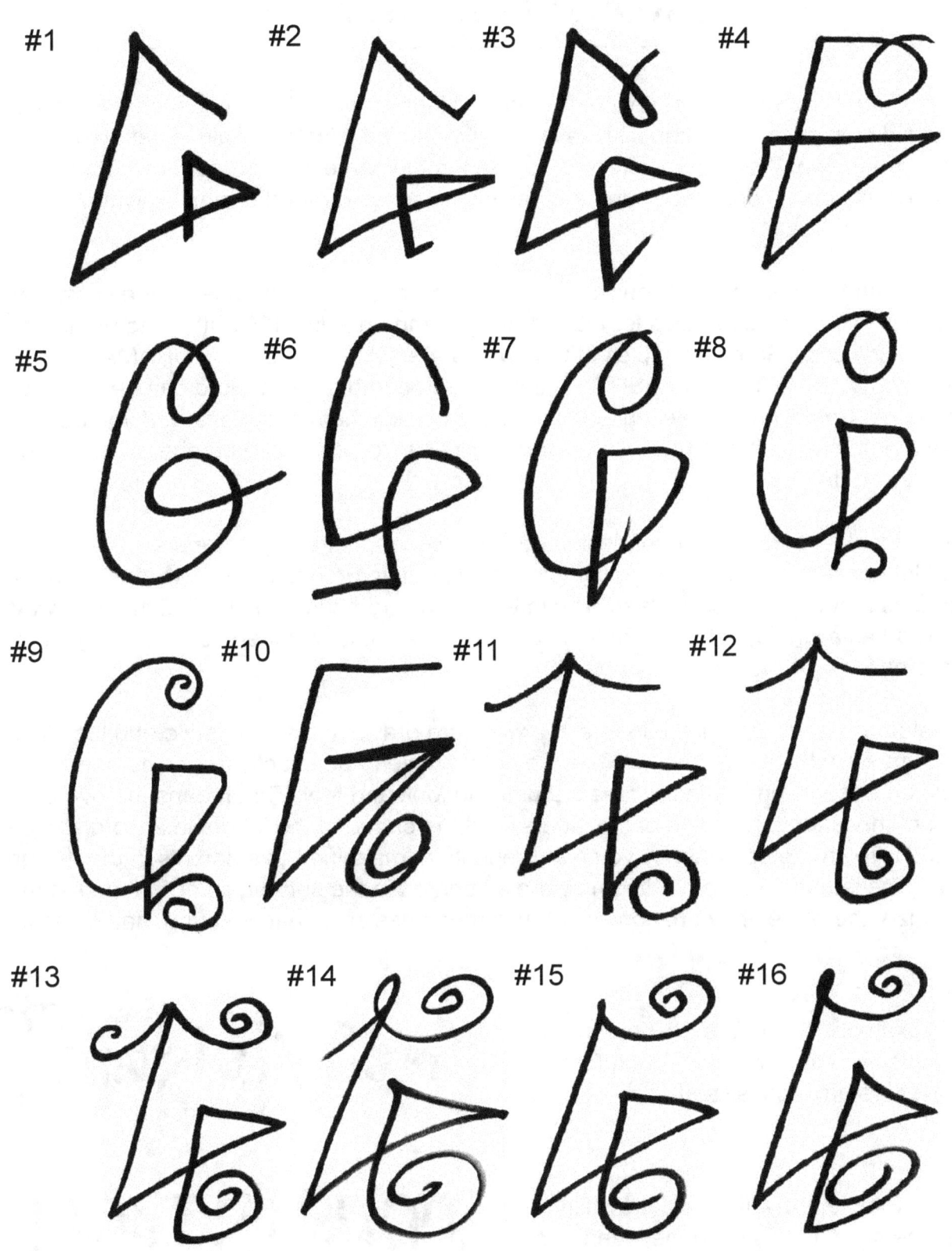

#1 #2 #3 #4 #5 #6 #7 #8 #9 #10 #11 #12 #13 #14 #15 #16

NEW FINISHED TAG LETTER

CHAPTER FOUR
TAG ALPHABET STYLES

Now that you have some experience drawing tag letters, we will put those letters to practical use drawing tags. You can also say writing tags. Technically speaking, letters are written, not drawn. We tend to approach tagging in the same way we approach drawing a picture with lots of loose sketching and revisions, so we prefer the term drawing. Use whichever you like.

Your tag can be anything that you want it to be: a name, a word, numbers, or a combination of these. We discuss strategies for picking a tag name on Page 106. Often tag names are just regular words. Some examples of tag names are "SPADE", "BUG", "DRAMA", "CAT", "SEEN", "COVE", "WINK", "FLASH".... the list goes on and on. Any word can be used for a tag name. Some writers even invent words or misspell them intentionally. If you decide to use a name that is already in use by someone else you can put a number after it, like "SPEK 2" or "JAZZ 3".

Now let's look at some important design rules concerning lettering in general. The function of letters is to be read. Letters combine together into groups to form words. Words are messages that communicate ideas. The letters in a word need to be unified in some way, to be read as a whole, not as individual parts. The way to unify letters is by making them **consistent**.

Consistency means that all the letters in a word are drawn in a similar style and look like they come from the same family. While they don't have to be exactly the same, there should be enough similarities to create a unifying look and feel. That means the overall height of the letters, the angle of the letters, and the shape of the letters in a word should all match. To create consistency you need repetition, meaning the elements in the design repeat. The letters you are reading now are all printed in the same type or font and at the same size, therefore, they are consistent. It is much easier to read lettering that is consistent.

In this example, the letters are drawn in completely different styles. Therefore these letters are inconsistent.

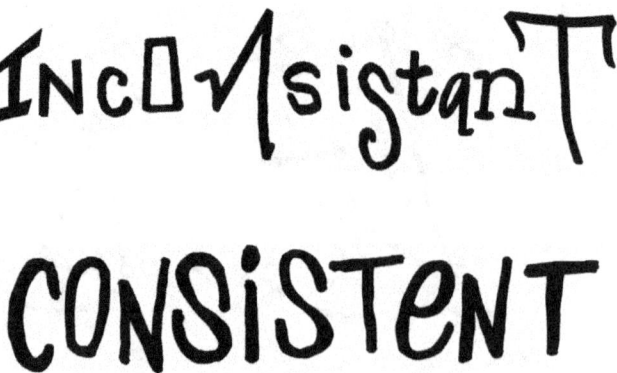

In this example, the letters are drawn in the same style. In this word the letters are consistent.

EXERCISE: DRAW CONSISTENT LETTERS IN A WORD

Here is a fun way to practice consistency in a word. Think about a word, remembering the expressive and descriptive vocabulary that we used for lines and single letters. Think about that word and draw it out using any style of letters that you want in a way that represents the literal meaning of the word. For example, think about the word BROKEN and draw letters that are broken up into pieces. Or think about what speed feels like and draw the word SPEED using fast, speedy letters. Or think about what floating feels like and draw the word FLOAT using wavy, rippling letters. Or think about what a crowd looks like and draw the word CROWD with letters that are squeezed together. These are not necessarily tag letters you are working with here, just random letters in any style that represents the literal meaning of a word. These are known as "Illustrated words".

Some other examples you might like to try are SHAKY, MELT, SWIRL, BUBBLE, WET, FIRE, CRASH, CRACK, SMILE, DRY, SIZZLE, HAIRY, or just make up your own. You can draw them any way you want, just remember that all the letters in each word need to be similar enough to match. If you need ideas look on the internet. Search the term "Illustrated words" in a search engine and see what comes up.

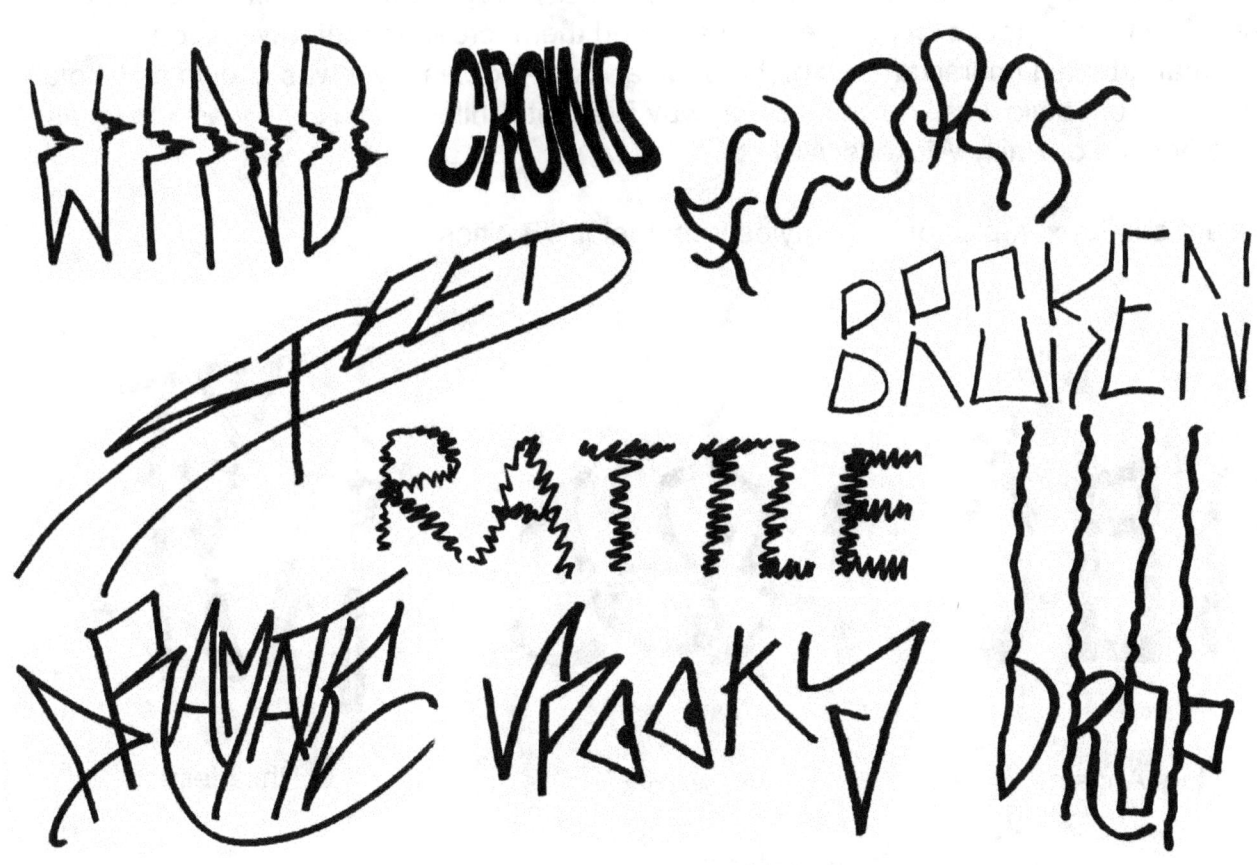

CONSISTENCY IN TAG LETTERS

Now we can apply the same rules of consistency to tag letters. The easiest way to draw consistent tag letters is to first organize them into different groups or styles using descriptive and/or expressive characteristics. For example, a square tag alphabet has all the letters from A to Z drawn in a squarish, blocky manner. The same applies to round, angular, or tall tag letters. If you draw all of the letters of a tag in a similar, consistent style, you will be able to create a tag that makes a clear, powerful statement. Maybe your statement just says "HERE I AM". That's a great statement.

How can you create consistency in your tag letters? Maybe you draw all your letters with sharp angles? Or maybe you draw all of your letters leaning way over to the left. Or maybe you add lots of extensions and loops to the ends (we'll talk more about extensions later). The particular style and details of your tag letters are totally up to you as long as the letters remain somewhat consistent.

That brings us to the heart of this topic. How do we take fifty plus years of graffiti tagging history and boil it all down into a few simple ideas that we can present to you as guidelines to get you started drawing your own tags? There is so much culture, tradition, and skill involved in this art form. So we'll sum it up like this. Throughout the history of graffiti tagging, different handstyles developed with unique characteristics in different regions of the country. These handstyles became recognizable by the city they originated from. Aspiring writers were influenced by these local styles and adapted them, creating their own unique handstyles that retained characteristics of the original. Los Angeles style was known as Cholo style. New York style was known as Broadway Elegant. Philadelphia style was known as Gangster style or Philly Wickeds/Wickets.

Here are some examples of letter styles from major US cities:

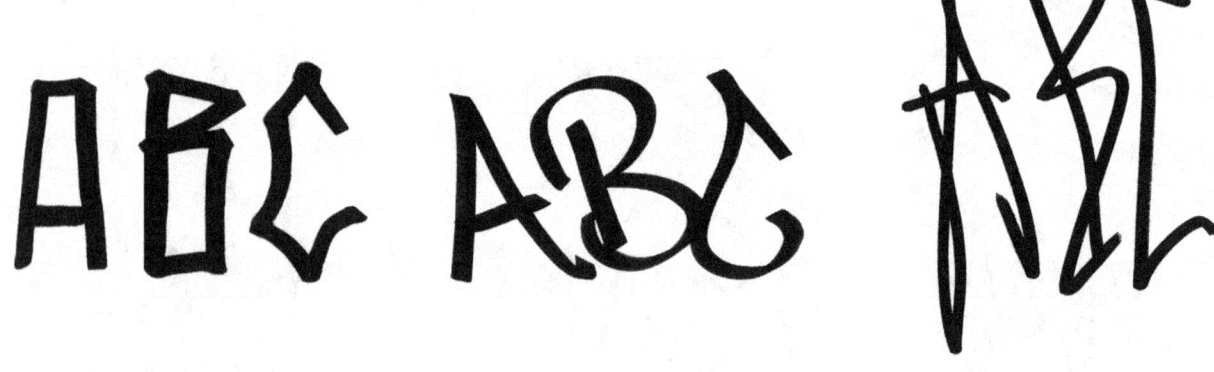

Los Angeles   New York   Philadelphia

EXERCISE: TAG LETTER STYLES

Because a tag is a word drawn with letters that are expressive, there is a lot of drama contained in a tag. With practice, you will develop your own letter styles, but you need some place to begin. Below are five generic tag letter alphabets. All five are based loosely on traditional tag letter styles. Copy each set of letters on a sheet of paper. These are just general categories to get you started.

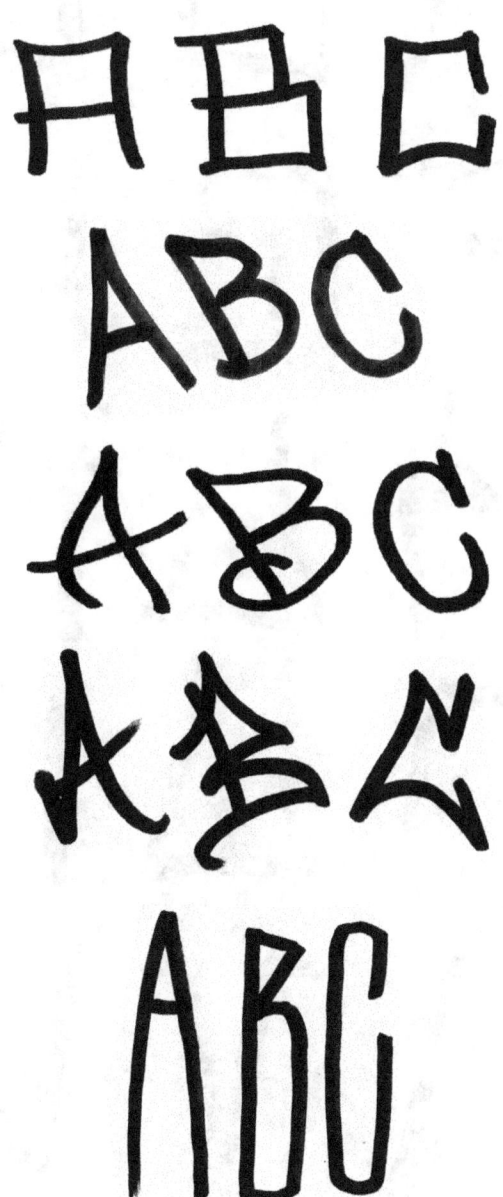

Square Tag Style

Basic, Backslanted Tag Style

Curvy, Elegant Tag Style

Sharp, Angular Tag Style

Tall, Skinny Tag Style

On the following pages are completed alphabets for each of these five styles. Each alphabet has a worksheet you can use to practice drawing the letters. The only way to learn is by doing, so complete the exercises included with each tag alphabet using the letters shown for that style. You might not use all of the worksheets all at once, but try a few out and see which ones you like. Next, copy each complete alphabet once or twice. Feel free to modify the worksheets any way that you want. If you prefer to trace the letters, that's fine, too.

SQUARE TAG ALPHABET STYLE

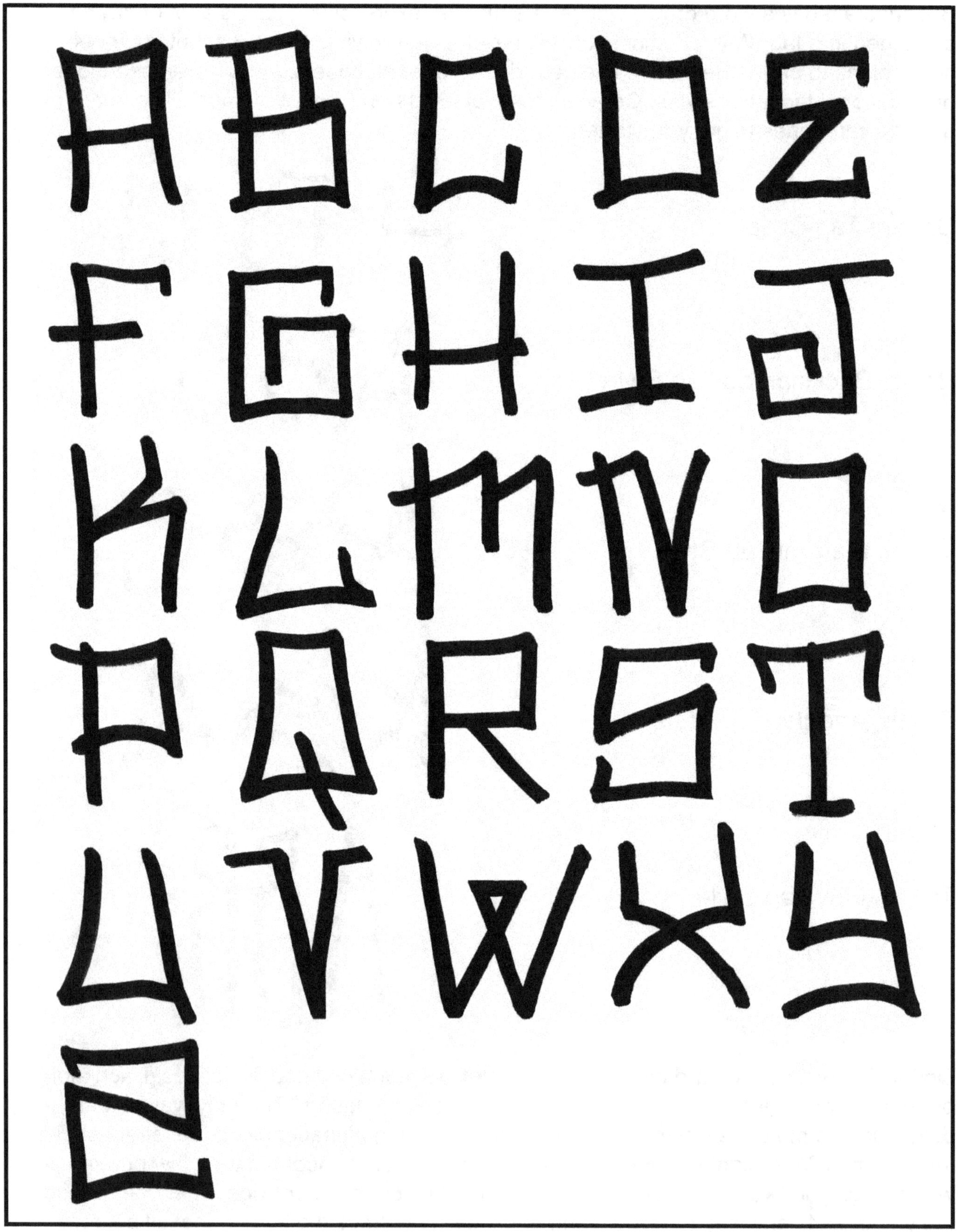

Using tag letters from the Square Tag Alphabet on the opposite page, write out each word on the line above it using square tag letters. At the bottom use square tag letters to write your own name. You can trace the letters if you like. See answers on Page 54.

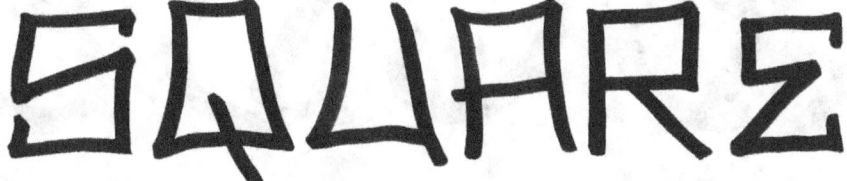

SQUARE

ANGELS

COAST

SKATER

YOUR NAME HERE

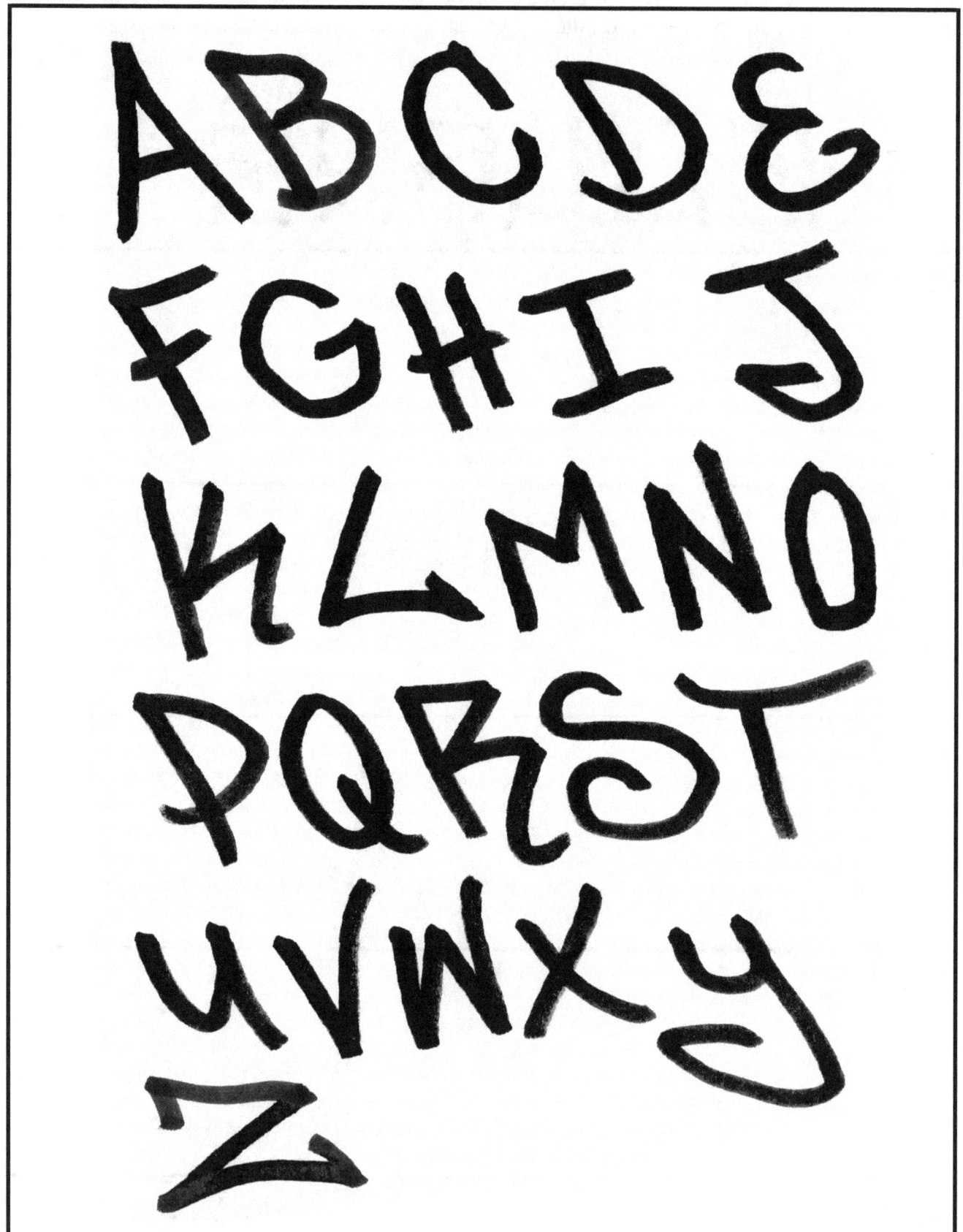

Using tag letters from the Backslanted Tag Alphabet on the opposite page, write out each word on the line above it using backslanted letters. At the bottom use backslanted tag letters to write your own name. You can trace the letters if you like. See answers on Page 54.

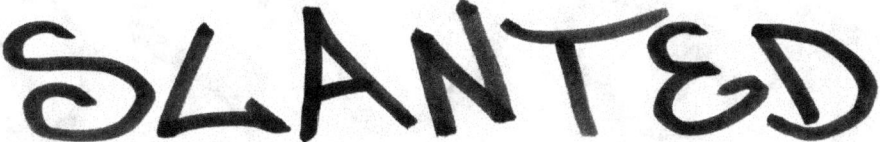

SLANTED

_____

TRUE

_____

STREET

_____

STYLE

_____

YOUR NAME HERE

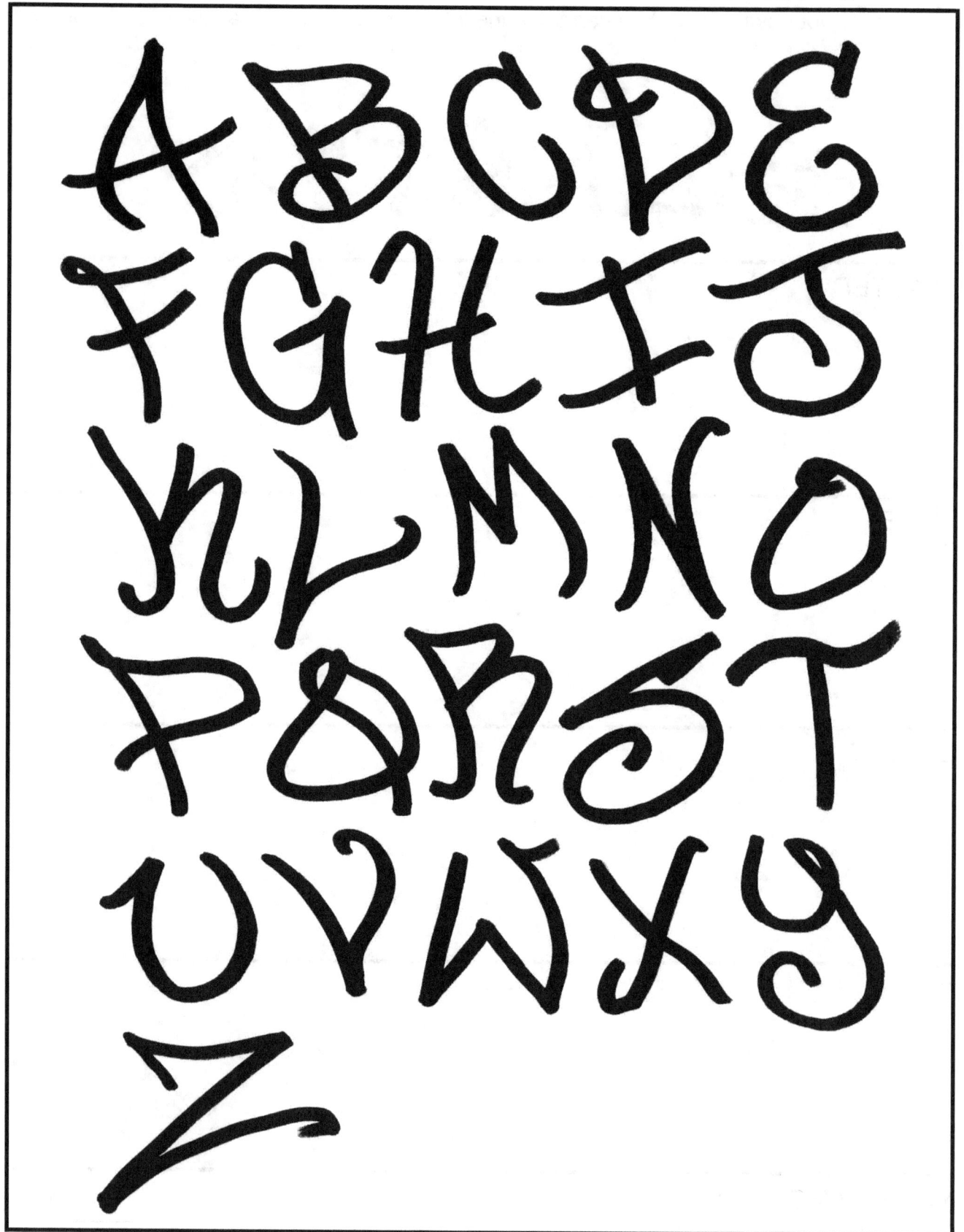

Using tag letters from the Curvy, Elegant Tag Alphabet on the opposite page, write out each word on the line above it using curvy, elegant tag letters. At the bottom use curvy, elegant tag letters to write your own name. Trace the letters if you like. See answers on Page 55.

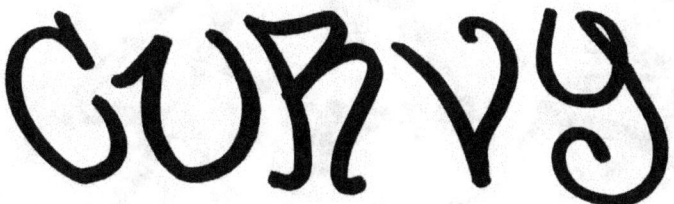

CURVY

ELEGANT

URBAN

CLASSIC

YOUR NAME HERE

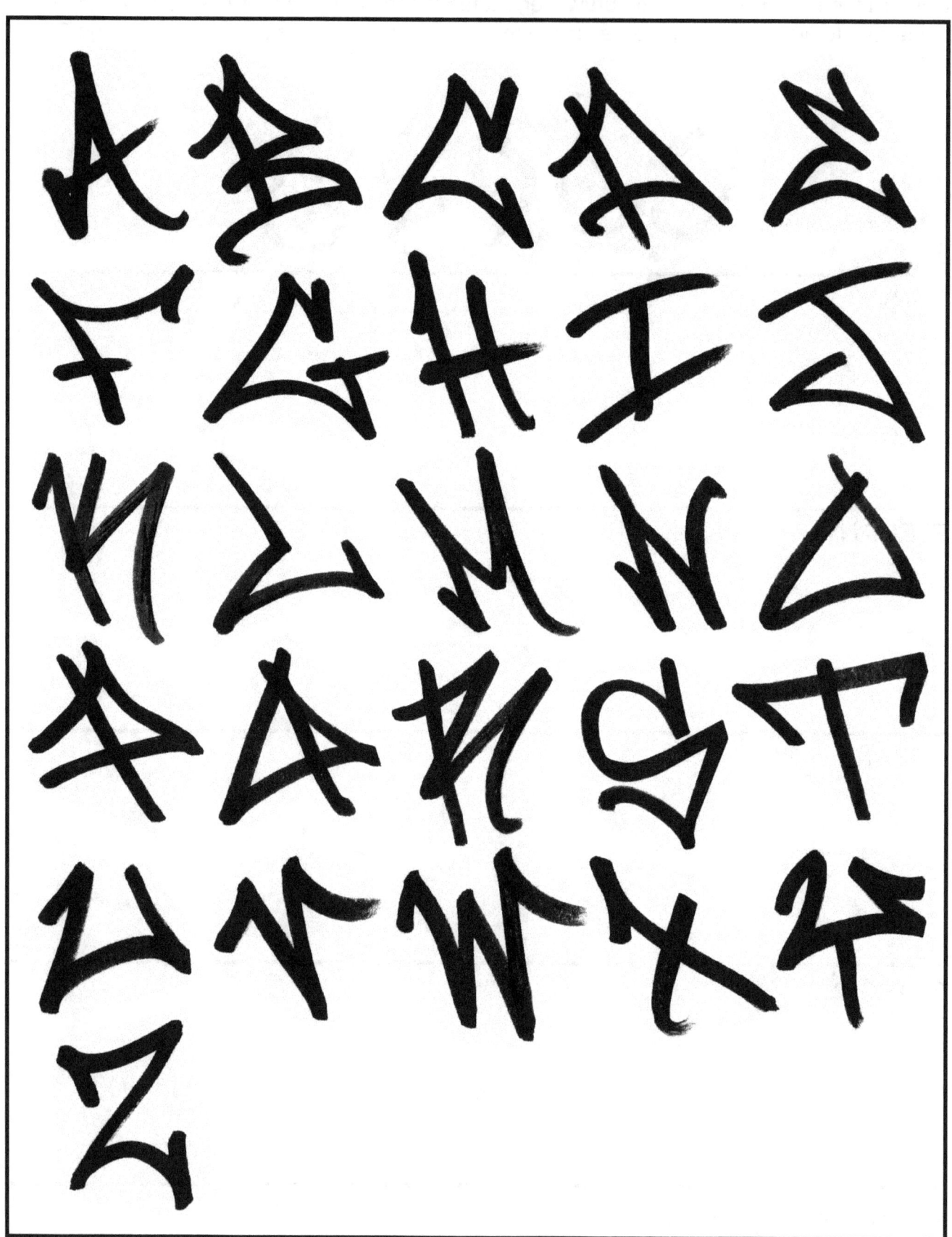

Using tag letters from the Angular Tag Alphabet on the opposite page, write out each word on the line above it using angular tag letters. At the bottom use angular tag letters to write your own name. You can trace the letters if you like. See answers on Page 55.

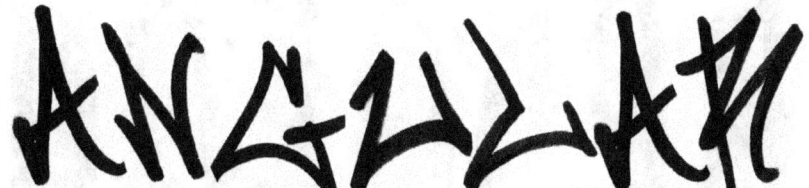

ANGULAR

SHARP

FIERCE

GRAFF

YOUR NAME HERE

ABCDEFGHI
JKLMNOPQ
RSTUVWXYZ

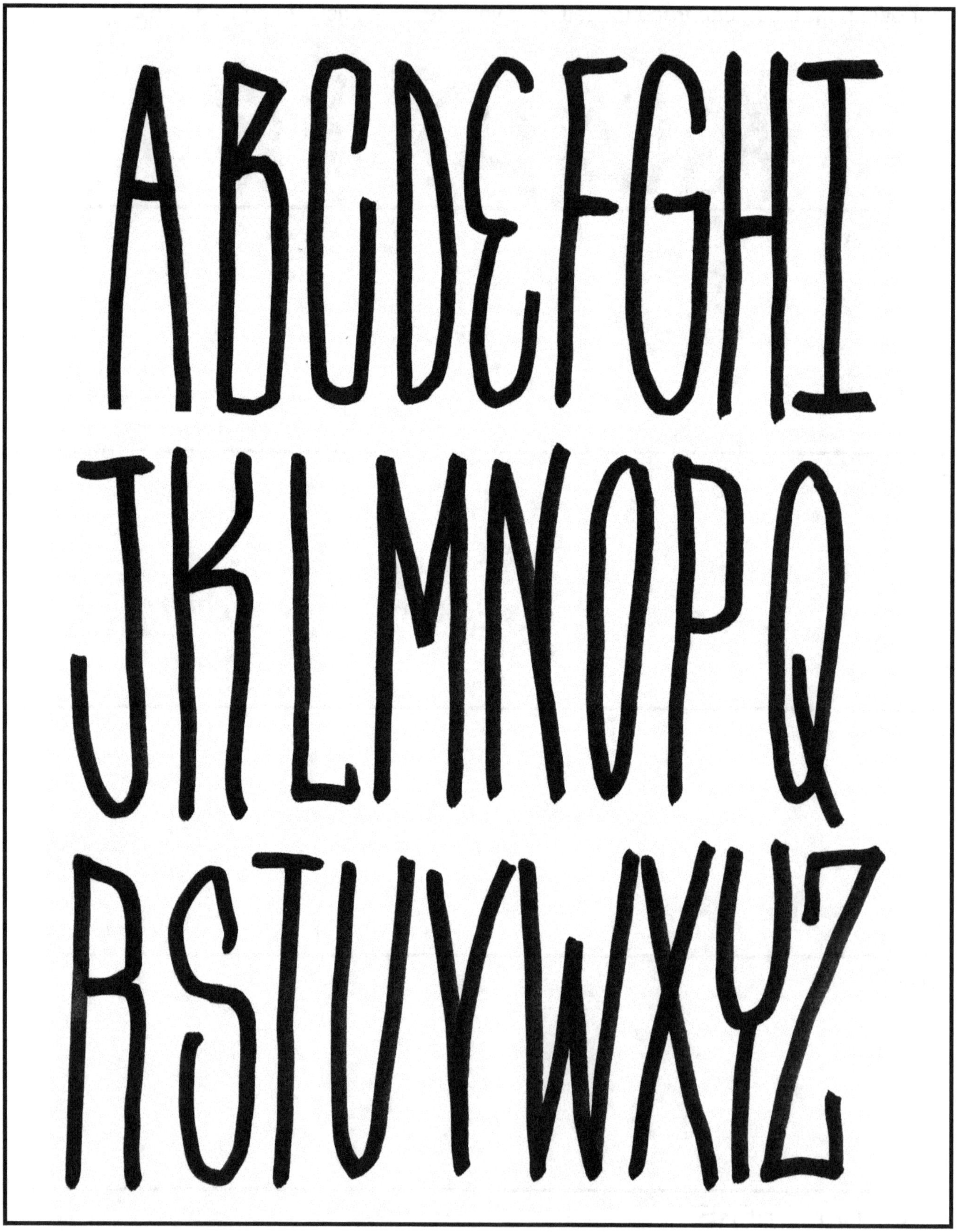

Using tag letters from the Tall Tag Alphabet on the opposite page, write out each word on the line above it using tall tag letters. At the bottom use tall tag letters to write your own name. You can trace the letters if you like. See answers on Page 56.

_____   _____
TALL   SKILL

_____
WRITER

_____
YOUR NAME HERE

Drawing backslanted letters can be difficult at first. Here's a helpful trick:

The chart on the opposite page has 26 boxes for the alphabet. Fill in the boxes with A thru Z using backslanted letters. The letters can be round, square or angular. Lean the letters way over to the left and fit them inside the boxes. Like this:

BACKSLANTED TAG LETTERS

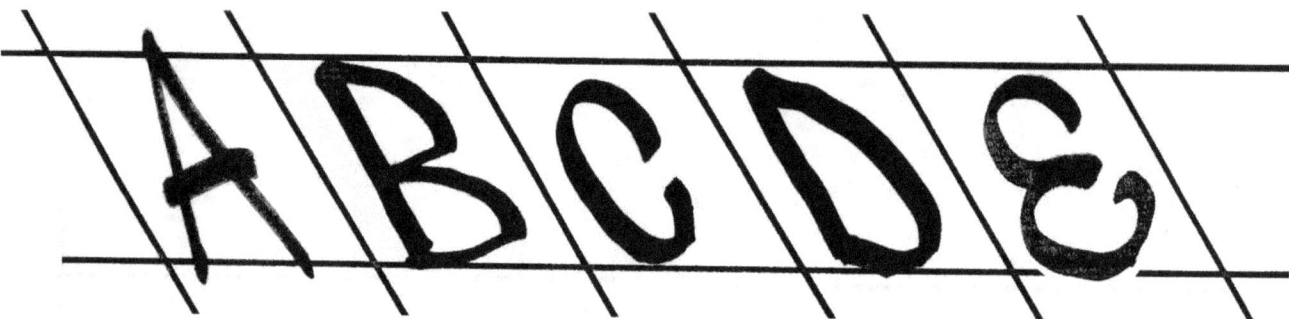

You can copy the graph before you fill it in so that you'll have an extra copy to continue practicing on. To copy the graph, place a piece of tracing paper or very thin copy paper on top and trace the lines with a pencil and a ruler.

Question: How far can a tag letter backslant? Answer: As far back as you want it to!

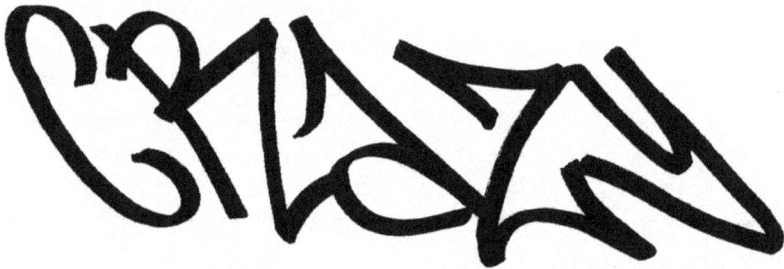

This technique also works the other way with letters that slant over to the right like *italic* letters. To create a right-slanted graph, copy the same blank graph on tracing paper, flip it over with the vertical lines tilting the other way and fill in the boxes. Like this:

ITALIC TAG LETTERS

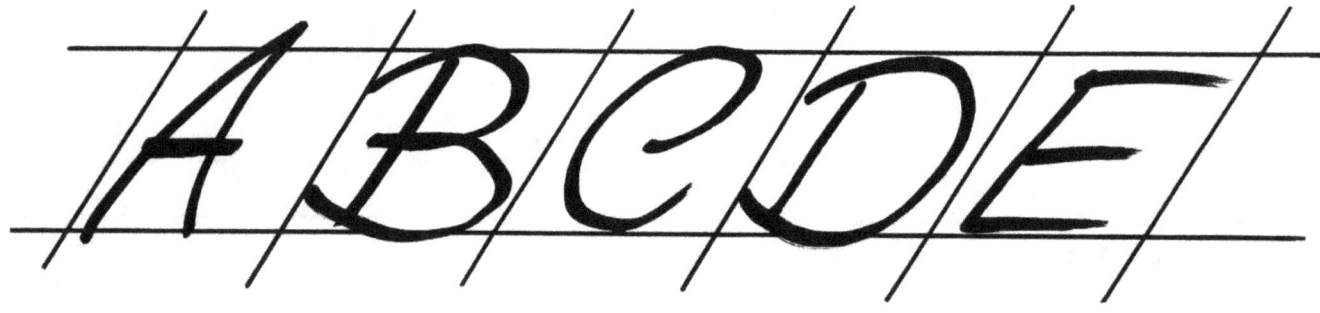

EXERCISE: FILL IN THE BOXES WITH LETTERS A to Z

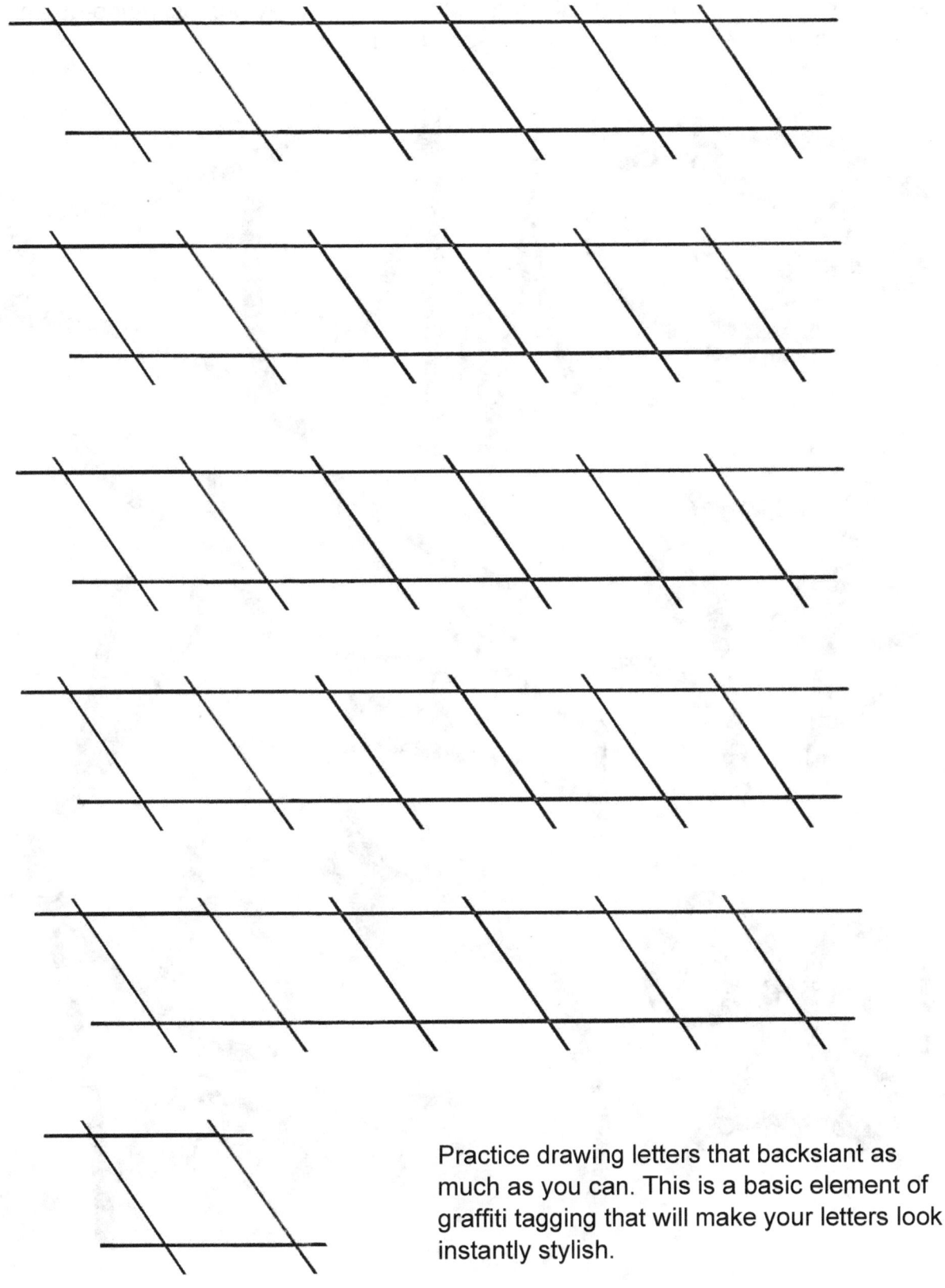

Practice drawing letters that backslant as much as you can. This is a basic element of graffiti tagging that will make your letters look instantly stylish.

MIX AND MATCH DIFFERENT ELEMENTS OF DIFFERENT STYLES AND INVENT SOME OF YOUR OWN TAG LETTERS. JUST MAKE THEM UP!

These are not based on any particular tag alphabet style. They are just made-up and fun. There are no right or wrong ways to draw a tag letter.

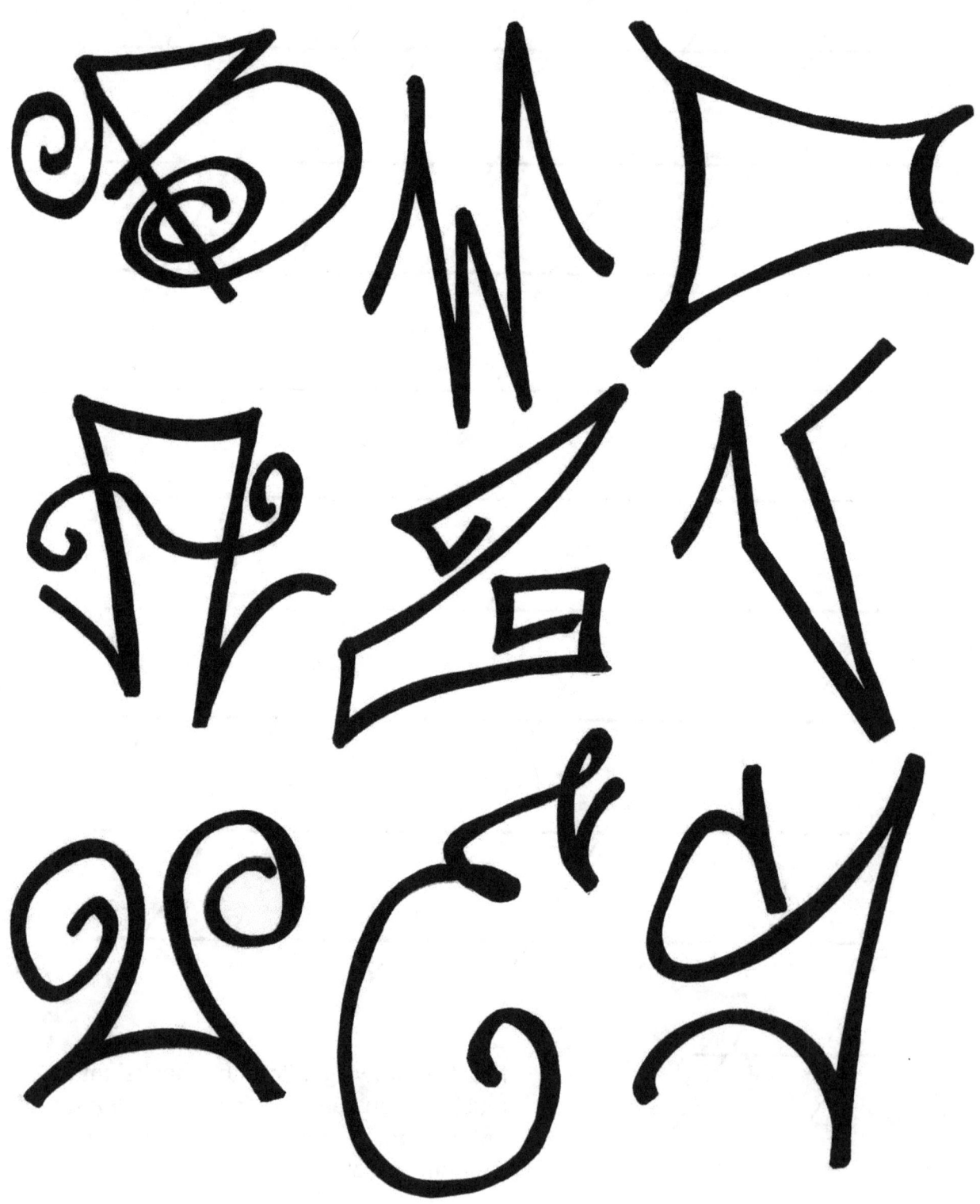

The alphabet styles we have shown you are just a few examples of the many styles of tag letters you can experiment with. Try different variations with little bits of different styles mixed up together and see what you can come up with. Combine round and curvy letters or square and angular letters. In time you will develop a unique style that is all your own. A dry erasable whiteboard or black chalkboard mounted on a wall is a useful tool you can use to draw your letters over and over without using up so much paper. Draw with your whole arm and body, not just your wrist and hand.

A few more tag letter features we want to point out:
•   Philadelphia Wickeds or Wickets have unusually shaped bottoms.
•   Cholo letters from Los Angeles have diamond shaped, triangular bottoms.
•   Ornamental, scripted styles are used by tattoo artists to create letter art on skin.
The main rule you have to remember is to keep the style of all the letters in your tag consistent and you will be on your way to drawing graffiti tags.

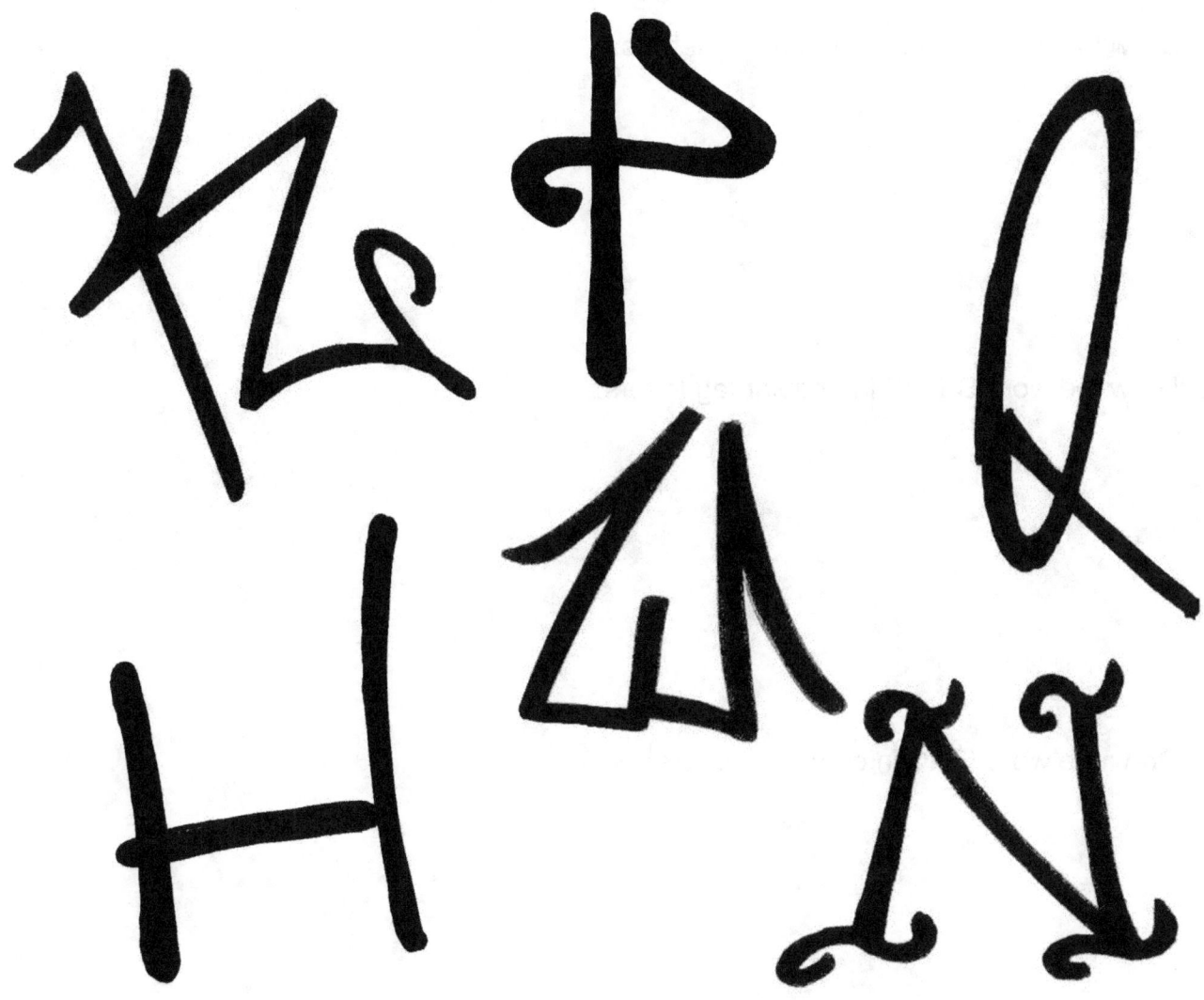

PRACTICE WORKSHEET A - Answers on Page 57

Draw a SQUARE TAG LETTER **A** in the box below	Draw an ANGULAR TAG LETTER **A** in the box below	Draw a CURVY TAG LETTER **A** in the box below

1. Draw the word CHILL in square tag letters.

2. Draw the word B-BOY in angular tag letters.

3. Draw the word EPIC in curvy tag letters.

Complete the exercises below. Write each word on the left - Tag each word on the right using any style of tag letter. Just make sure to keep the letters in each word consistent. Make up your own tag style if you like.

Write the word ME

Tag the word ME

Write the word ART

Tag the word ART

Write the word FUNNY

Tag the word FUNNY

Write the word WILD

Tag the word WILD

---

1. 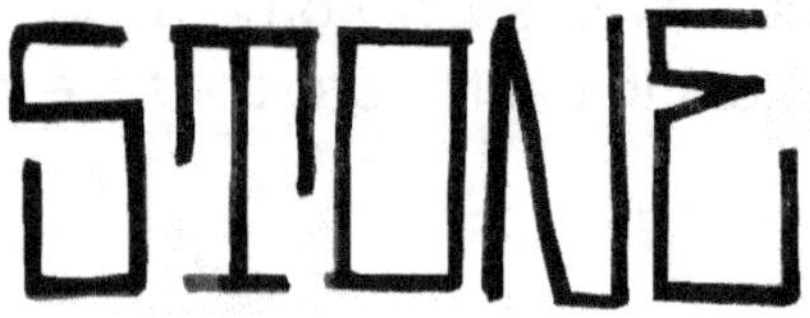 STONE

Write the word NOTES
using the letters in STONE

_____

Write the word TEST
using the letters in STONE

_____

Write the word BONES
using the letters in STONE

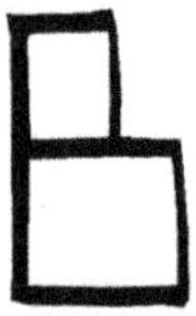

B

_____

2. 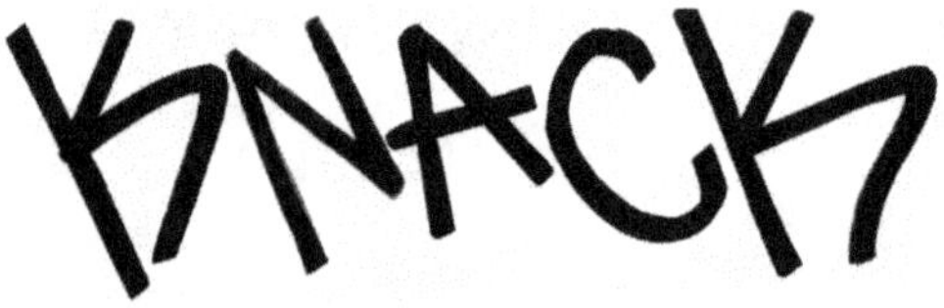 KNACK

Write the word CAN
using the letters in KNACK

_____

Write the word TANK
using the letters in KNACK

T

_____

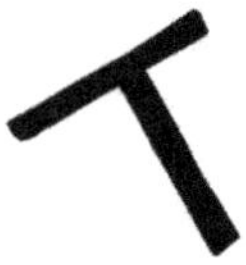

Write the word ACT
using the letters in
KNACK and TANK

_____

3. RACE

Write the word CAR
using the letters in RACE

Write the word ACRE
using the letters in RACE

Write the word SCARE
using the letters in RACE

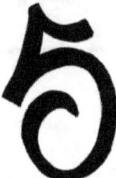

4. COOL

Write the word LOCO
using the letters in COOL

Write the word POOL
using the letters in COOL

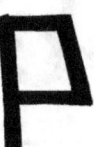

Write the word LOOP
using the letters in
COOL and POOL

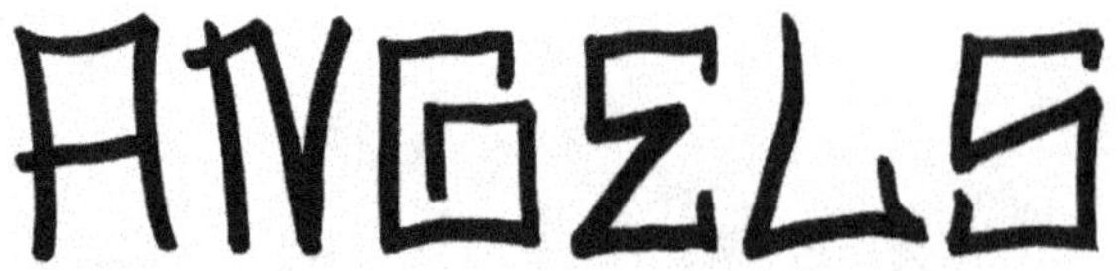

ANGELS

ANGELS

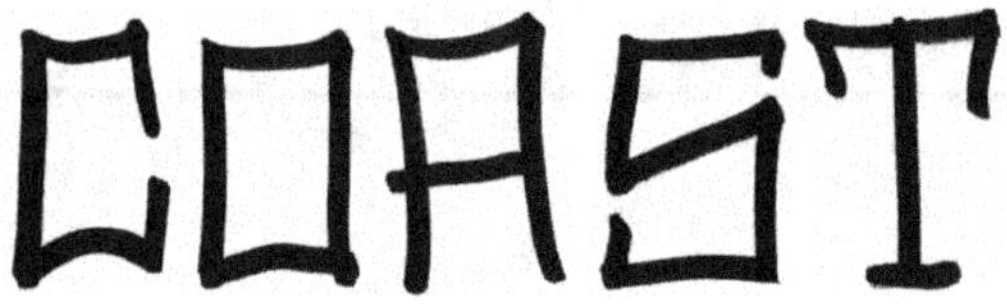

COAST

COAST

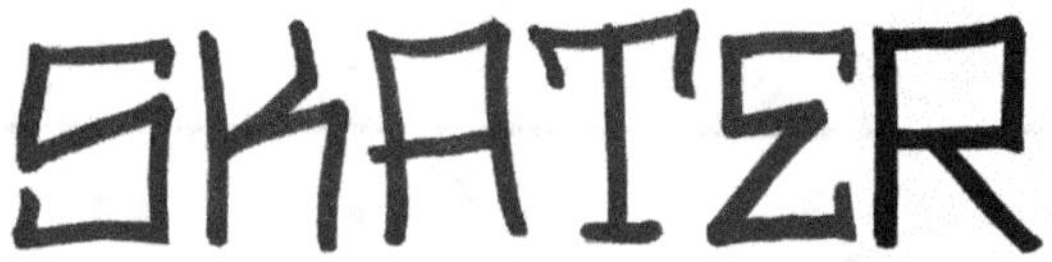

SKATER

SKATER

Solutions to Exercise on Page 39

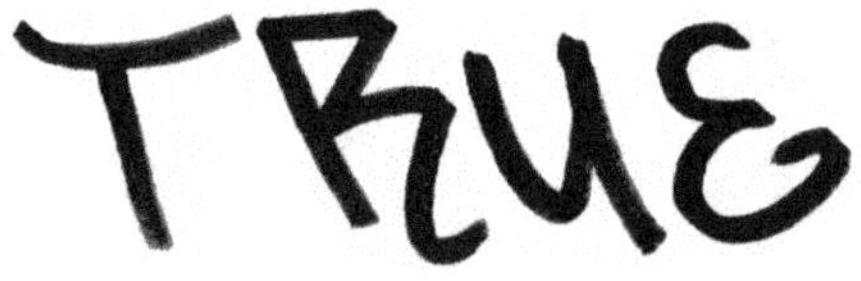

TRUE

TRUE

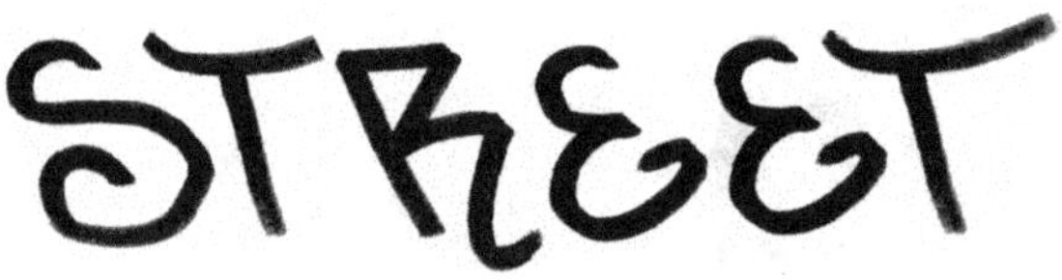

STREET

STREET

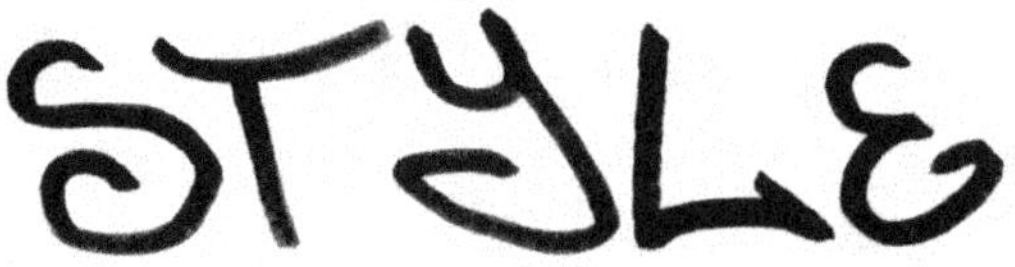

STYLE

STYLE

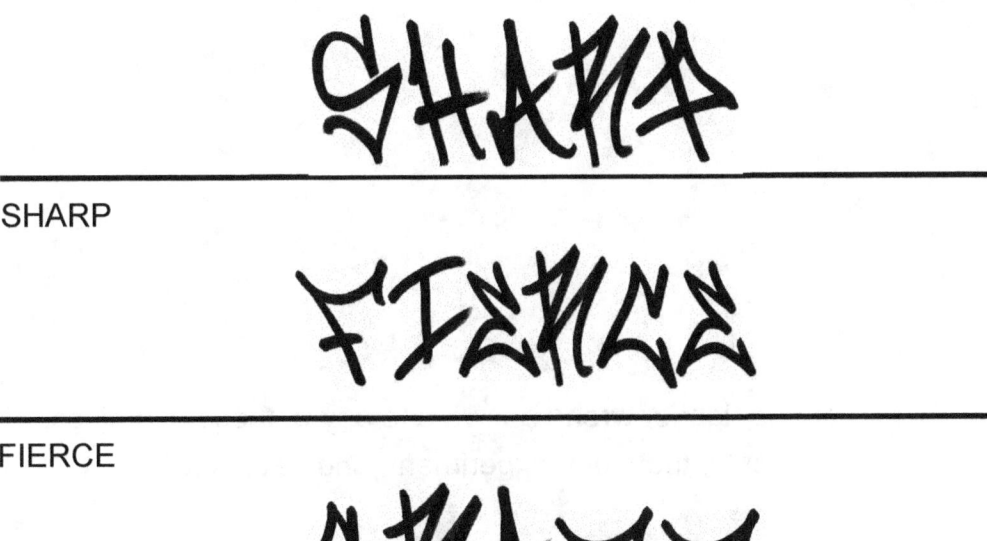

ELEGANT

URBAN

CLASSIC

Solutions to Exercise on Page 43

SHARP

FIERCE

DANGER

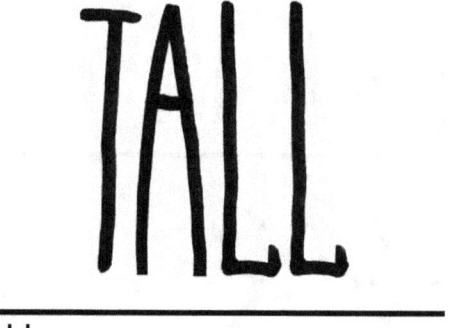

TALL

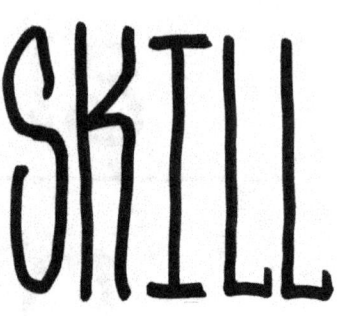

SKILL

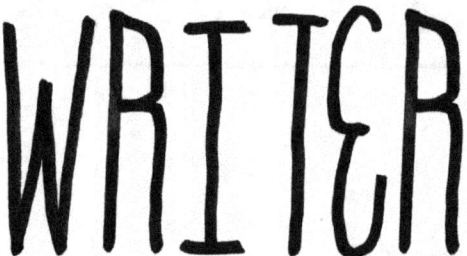

WRITER

There are no right or wrong answers to any of these exercises.
Just try them out, experiment, and have fun!

Draw a SQUARE TAG LETTER **A** in the box below	Draw an ANGULAR TAG LETTER **A** in the box below	Draw a CURVY TAG LETTER **A** in the box below
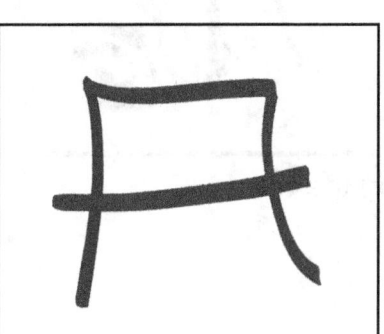	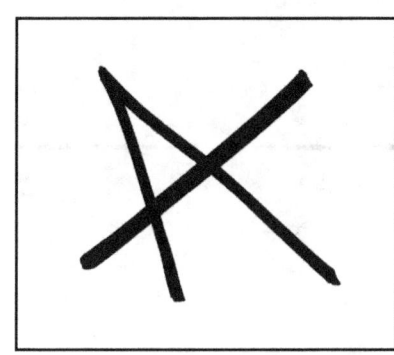	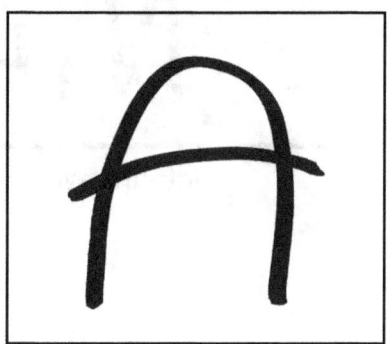

1. Draw the word CHILL in square tag letters.

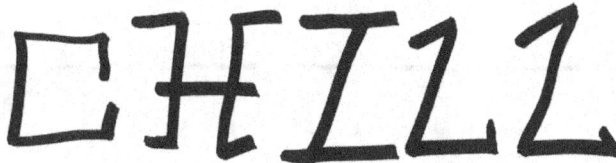

2. Draw the word B-BOY in angular tag letters.

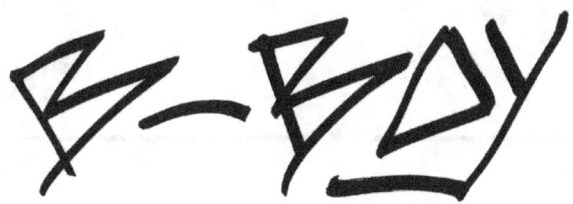

3. Draw the word EPIC in curvy tag letters.

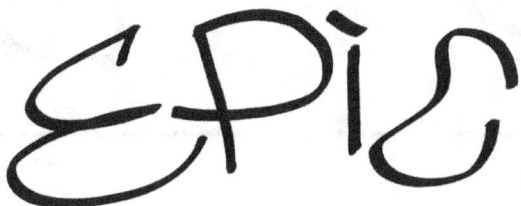

SAMPLE OF STUDENT'S COMPLETED WORKSHEET B FROM PAGE 51 -
There are no right or wrong answers.

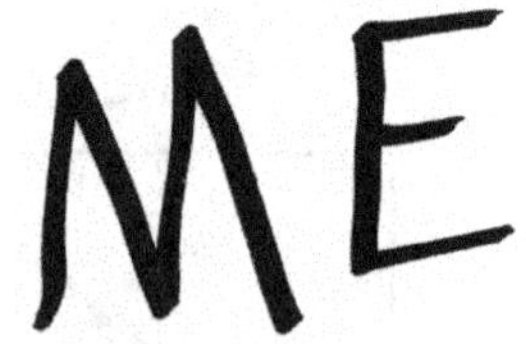

ME

Write the word ME

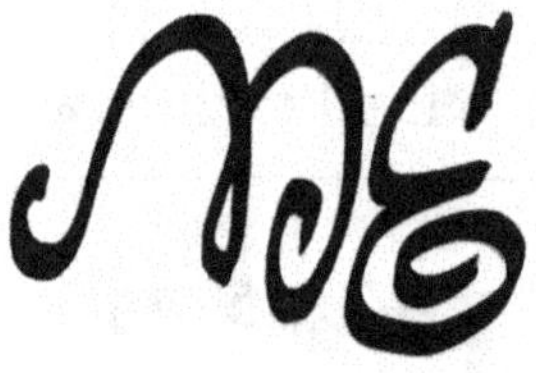

ME

Tag the word ME

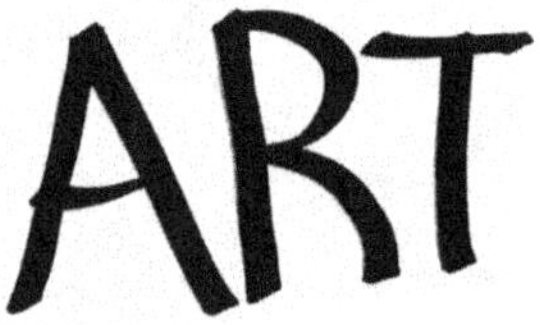

ART

Write the word ART

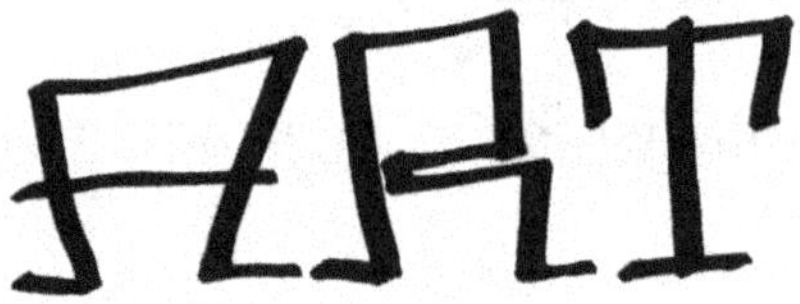

ART

Tag the word ART

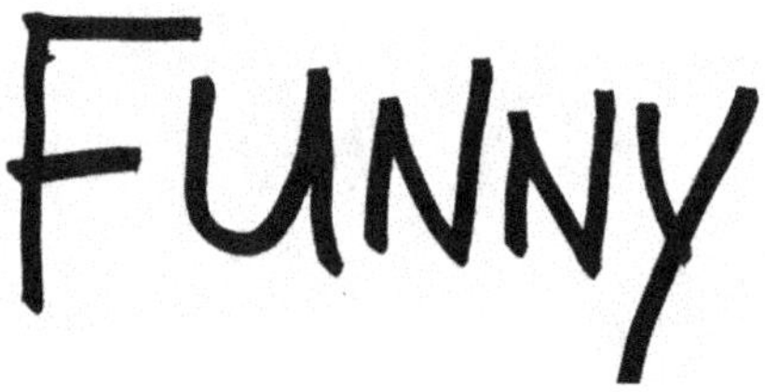

FUNNY

Write the word FUNNY

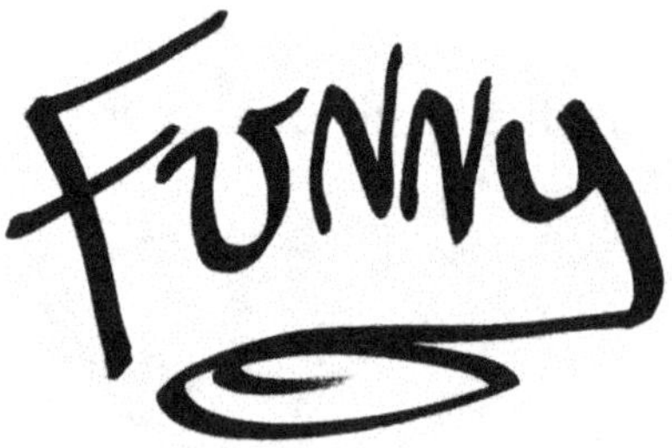

Funny

Tag the word FUNNY

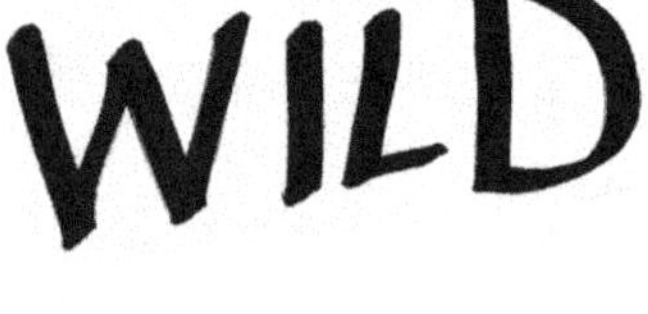

WILD

Write the word WILD

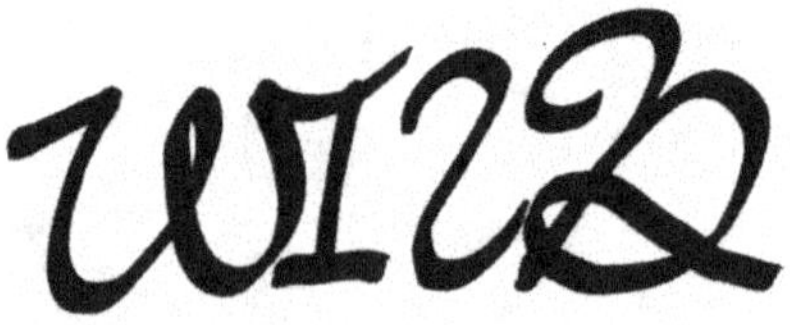

WILD

Tag the word WILD

1.

NOTES

TEST

BONES

2.

CAN

TANK

ACT

3.

CAR

ACRE

SCARE

4.

LOCO

POOL

LOOP

CHAPTER FIVE
LAYOUT WITH GUIDELINES

So far we have explored the concepts of line, tag letter structure, and consistency. Now it is time to think about how a graffiti tag should be planned and organized. The technical term for this is the layout. Layout refers to how elements in a design are arranged on a page. In graffiti tagging terms, layout refers to the positioning of the letters in a tag.

Spacing is important when laying out a block of text, like the words you are reading now. The space between each letter is roughly equal, as are the spaces between each word. If you squint at this page, the individual paragraphs look like gray blocks. The gray blocks are arranged evenly in between the edges of the paper. By grouping the words into blocks it is not that difficult to arrange them on the page in a balanced, effective manner. Proper spacing is the foundation of good typography (typography is the art of arranging letters).

Graffiti tag design is a little different, however, because it is more like drawing a picture than writing text. As a tag design progresses, the letters are modified and manipulated in ways that don't necessarily conform to the basic rules of traditional typography. When a tag design is complete, it resembles a symbol or a logo rather than a written word. But even a graffiti tag design needs a place to start and that is where layout comes in. Before you can begin to develop a tag you need to decide on what the layout of the letters are going to be.

WORKING WITH GUIDELINES

To create a layout you use guidelines. Guidelines are lines which serve as a reference to show you where things go. In a layout two guidelines are needed, one above the letters and one below. The two guidelines are drawn first and then the letters are placed in between them. The guidelines make it easy to keep the letters equally sized and moving in the same direction.

To start a layout, first draw two guidelines **lightly with a pencil**. You will be erasing them in a minute. Make the guidelines parallel to each other and as far apart as you want. Next, draw the letters of your tag in between the guidelines. The tops of the letters should almost touch the top guideline, and the bottoms of the letters should sit on the lower guideline. The lower guideline is also known as a **baseline**. Stretch and mold the letters to fit. When you are done, erase the guidelines. You now have a Starting Point that you can use to design your tag.

BASIC LAYOUT WITH GUIDELINES

STEP 1. With a pencil draw two guidelines parallel to each other.

TOP GUIDELINE

_____

BOTTOM GUIDELINE OR BASELINE

STEP 2. Draw tag letters inside the guidelines. The top of the letters should be near the top guideline and the bottom of the letters should sit on the bottom guideline or baseline as much as is possible.

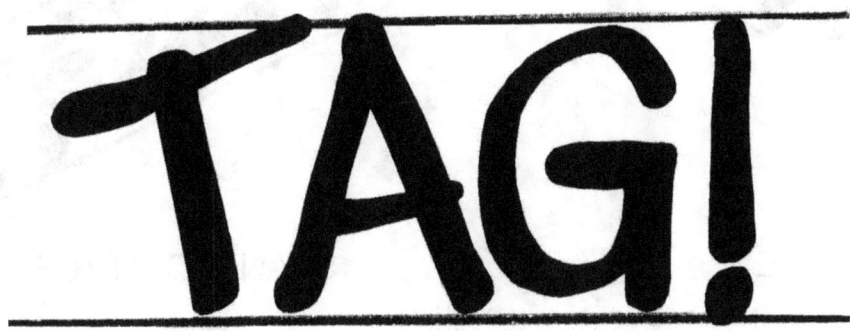

STEP 3. Erase the guidelines. This is your Starting Point for a tag design. Chapter Eight shows you how to use your Starting Point to design a tag.

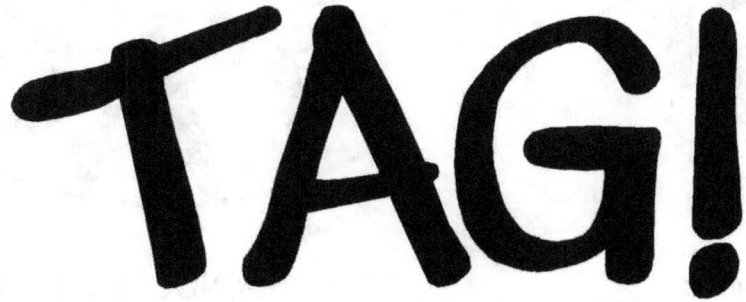

There are four basic layout styles you can refer to when designing a tag. They are Straight Style, Slanted Style, Rainbow Style and Wave Style. In these layout styles, the guidelines are parallel to each other.

STRAIGHT STYLE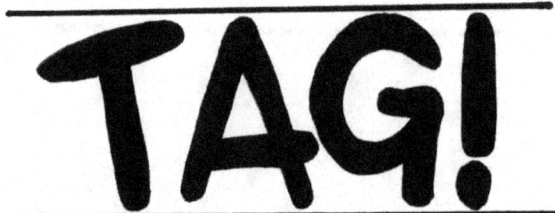

You can change the direction or bend the guidelines in different ways. In Slanted Style the guidelines move either in an upward direction or in a downward direction.

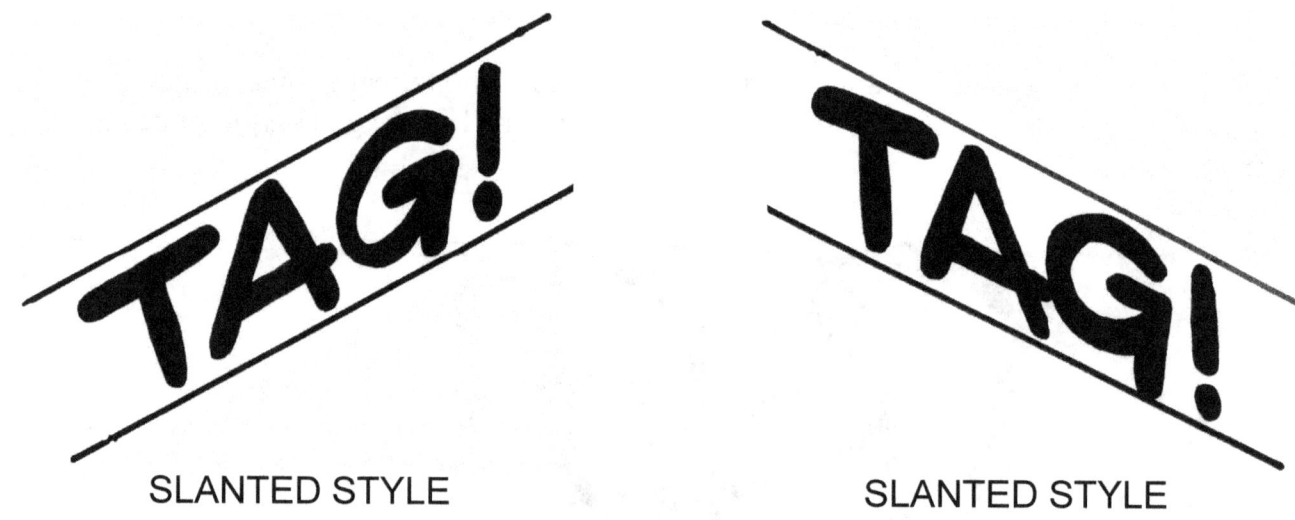

SLANTED STYLE   SLANTED STYLE

In Rainbow Style the guidelines curve upward or curve downward. The letters fit in between the guidelines just like in Straight Style.

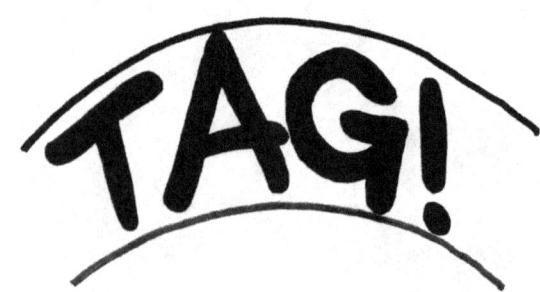   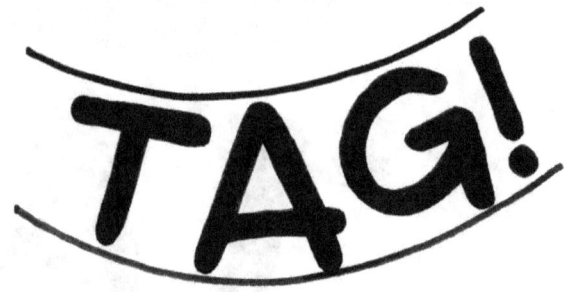

RAINBOW STYLE   RAINBOW STYLE

This is Wave Style. In this style, you can bend the guidelines in several places, still keeping the lines parallel. This style is a little harder to do, but the rules are the same. First draw the guidelines with a pencil, then stretch and mold the letters to fit in between the guidelines, following the contours of the waves.

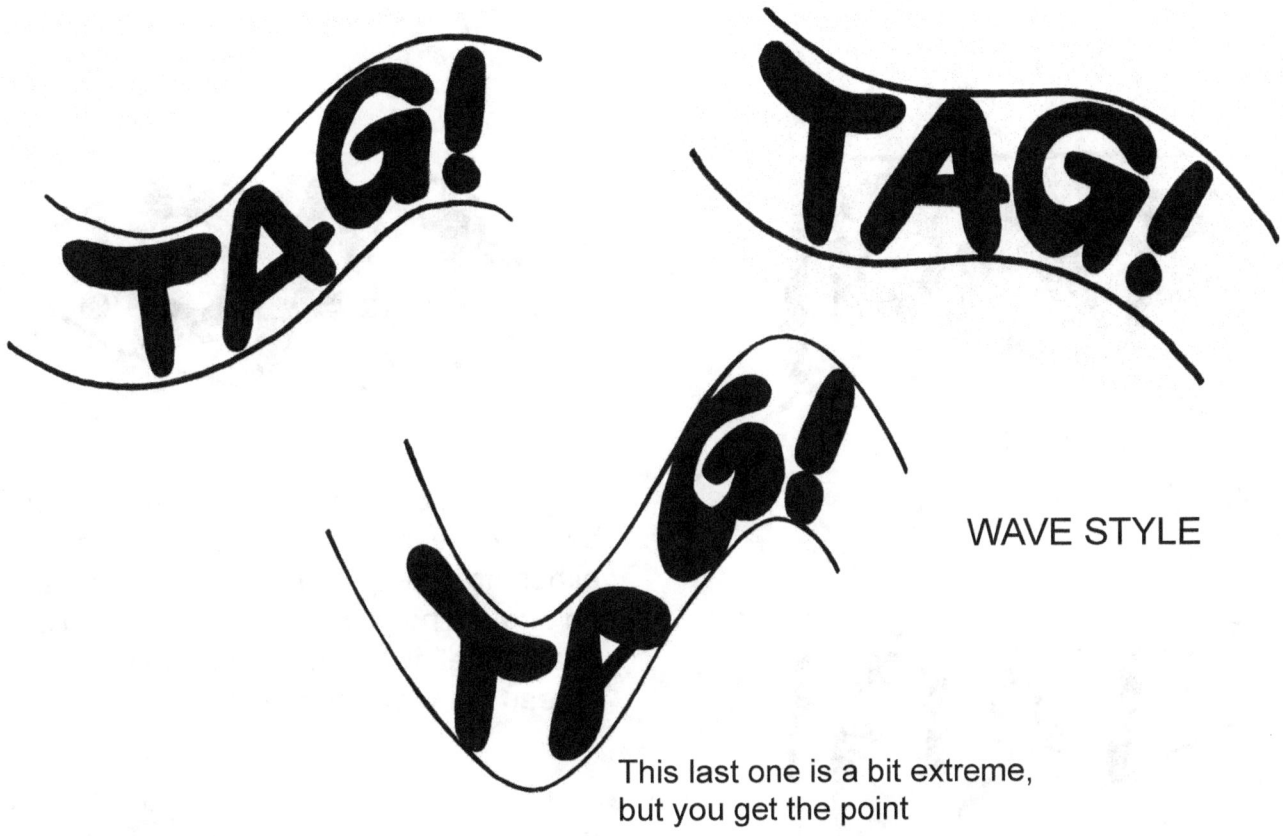

WAVE STYLE

This last one is a bit extreme, but you get the point

You can play around with the guidelines and try bending them in different ways. There are no exact rules for laying out a word.

EXERCISE: MAKE A DUMMY LAYOUT WITH CUT-OUT LETTERS

If you find it difficult to work with the curved guidelines, you can make a dummy layout with cutouts of the letters. With this technique, you can try out lots of different layouts and see what works best.

INSTRUCTIONS
1. Draw your letters on paper really big. Cut them out.
2. Draw guidelines on another piece of paper and lay your cut-out letters on top.
3. Shift them around until you find a layout you like, then tape them down.
4. Trace the word on a clean sheet of paper, scan it into your computer, or take a photograph. Try several different layouts and compare them.

VARIATIONS ON BASIC LAYOUT STYLES

Here are some alternate layout styles that don't really have a particular name. What makes these examples different from Straight style, Slanted style, Rainbow style and Wave style is that here the two guidelines are not parallel.

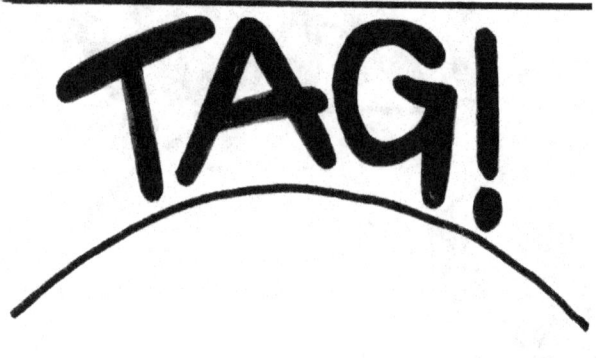

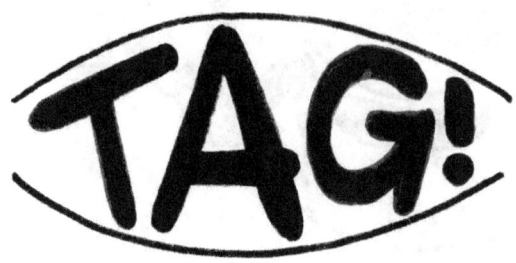

You can also arrange the guidelines vertically. The letters are placed between them either straight up and down or rotated at an angle. The guidelines can be parallel at an equal distance apart or they can spread out wider at one end.

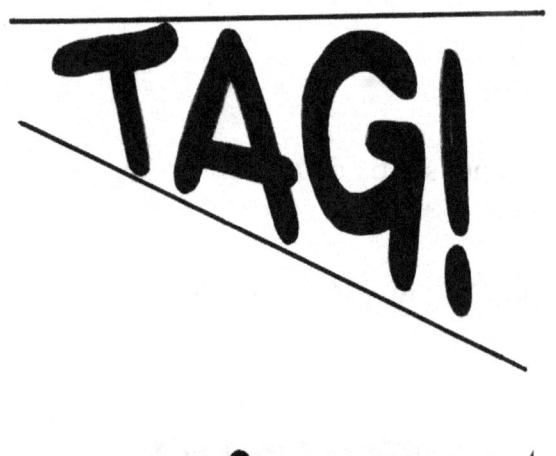

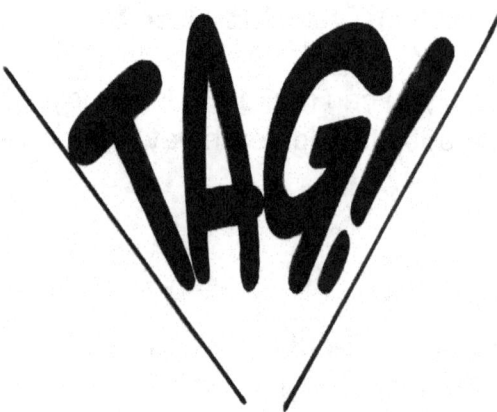

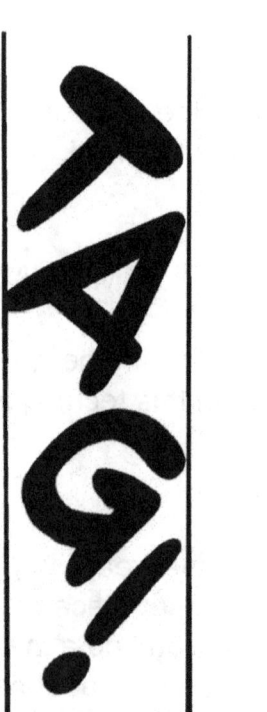

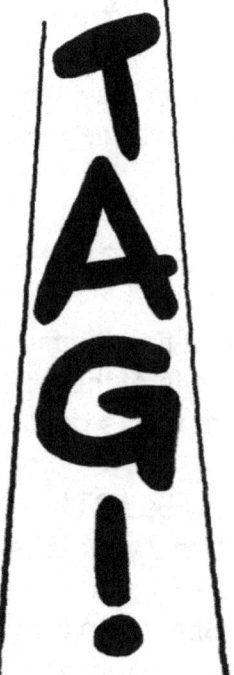

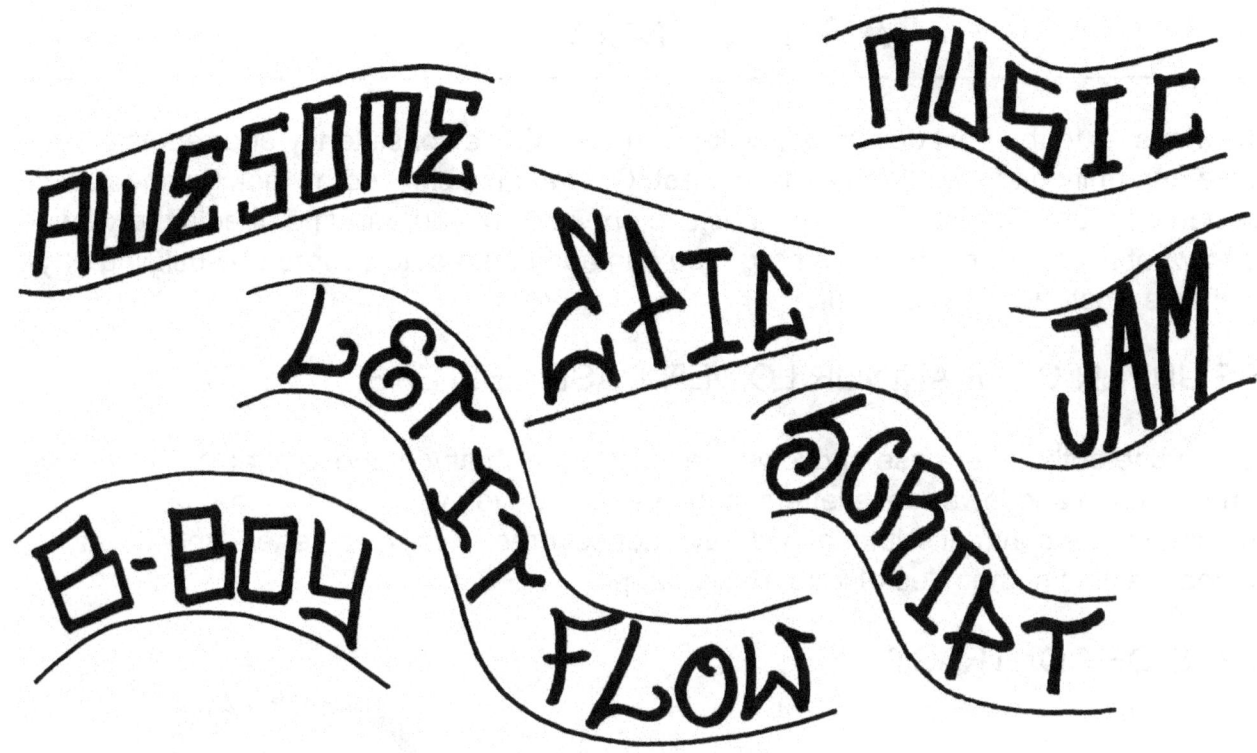

NON-TRADITIONAL LAYOUT STYLE: UNEVEN ALIGNMENT

That brings us to the last layout style, letters drawn to an uneven alignment. This means the letters move up and down in between two guidelines without any set pattern and can rotate at different angles. There are no set rules on how the design should be constructed so this layout is a little more challenging. The goal is the same as with all other layout styles, however - to create a good design. All you really have to go by here is your own individual taste to determine if the layout looks good to your eyes. Is the design balanced? Does it flow? Do the letters look like they belong together? Do they fit well in the space? Is the overall shape of the finished tag interesting? Are the white spaces evenly distributed? These are very subjective measurements, but with practice, you will develop a sense for how letters should be placed.

UNEVEN ALIGNMENT

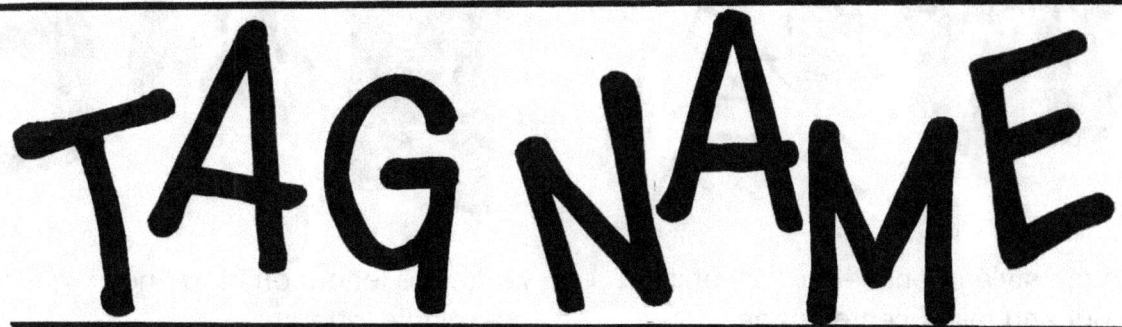

CHAPTER SIX

TAG STYLING OPTIONS

This brings us to the next design principle, Contrast. While consistency and repetition organize and unify a tag, contrast adds interest. Contrast is achieved by making one part of a design different. Contrast adds emphasis to one area of your tag and directs the viewer's eye to what is important about your tag. You can add contrast to your tag by utilizing any of the effects illustrated in this chapter.

USE UPPER-CASE AND/OR LOWER-CASE LETTERS

You can use both upper-case and lower-case letters with any of these effects. By combining upper-case and lower-case letters in the same tag, you will increase your design options and create contrast. Although we have not covered lower-case letters specifically in this book, all the same rules of letter design apply.

TYPES OF CONTRAST

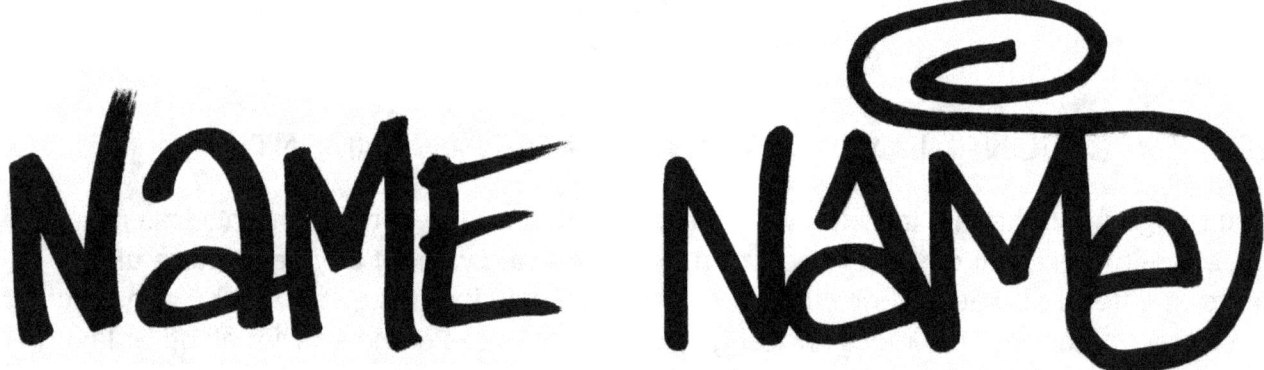

Mix upper-case and lower-case letters.

Stretch out the first or last letter.

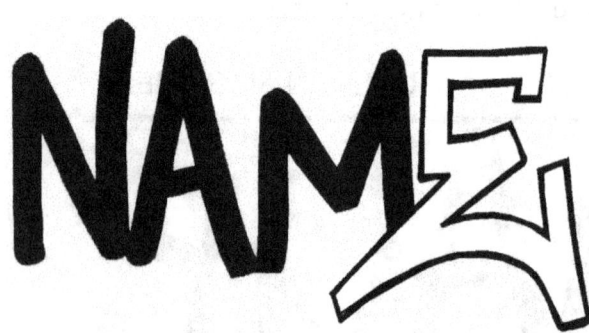

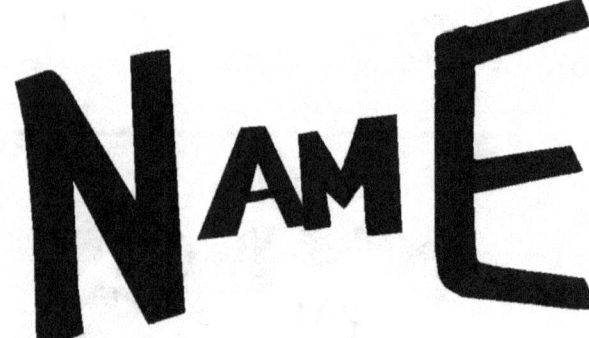

Change the style of one letter so that it stands out and takes center stage.

Make the letters on both ends bigger than the middle letters.

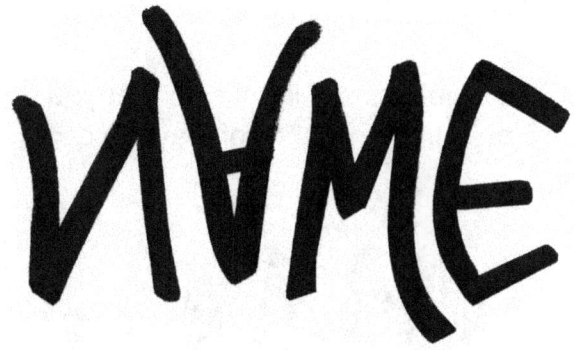

Turn some letters upside down, backward or sideways.

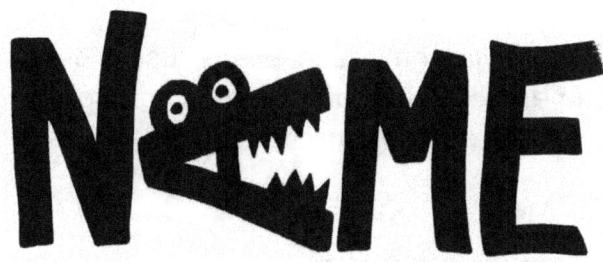

Substitute a letter with a symbol that has a similar shape.

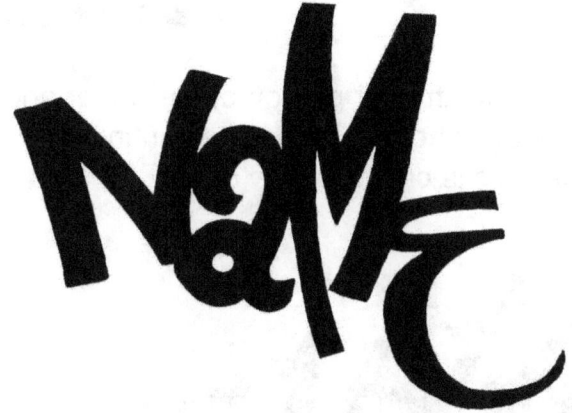

Stretch and mold the shapes of the letters so they fit together like puzzle pieces. Rotate the letters at different angles.

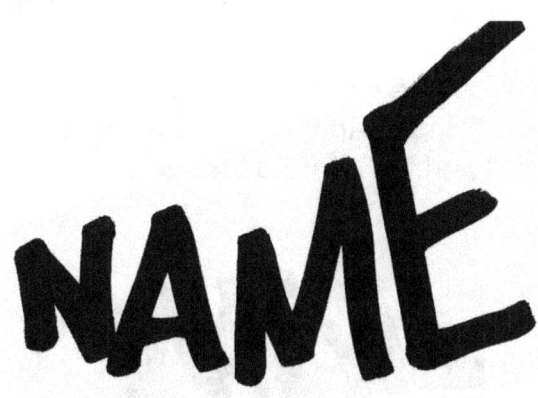

Make the letters larger toward one end.

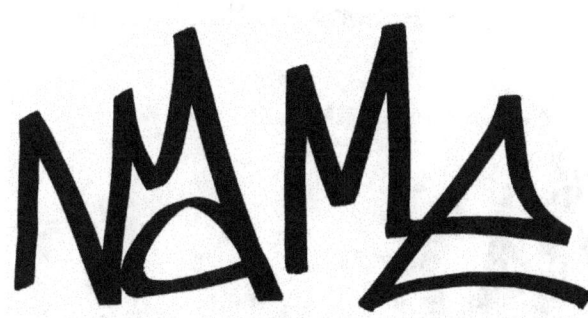

Connect some of the letters.

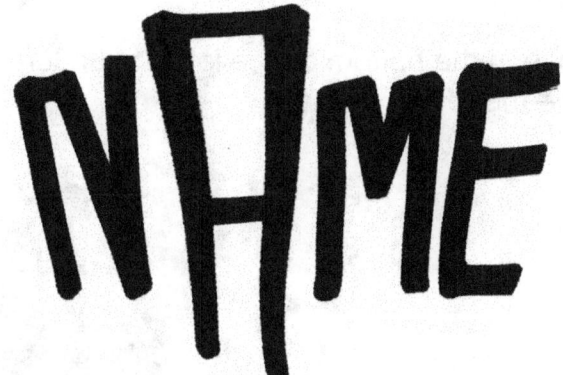

Make one letter much bigger or smaller than all the rest.

Adding some kind of contrast to your tag will increase its visual impact. Contrast makes a tag more interesting so the reader is more apt to pay attention to it.

MORE TAG DESIGN IDEAS USING CONTRAST AND/OR CONSISTENCY

When trying out these effects, use a pencil and sketch your letters out lightly, so that you can erase and modify them as you go along. There are an infinite number of ways to design a tag, so experiment with some of these techniques.

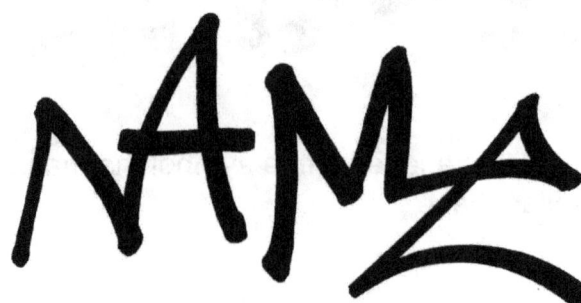

Use the same line to form two different letters. The "N" and "A" share a line, and the "M" and "E" share a line.

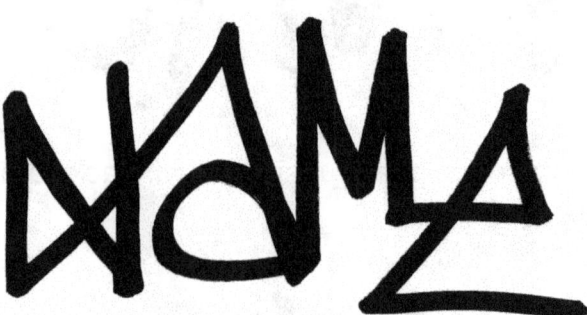

Try not to lift your pen off of the paper and draw the whole tag with one continuous line. This is called a *One Liner*.

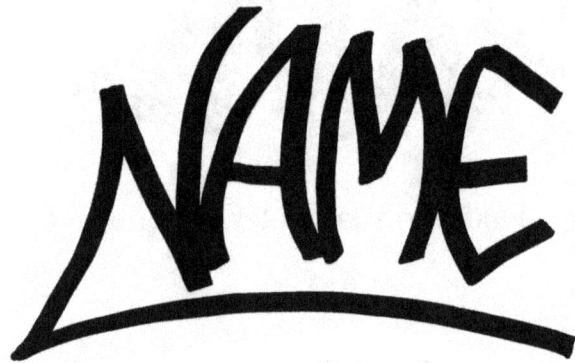

Extend the bottom of one letter to underline the rest of the tag.

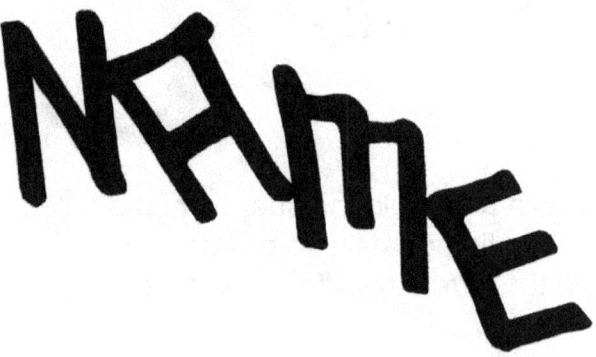

Draw the letters on a slanted baseline.

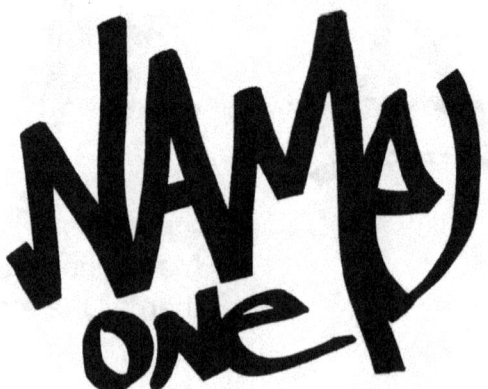

Combine letters with a number or numeral.

WHY WRITE WHEN YOU CAN TAG

Using any of these effects in your tag will make it more dramatic and distinctive. You don't have to reinvent the wheel here because these are all established effects that graffiti writers have used for decades. These are not our inventions. But you can experiment with your own ideas and mix-and-match these effects to create something unique and eye-catching.

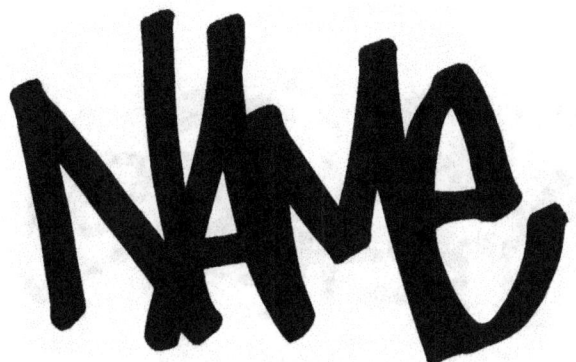

Overlap all of the letters.

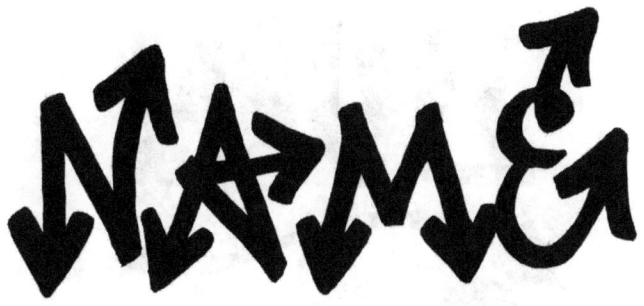

Add arrows to the ends of letters.

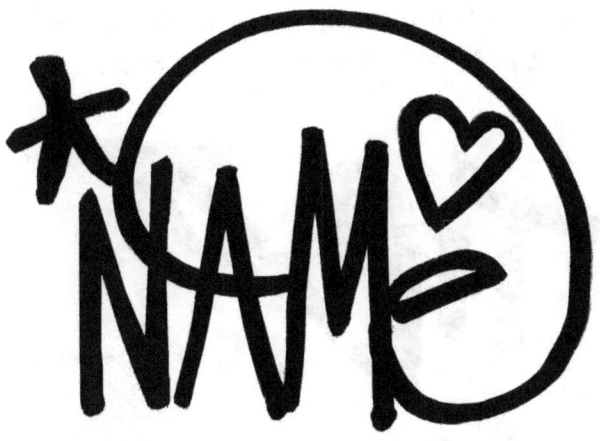

Add extra elements, like stars, hearts, dots or swirls.

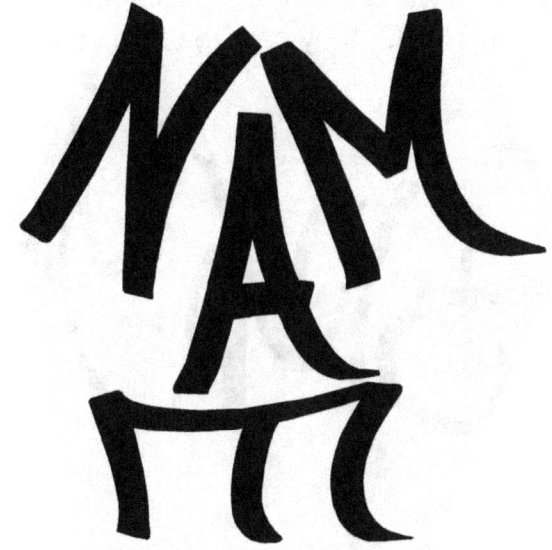

Scramble the layout of the letters and arrange them in an interesting pattern.

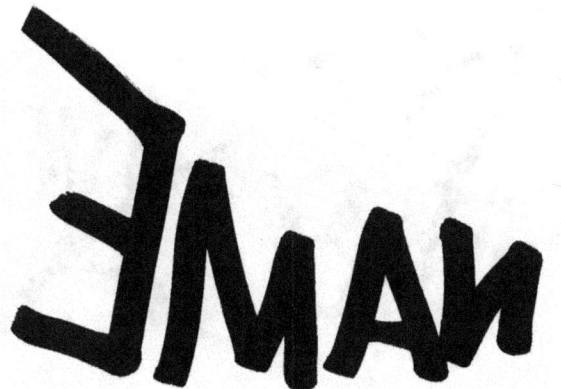

.sbrawkcab gat ruoy etirw neve nac uoY
Sorry, I couldn't resist the temptation.

You can even write your tag backwards.

ADDING ARROWS TO A TAG - SO MUCH STYLE

Graffiti tagging has a unique set of elements that you can add to your letters to make them more interesting. Arrows are the most popular element. At first graffiti writers added arrows to underline their tags like in these "JUAN" and "FATZ" tags.

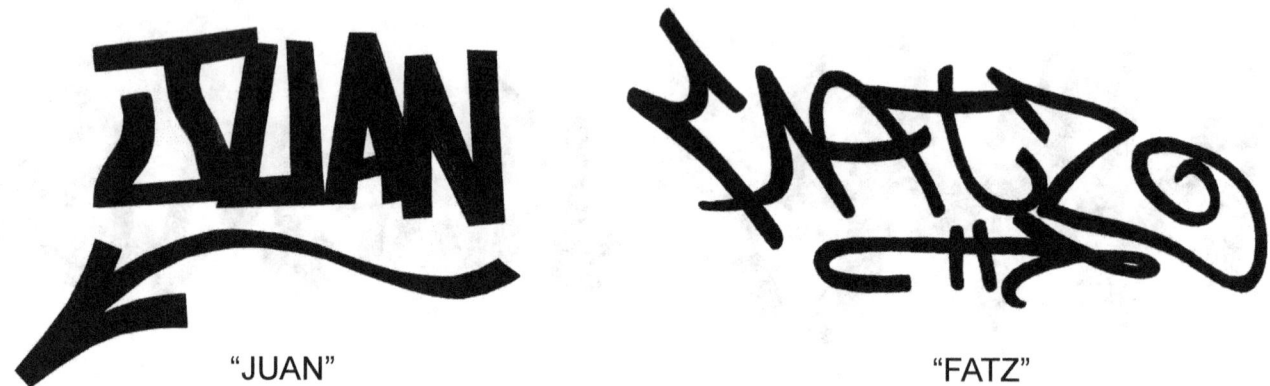

"JUAN"

"FATZ"

Then writers had the brilliant idea of attaching arrows to the letters themselves, and a new letterform was born! Letters with arrows can be drawn very simply like the **K** in SICK and the **e** in TIE. Or they can be more complex like in the **Z** in NEPZ(?) and the **C** in ROC.

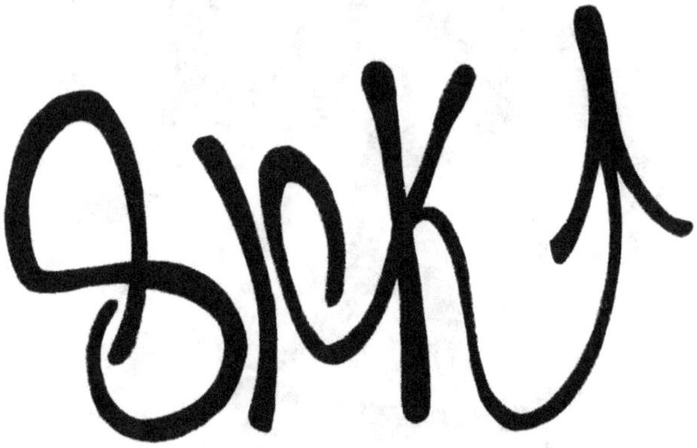

"SICK"

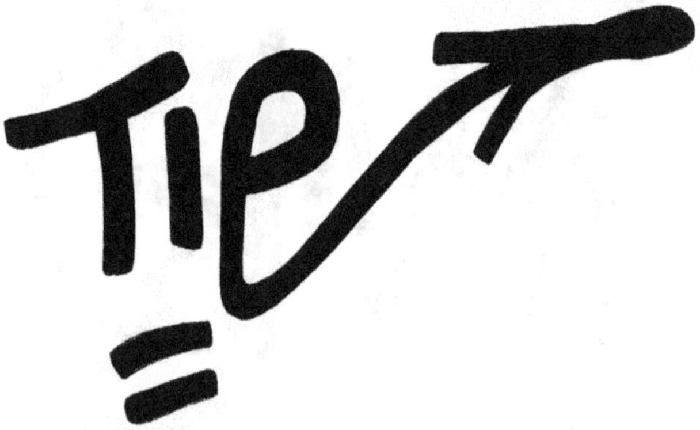

"TIE"

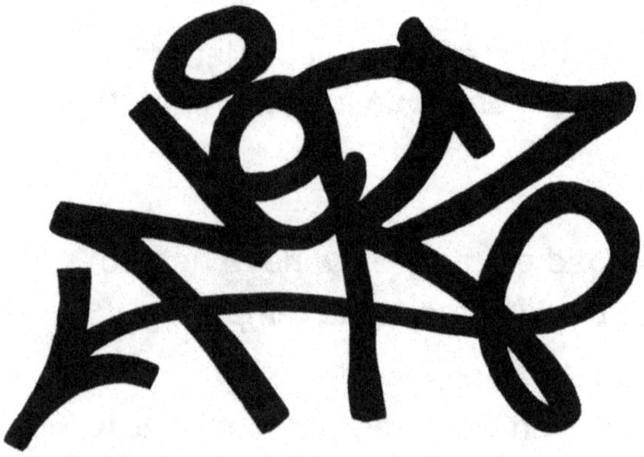

"NERZ" or "NEPZ"

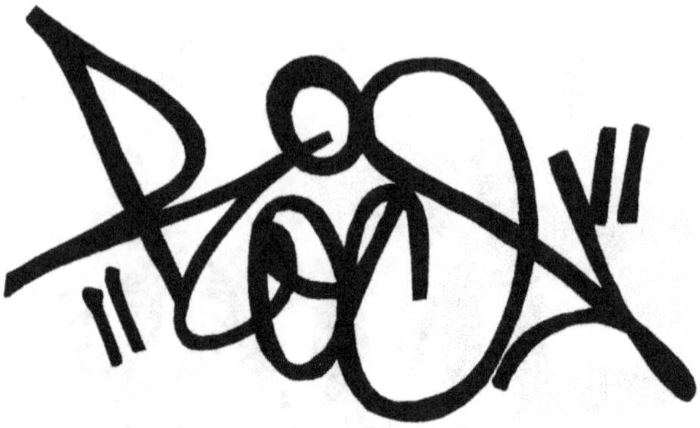

"ROC"

You can add arrows to a letter anywhere you want. An arrow can flow smoothly from the end of a letter in a straight or curving line. Or it can jump off unexpectedly at a sharp angle. You can even add multiple arrows to a single letter or multiple points to the same arrow.

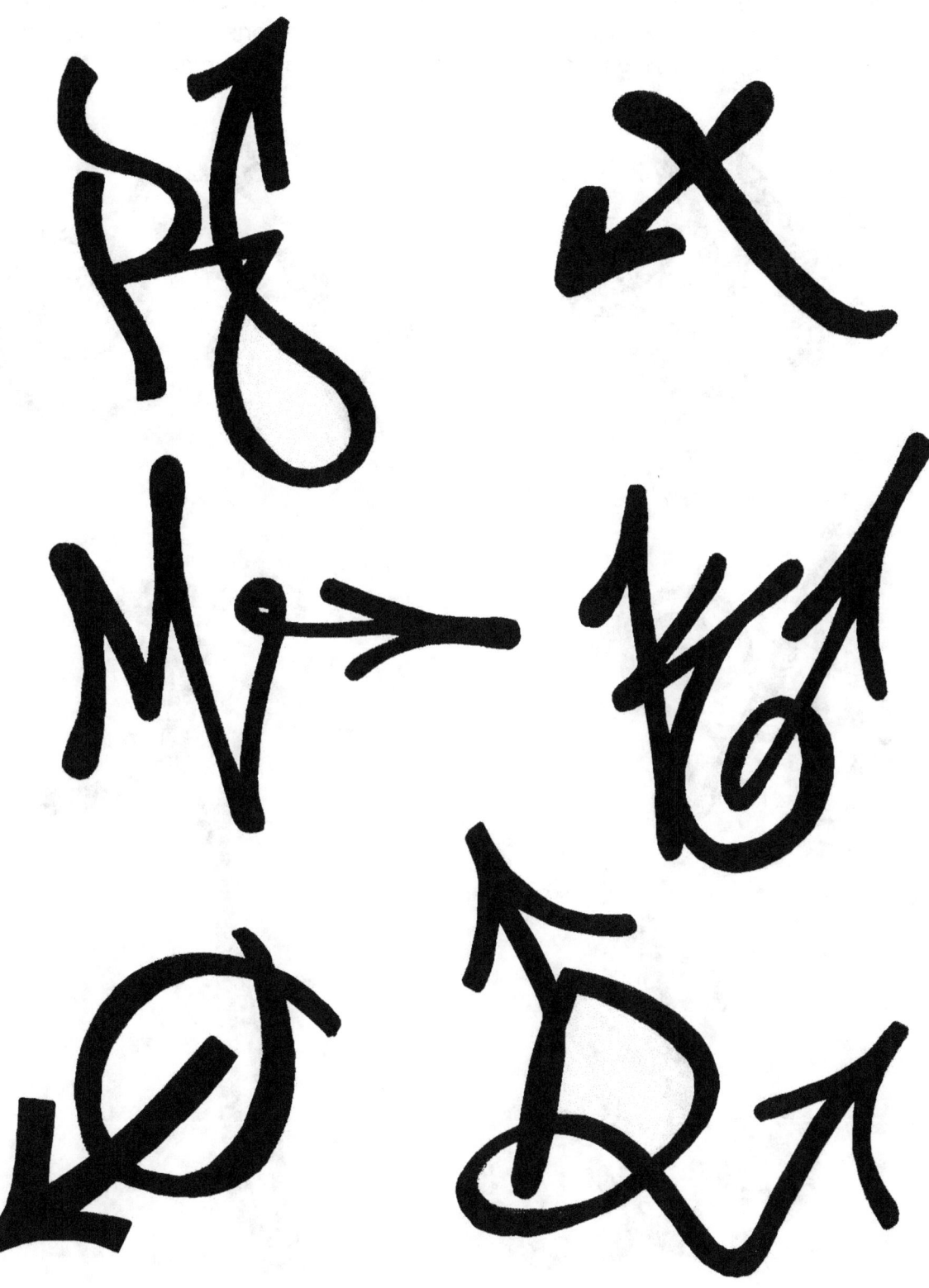

EXTENSIONS AND FLOURISHES

Extensions or flourishes are extra parts that can be added to the ends of the strokes of letters to fill space and add unexpected interest. These parts can be drawn as rounded loops or sharp, angular points. They should follow the flow of the strokes of the letter and compliment it. The more you practice drawing tag letters with extensions and flourishes, the better you will get at figuring out where these extra parts can logically be placed.

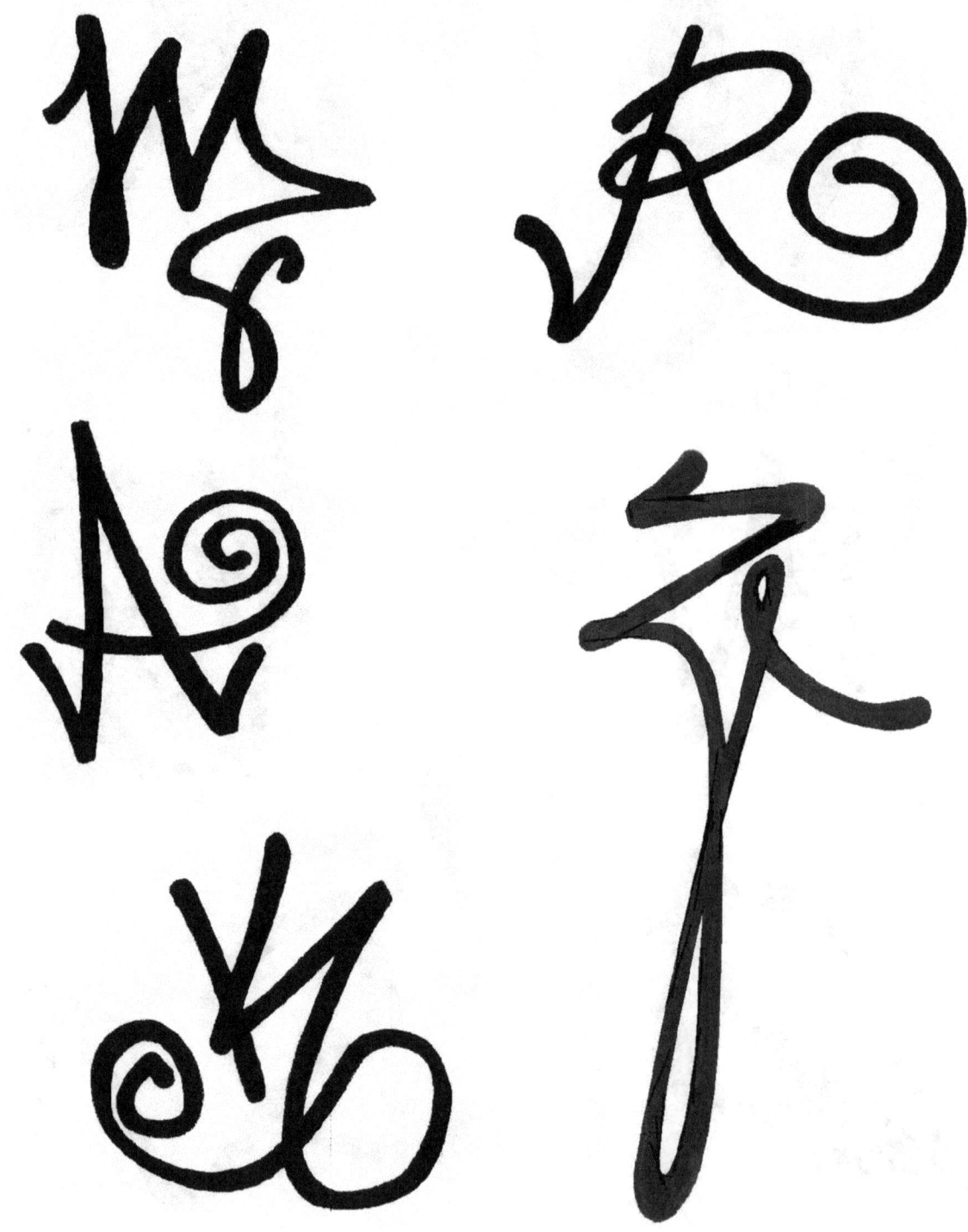

WHY WRITE WHEN YOU CAN TAG

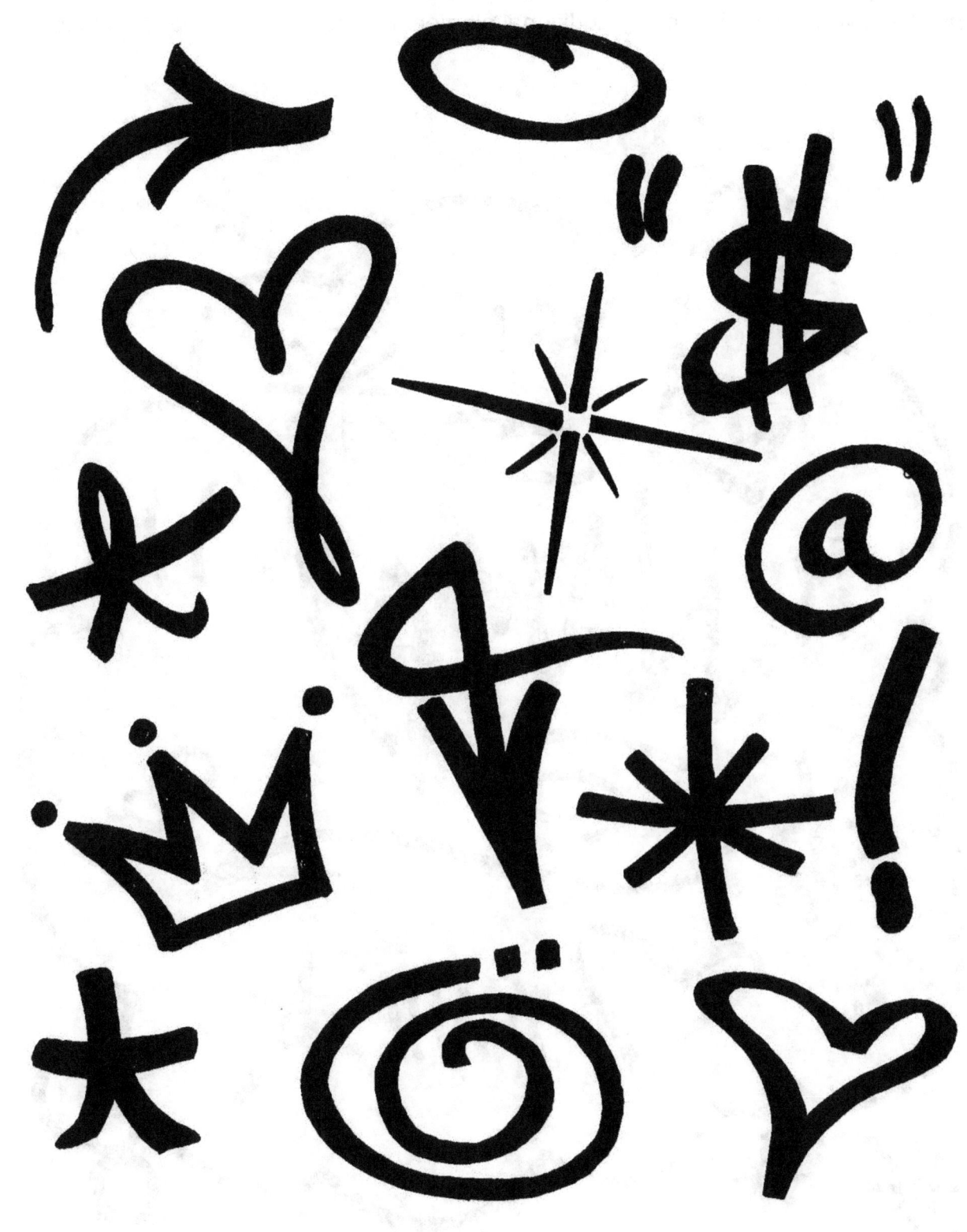

BACKGROUND SHAPES

So you have finalized your tag letters, layout, and other details. What now? Maybe you want to put your finished tag name inside a tag cloud or in the middle of an explosive shape. Then you can add as many additional elements as you like to fill up the space.

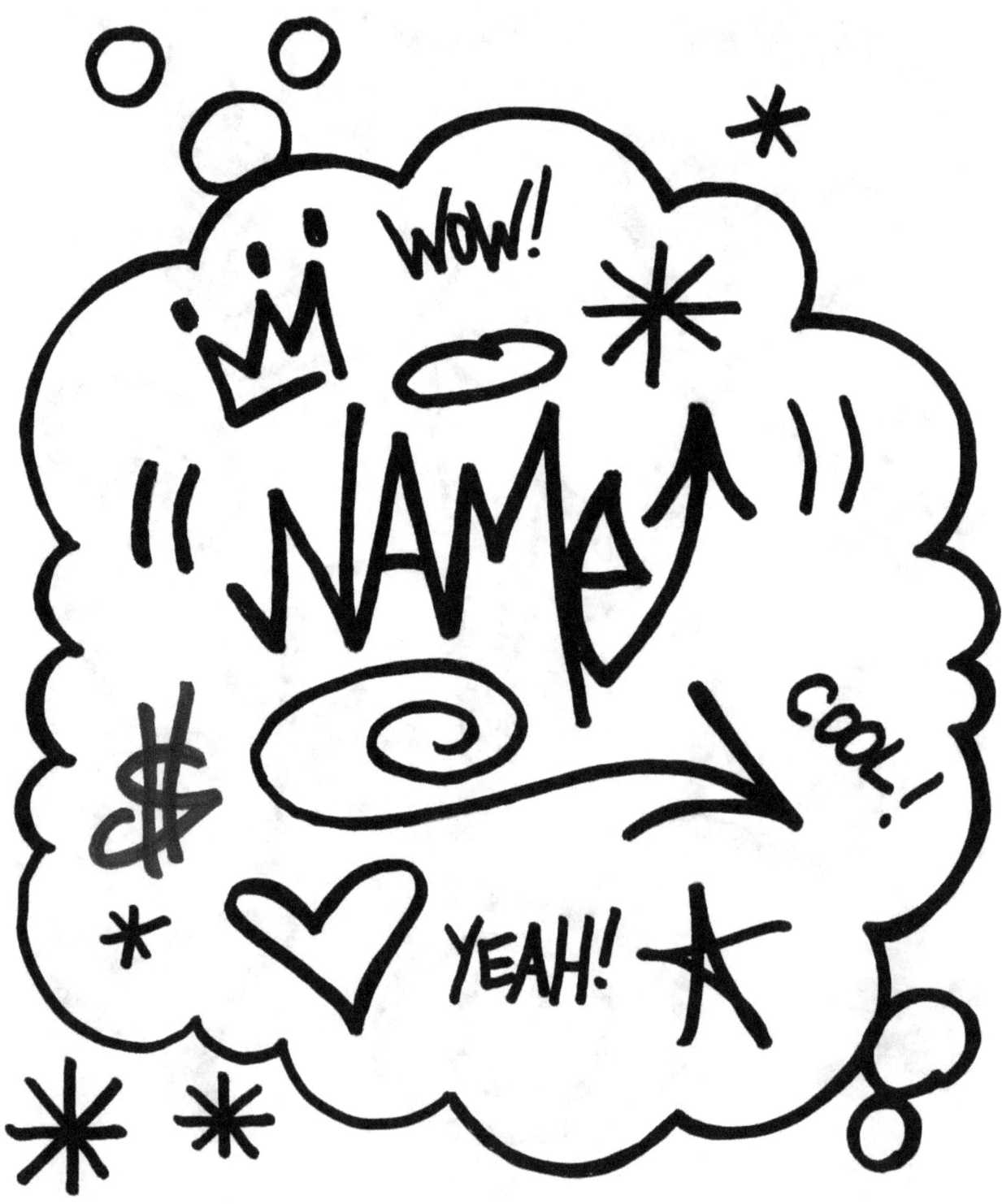

Comic books are a great place to look for ideas on different ways to use clouds, explosions, and other background shapes.

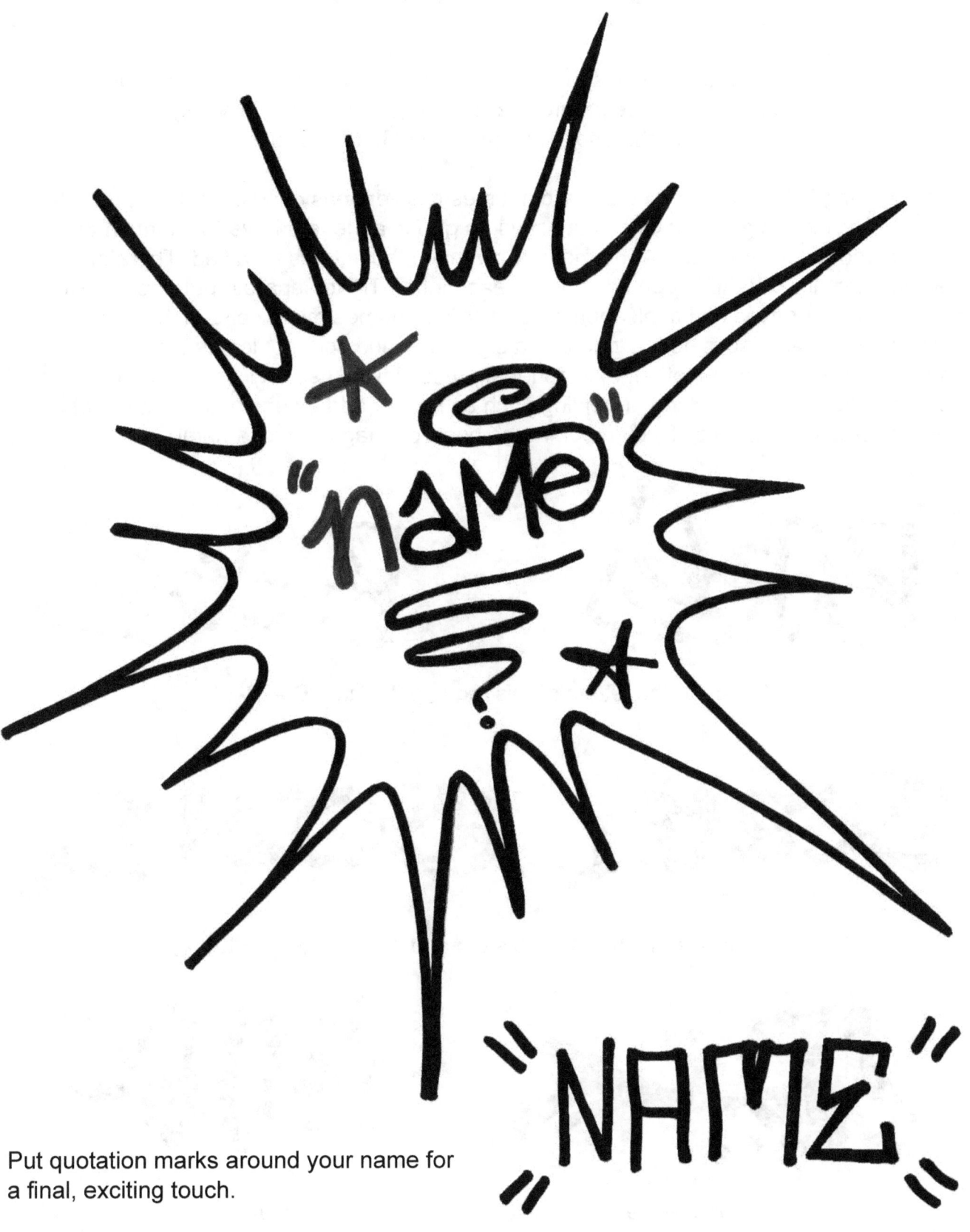

Put quotation marks around your name for a final, exciting touch.

"For those who learn to read tags, a world of aesthetic expression and communication opens up. Tags are a universal language, the jazz of lettering"
- From the book "Tag Town" by Martha cooper

Reading a tag is like solving a puzzle. Sometimes it is very easy and other times it is almost impossible to figure out what a tag says. In graffiti art letters have to maintain their structure, so an "A" is still an "A" no matter how much the letter is modified. Therefore when viewing a tag, look at the shape and form of each letter. Try to separate out each individual letter with your eyes and think about what words or names might contain those letters. Keep in mind that a tag is both a logo and a signature, and communicates a story. So a writer may blend letters together, overlap letters, use initials, use an intentionally incorrect spelling, add numbers, include an ending such as *ism*, or add extensions and other elements to create complexity. Remember, at the heart of a tag lies just a name.

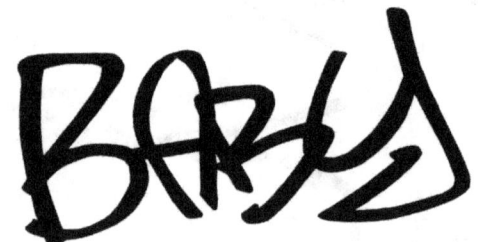 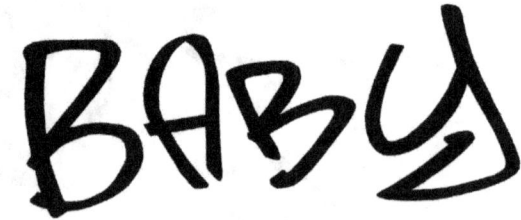

Separate the letters of this tag and it reads "B-A-B-Y".

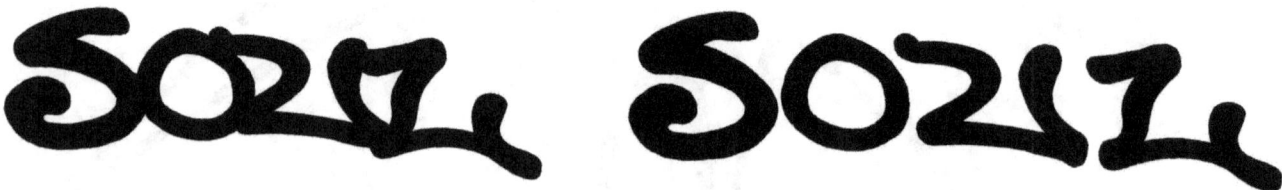

Separate the letters of this tag and it reads "S-O-U-L".

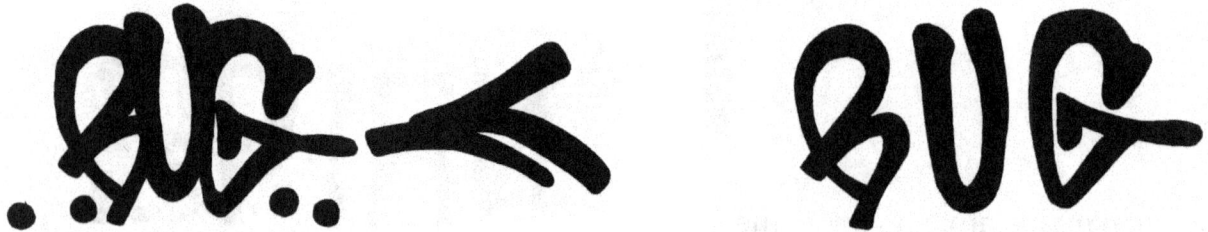

Separate the letters of this tag and it reads "B-U-G".

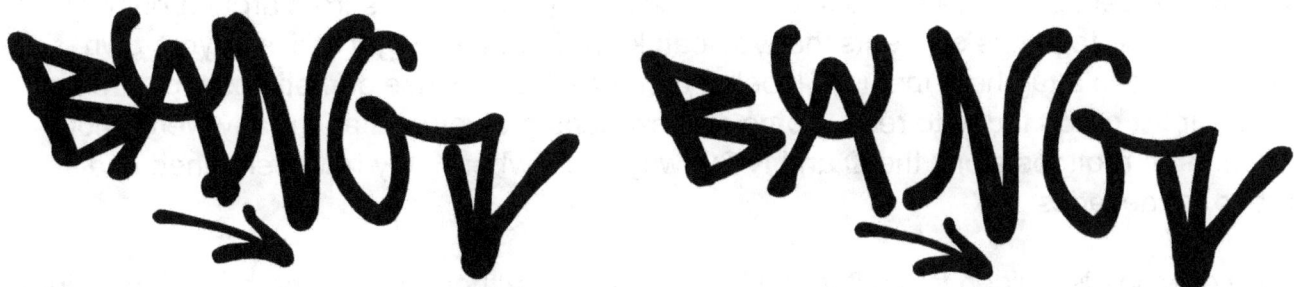

Separate the letters of this tag and it reads "B-A-N-G".

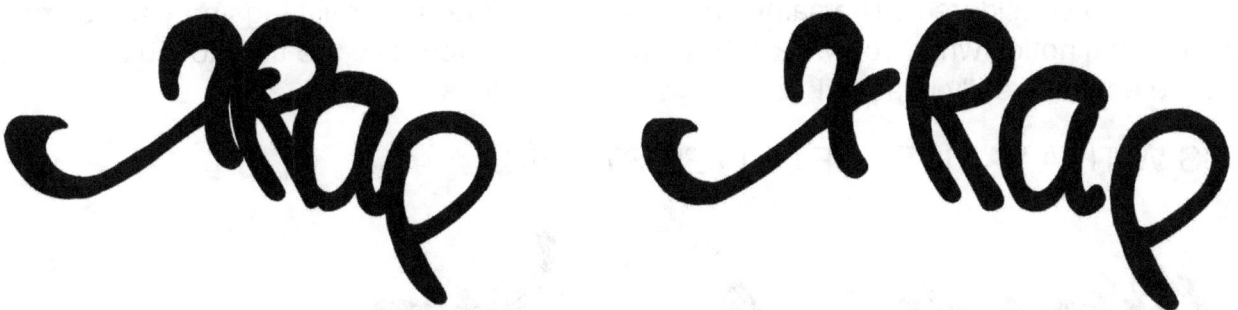

Separate the letters of this tag and it reads "X-R-A-E" (we think).

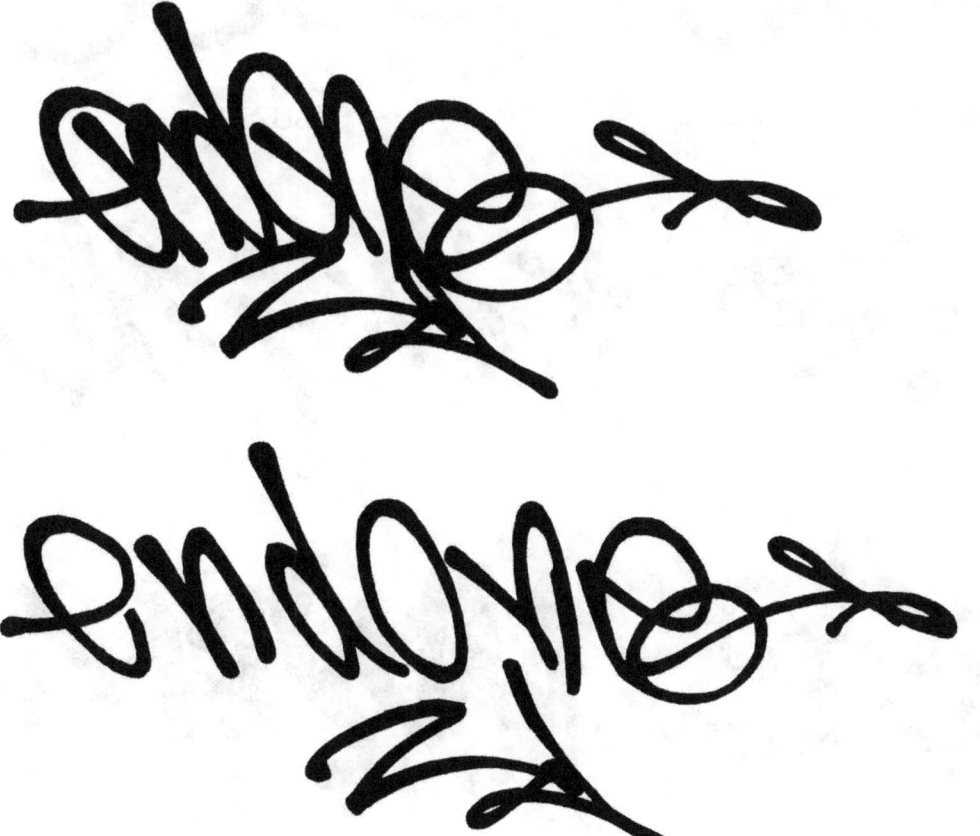

Separate the letters of this tag and it reads "E-N-D O-N-E".

Trying to read a tag like this one is kind of like trying to untangle a bowl of spaghetti. It has a great handstyle with lots of overlapping elements that create complexity. But at the end of the day it's still just letters and a name.

Now we present to you a collection of tags drawn by graffiti writers from around our city. Each of these tags has elements that you can learn from and might utilize in your own tags. If there is a tag here that isn't labeled correctly, it's because sometimes tags are just too complex or too faded to read. Some of these tags are very old and many were photographed on rooftops along the Q and N Subway lines, where they have remained undisturbed for decades.

This collection is divided into different style categories, although many of these tags fit into multiple categories. We just needed a simplified way to organize them. In his book "Hand Job: A Catalogue of Type" Micheal Perry says " ...One of my own motivations for copying type from signs and photos (is) to pay homage to the people whose handiwork is all around me, yet rarely considered". The same can be said about tags. Graffiti tags may not be the first thing you notice when you walk down a street, but if you take the time to look, some of them are actually really beautiful.

TAGS WITH A VARIETY OF LETTER STYLES

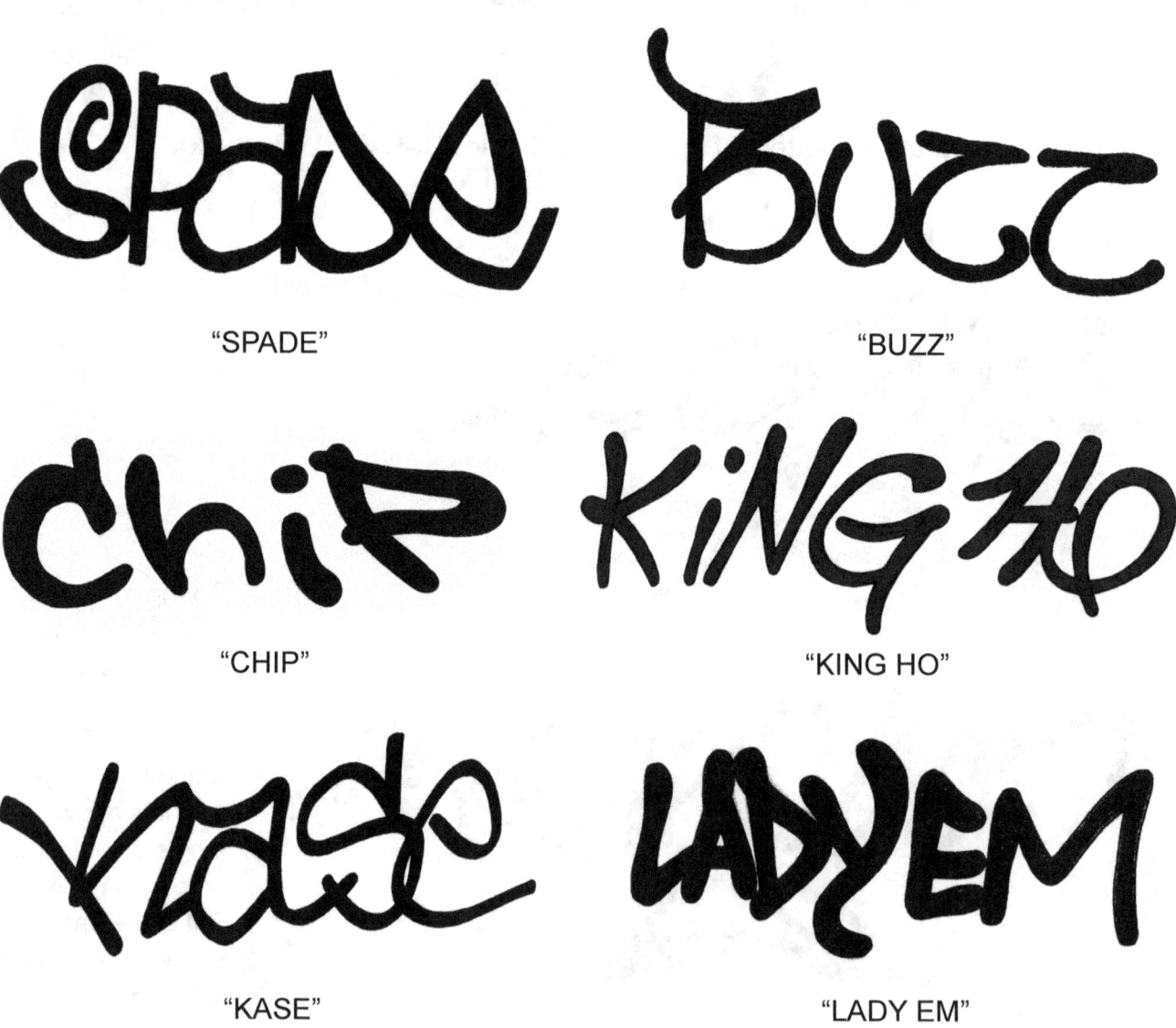

"SPADE"

"BUZZ"

"CHIP"

"KING HO"

"KASE"

"LADY EM"

WHY WRITE WHEN YOU CAN TAG

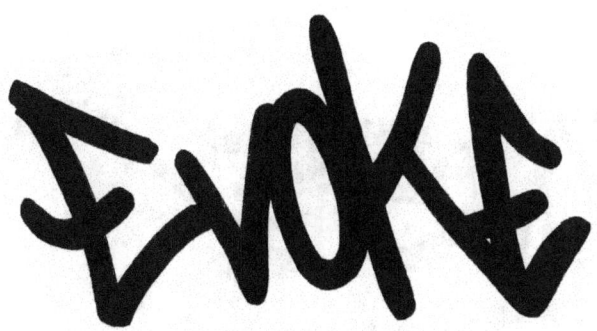

"EVOKE"

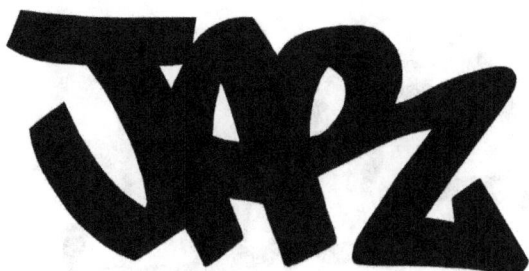

"JAR"

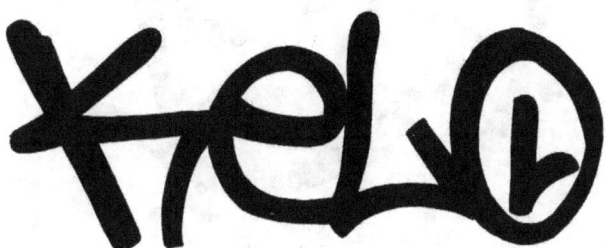

"KELO

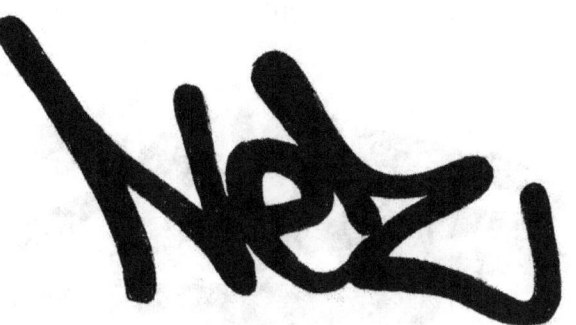

"NEZ"

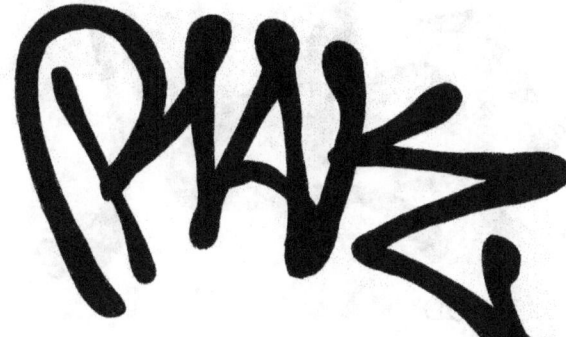

"RAK"

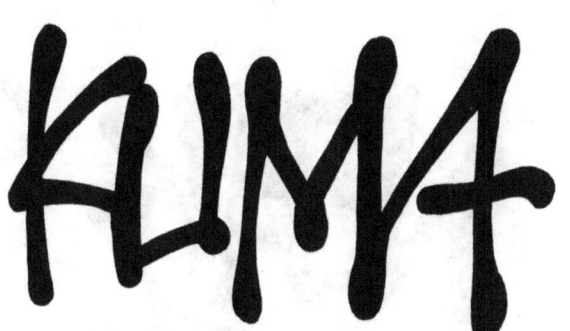

"KUMA"

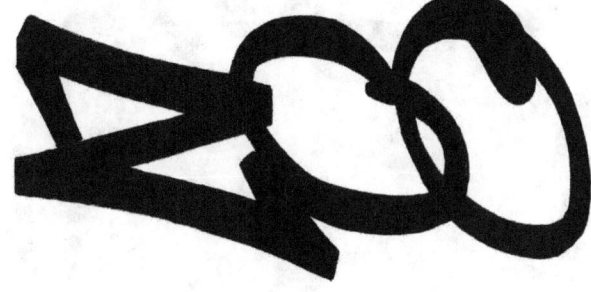

"ZOO"

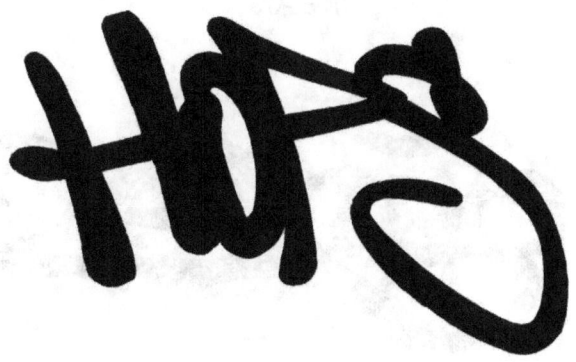

"HOPS"

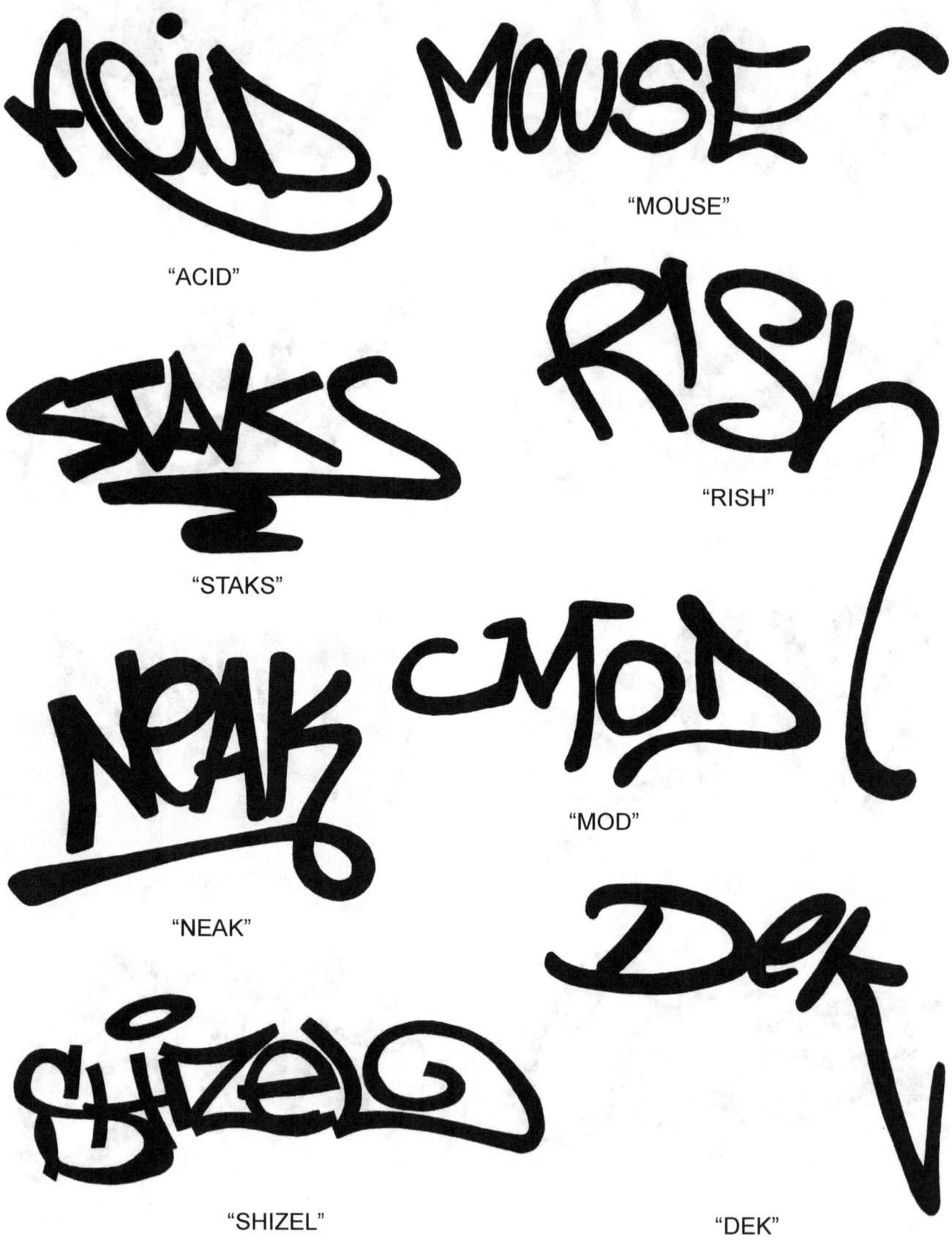

"ACID"

"MOUSE"

"STAKS"

"RISH"

"NEAK"

"MOD"

"SHIZEL"

"DEK"

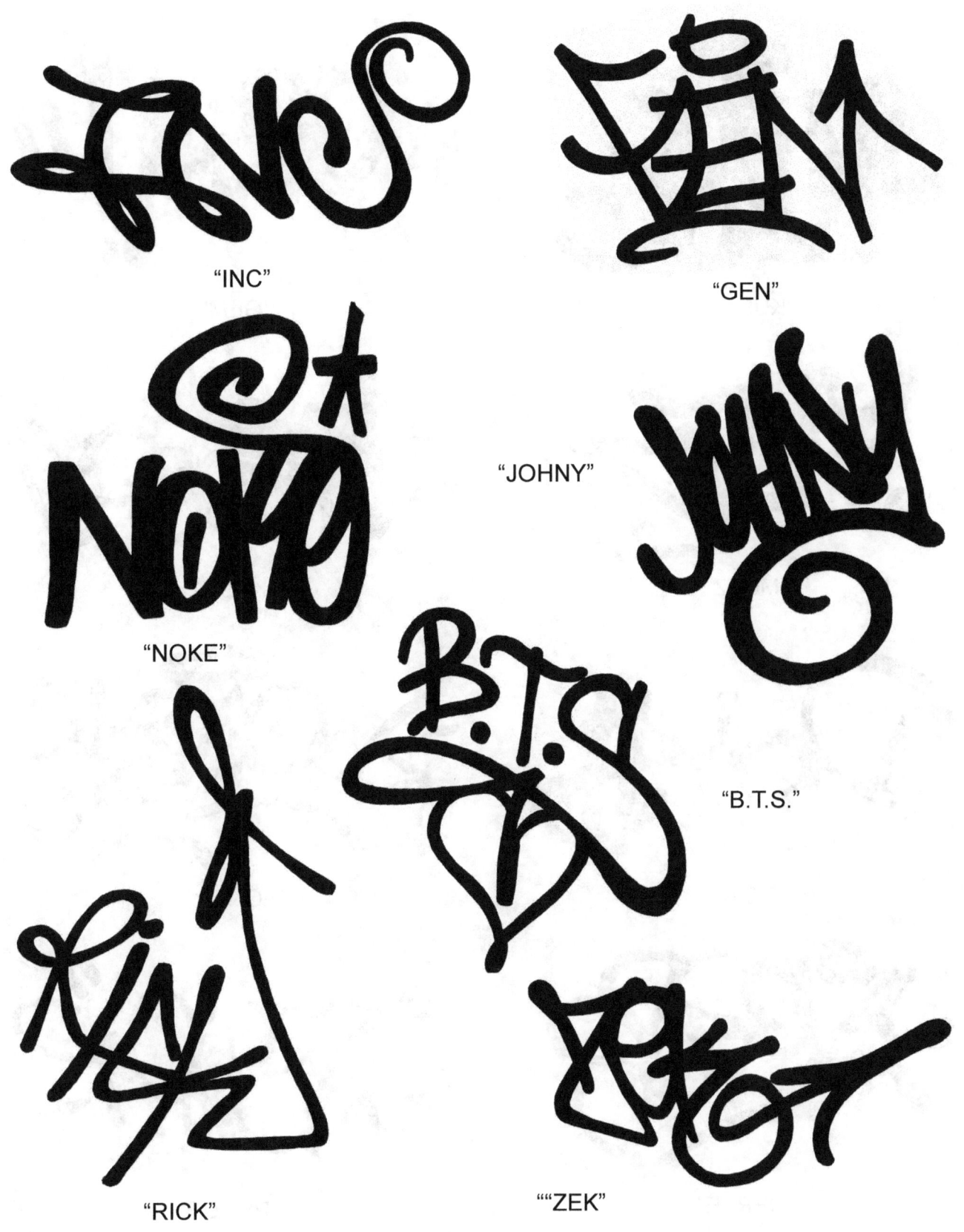

"INC"

"GEN"

"JOHNY"

"NOKE"

"B.T.S."

"RICK"

""ZEK"

TAGS WITH ELEMENTS ADDED OR SUBSTITUTED FOR PARTS OF LETTERS

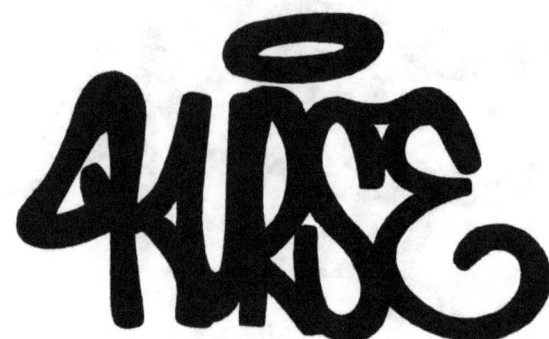

"KURSE"

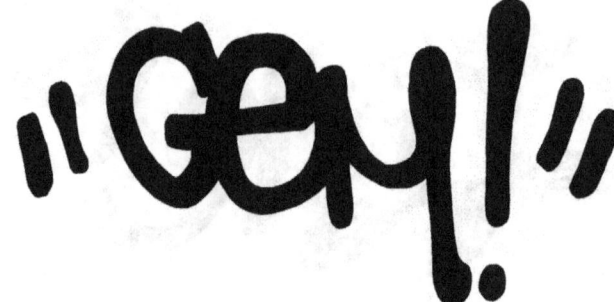

"GEM"

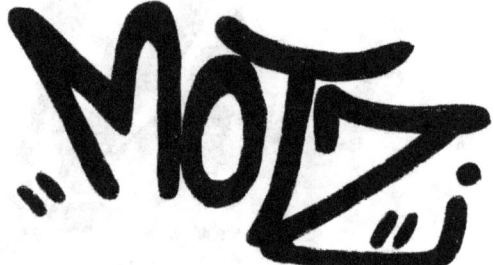

"MOTZ"

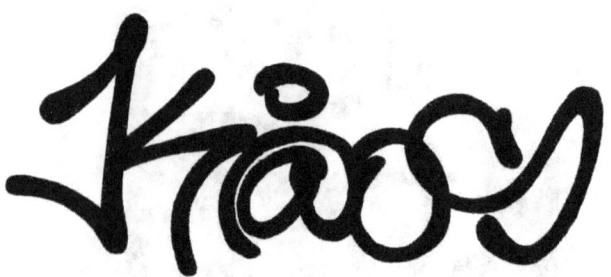

"KAOS"

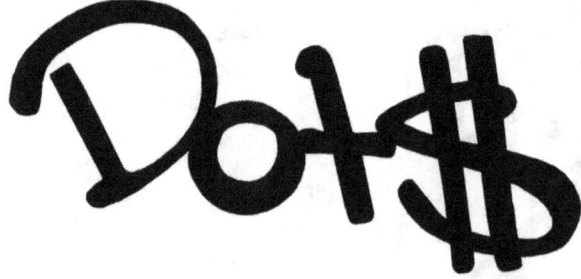

"DOTS"

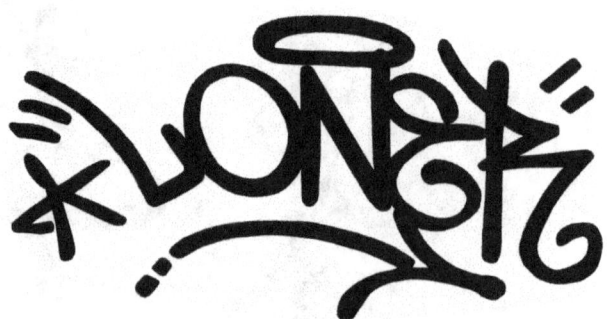

"LONER"

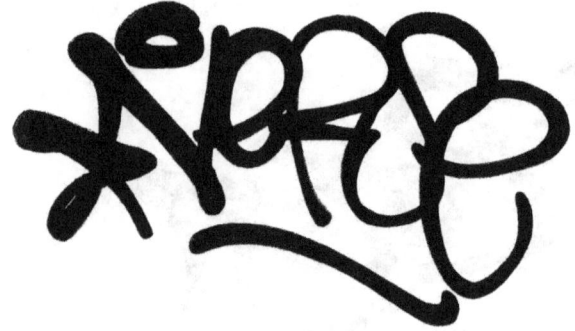

"NERSE"

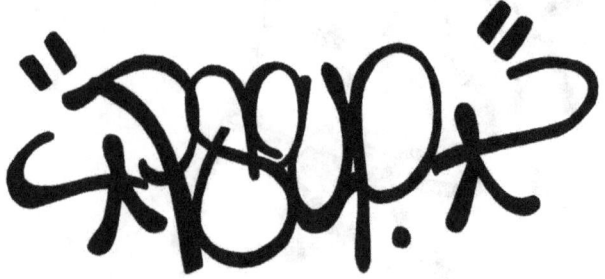

"PSOUP"

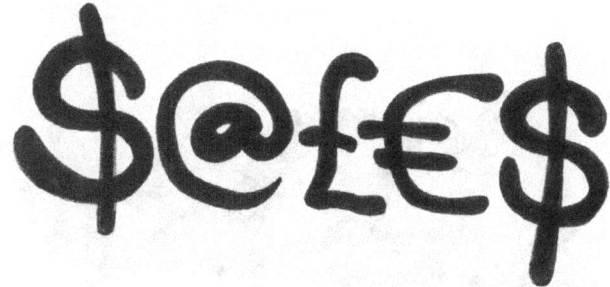

"SALES"

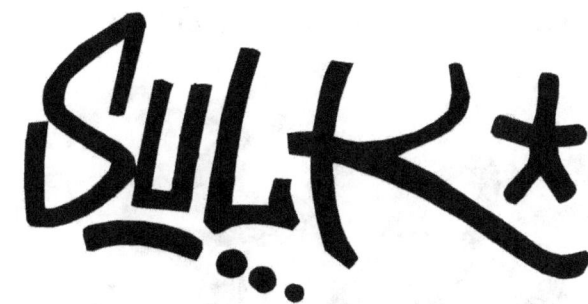

"SULK"

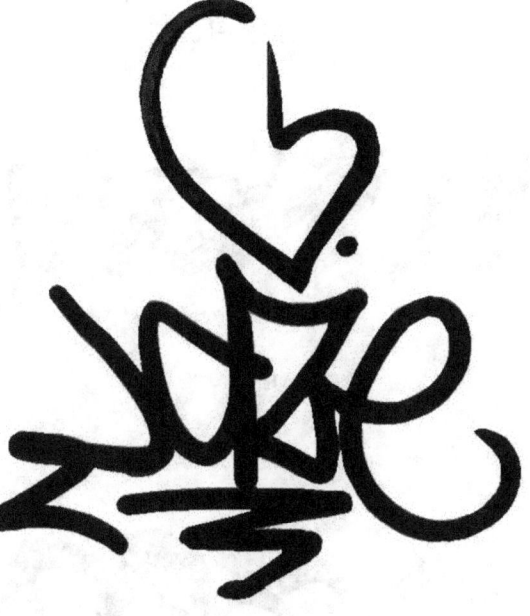

"JORE"

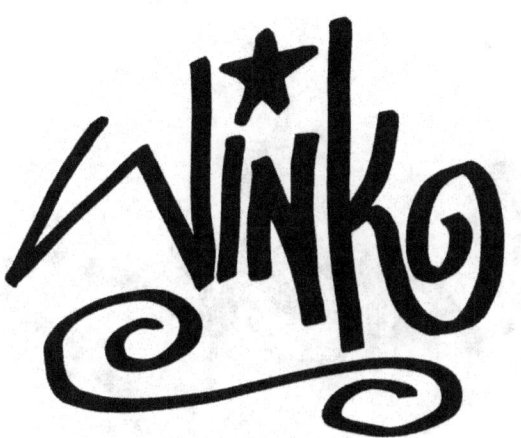

"WINK"

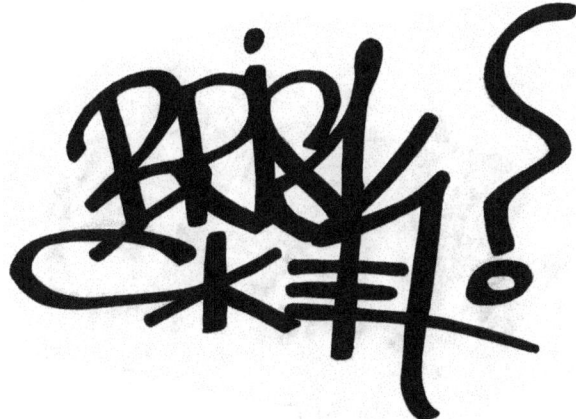

"BRISK"

"SOG CREW"

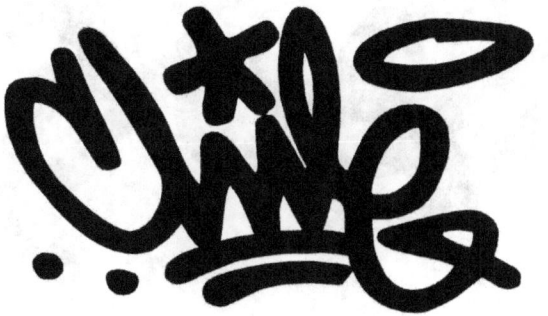

"CHILE"

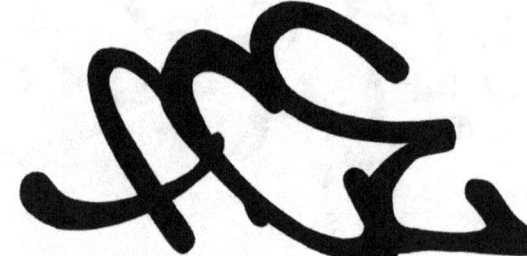

"ACE"

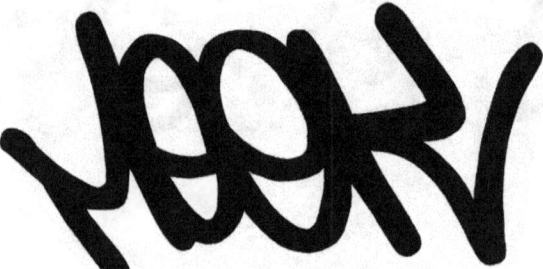

"MEEK"

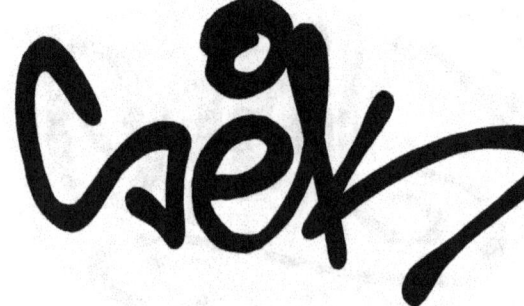

"SEK"

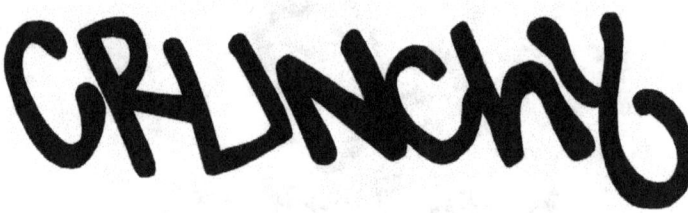

"CRUNCHY"

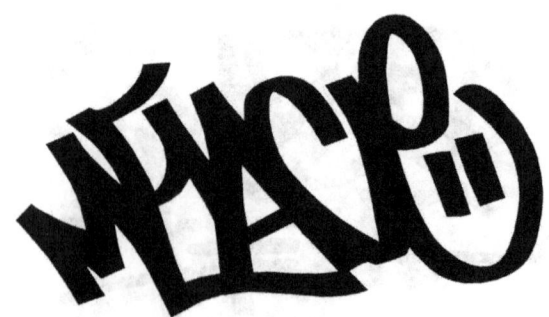

"MFACE"

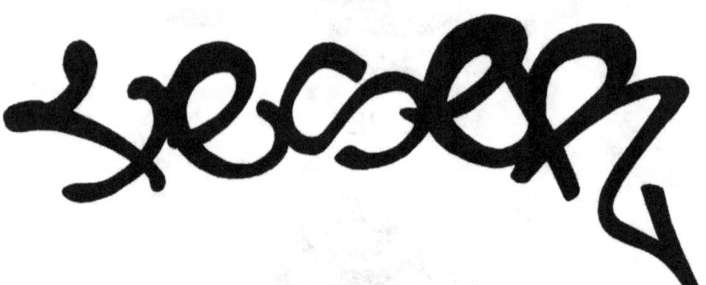

"FESER"

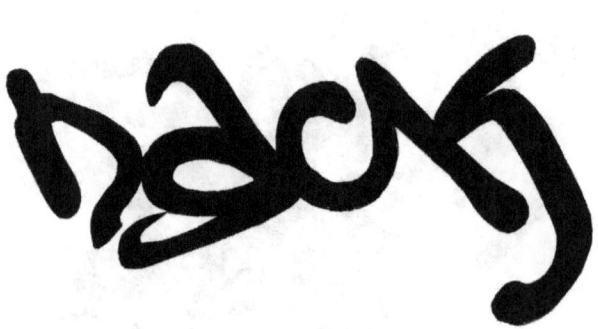

"DACK"

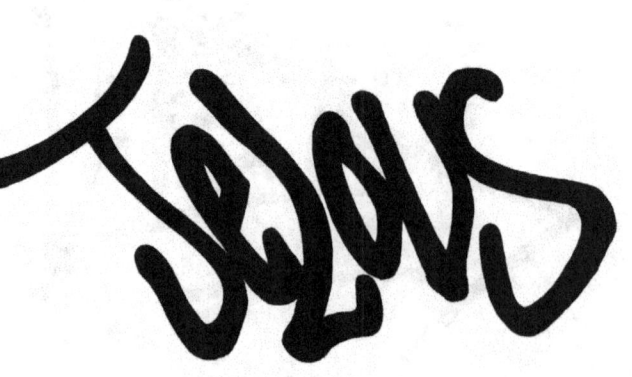

"JEALOUS"

WHY WRITE WHEN YOU CAN TAG

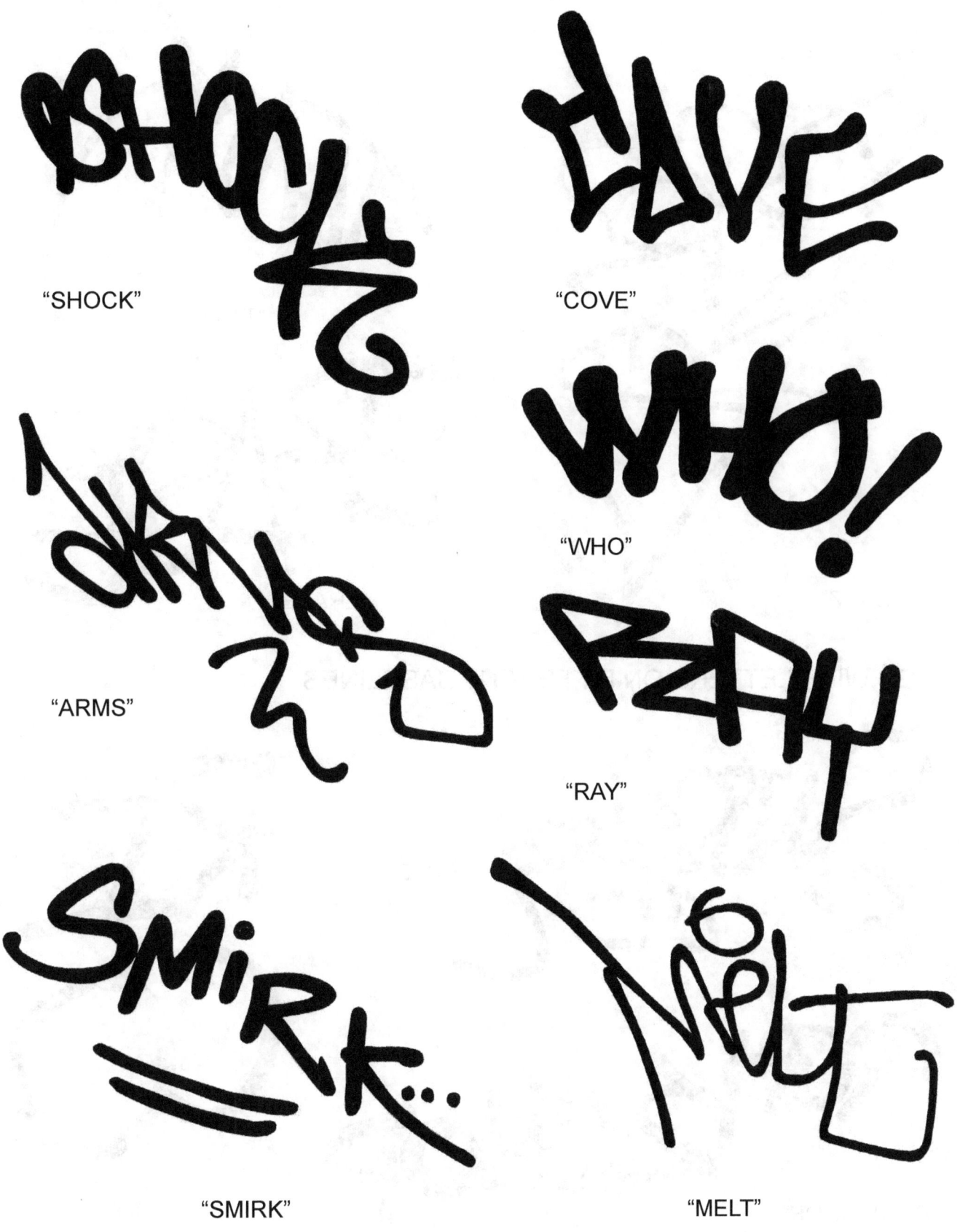

"SHOCK"

"COVE"

"WHO"

"ARMS"

"RAY"

"SMIRK"

"MELT"

MORE TAGS WITH CURVED OR SLANTED BASELINES

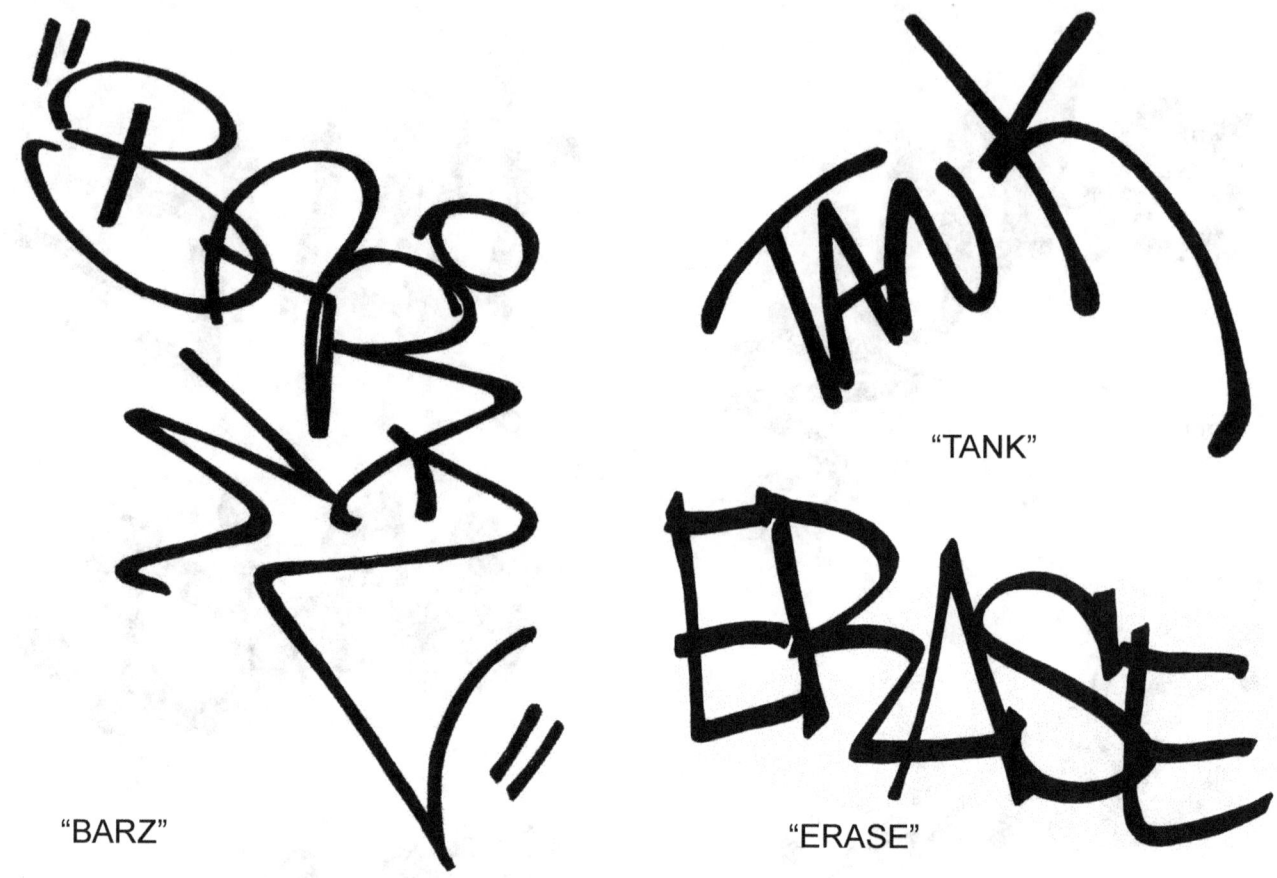

"TANK"

"BARZ"

"ERASE"

TAGS WITH LETTERS ON DIFFERENT BASELINES

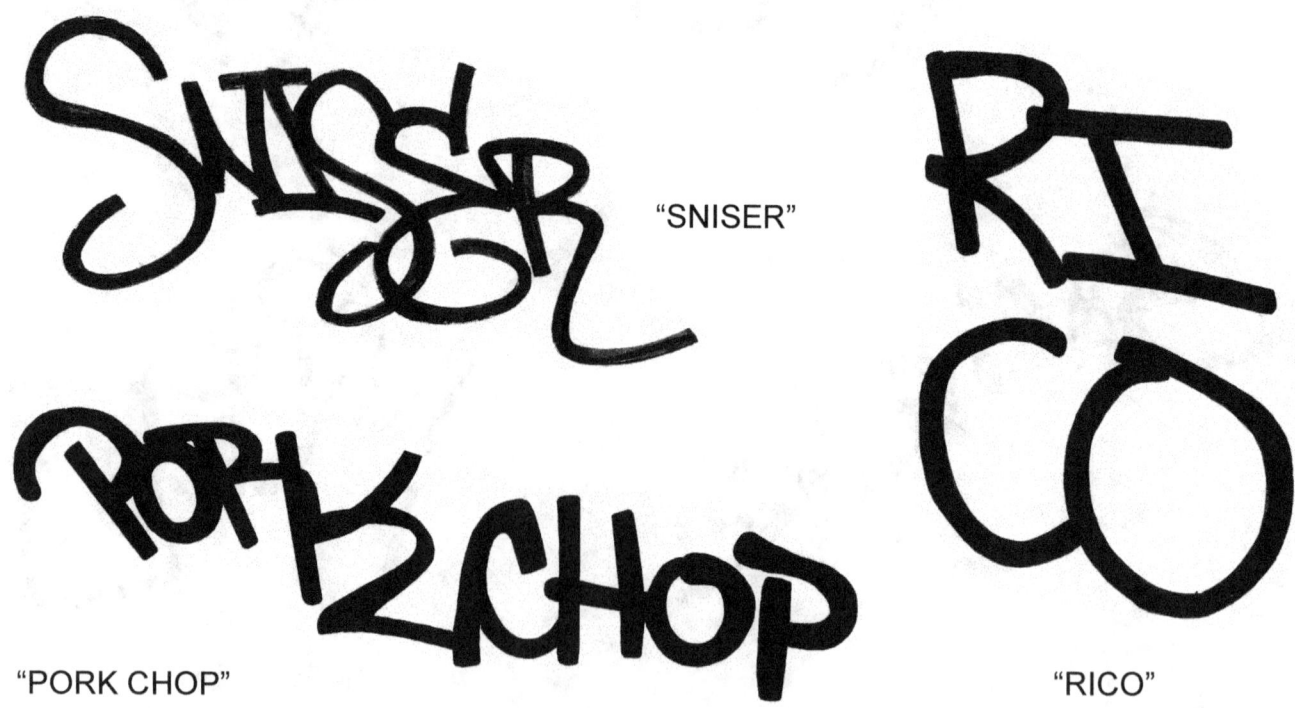

"SNISER"

"PORK CHOP"

"RICO"

WHY WRITE WHEN YOU CAN TAG

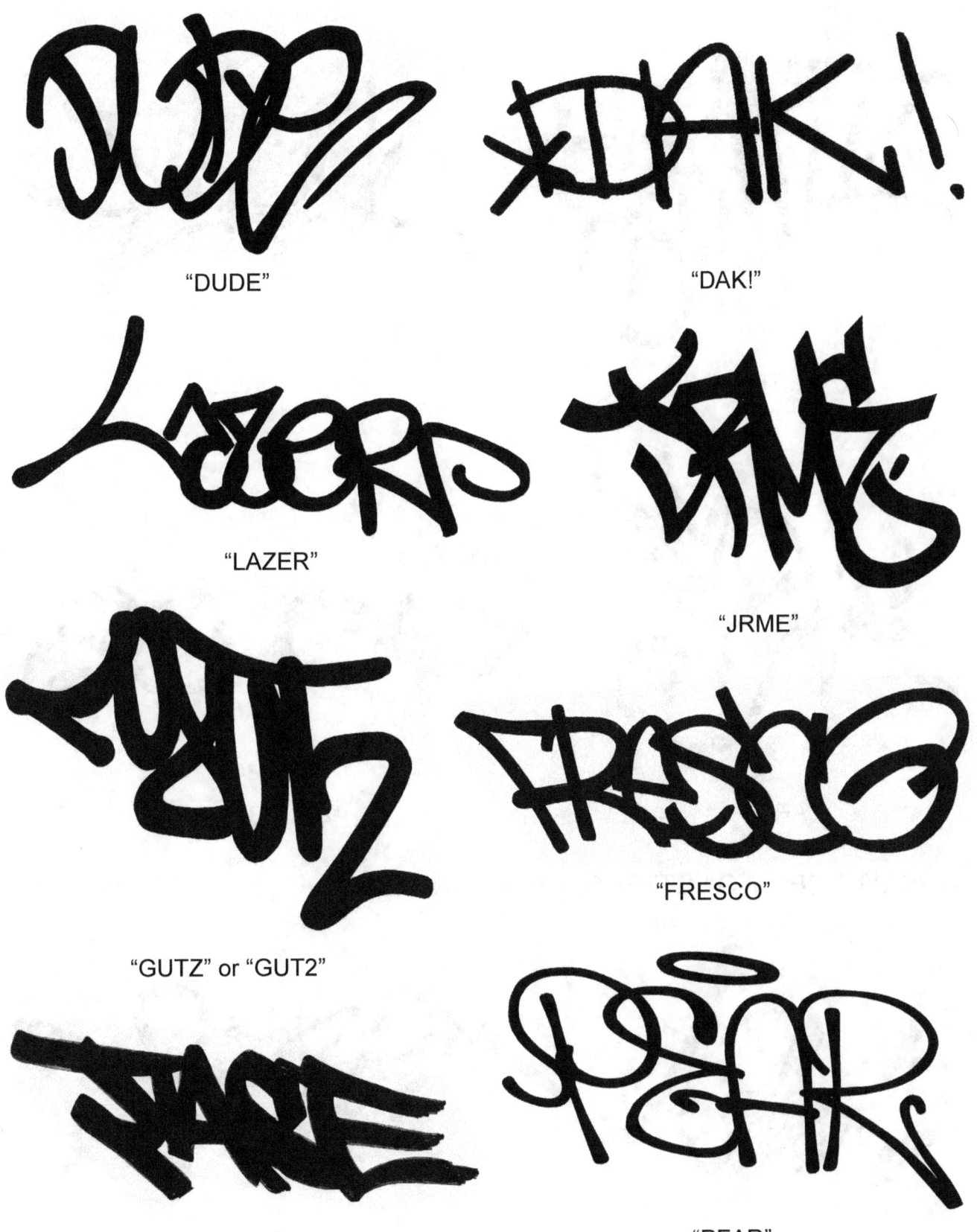

"DUDE"

"DAK!"

"LAZER"

"JRME"

"GUTZ" or "GUT2"

"FRESCO"

"JASE"

"PEAR"

TAGS WITH SOME LETTERS THAT ARE CONNECTED

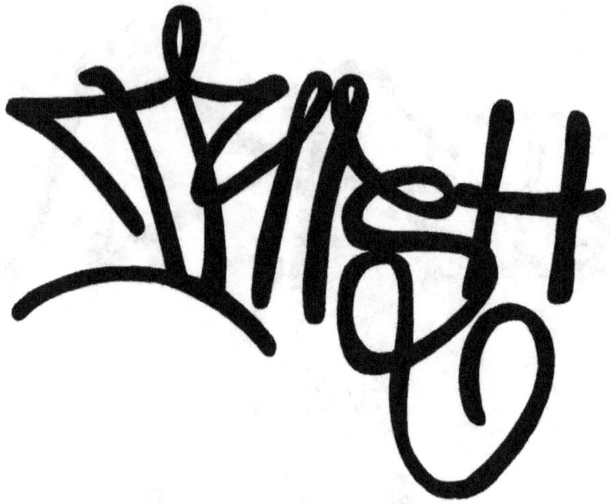

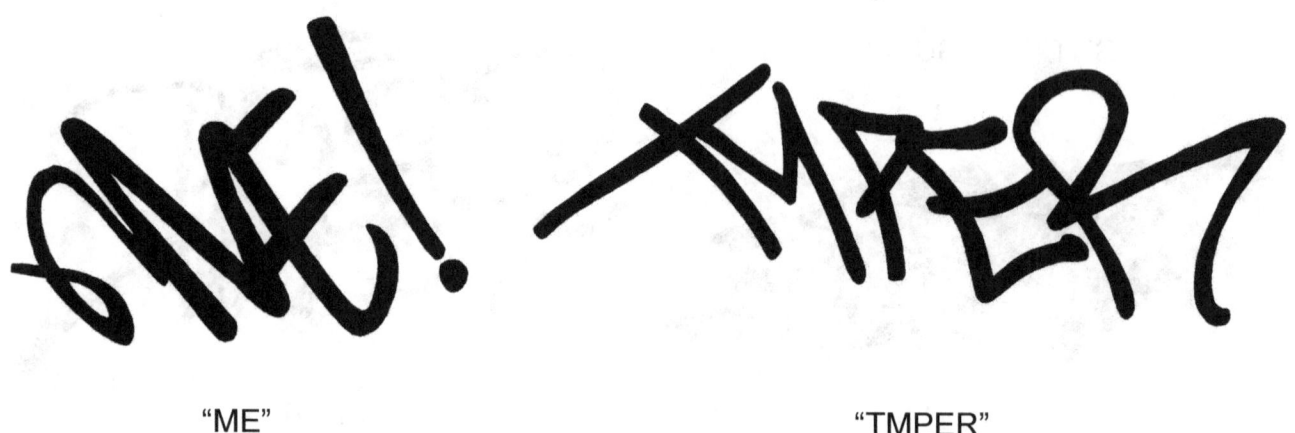

"TRISH" ?

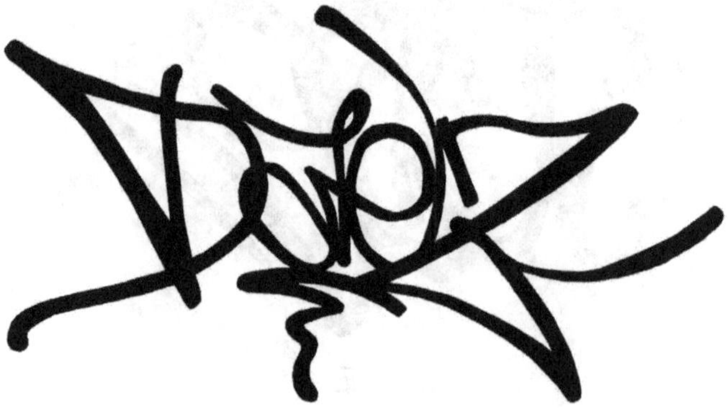

"DAEZ"

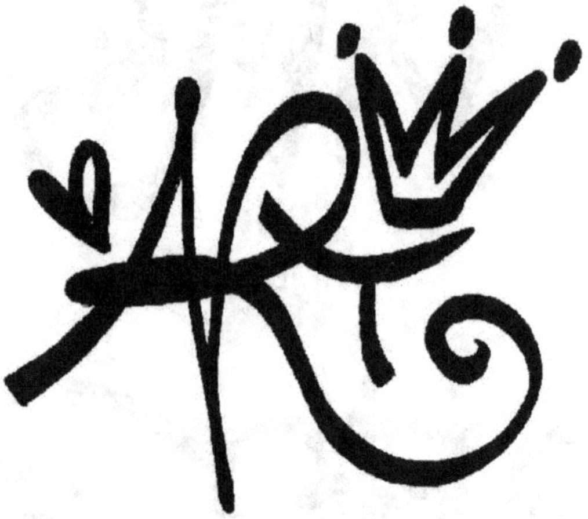

"ART"

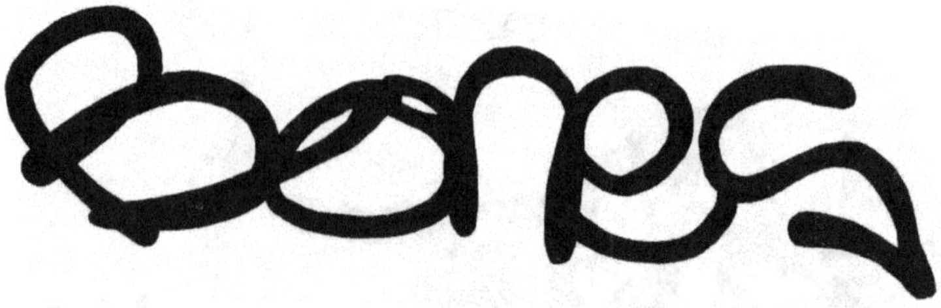

"BONES"

TAGS WHERE TWO LETTERS SHARE ONE LINE

"ME"

"TMPER"

WHY WRITE WHEN YOU CAN TAG

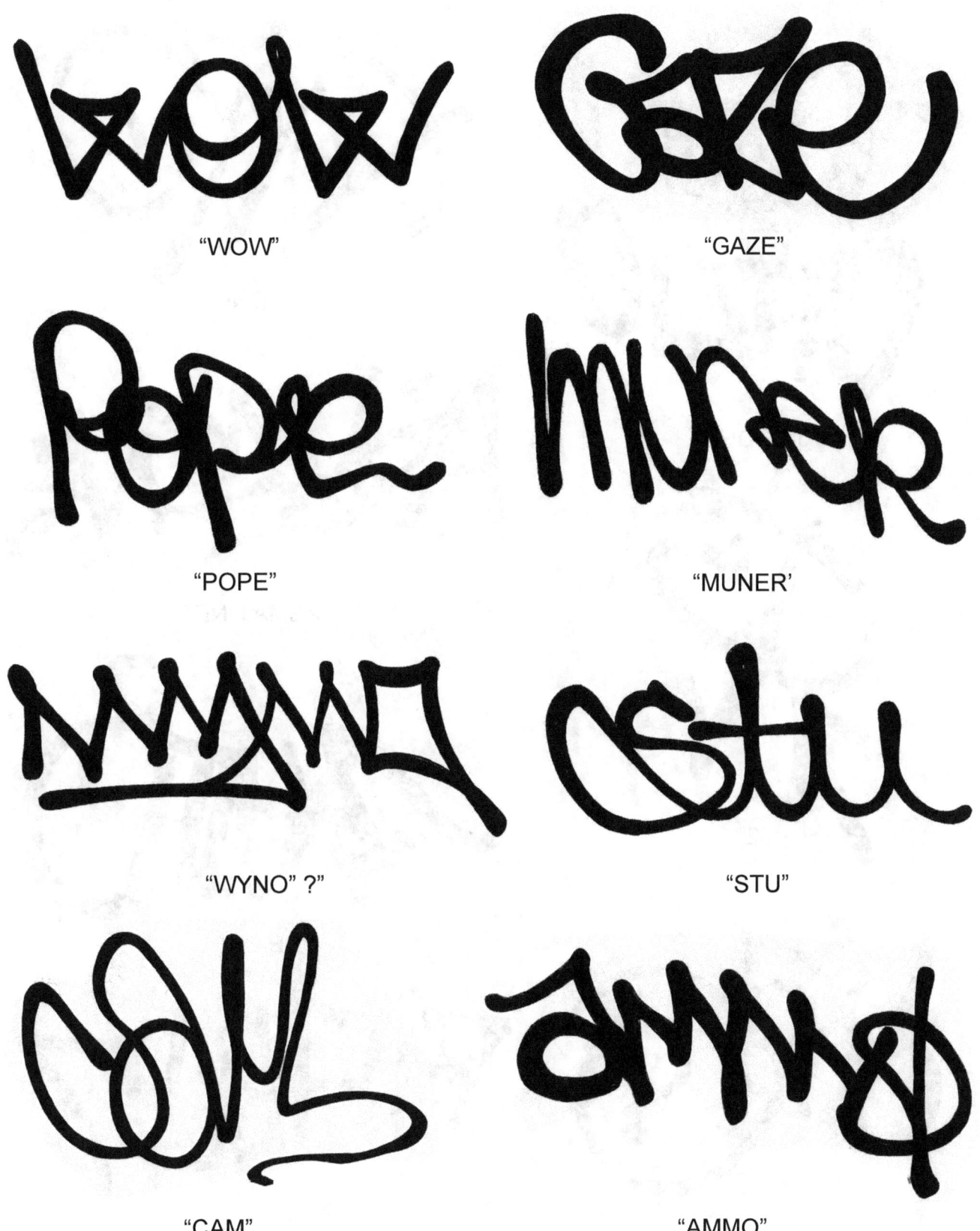

"WOW"

"GAZE"

"POPE"

"MUNER'

"WYNO" ?"

"STU"

"CAM"

"AMMO"

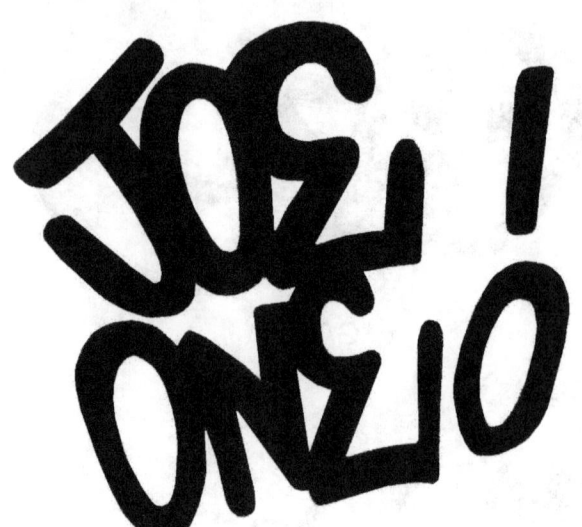

"JOE ONE"

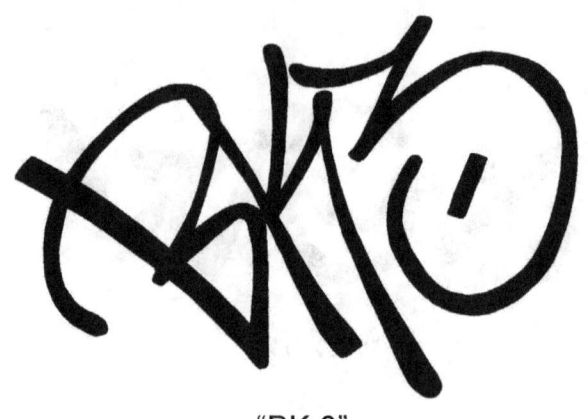

"BK 3"

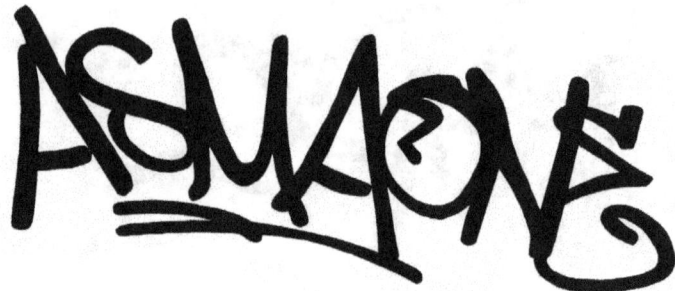

"ASMA ONE"

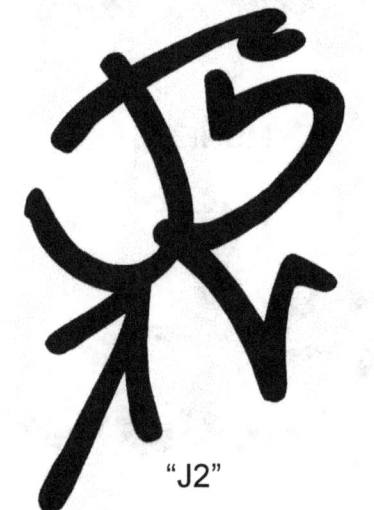

"J2"

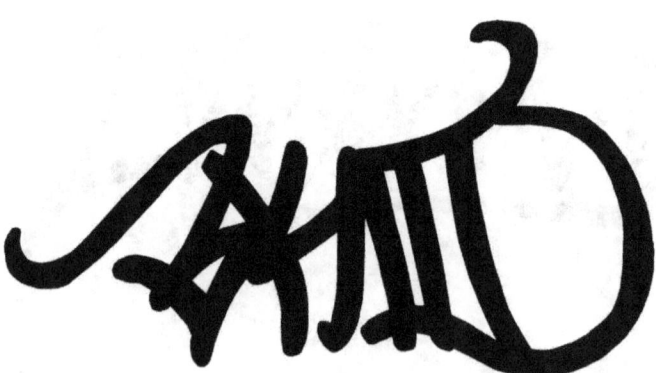

"BK III"

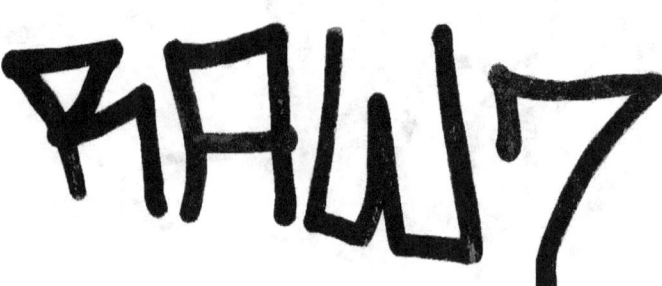

"RAW 7"

"WA ONE"

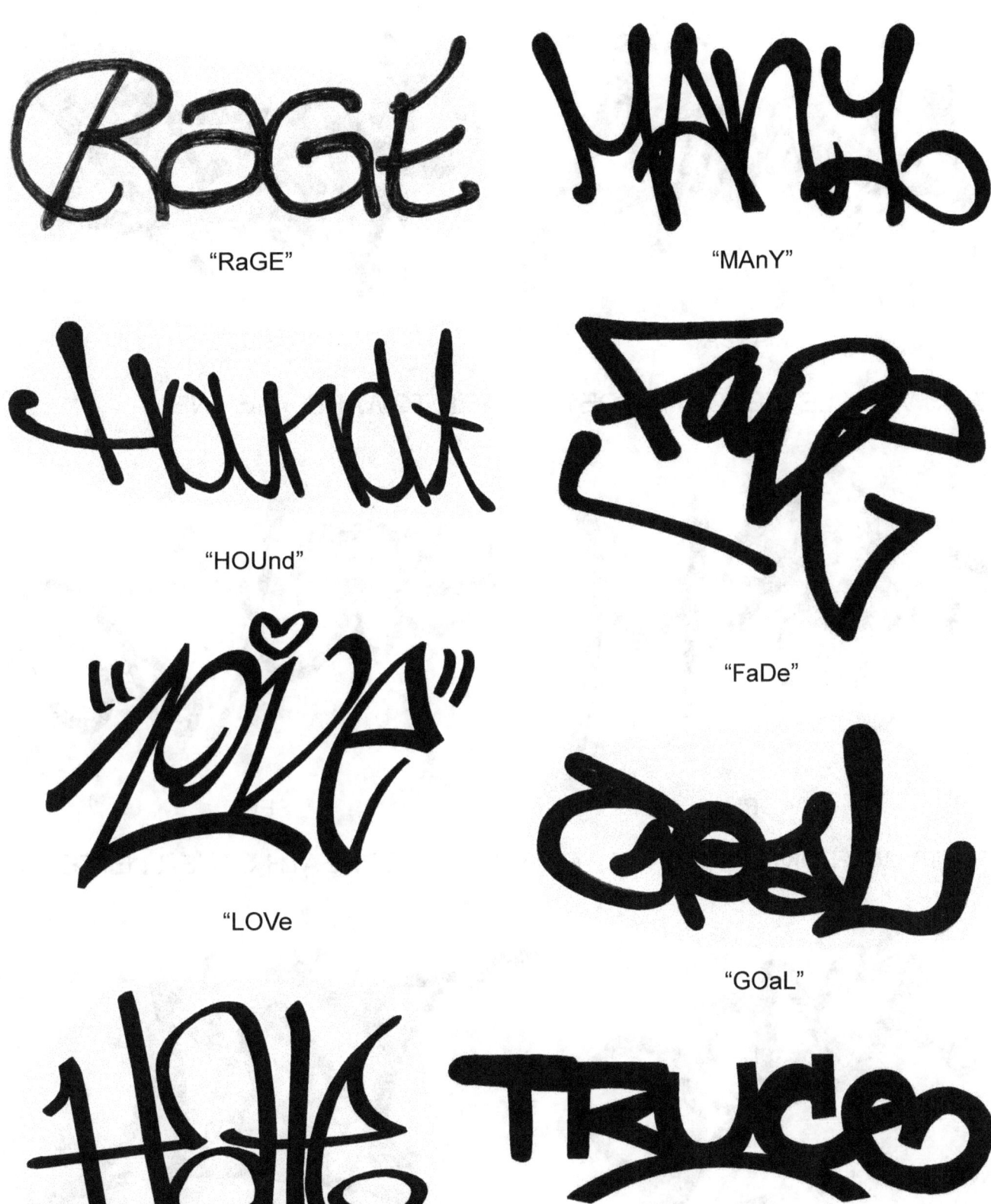

"RaGE"

"MAnY"

"HOUnd"

"FaDe"

"LOVe

"GOaL"

"Hate"

"TRUCe"

TAGS WITH THE FIRST AND LAST LETTER LARGER THAN THE REST

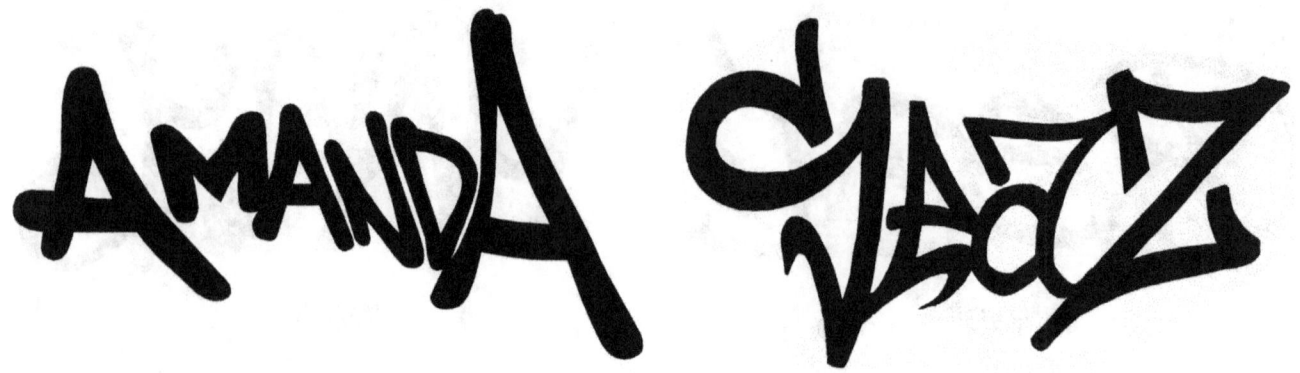

"AMANDA"   "SEAZ"

TAGS WITH LETTERS THAT GET LARGER TOWARD THE END

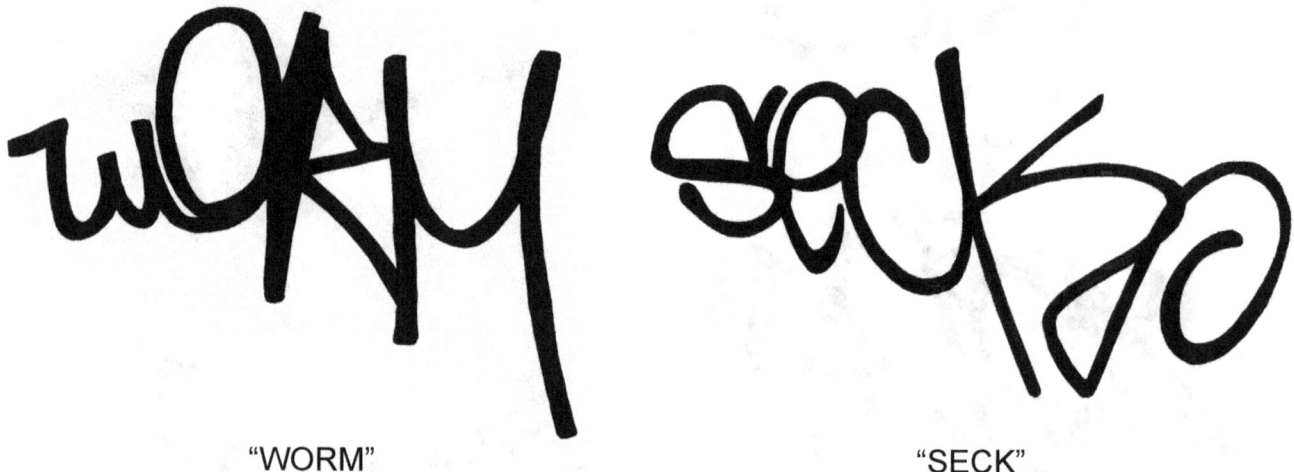

"WORM"   "SECK"

TAGS WITH ONE LETTER EXTENDING UNDERNEATH OTHER LETTERS

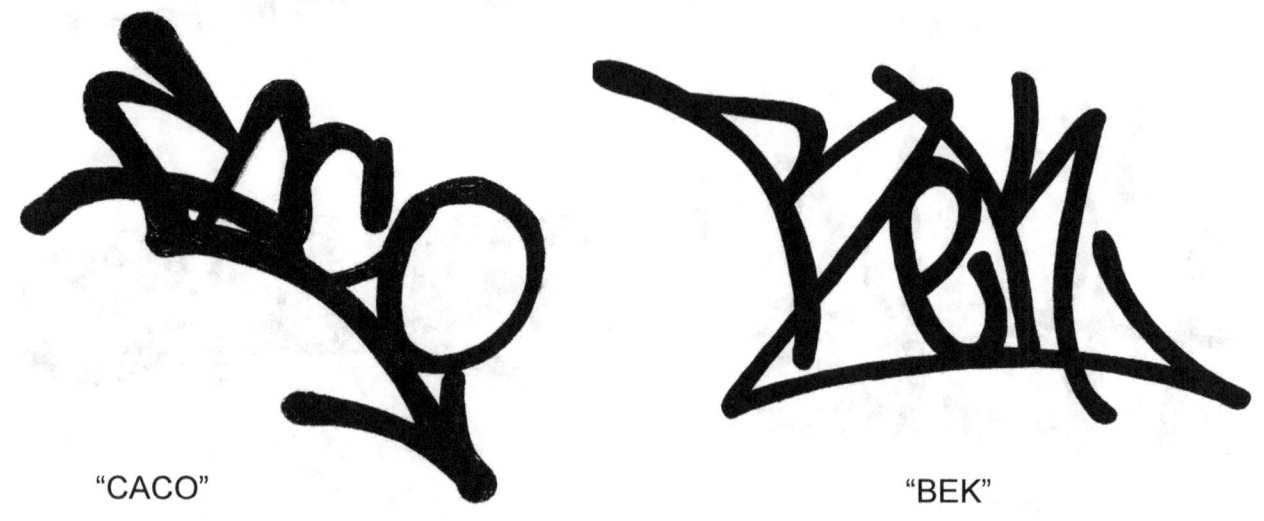

"CACO"   "BEK"

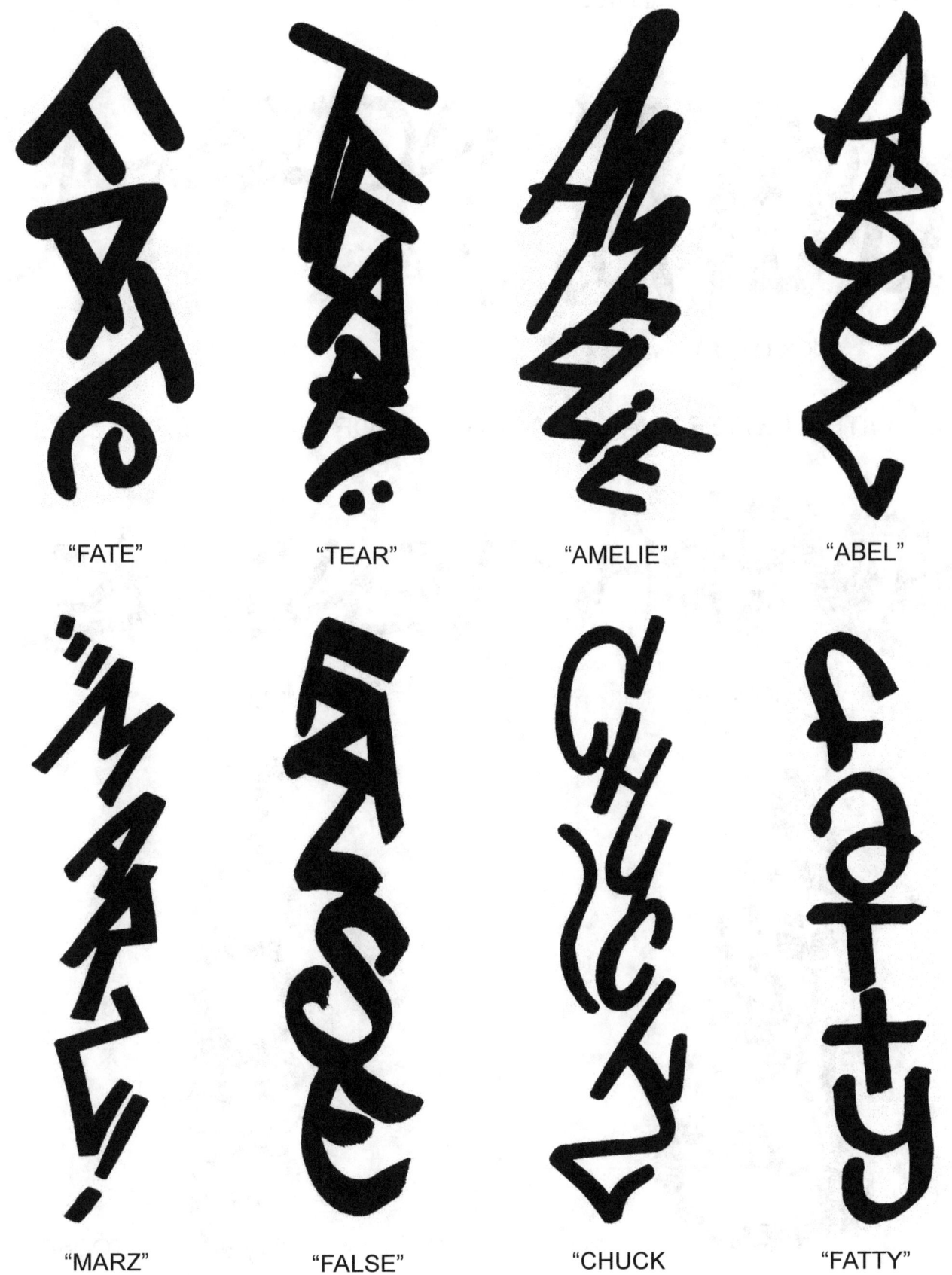

"FATE"

"TEAR"

"AMELIE"

"ABEL"

"MARZ"

"FALSE"

"CHUCK

"FATTY"

TAGS WITH AN *ER* OR *ISM* ADDED TO THE END. YOU CAN ALSO ADD
JUST AN *R*, AN *ISH* OR AN *ING*

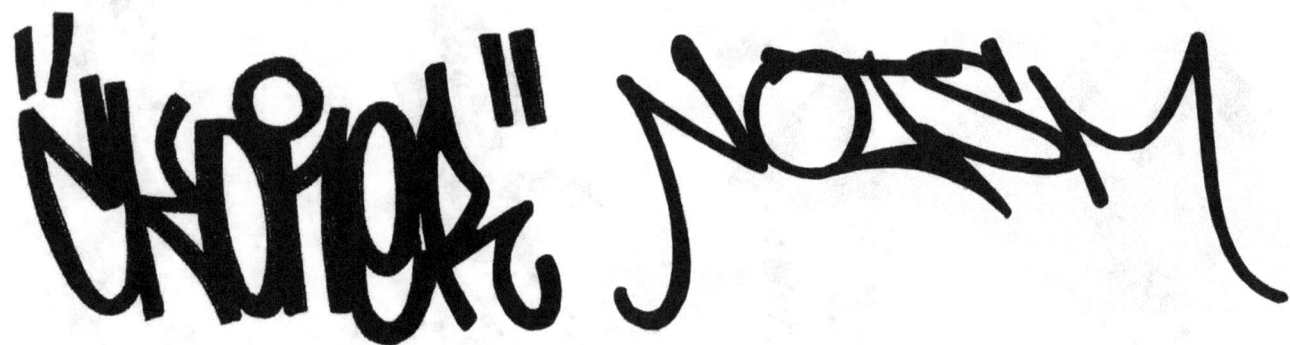

"CK ONER"   "NOISM"

TAGS WITH A LETTER THAT IS BACKWARDS OR SIDEWARDS

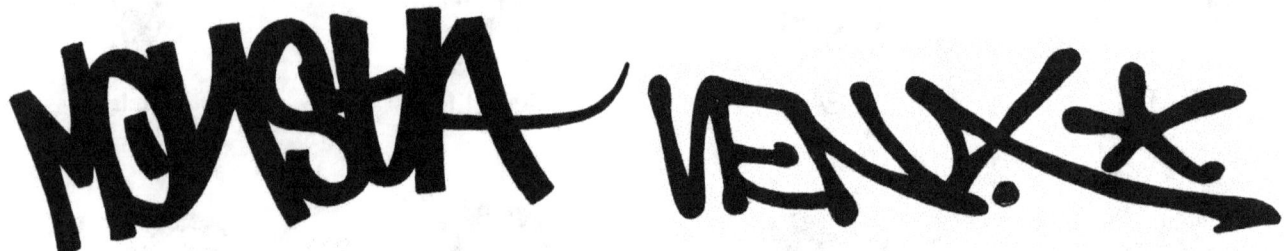

"MONSTA"   "NENA" ?

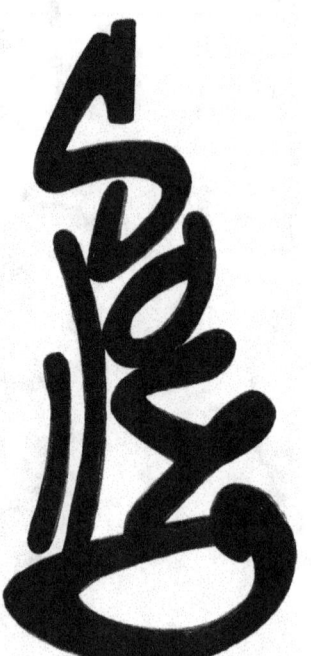   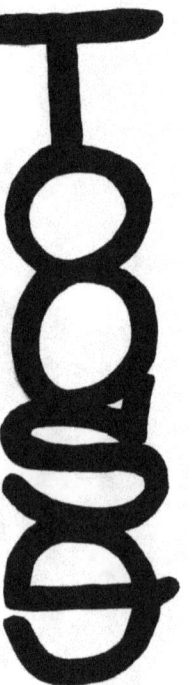

"SOUD"   "TOOSE"

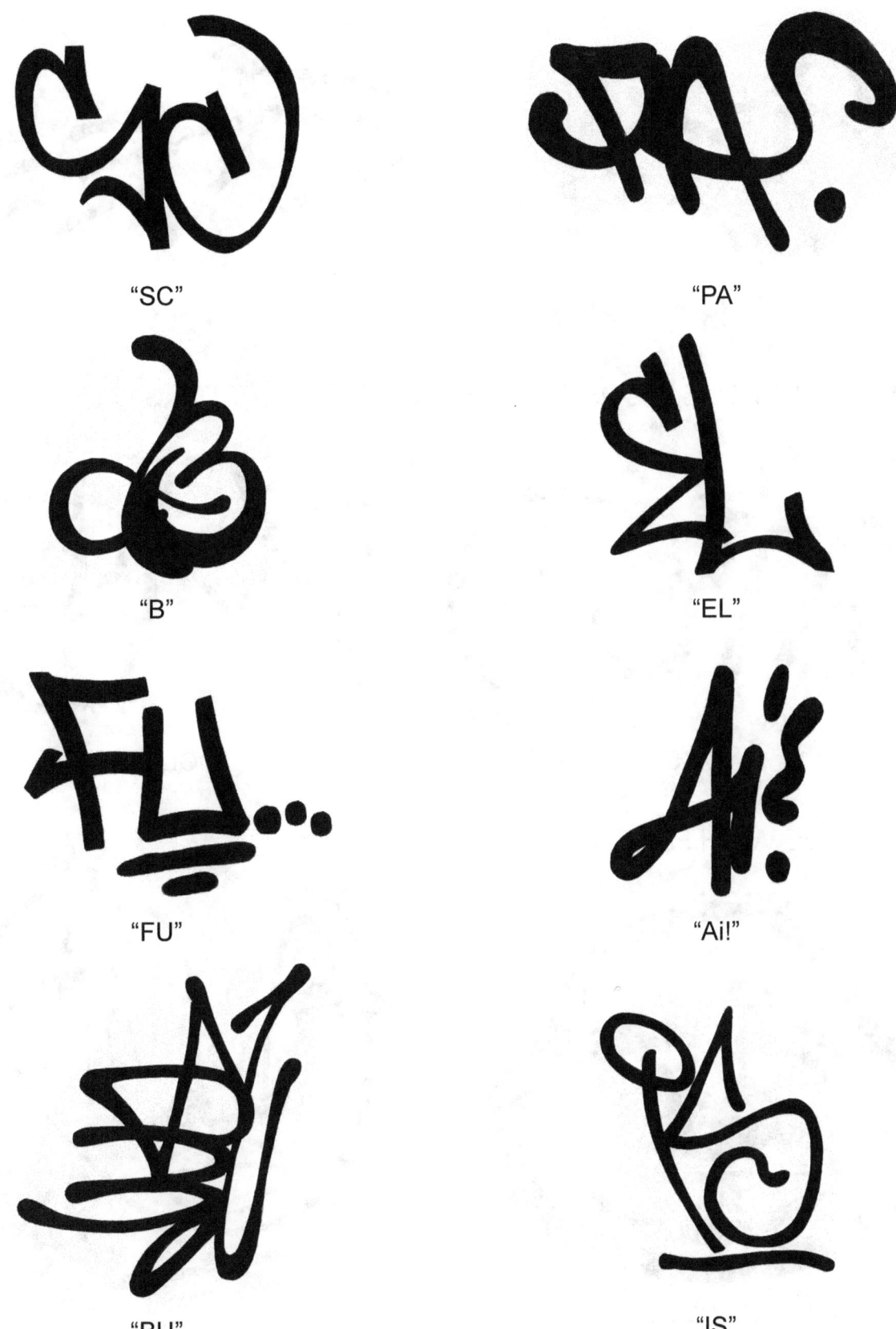

"SC"

"PA"

"B"

"EL"

"FU"

"Ai!"

"BU"

"IS"

TAGS WITH PART OF A LETTER LEFT OUT

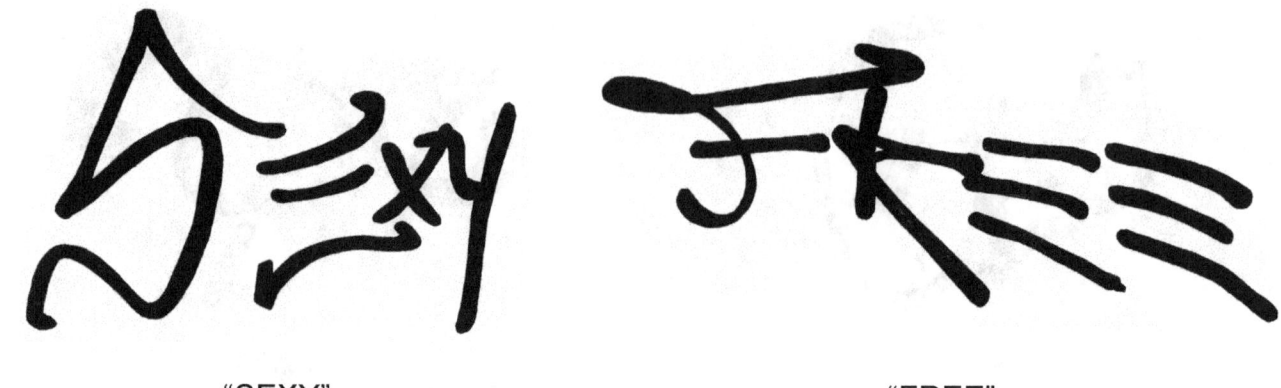

"SEXY"   "FREE"

TAGS WITH A FACE INCORPORATED INTO THE LETTERS

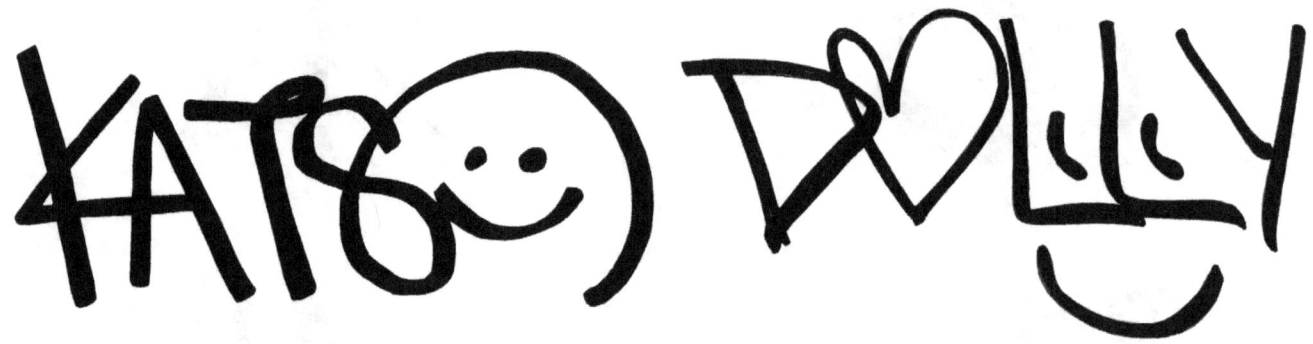

"KATS"   "DOLLY"

TAGS MADE WITH FACES

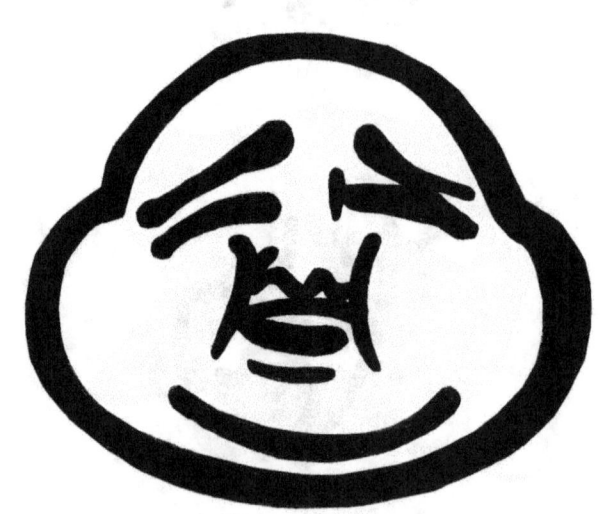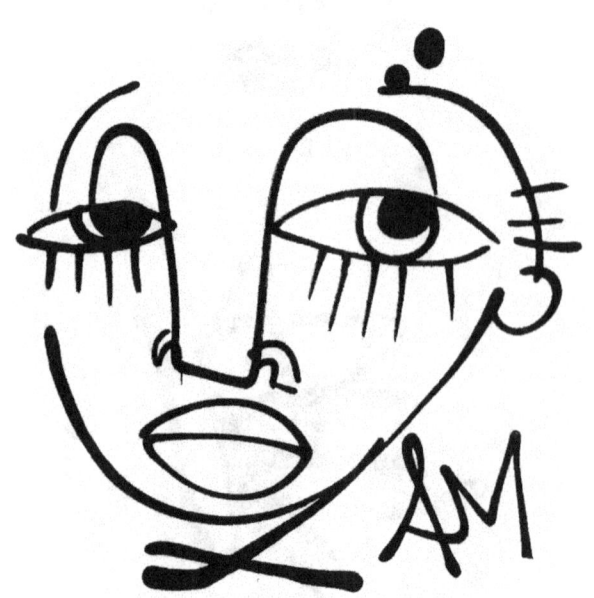

"WYNO" ?   "AM"

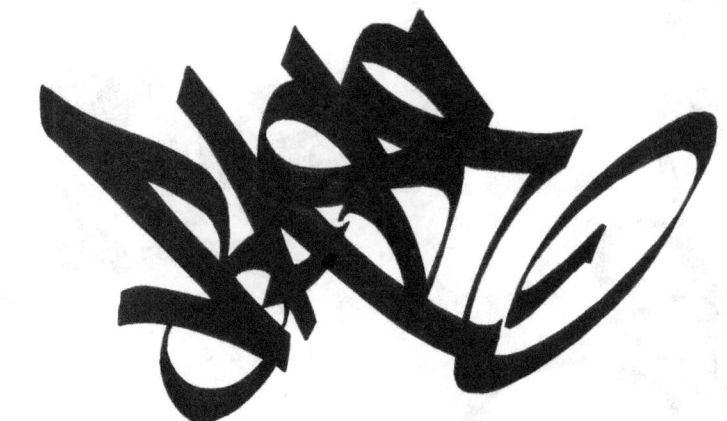

"BASE"

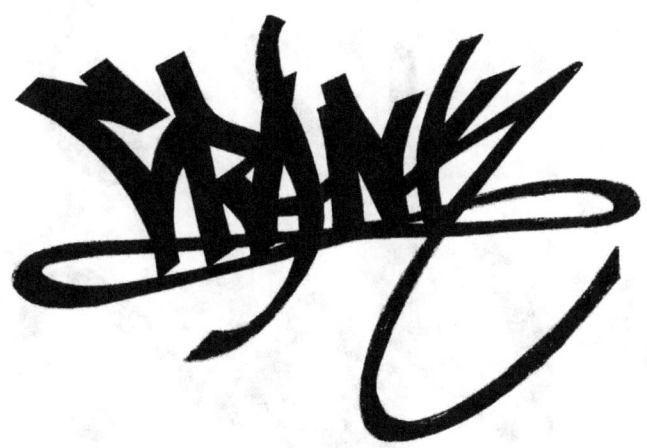

"CRANK"

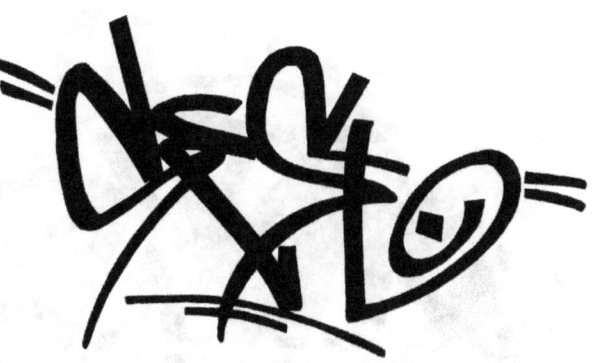

"SEST" ?

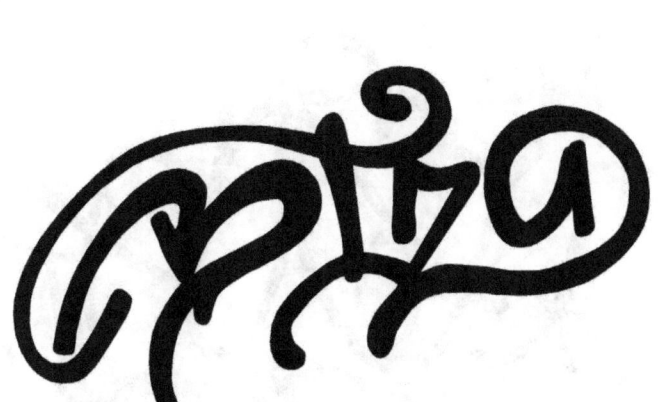

"BIZA"

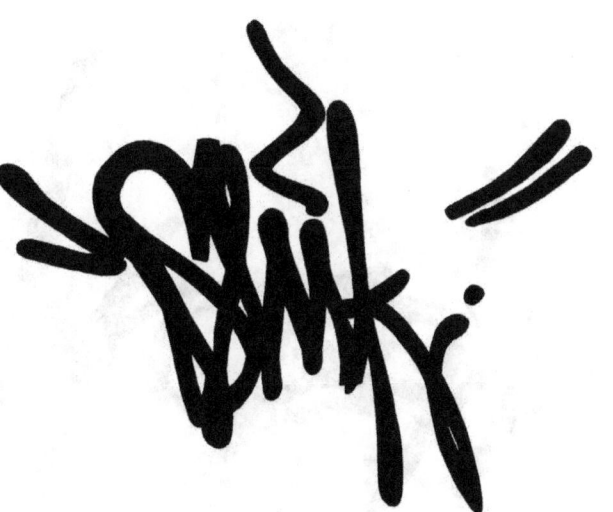

"SHIK" ?

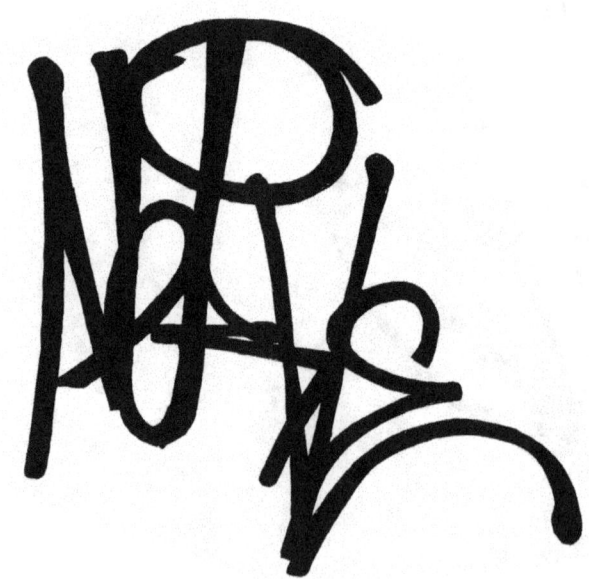

"NERVE"

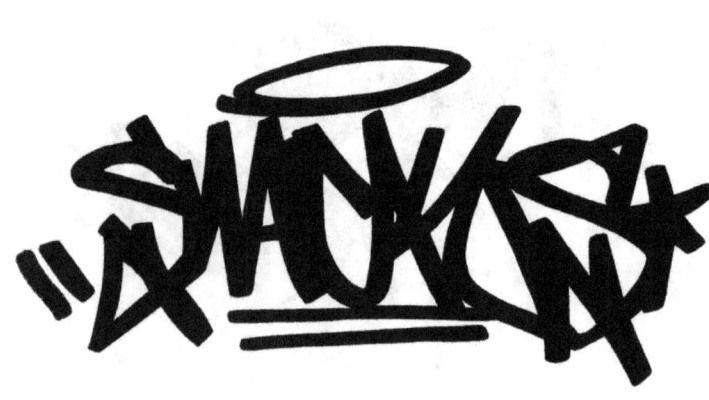

"SNACKS"

"XCUSE"

"TES"

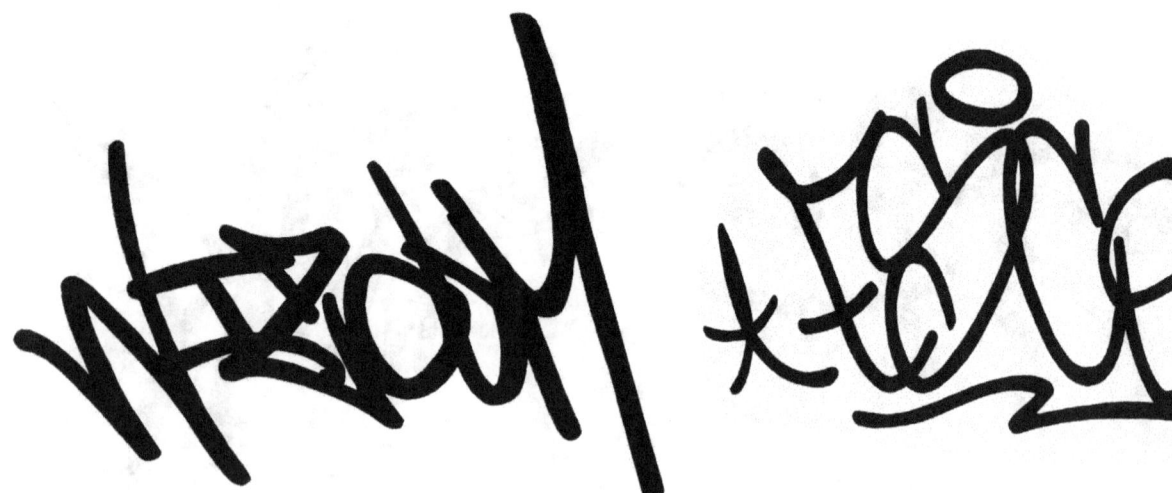

"WIZDOM"

"ESCO"

WHY WRITE WHEN YOU CAN TAG

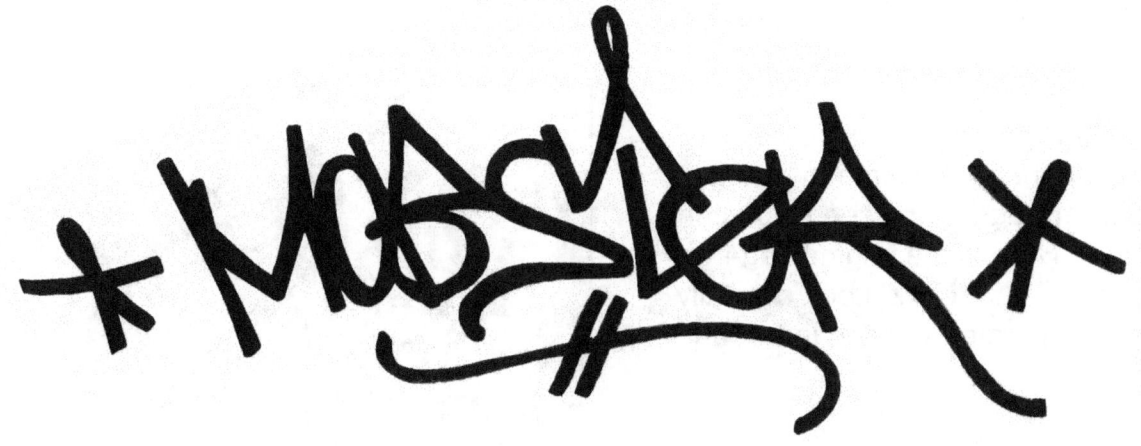

"MOBSTER"

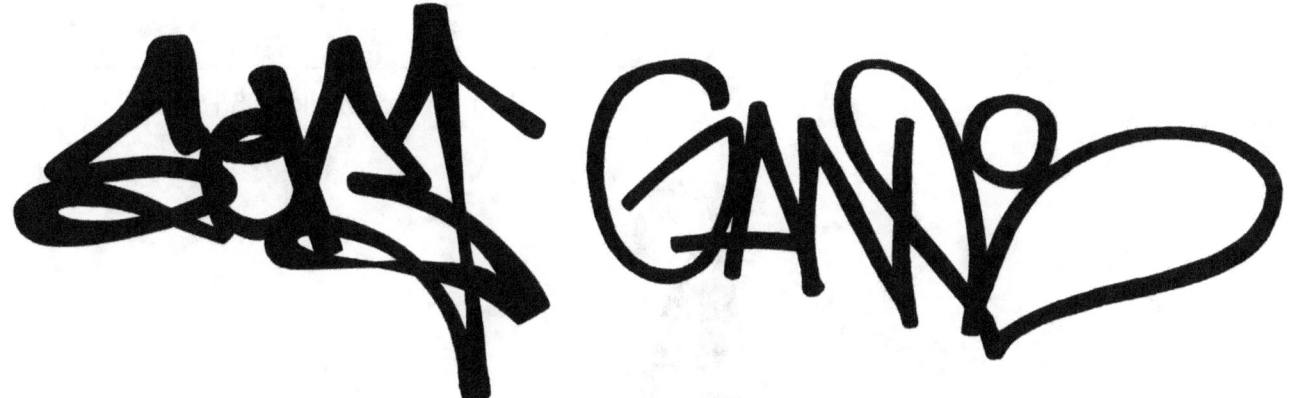

"SOB"

"GANG" or "GAN" ?

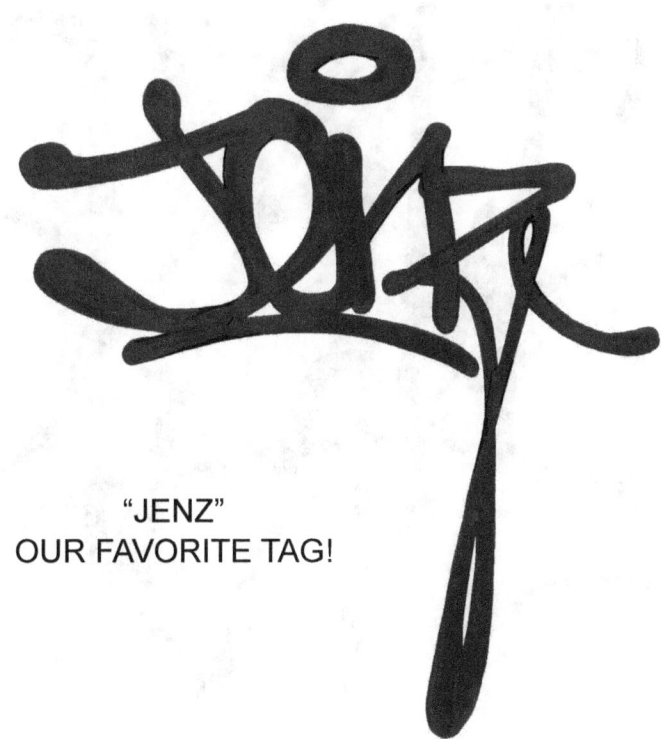

"JENZ"
OUR FAVORITE TAG!

READY TO SOLVE THIS TAG PUZZLE?

So now that you have plenty of tag reading experience it's time to revisit the tag from Page 4 and see if you can decipher it. Here is the original tag from the sidewalk at 5 Pointz. Look carefully and try to separate out each individual letter.

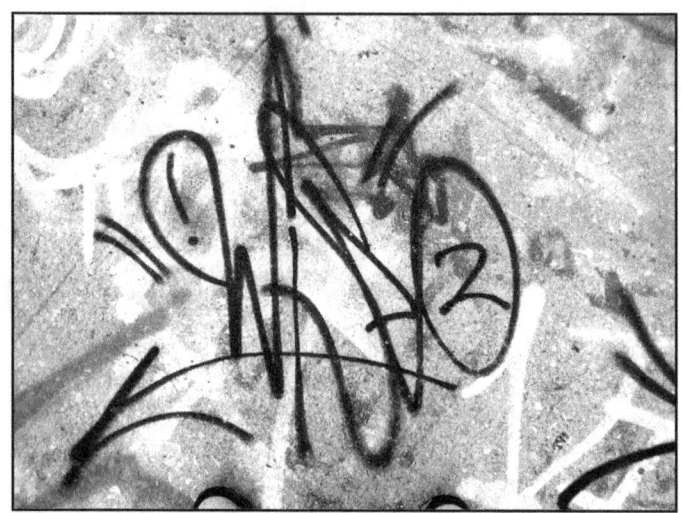

Tag on sidewalk at 5 Pointz

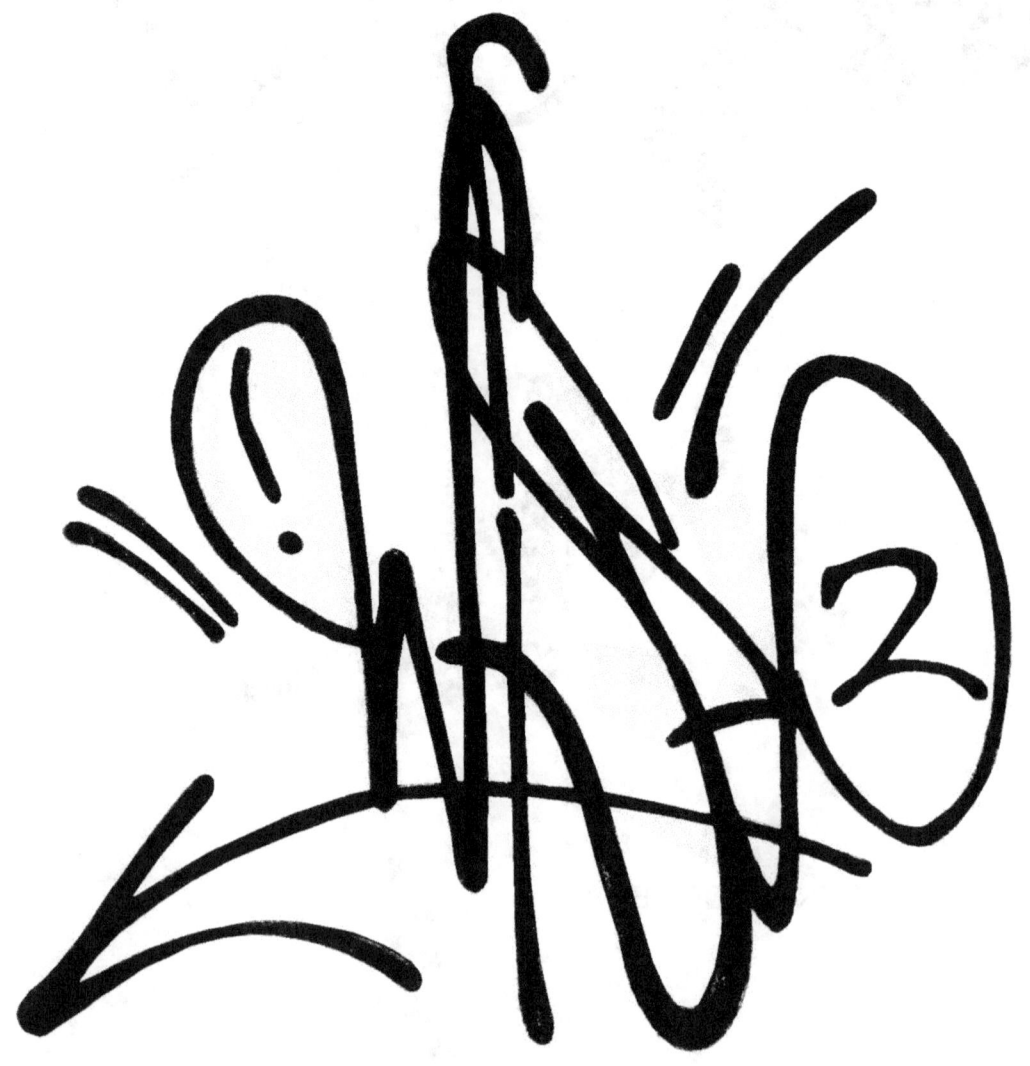

Here's what we think is in this tag:

1) letter "W"
2) letter "I"
3) letter "S"
4) letter "E"
5) two quotation marks
6) one exclamation point
7) one numeral "2"

We are convinced that this tag says "WISE 2". But that's just a guess. What do you think it says? One thing is for sure. This tag has great handstyle.

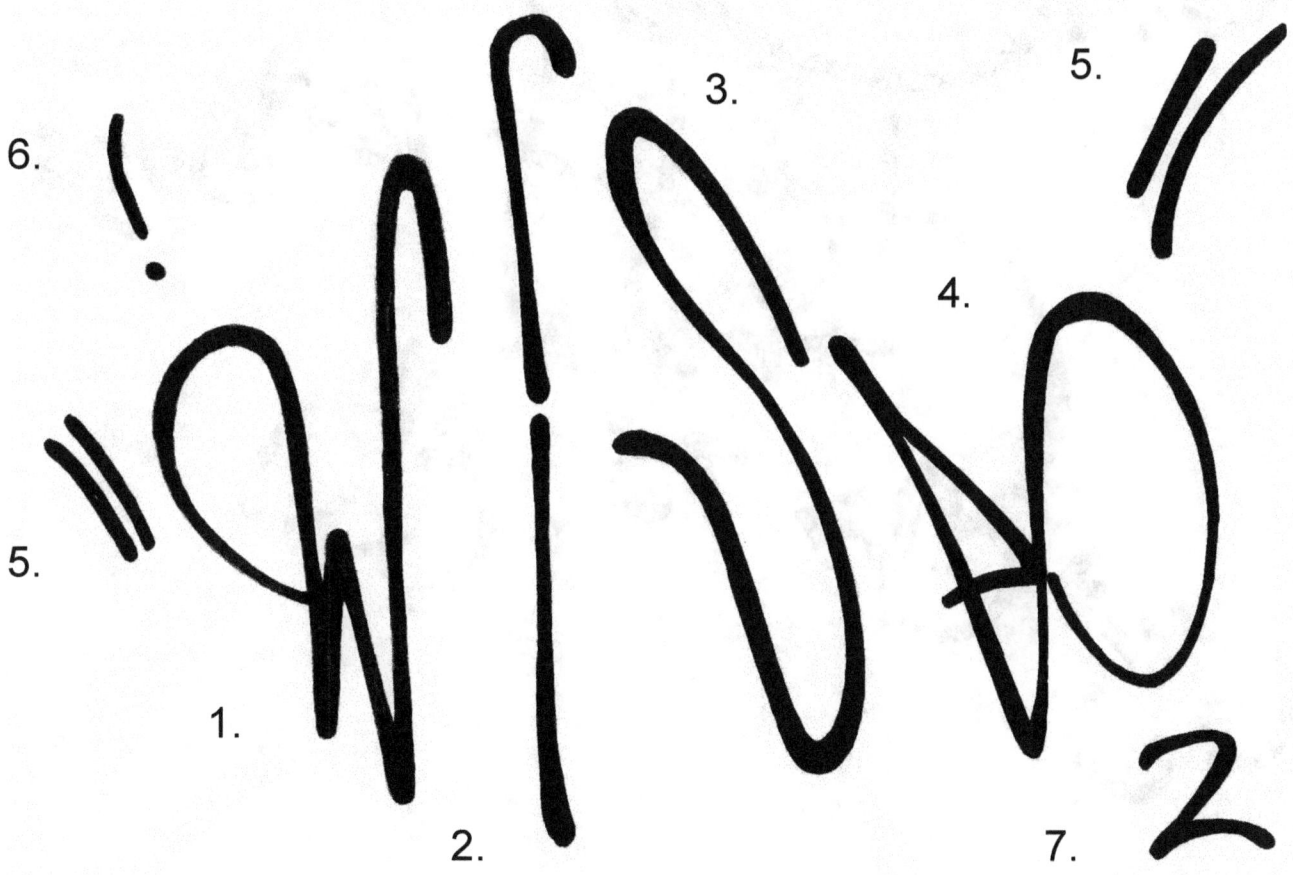

What a great puzzle. Now you know why we love graffiti tagging!

We found this amazing tag in an old textbook on Afro-Asian Culture Studies at Lafayette High School in Brooklyn, New York. It was drawn around 1974. It is an excellent example of graffiti tagging in its formative years and perfectly illustrates the different tagging motifs that were popular at that time: arrows, hearts, street addresses, and bones. This tag reads "JEFF 16 st. Boss". The '74 and '75 are abbreviations for 1974 and 1975. Amazing tag!

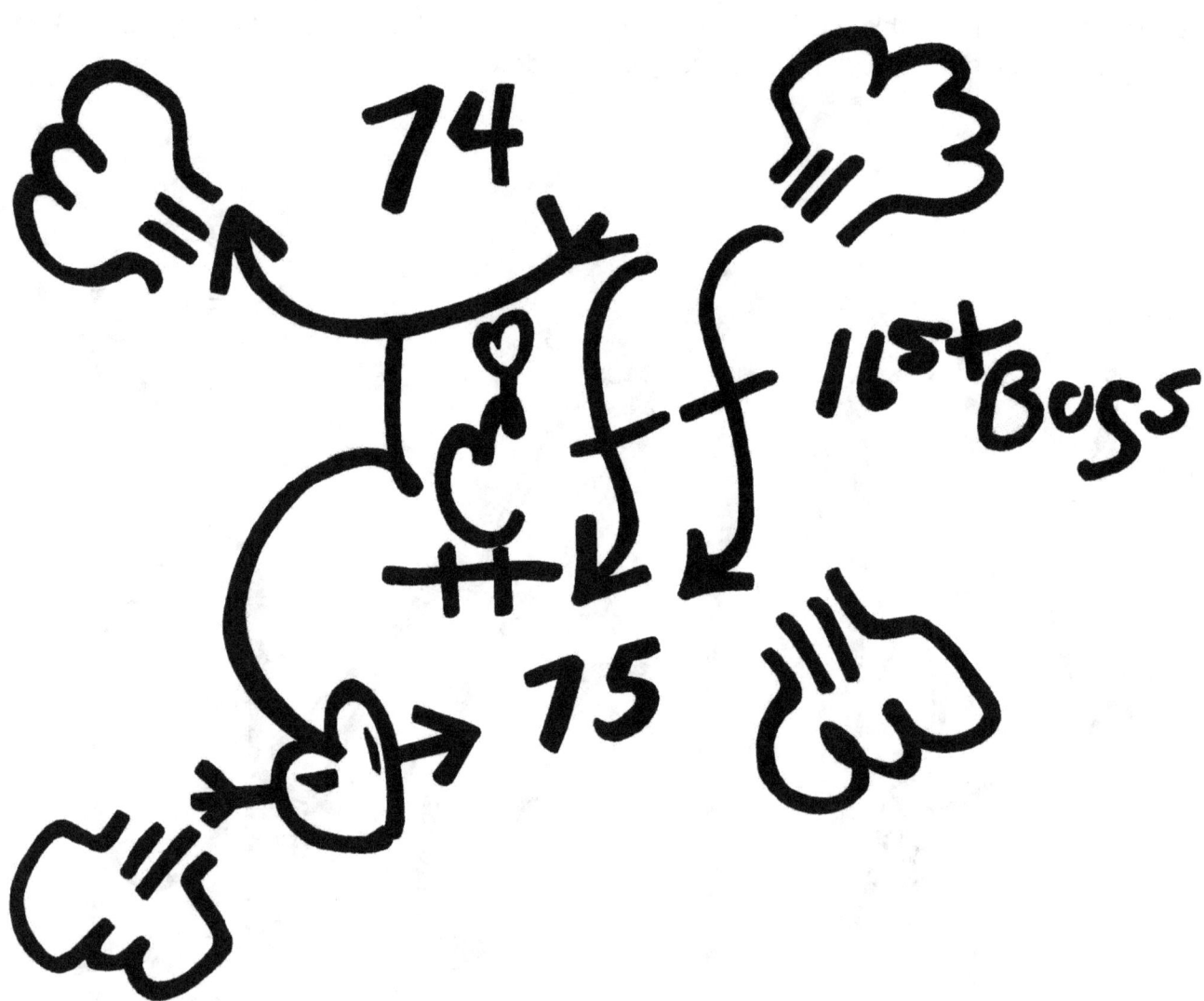

Here is another outstanding example from a textbook on Economics, also from Lafayette High School in 1974. The graphic shows a bubble letter piece that says "FIN" with a "FIN" tag in the bottom right corner. Notice the extreme back-slanting of the "F". We stumbled across these amazing examples while cleaning out some old bookshelves.

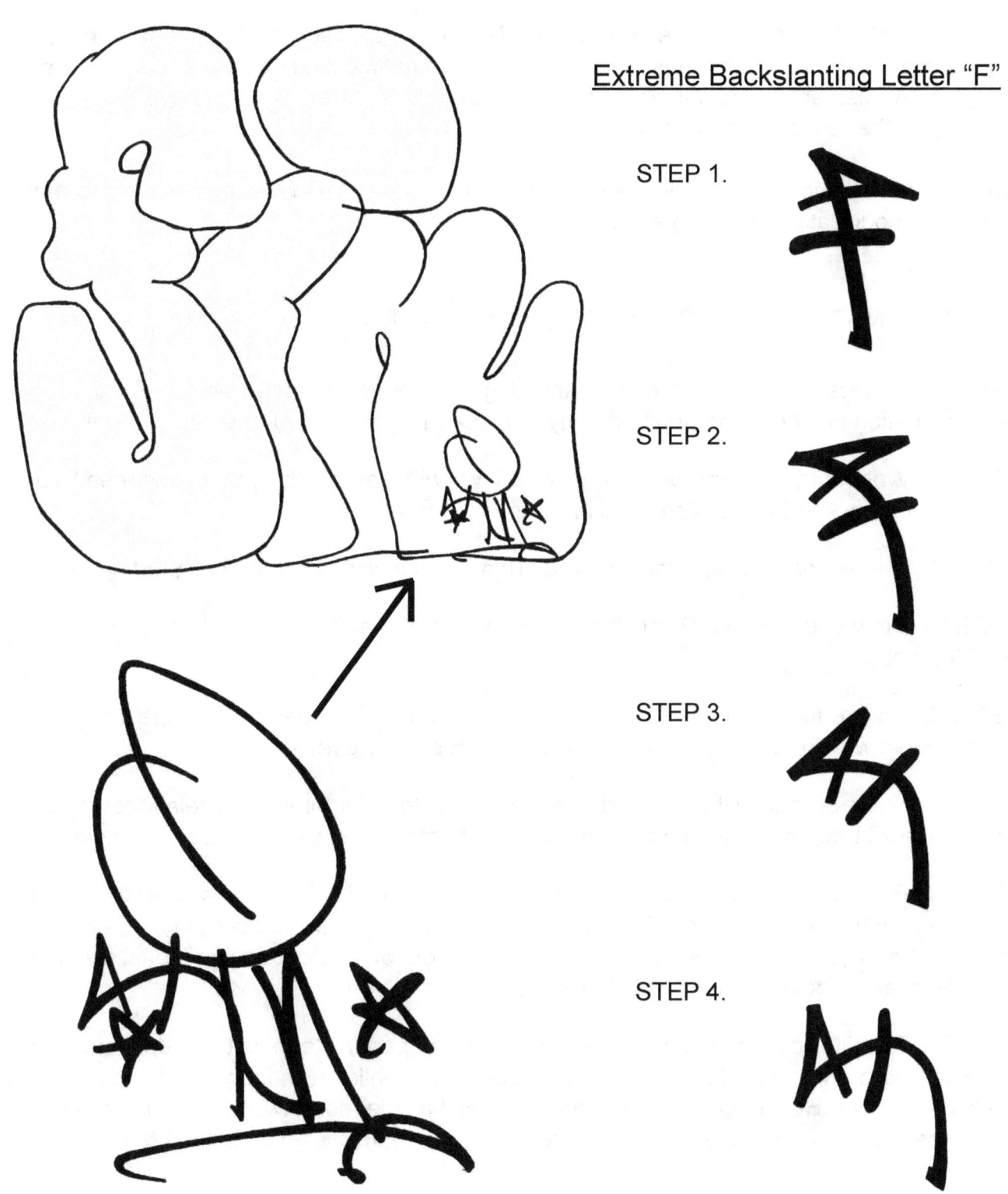

Extreme Backslanting Letter "F"

STEP 1.

STEP 2.

STEP 3.

STEP 4.

CHAPTER EIGHT
DESIGNING A TAG

We love this line from the movie "The Matrix'. Morpheus says to Neo "I can only show you the door. You're the one that has to walk through it." That's exactly how it works with graffiti tagging. We can show you our whole process from start to finish, but you have to practice and figure the rest out for yourself.

So now we will show you how to design your own tag. You already know the basic formula. It's letter modification and progression!

BASICS INSTRUCTIONS FOR DESIGNING A TAG

STEP 1. Choose a tag name. It can be anything that you want, a nickname, a word, initials, a combination of letters and numbers, anything (see Page 106 for more suggestions).

STEP 2. Write out your name with tag letters. Try it with several different styles (see Page 107). Refer back to the tag alphabets in Chapter Four for ideas.

STEP 3. Choose one drawing that you like. This drawing will become your Starting Point.

STEP 4. Draw your Starting Point on a clean sheet of paper. Make it big so you can really see the details.

STEP 5. Now redraw your Starting Point on a clean sheet of paper, but change it slightly. The easiest way to redraw it is to trace it. Or just copy it by eye.

STEP 6. Trace or redraw it again and again. Begin to look for interesting relationships between the letters. Try adding some additional elements, like stars, arrows or extensions.

STEP 7. Redraw your tag name over and over. People laugh when we say 200 times, but that is really the secret to designing a tag. Number the pages as you go so you have a record of how your tag developed. Experiment with lots of different design ideas. Eventually you will reach a point where the design looks finished to you.

STEP 8. Redraw your finished tag on a clean sheet of paper. Redraw it a couple of times. Make it sharp and crisp. Hang it up and stare at it for a while. Turn it upside down and stare at it some more. Hold it up to a mirror and stare at it a little more. Make any corrections you feel it needs and redraw it again. If you are happy with it, this is your finished tag.

HOW DO YOU KNOW WHEN YOUR TAG IS FINISHED?

That's a great question. The answer is <u>when it starts to flow</u>. When writing the tag begins to take on an automatic feeling, like you are tracing a well-worn path. You can draw it with your eyes closed. When you have memorized the curves, the angles, the details, that's when you know your tag design is complete. And when it looks good to you. That's important, too.

But it doesn't end there. If you continue to draw this tag over time, maybe years, it will change. Think of the Chinese calligrapher who spends a lifetime mastering the execution of a single Chinese character. In our experience, it takes approximately 200 drawings to create a good tag. But one of our students created her tag in just fourteen drawings. So there is no specific number. Designing a tag is not an exact science. Trial, error, and practice-these are the main ingredients of tag design. Anyone can do it. It just takes patience and a desire to want to design a really good tag!

Below is our example of a Starting Point and a Finished Tag. On the following pages, we have illustrated the modification and progression of this tag from start to finish, starting on Page 108. Study the examples and then try the same exercise with a tag of your own. Although there were originally 200 drawings in the construction of this tag, we boiled it down to 50 drawings that we thought most clearly demonstrate the evolution from one step to the next.

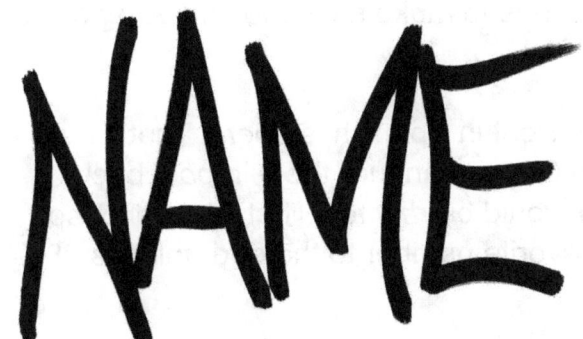

This is our Starting Point.

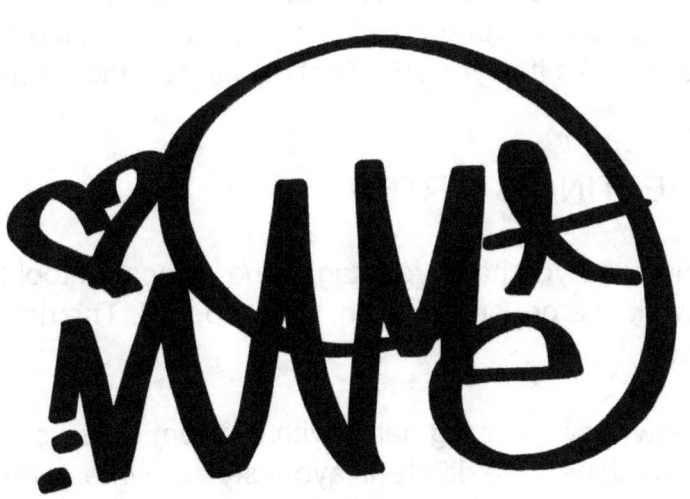

This is our Finished Tag.

CHOOSING A TAG NAME

You can use any thing that you like as a tag name. Your real name will work just fine, but you can use a variation of it, shorten it to just a few letters, use your nickname, or just your initials. The tag name you choose should mean something to you or have something to do with your personality. You can make up a word, too, just keep it short. Long names are harder to write. Sometimes a writer will choose a tag name simply because the letters work well together. You can have as many tag names as you like and you can try different names out to see what works. Use unusual spellings. Or try these ideas for a tag name: a pet's name, a favorite song, a sports team, a color, a car model, an animal, a favorite character in a movie…anything that makes sense for you.

In the book "Getting Up" by Craig Castleman, there's a quote from Wicked Gary who says "Writing your name identifies who you are. The more you write your name, the more you begin to think about and the more you begin to be about who you are. Once you start doing that, you begin to assert your individualism and when you do that, you have an identity". So your first step is to find a tag name that you think best represents you.

If you still can't think of a tag name try this exercise:
Make a list of five things about yourself that you like. Use one word to describe each thing. Choose one of those things and look up synonyms (words that mean the same thing) for that word. Look up translations for the word in different languages. Pick from one of those options. Abbreviate the word if it's too long. Add a number to the end of the word. Don't worry if it doesn't make sense to anyone else, it just has to make sense to you. After all, a tag name is kind of like a secret code anyway.

Here is an example: Let's say you are a great poet. Poet in Spanish is *poeta*. That would make an interesting tag name. In French it's *poete*. Or you can turn the *e* in *poet* back-wards, which looks pretty cool. A synonym for *poet* would be *rhymer*. That's too long, so take out the *h* and *e* and shorten it to *rymr*. Add a favorite number to the end (mine is 28) and make it "R*ymr 28*". That's your new tag name.

GETTING STARTED

So once you have your tag name, choose a tool to draw with. Any kind of magic marker will work fine or use a crayon, pen or pencil. The darker, the better so it's easier to trace later on.

Now draw your tag name with different styles of tag letters. Draw it several times in different variations. Use different layout styles. Write it with a mixture of upper-case and lower-case letters. Try turning one letter sidewards, backward or up-side down. Start small, finish big. Try angular letters or tall letters or a mixture of both. Use curves or sharp lines.

WHY WRITE WHEN YOU CAN TAG

Now choose one of the drawings that you like for your Starting Point. Keep in mind that the Starting Point drawing will be changing, so it's not that big of a deal which variation you choose. Just pick one and move on to the next step.

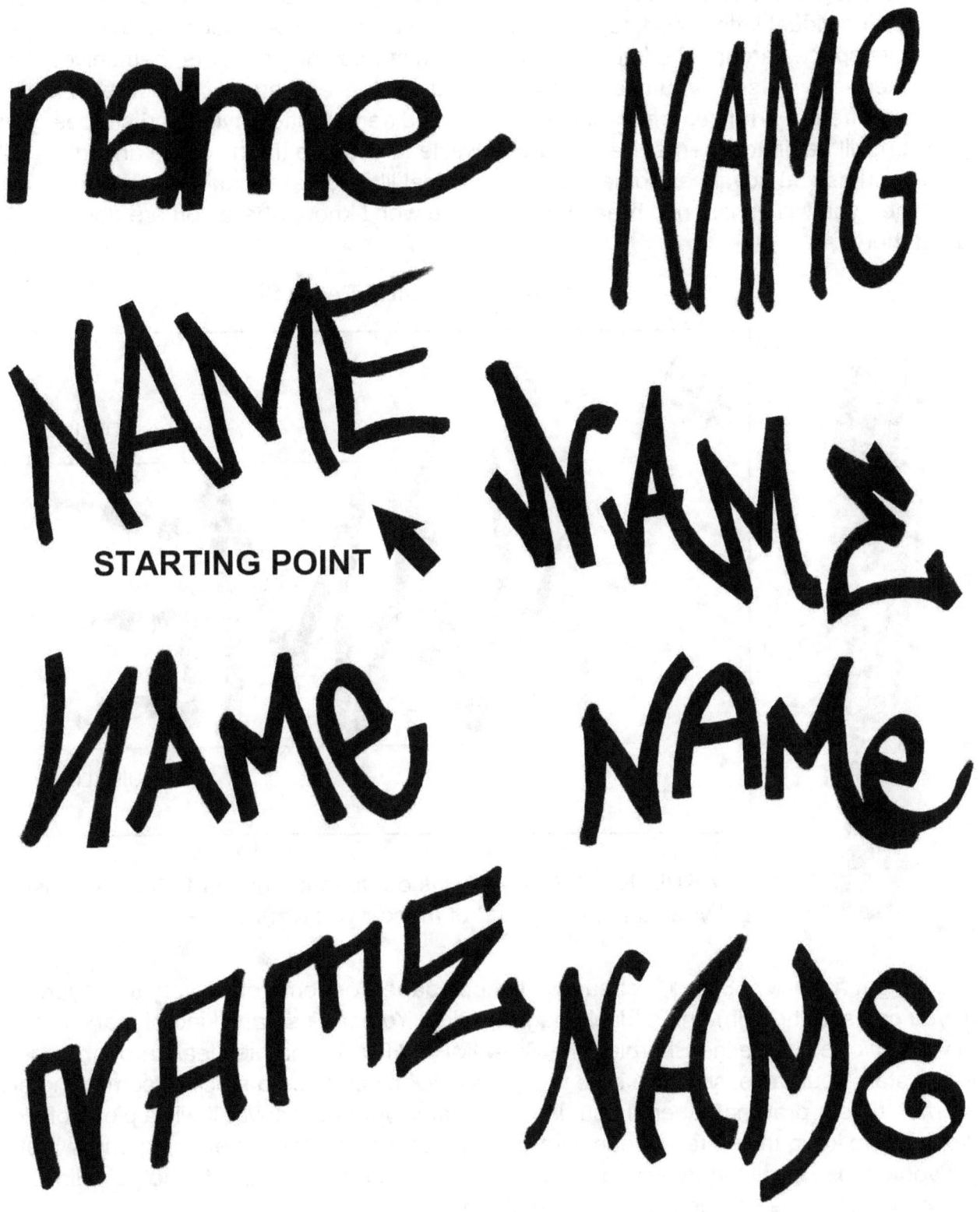

STARTING POINT

NOW IT'S TIME TO DESIGN YOUR TAG

The process you use to create a tag is exactly the same one you used to create a single tag letter; letter modification and progression. Except now you will be modifying all of the letters in the tag at the same time. When modifying a tag, you have to pay close attention to how the individual letters work together to form the whole tag. Attention should be given to the white spaces around the letters, as well as the strokes of the letters themselves. The only problem-solving skills you need to create a tag are trial and error. Through experimentation with different arrangements, extra details, and different letter styles and shapes, your tag design will begin to emerge. Each drawing will lead you into the next one and ideas will come to you as you advance. Sometimes you will feel like you are making no progress at all, but then you will experience breakthroughs. You won't know where you are going until you get there.

STARTING POINT PAGE SET-UP

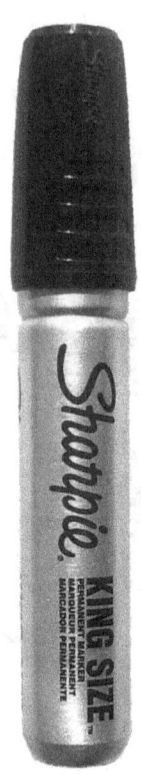

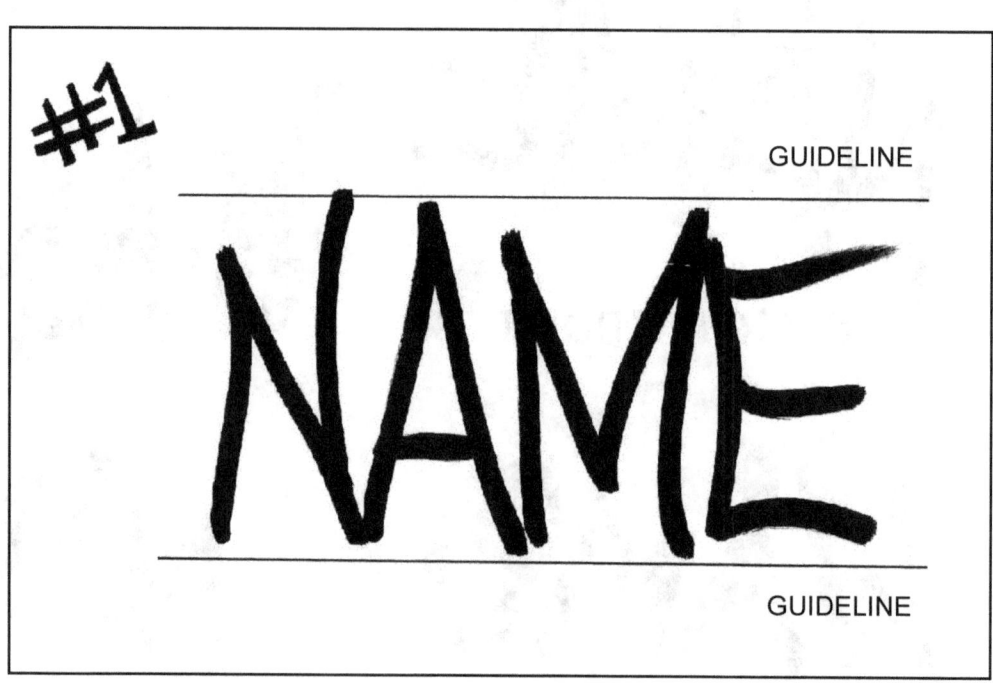

SHARPIE KING SIZE - This is our favorite marker for this exercise, but you can use any kind of marker you want.

To begin, get a stack of 8.5"x11" cheap white copy paper (or some other very thin paper that you can see through) and a black magic marker. You can use any kind of marker that you wish. We really like the Sharpie King Size. IMPORTANT: Sharpies leak through paper and will stain your table, so make sure you put a thick piece of card stock or something else underneath your drawing paper. If you use a light box, you must cover it will a piece of clear cellophane to keep the surface clean. Draw two guidelines on the paper using any layout style you choose and then draw your Starting Point from Page 107 inside the guidelines. Put a #1 in the top left or top right corner of the page.

MODIFICATION AND PROGRESSION

Now let's start. Place a clean sheet of paper on top of Page #1 and put a #2 in one corner. Copy your Starting Point drawing or trace it. As you redraw your Starting Point drawing on page #2 look for some way you can change it a little. Add an element like an arrow or a star. Just a tiny change is enough. Then put page #1 aside and lay a clean piece of paper on top of page #2 and place a #3 in the corner. Redraw the tag again and change it a little again. Continue this process. Number each page consecutively as you go. Look for interesting relationships between the letters. Try some of the effects from Chapter Six. Keep going until you think your tag is done. See our tag progression on Pages 109-117. You don't have to copy our examples, just study our drawings and see how the tag progresses from one step to the next. Then try this with your own tag name.

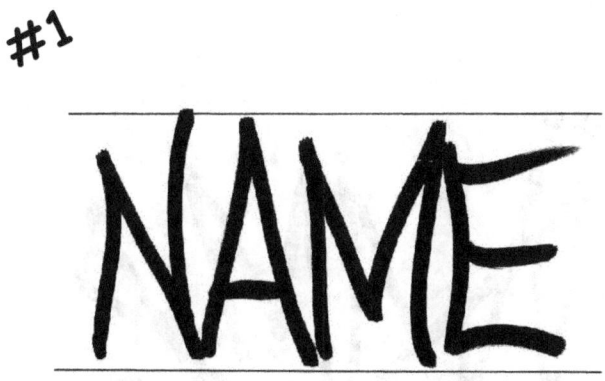

STEP 1. Draw your Starting Point on an 8.5"x11" piece of paper. Place a clean sheet of paper on top.

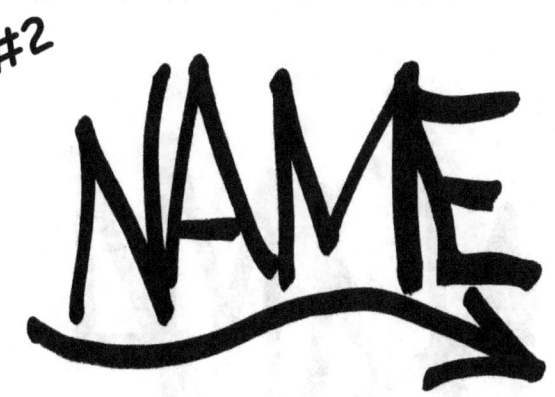

STEP 2. Begin to modify the letters. Draw a curving arrow underneath.

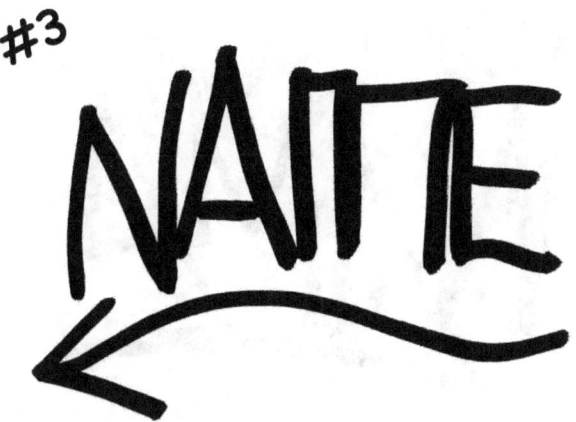

STEP 3. Reverse the arrow and change the "M" to a square tag letter.

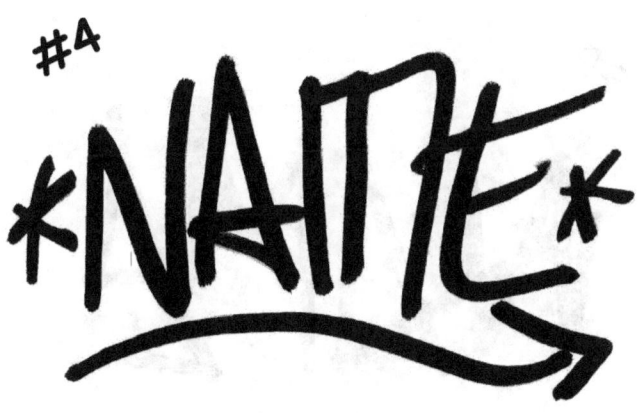

STEP 4. Turn the arrow back around and add two stars on the sides. Draw the "A" with one line.

#5

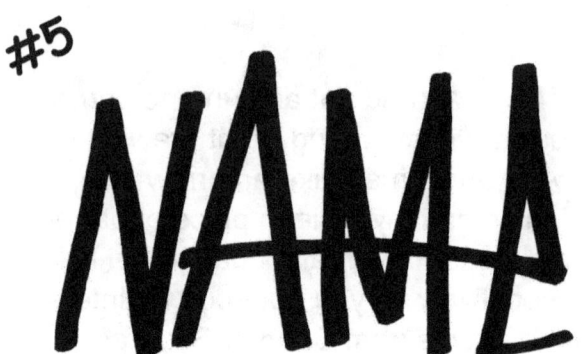

STEP 5. Remove the arrow. Change the upper case "E" to a lower case "e". Extend the middle bar of the "e" to complete the "A".

#6

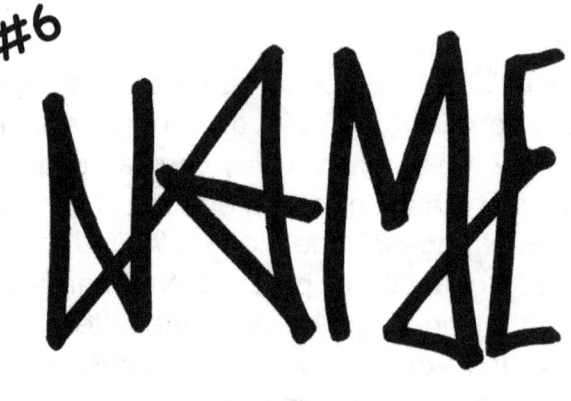

STEP 6. Go back to an upper case "E". Connect the "N" and "A", and the "M" and "E".

#7

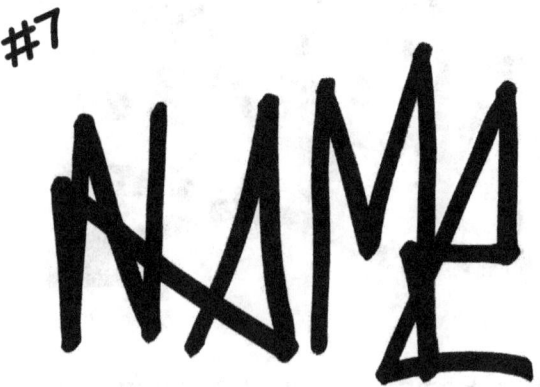

STEP 7. Change the upper case "E" to a lower case "E" and connect it to the "M".

#8

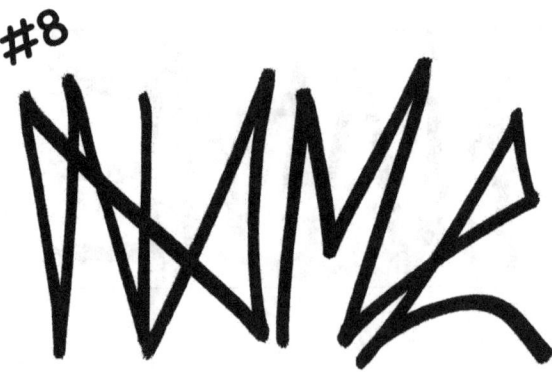

STEP 8. Redraw again, but simplify the connection between the "M" and the "e".

#9

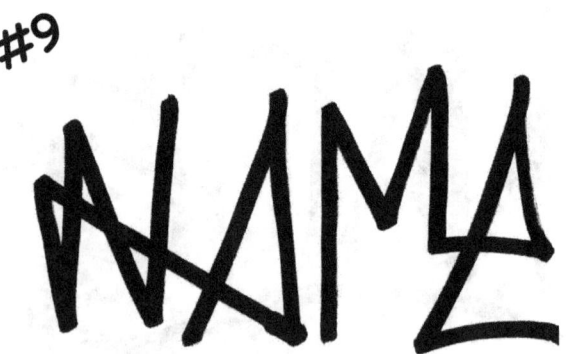

STEP 9. Shorten the right side of the "M" and connect the "M" and the "e" at the mid-line

#10

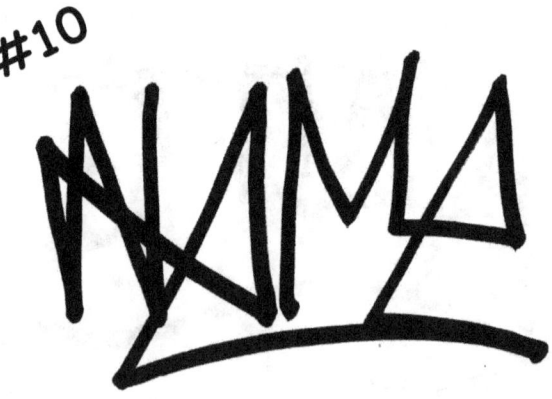

STEP 10. Connect the bottoms of the "A" and the "e" with a line underneath.

WHY WRITE WHEN YOU CAN TAG

Continue numbering...

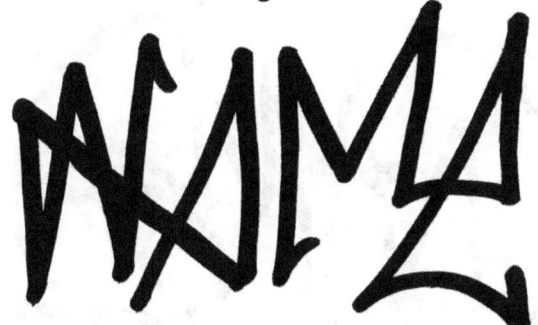

STEP 11. Add serifs to the letters in some places (serifs are little decorative strokes at the ends of some letters).

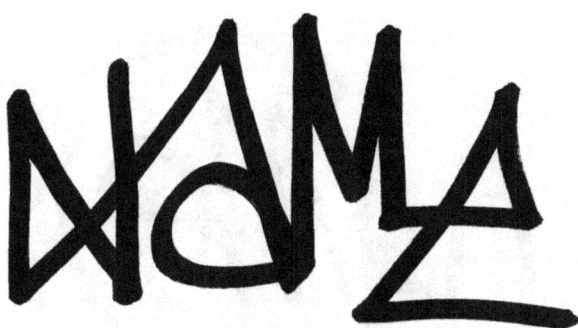

STEP 12. Change the upper case "A" to a lowercase "a" and draw all the letters with one continuous line (one liner tag).

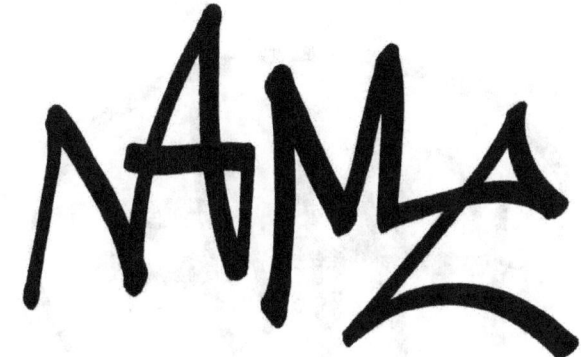

STEP 13. Connect just the "N" to the "A", and "M" to the "E" using one line to form two letters.

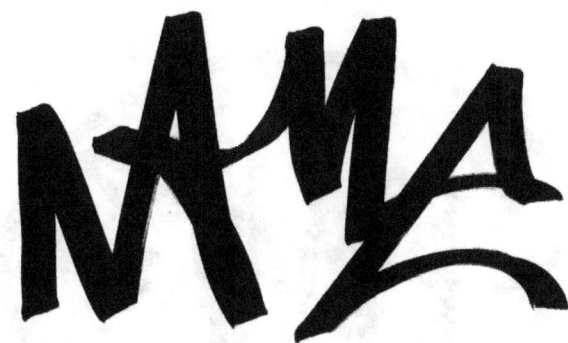

STEP 14. Switch to a thicker marker and draw the tag with one continuous line. It looks very different.

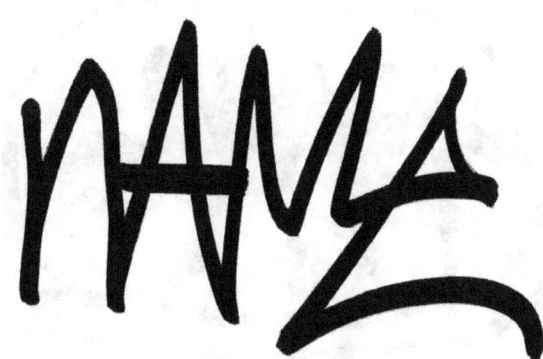

STEP 15. Change the upper case "N" to a lowercase "n".

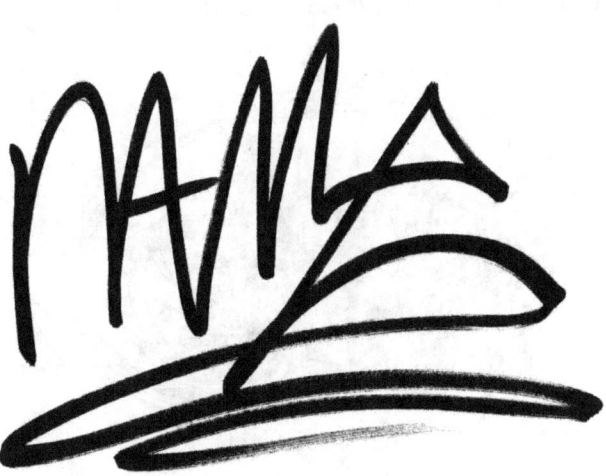

STEP 16. Extend the bottom of the "e" into a squiggly flourish underneath.

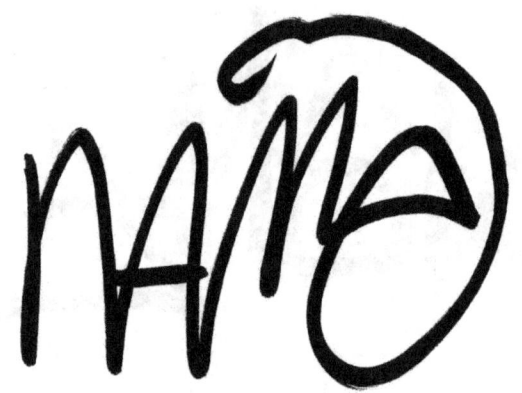

STEP 17. Curl the end of the "e" up and over the top.

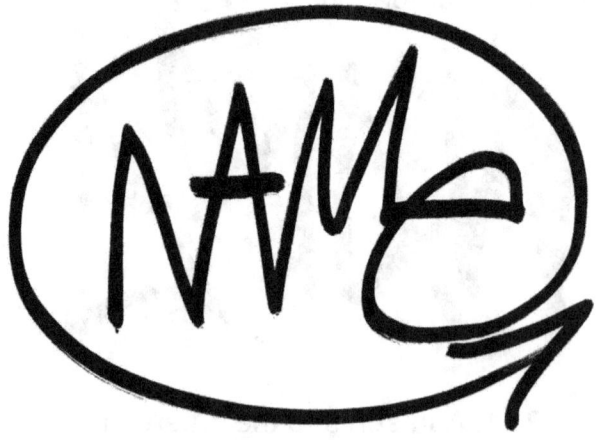

STEP 18. Change back to an upper case "N" and swing the end of the "e" around to encircle the whole word. Add an arrow.

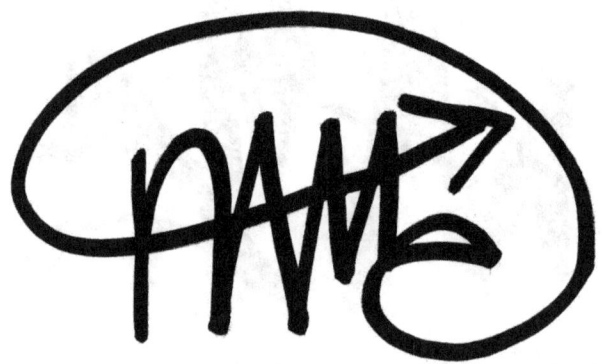

STEP 19. Switch back to a lowercase "e". Slash across the word using the extension of the "e" to form the crossbar of the "A".

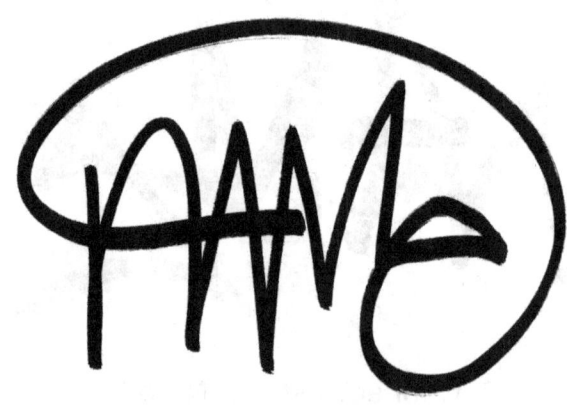

STEP 20. Remove the arrow and shorten the extension.

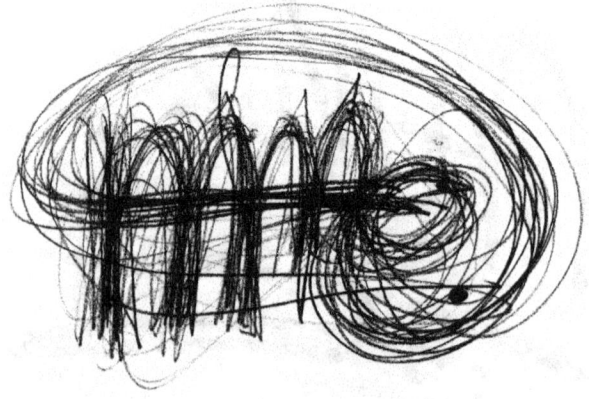

STEP 21. Sometimes we get stuck and just scribble until another idea comes along.

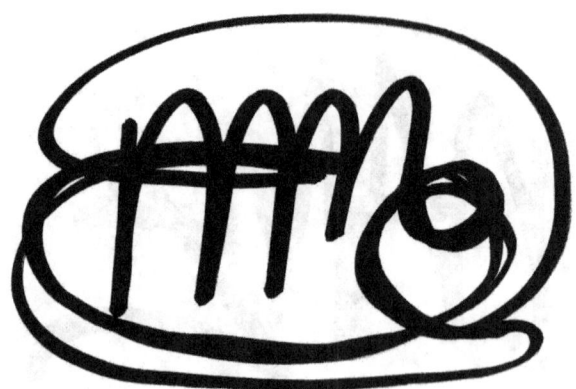

STEP 22. At this point we are totally confused. Ya think?!

WHY WRITE WHEN YOU CAN TAG

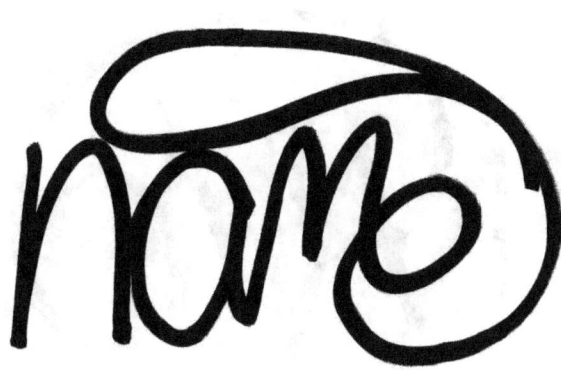

STEP 23. Change to a lower case "a" and loop the curled line over the top.

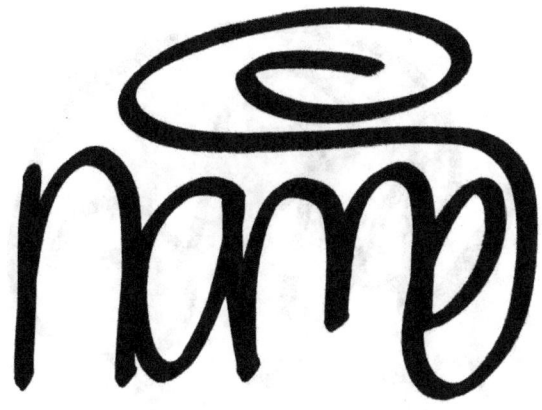

STEP 24. Make a nice, neat swirl. Now we are getting somewhere.

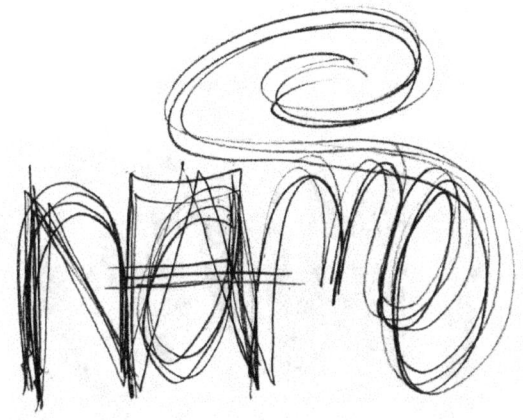

STEP 25. More scribbling and experimenting. Change lower case "N" back to an upper case "N".

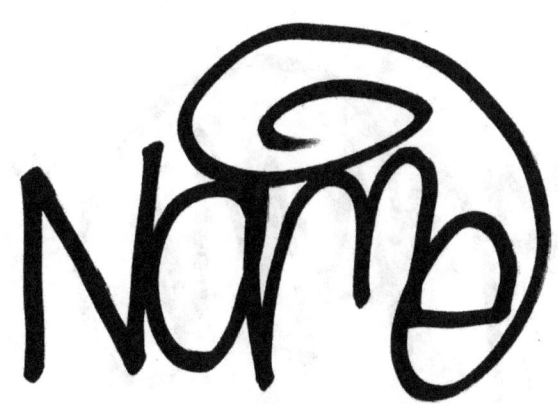

STEP 26. Flip the curl downwards.

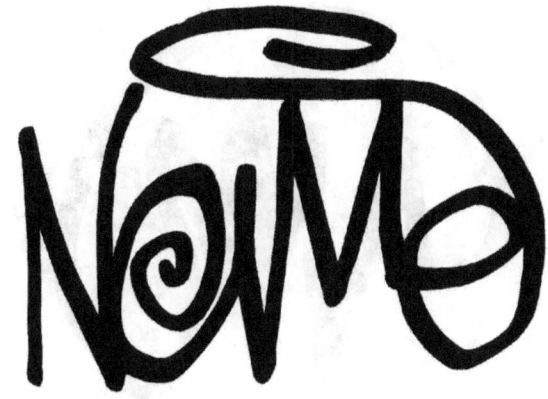

STEP 27. Make a swirly line inside the "a". Flip the top curl upwards again. Make the "M" more pointy.

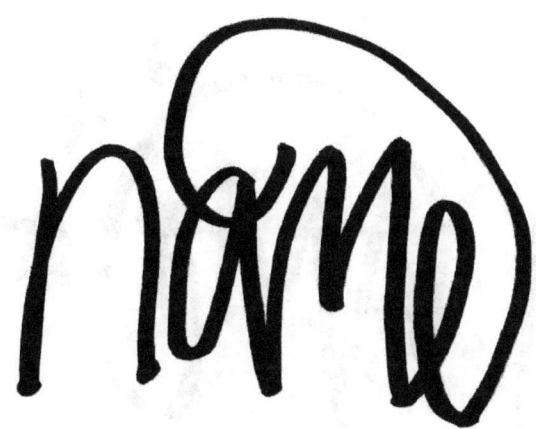

STEP 28. Switch back to a lower case "n". Shorten the top curl to overlap the top of the "a". At this point we are still pretty lost.

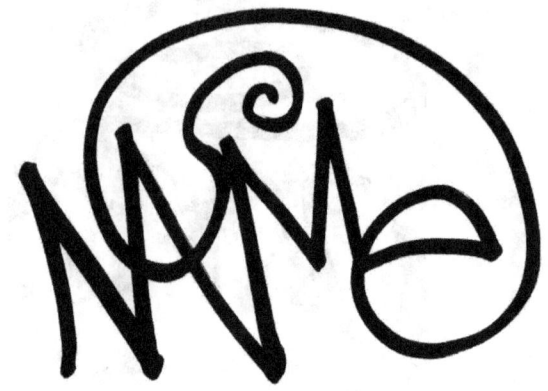

STEP 29. Switch back to a capital "N" and "A" and then connect them. End the top curl with a little curlicue.

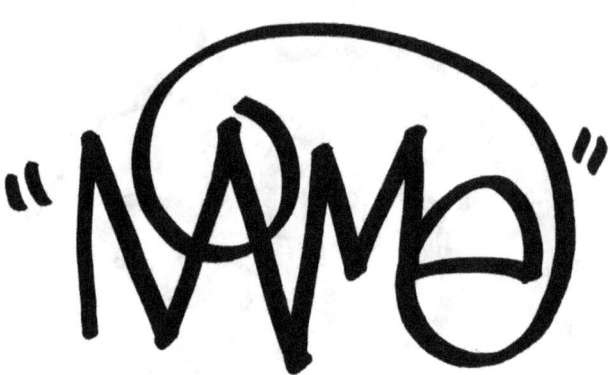

STEP 30. Shorten the top curl to act as just the crossbar of the "A". Add quotation marks.

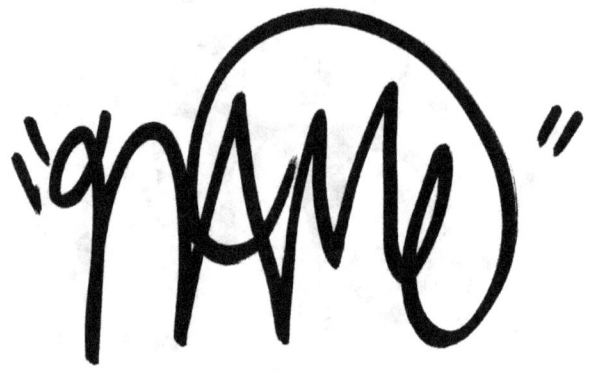

STEP 31. Switch back to a lower case "n" with a little curl on the end.

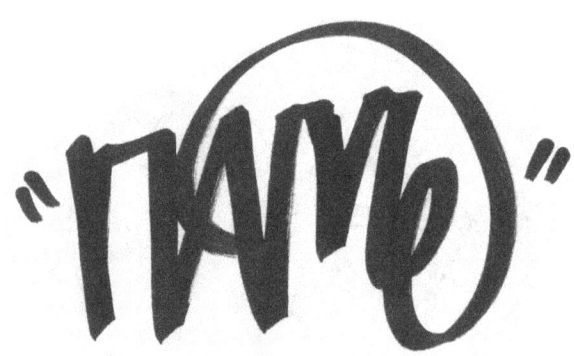

STEP 32. Redraw the tag with a thicker marker and make the letters more square.

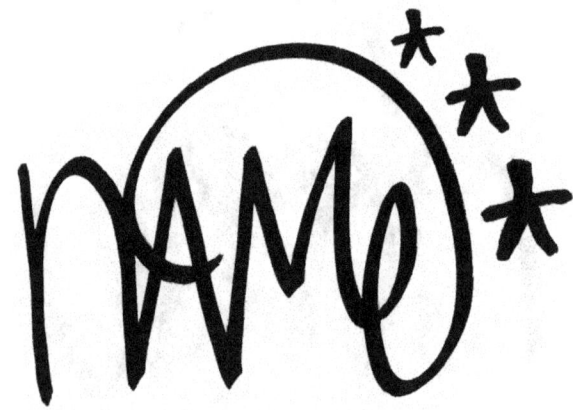

STEP 33. Change the letters back to rounded letters. Add three little stars.

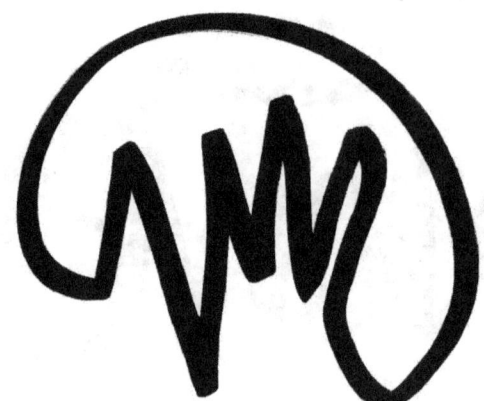

STEP 34. This is where it gets a little weird. Looks like the Abominable Snowman's teeth from Rudolph movie. Never mind!

WHY WRITE WHEN YOU CAN TAG

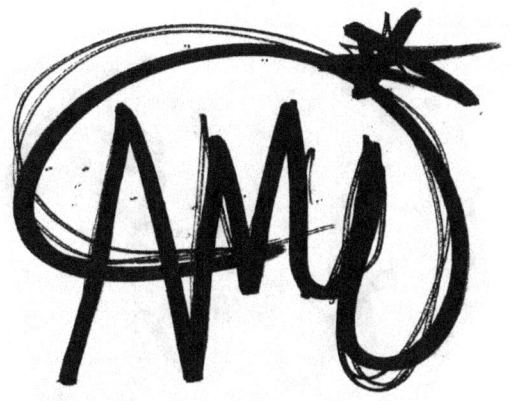

STEP 35. We got to thinking we could drop the "n", change the "e" to an "i" and make the word "AMI", which means friend in French.

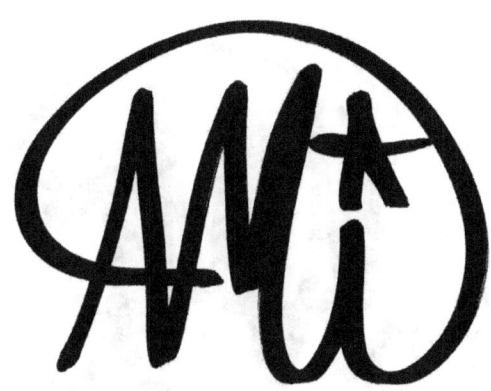

STEP 36. Put the star inside the circle and neaten it up. That looks pretty good.

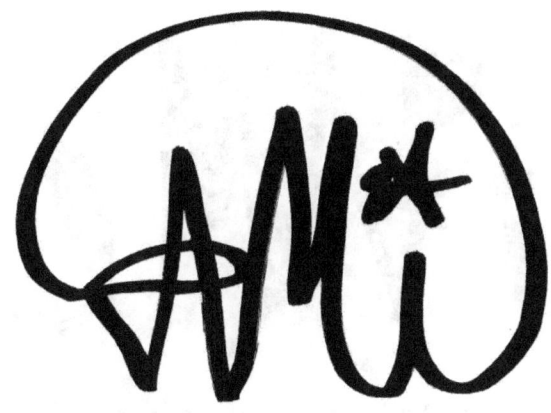

STEP 37. Draw all the letters with one continuous line, plus the star.

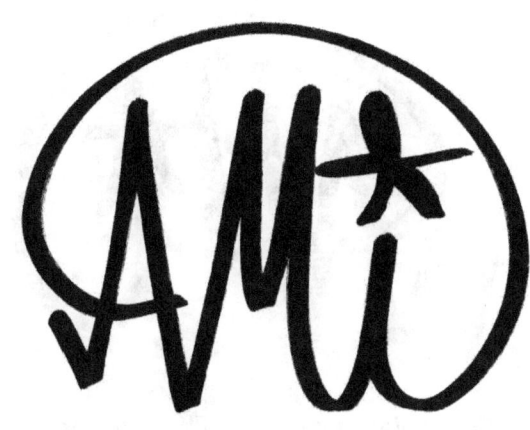

STEP 38. Put a serif on the bottom of the "A".

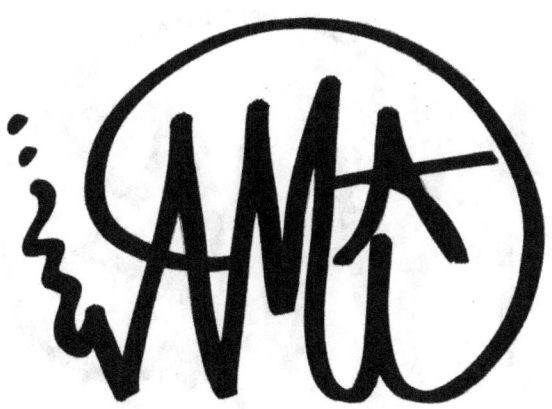

STEP 39. Extend the serif into a wiggly line with a few dots on the end.

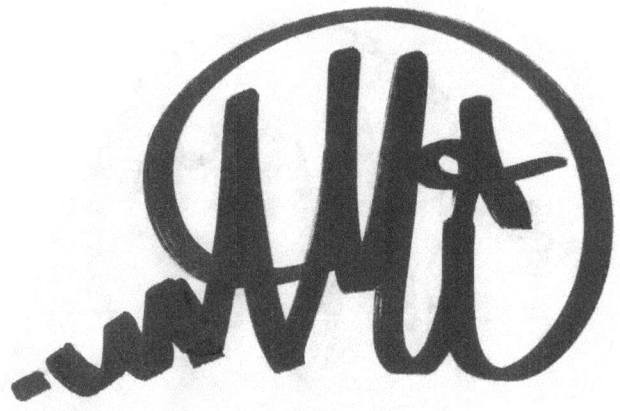

STEP 40. Use a thicker marker. Point the wiggly line downwards.

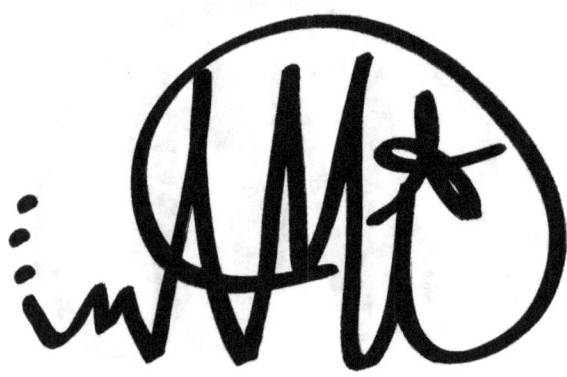

STEP 41. Shorten the wiggly line.

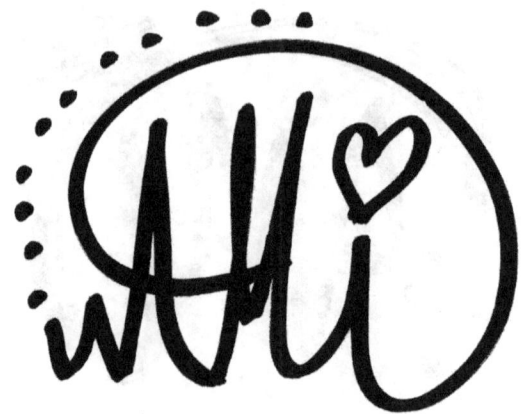

STEP 42. Draw more dots going over the top. Change the star to a heart.

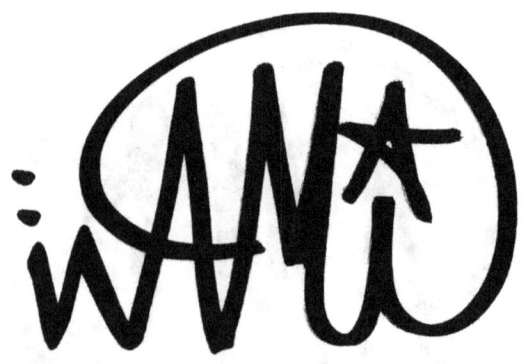

STEP 43. Wait a minute. The wiggly line looks like an "n". So...........back to the word "NAME".

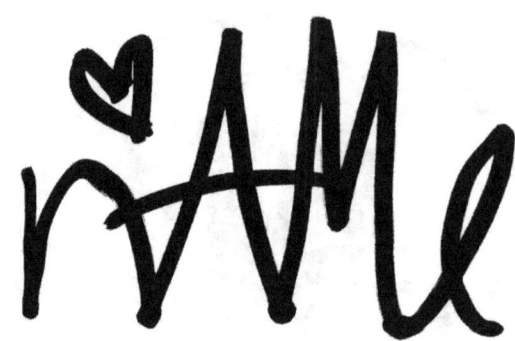

STEP 44. Add a heart over the "n". Take out the big cuvly line over the top.

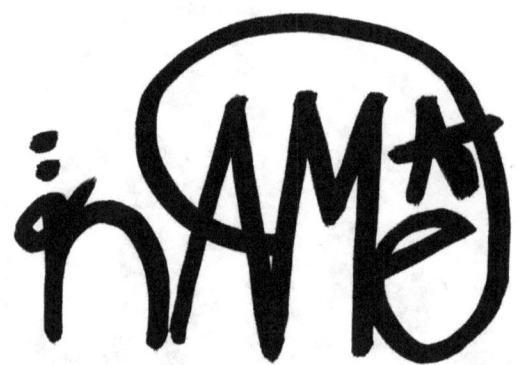

STEP 45. Put back the curving line up over the top again. Then add a star.

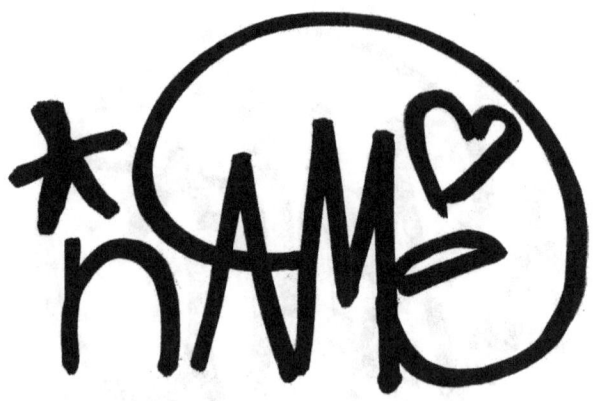

STEP 46. Put the star over the "n" and a heart over the "e".

WHY WRITE WHEN YOU CAN TAG

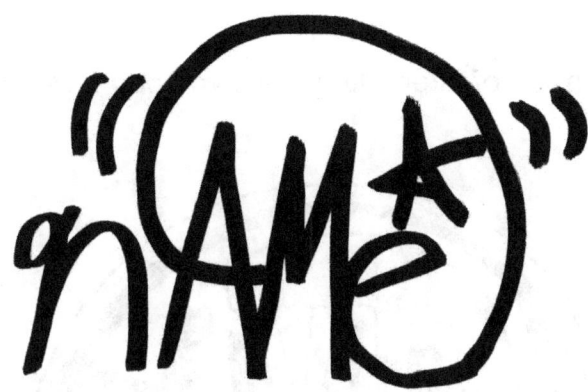

STEP 47. Add quotation marks. Move the star back over the "e".

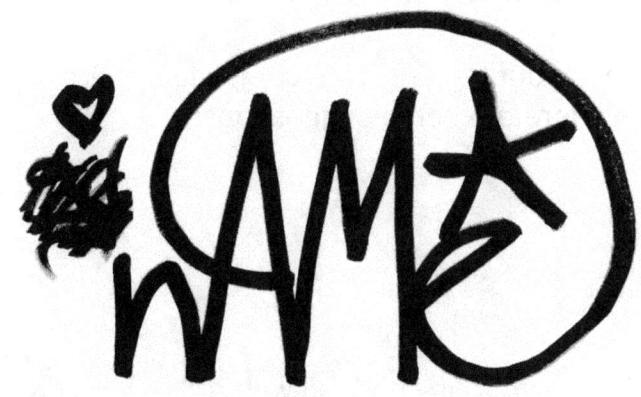

STEP 48. Put a heart over the "n".

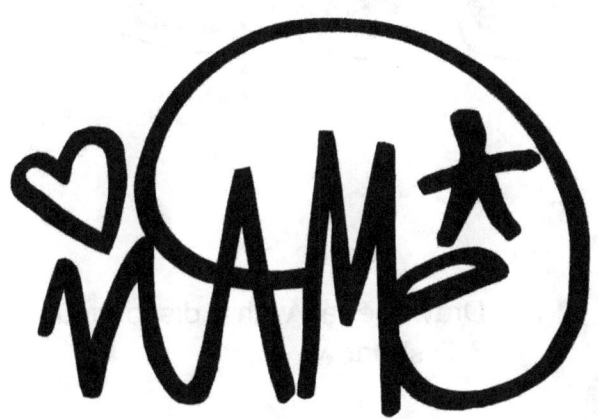

STEP 49. Redraw.

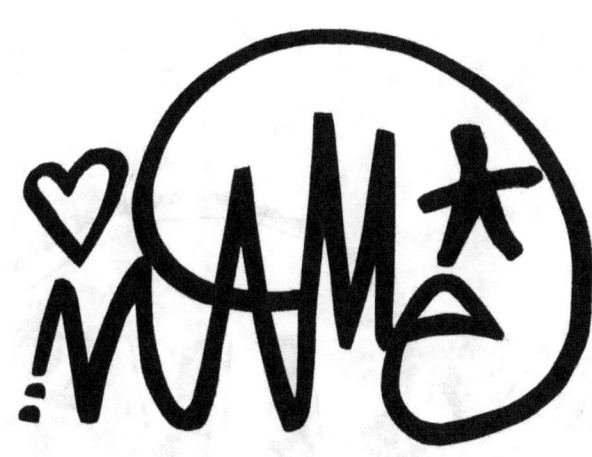

STEP 50. Draw all the letters with one continuous line. Add a few dots at the tip of the "n".

FINISHED TAG!!!

Redraw with a thicker marker. This is the finished tag.

As a reminder, this was the Starting Point.

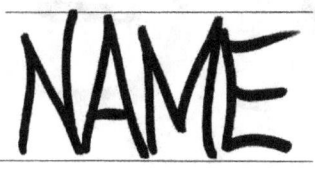

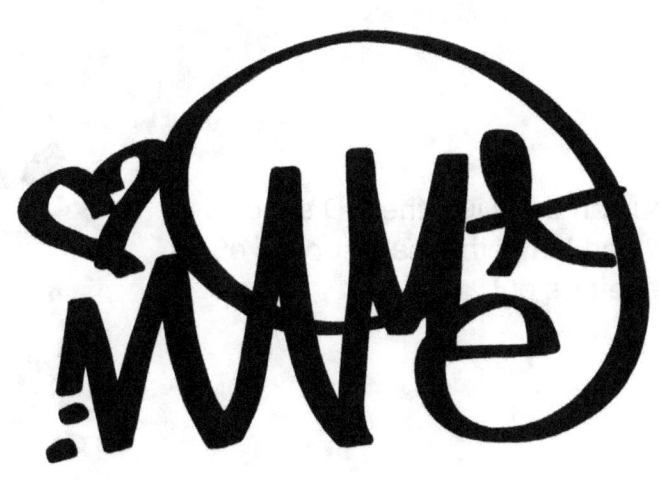

FINISHING TECHNIQUES

Once your tag design is completed, there are a number of interesting ways you can finish it off. Here are some suggestions:

Outline your finished tag with a fine-point magic marker. Make the outline about 1/8" to 1/4" from the edges of the letters.

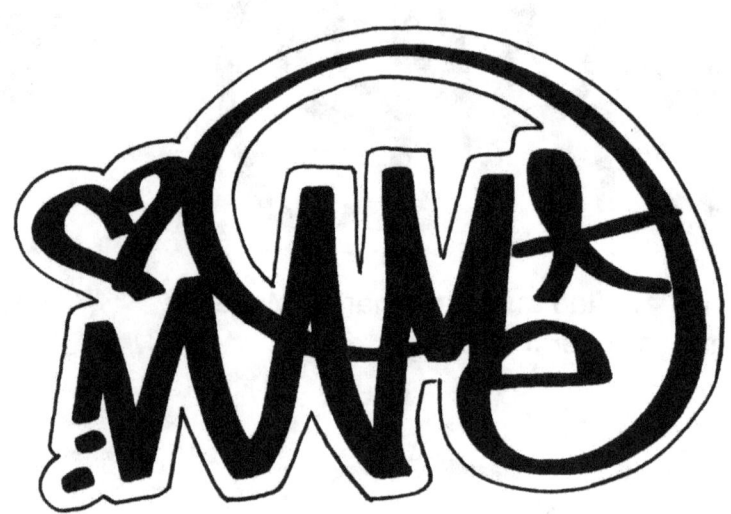

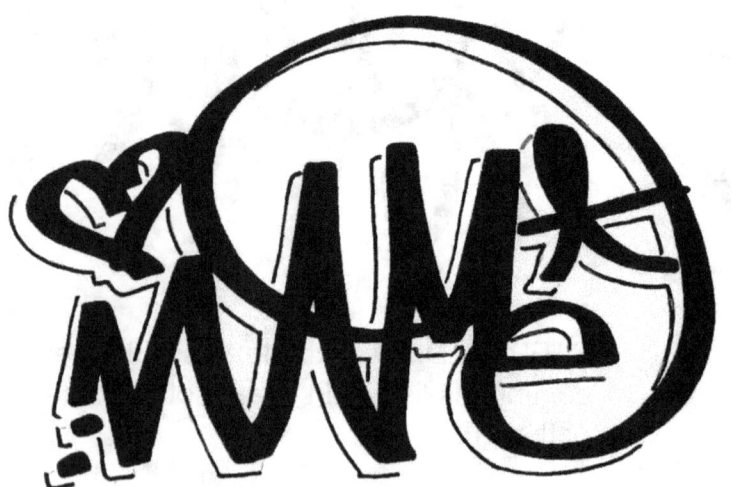

Draw the tag with a discontinuous 3-D shadow.

You can draw just the 3-D shadow and leave the main strokes of the letters out.

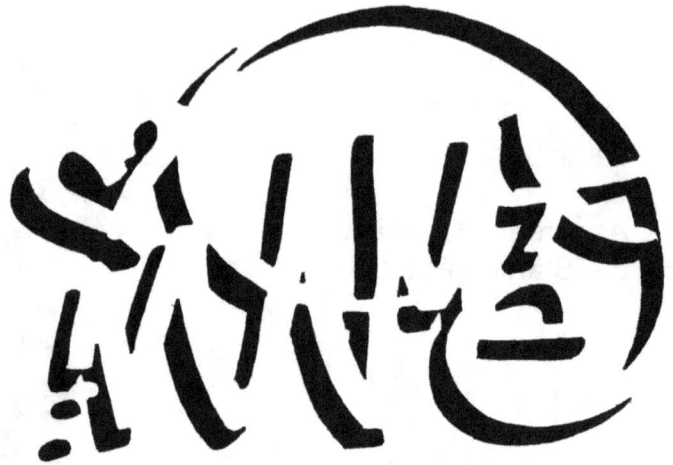

This tag has a 3-D block outline drawn with a fine-point marker.

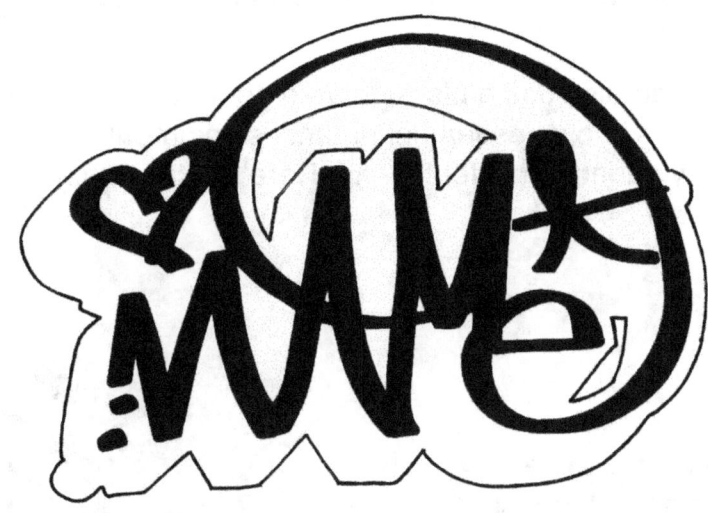

What about drawing your tag as an outline with a drop shadow?

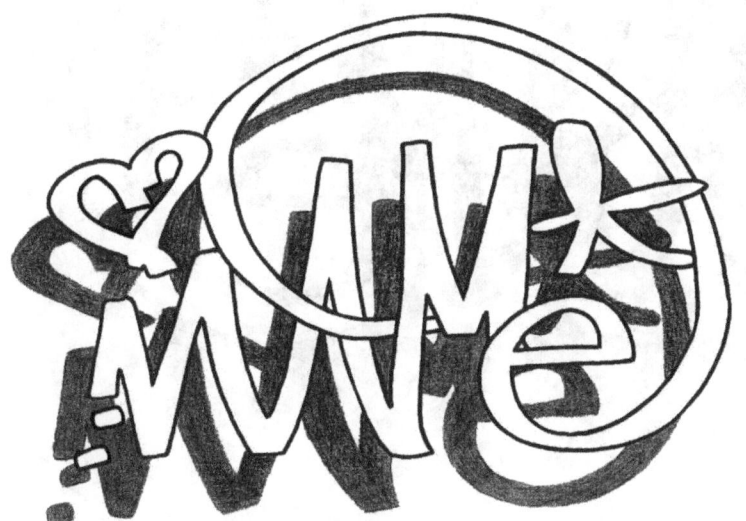

Add a tag cloud. When creating a tag cloud, follow the shapes of the letters and center your tag inside the cloud. Add some bubbles around the outside edge.

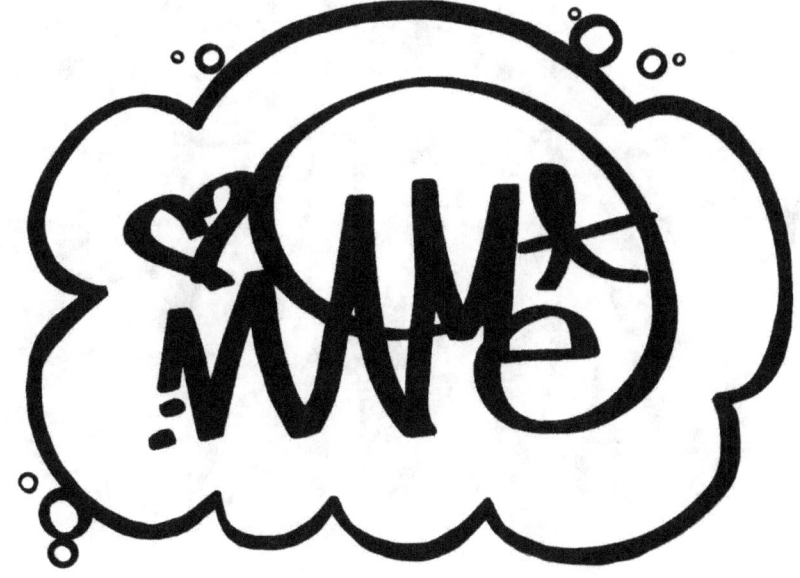

ADVANCED FINISHING TECHNIQUES

You can also use a black colored pencil and give your finished tag a graded look. This technique is known as feathering and is commonly found in tattoo lettering design. There are many variations of feathering. Here's just a few ideas you can experiment with:

Put shading in cut-out area

Draw an outline with a black pencil about 1/4" from the edges of the letters and feather shading all around the outside edges. Add shading inside the little cut-out.

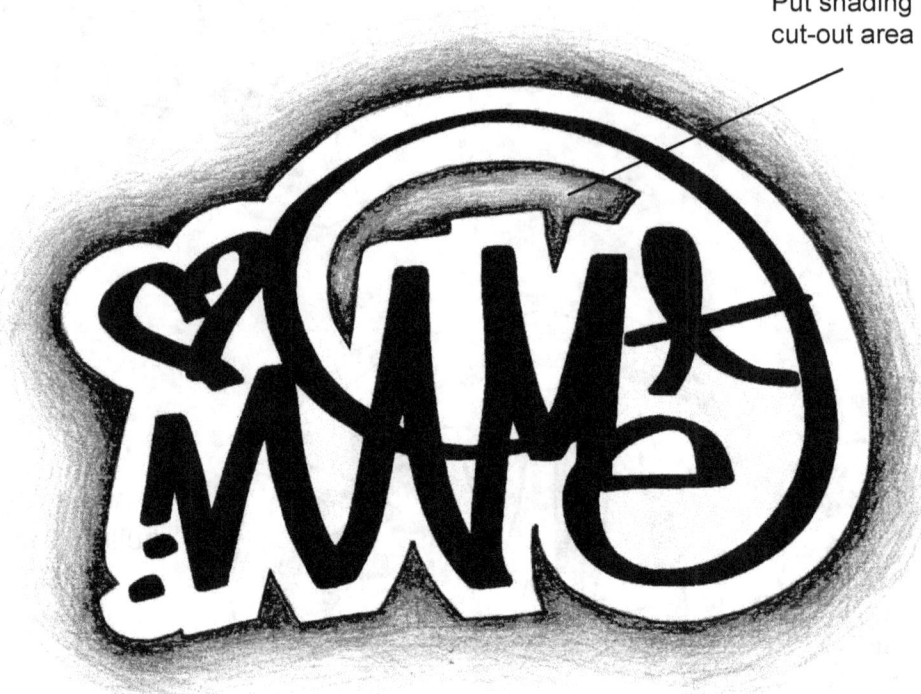

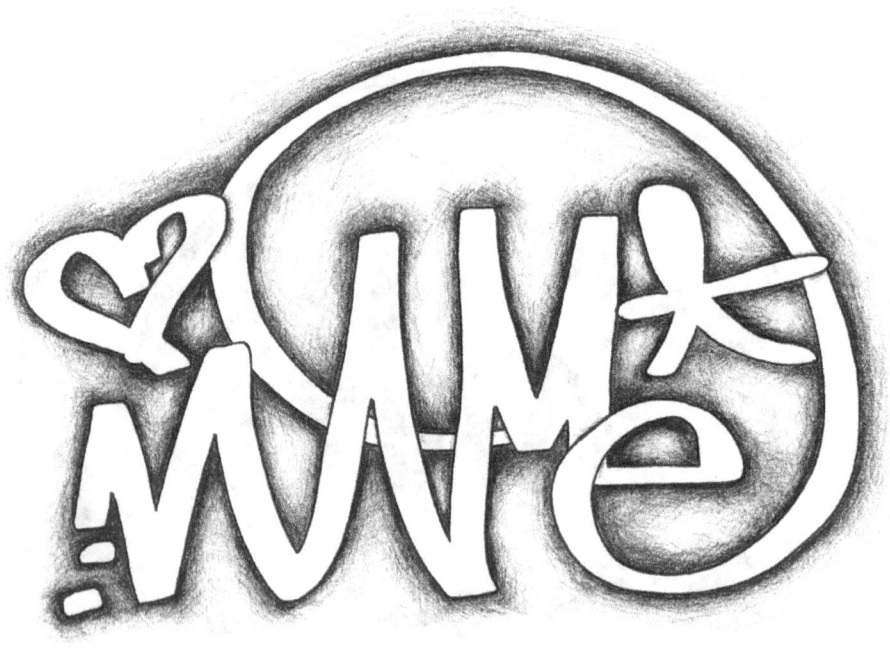

Or draw the outline of the letters with a fine-point marker. Then add soft shading surrounding the outline with a black pencil. Feather the shading outwards until it disappears.

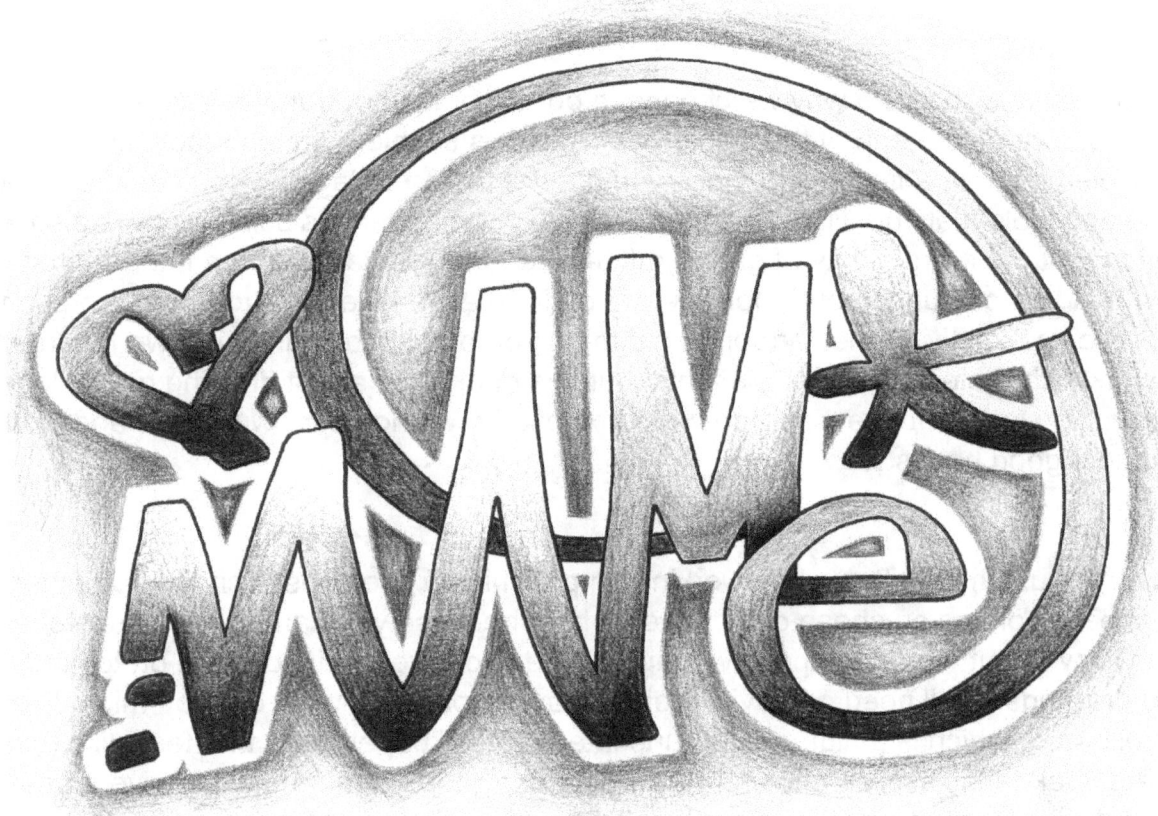

You can draw the outline of your tag with a fine-point marker and then add graded shading inside the letters and feathering around the outside, like in the example above. This technique looks really professional and using it will make your finished tag into a real work of art. You can try this feathering method with multiple colors, using pastels or colored pencils. We prefer colored pencils because they allow greater precision and control. If using pastels, you can use your finger or a Q-tip to smear and soften the edges. Pastels are messy and can be hard to control in fine detail areas but they are fun to experiment with. Watercolor pencils are another great tool to try.

REVIEW

To design a tag, pick a tag name that you like. Draw the tag name in several different tag letter styles. Choose one drawing as your Starting Point. Pick a layout. Place your letters in between guidelines and begin to modify them. Redraw the tag over and over. Make small changes. Look for interesting relationships between the letters. Try out extra elements, such as arrows, stars or swirls. Keep the letters consistent. Add some kind of contrast. Draw the letters instead of writing them. Memorize the paths of the lines and the curves. Continue to redraw the tag until it looks finished to you and begins to flow. Try out some of the finishing techniques shown in this chapter.

CHAPTER NINE
TOOLS AND TECHNIQUES

You are probably wondering why we choose to put such an important topic like Tools and Techniques towards the end of this book. The reason is simple. Although tools are an essential element in graffiti tagging, once you master the art of tagging you can draw your tags with any tools that you wish. Even if you use a crayon, a tag is still a tag. We also want to mention that there are plenty of great graffiti-style fonts available on the Internet that you can download onto your computer for free or buy from a type website (foundry). You can use those fonts exactly as they are or as a jumping off point to design your own letters. It's fine to work with professionally made fonts, but this book is all about drawing graffiti lettering by hand, so we want to encourage you to practice drawing your own letters and work at developing a good handstyle.

Paper
The paper we use most often when working on preliminary sketches is cheap computer printer paper. Working on cheap copy paper is best because you can do lots of sketches and not worry about wasting expensive paper. When you are ready to move on to your finished drawings you'll need a heavier weight drawing paper to work on. You might like to try Bristol board, which is a high-quality, uncoated, artists' paperboard that feels like thin cardboard. Oak-tag is similar, cheaper and works okay, too. Another inexpensive art material that works well for tag practice is a roll of Kraft paper. You can place it on the floor or tack it up on a wall. Just make sure to protect the wall or floor from leaking markers. You can try using large colored sidewalk chalk on dark colored kraft paper as well.

Pencils
Number 2 pencils are the best tool for sketching. Keep a pencil sharpener nearby and some erasers. When applying color we like to use colored pencils, magic markers, pastels and even crayons. People are always surprised that we use crayons, but crayons are a great art tool, not just a toy. We also use oil pastels, acrylic paint, watercolor pencils, and watercolor pan paints.

Brushes and Ink
Brushes are a great tool and you can buy them in a variety of sizes with different shaped points from an art supply store. Some have round points and some have flat points. The best drawing inks to use with brushes are called India Ink or Sumi Ink, both water-soluble.

Markers
To draw tags we use Sharpies, Paper Mate Flairs, Montana Acrylic Paint Markers, Krink, and Pilot Super Color Markers. When using any of these markers (except Paper Mate Flairs) you must put a piece of cardboard underneath the paper you are working on because these markers will leak through the paper and stain your table.

There are two basic types of markers you need to know about. One type makes a wet mark that drips. These are called paint markers, squeeze markers and mops. The second type, called permanent markers and water-based markers leave a clean, sharp mark and don't drip. They all have a felt tip. Permanent markers work best for drawing outlines because they dry almost instantly and won't smear when wet. Unfortunately, all of these felt tip markers lose their sharp point fairly quickly so you need to keep replacements on hand if you are doing a lot of drawing.

Blackboards and Whiteboards

A black chalkboard or a whiteboard is a really great tool to have in your studio or art room. Drawing on a whiteboard or a blackboard is a great way to practice drawing while saving money on paper. When using a whiteboard only use dry erase markers made especially for whiteboards.

Light Box

A light box is a rectangular box with a piece of translucent glass or plastic on top and an electric fluorescent light inside. The bright light provides an evenly illuminated, flat surface which makes tracing designs, letters, and anything else really easy. You might consider investing in one if you draw alot. They are sold at art supply stores and on art websites.

Blackbook

A blackbook is a graffiti artist's sketchbook. Also known as a "piecebook", it is often used to sketch out graffiti pieces and to collect tags from other writers. The covers are a great place to put graffiti stickers. If you get really lucky you can have one of your favorite graffiti writers sign your book. This is a "TOOFLY" tag we got several years ago. What a score!

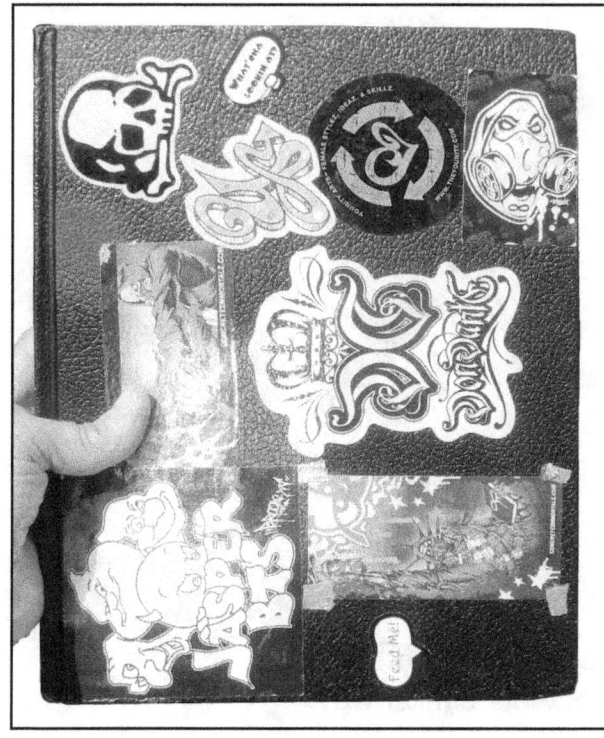
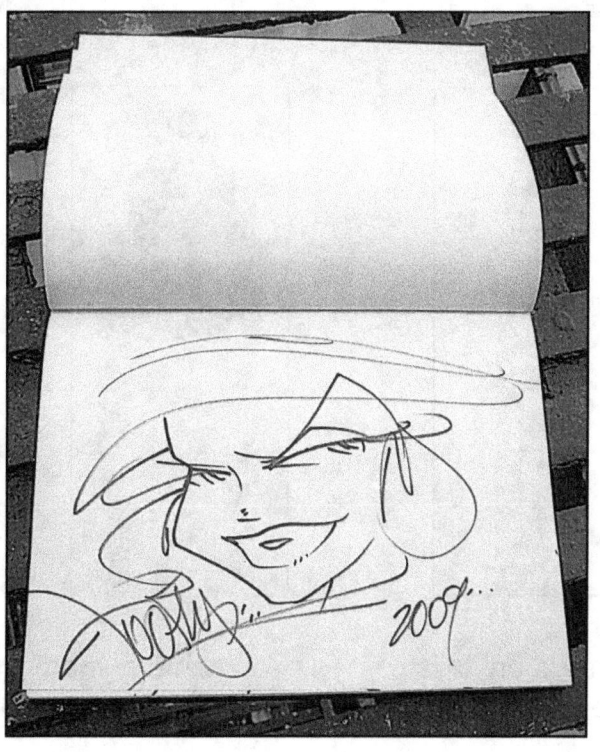

GRAFFITI TAGGING AND CALLIGRAPHY

In order to understand some of the concepts behind graffiti tagging, it is necessary to first talk about calligraphy. Calligraphy is an Ancient Greek word made up of two smaller words, kallos "beauty", and graphe "writing". So calligraphy is translated as "the art of writing beautifully". Calligraphy is written with ink and a special kind of pen that has a flat, wide tip or nib. The nibs come in different sizes. The pen is sometimes referred to as an italic pen or a broad pen. Fortunately, you don't have to know calligraphy to learn to tag, but understanding some of the concepts will help you learn.

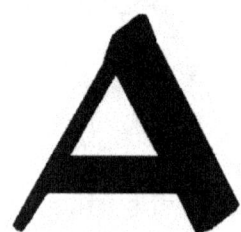

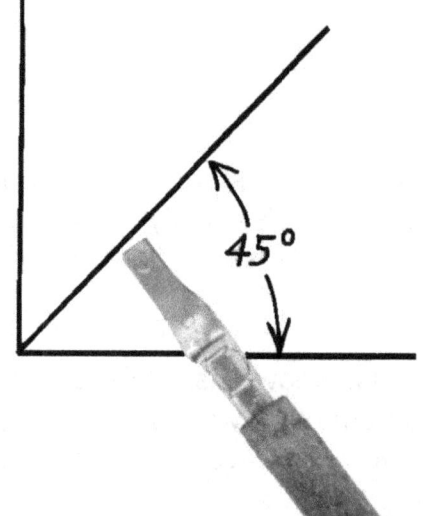

45°

The thick and thin lines are formed by holding the tip of the pen at a 45-degree angle.

When writing calligraphy the tip of the pen is held against the paper at a 45-degree angle. This angle creates lines or strokes that are both thick and thin, depending on which direction the pen is moving. Graffiti writers use this same technique to draw tag letters that have lines with varying widths. Instead of using an italic pen and ink, they use magic markers with a square, broad tip. These magic markers come in many different sizes, and they are available in both the wet, drippy style and the dry, permanent style. A marker with a broad, square tip is called a chisel-tip marker.

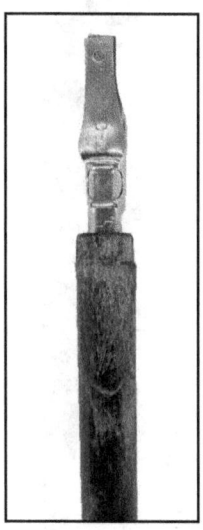

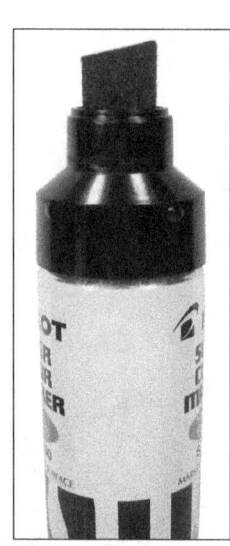

This is an italic pen with a flat nib.

You can buy magic markers with a broad, square tip called a chisel-tip that work in a similar way.

EXERCISE: PRACTICE STROKES

For this exercise, you will need a magic marker with a broad, chisel-tip. Hold the marker at a 45-degree angle. To test whether you are holding the marker at the correct angle, draw a lower-case t. Both the vertical stroke and the horizontal stroke should be the same thickness. Experiment with drawing these and then copy the rest of the practice strokes shown below. Use any width of chisel-tip marker that you have. The most important thing to remember is that the tip of the marker is held at a consistent 45-degree angle. Do not let it rotate. Practice drawing these strokes a few times.

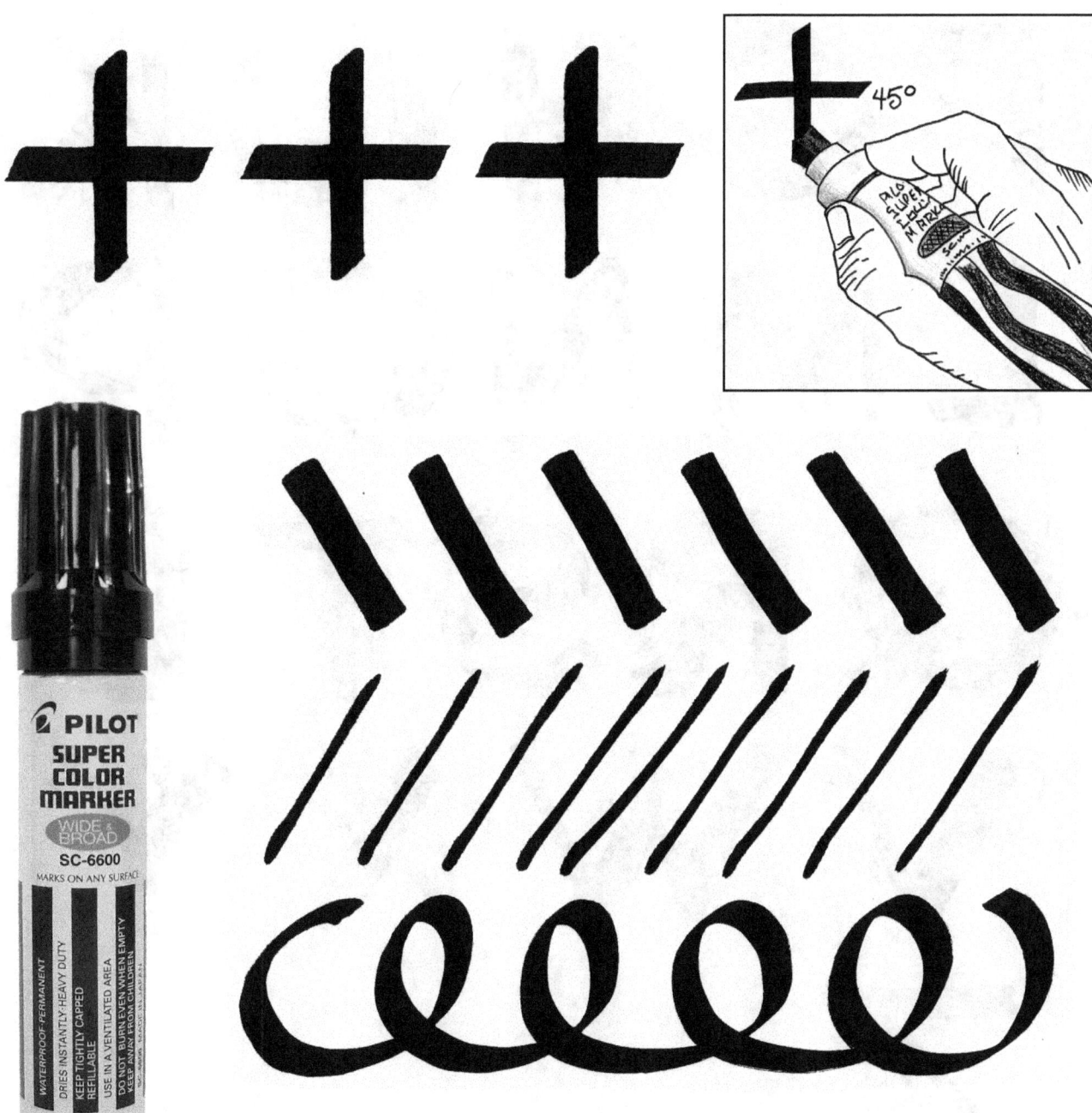

Hold the tip of your marker at a 45-degree angle and draw these strokes.

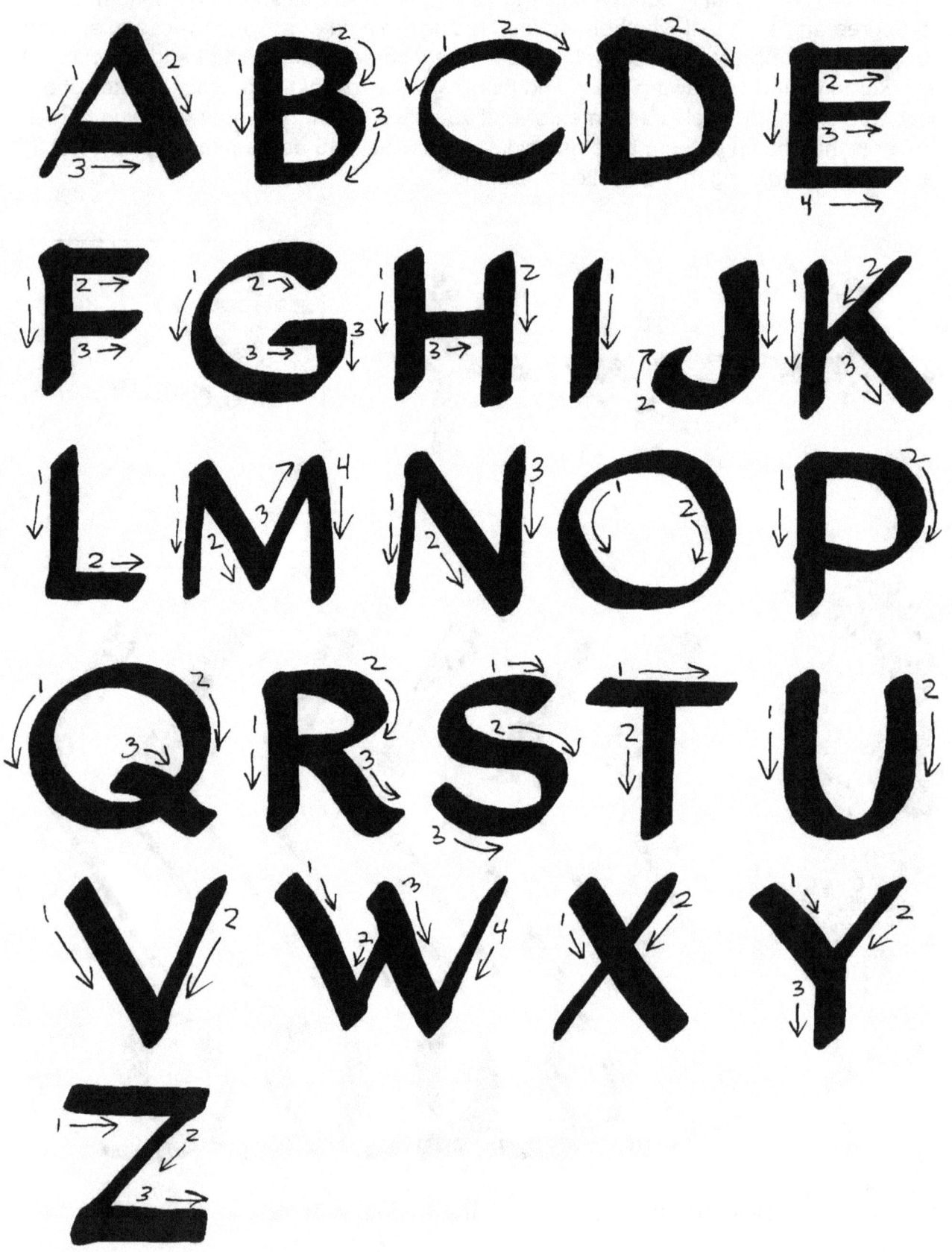

The alphabet on the opposite page is an example of a traditional Roman Alphabet used to learn calligraphy. The numbers indicate the order in which the strokes of each letter are drawn. The arrows indicate the direction of each stroke. You can copy this alphabet for practice. Notice where the thick and thin lines appear. You don't need to follow the numbers or arrows - we just wanted to give you an idea of how calligraphy works. Draw the letters as they appear and keep the tip of your marker at a constant 45-degree angle.

If you don't have access to a calligraphy pen or square tipped marker, you can still practice drawing this alphabet with a double-pointed pencil. To make one, tape two pencils tightly together with the points evenly placed. Hold the pencil at a 45-degree angle just like you would hold a broad pen or chisel tip marker. The pencil points act like a pen nib or marker tip and produce a drawing with two lines.

A double-pointed pencil held at a 45-degree angle will produce a drawing with thick and thin lines, just like a broad pen or square tipped magic marker. You can use this technique to draw any style of letter. It works especially well with back-slanted tag letters. You can close off the ends of the strokes and fill in the letter with a fine point marker.

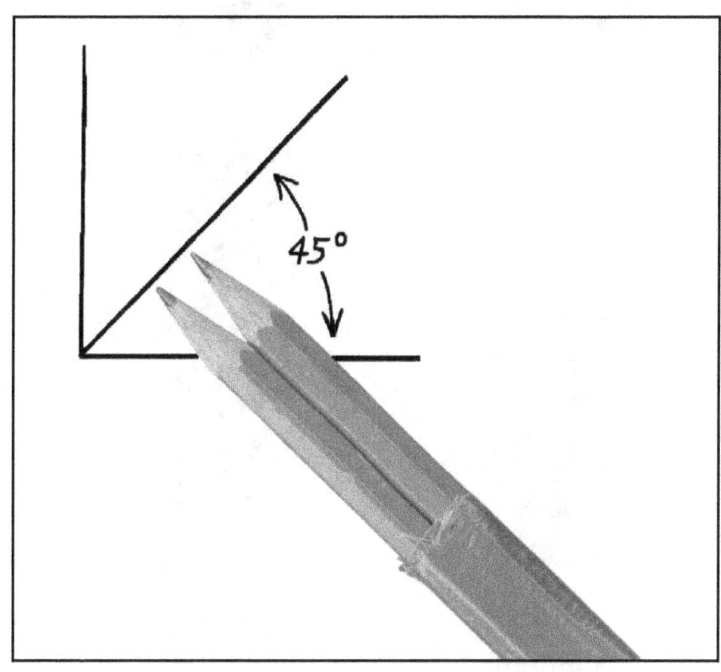

STEP 1. Draw a back-slanted tag letter "A" with a double pointed pencil.

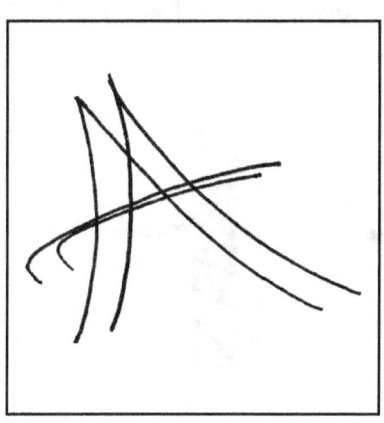

STEP 2. Draw small lines to close off the ends of the strokes.

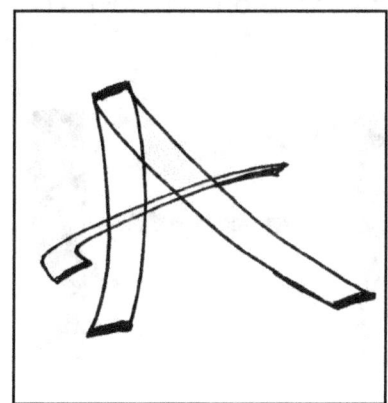

STEP 3. Fill in the letter with a fine point magic marker.

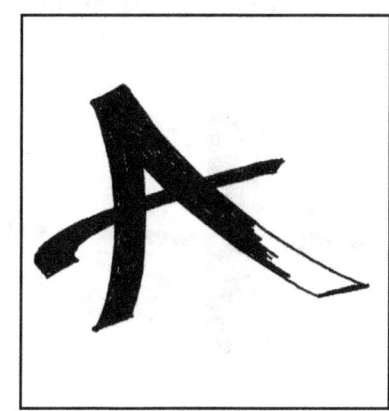

Here are some chisel-tip markers that we use a lot. These particular brands are known as permanent markers because the marks they make are water resistant. Permanent markers are great for drawing clean, sharp lines that don't drip. Just be aware they will leak through thin copy paper, so make sure to protect your table underneath. Important Note: Some of these markers have really strong fumes, so you will need to work in a well-ventilated area.

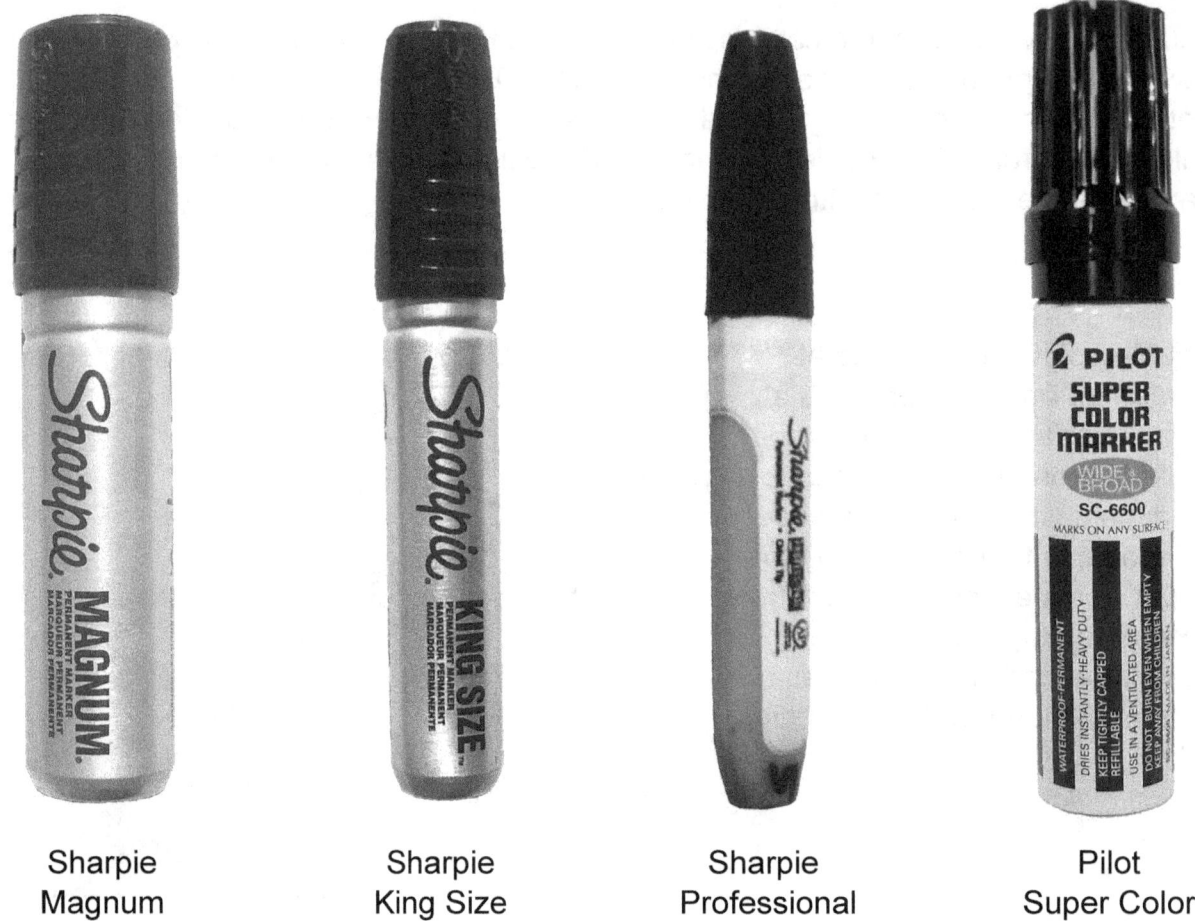

Sharpie
Magnum

Sharpie
King Size

Sharpie
Professional

Pilot
Super Color

If you choose not to hold the marker tip at a 45-degree angle you will get a thick vertical line and a much thinner horizontal line like the ones below. Try it out for yourself and see.

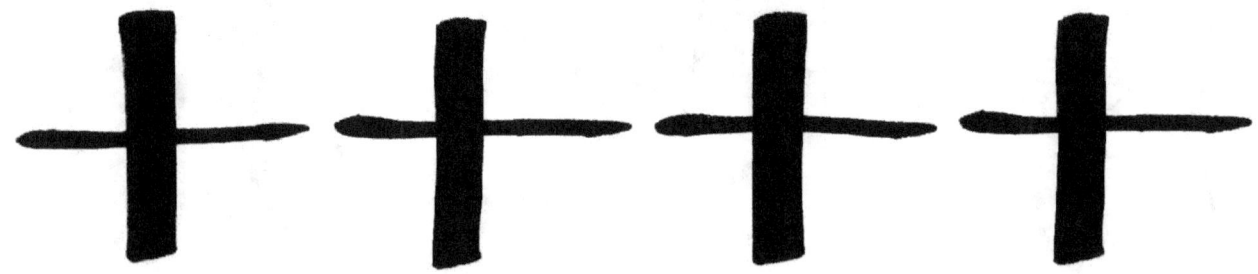

WHY WRITE WHEN YOU CAN TAG

Chisel-tip markers give you tag letters that look like this. Notice the alternating thick and thin lines. These markers have felt tips that get dull over time, so use brand new markers when you want your lines and corners to be extra sharp. You can also do touch ups to the edges with an ultra-fine point marker later on.

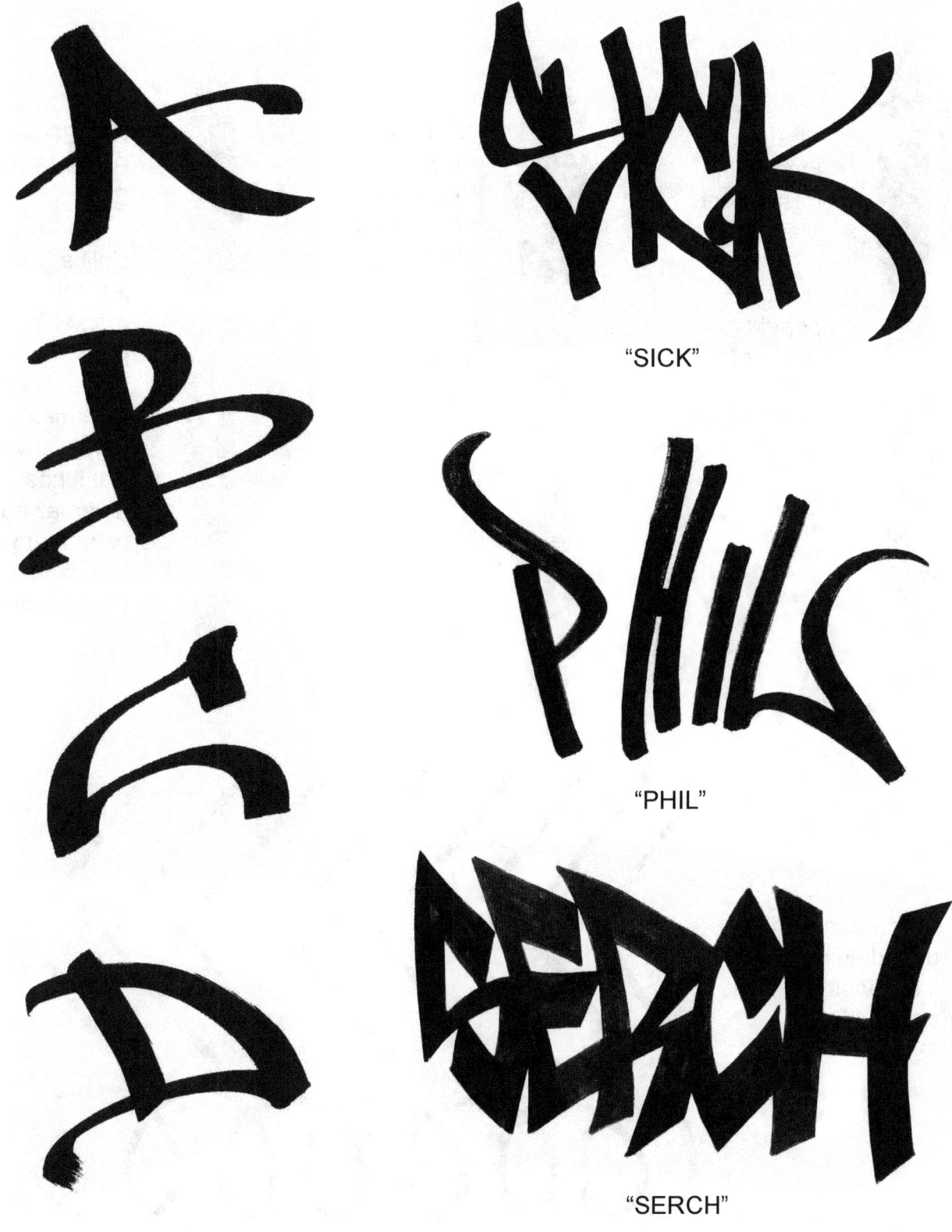

"SICK"

"PHIL"

"SERCH"

You can also buy permanent markers with a rounded tip. Unlike chisel-tips, a marker with a rounded tip creates lines that are uniform in thickness, so the lines are exactly the same width no matter what direction you are drawing.

Sharpie Fine Point Permanent Markers are the most popular marker for outlines.

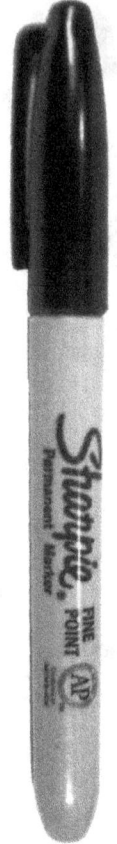

Sharpie
Fine Point
Permanent
Marker

Most
popular
marker for
outlines
and tags on
paper.

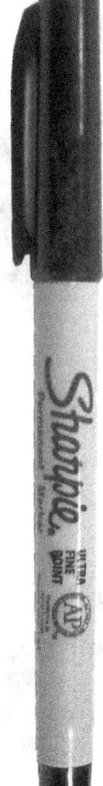

Sharpie
Ultra
Fine Point
Permanent
Marker

Good for fine
detail.

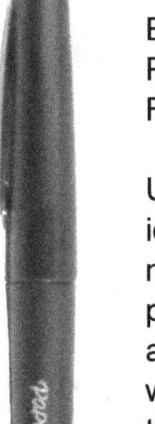

EXCEPTION
Paper Mate
Flair

Unlike Sharp-
ies, this
marker is not
permanent
and the lines
will smear if
they get wet.
But it has
an amazing
point that you
just can't find
on any other
marker.

When drawing with
a rounded tip mark-
er all the lines are a
uniform width.

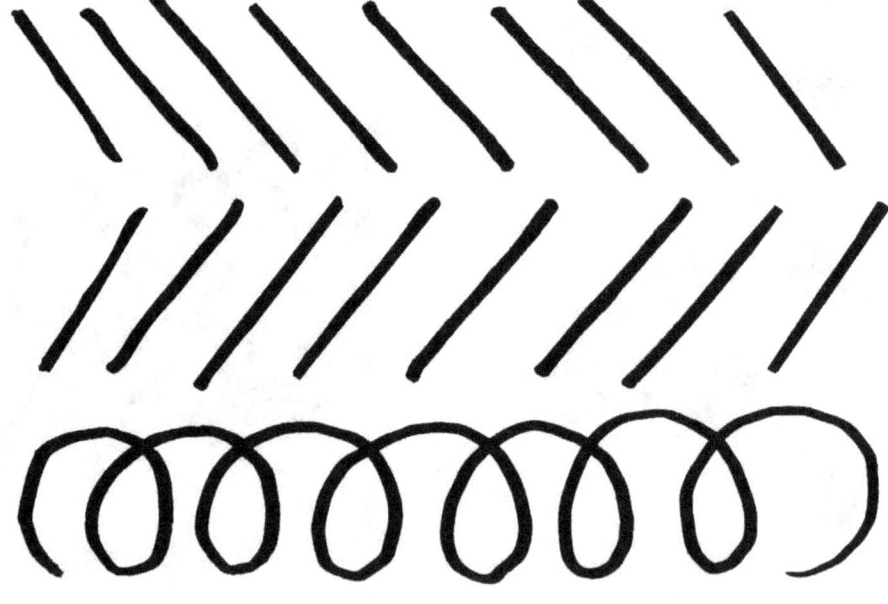

WHY WRITE WHEN YOU CAN TAG

All of these tags are drawn with rounded tip markers. These tags have a very different look then tags drawn with a chisel-tip marker. Notice there are no thick and thin lines. This might not be important to you at first, but once you have developed some skill drawing tag letters, you will want to experiment with chisel-tips to go to the next level.

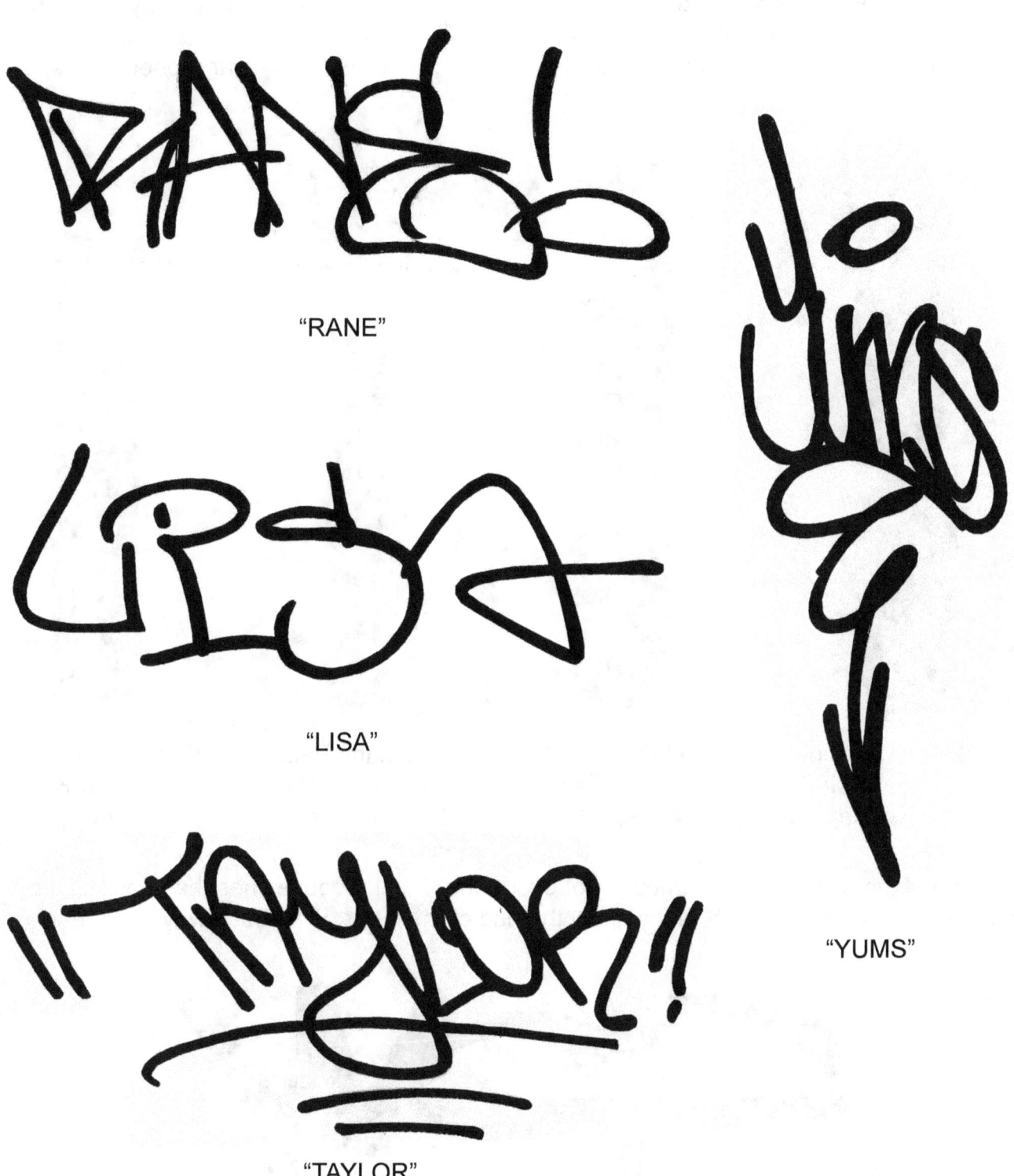

"RANE"

"LISA"

"YUMS"

"TAYLOR"

PAINT MARKERS AND MOPS

Graffiti paint markers and mops are a special kind of marker that produces a line that is wet and drippy. Some of these markers are pump action (you have to press down on the tip several times to release the paint or ink) and some of them are squeeze bottles. They are available in both chisel-tips and round tips. You should use a heavier weight paper when using any of these drippy markers because they saturate the paper. Cheap copy paper is just too thin. Working with these tools is a messy activity so read the directions and cover your work surface before you start drawing! You might even want to wear rubber gloves.

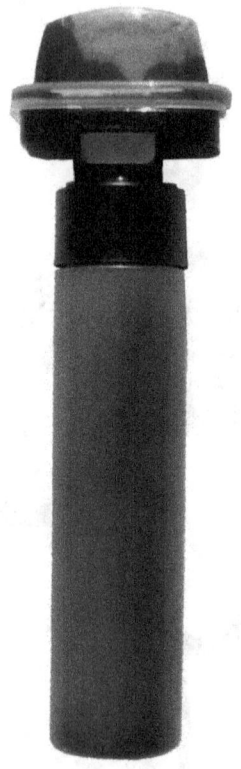  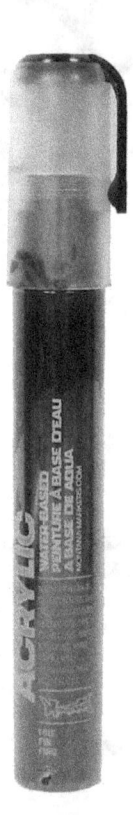 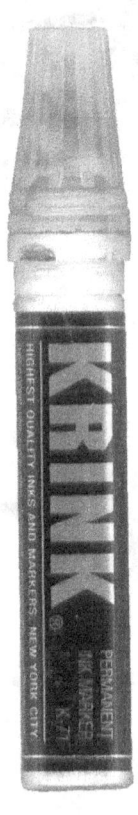

Montana Paint
Marker 30Mm
Black (square tip)

Montana Paint
Marker 15Mm
Black (square tip)

Montana Paint
Marker 7Mm
Black (round tip)

Krink Permanent
Ink Marker K-71
(square tip)

If the tip of the paint marker or mop is not overly wet, it will produce lines that look like they were drawn with a dry brush. Notice how the end of the letter "W" fades away at the end.

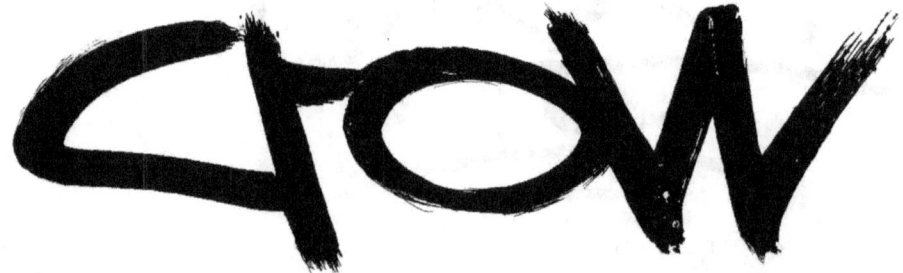

Pumping a marker or squeezing a mop produces lines that are saturated with paint or ink and drip like mad. With practice, you can learn to control how much paint or ink is released from the tip at one time and how the drips flow. We love the way a drippy tag looks. This "ALOT" tag was drawn with either an acrylic paint marker or a mop filled with ink. It's a great example of a drippy graffiti tag.

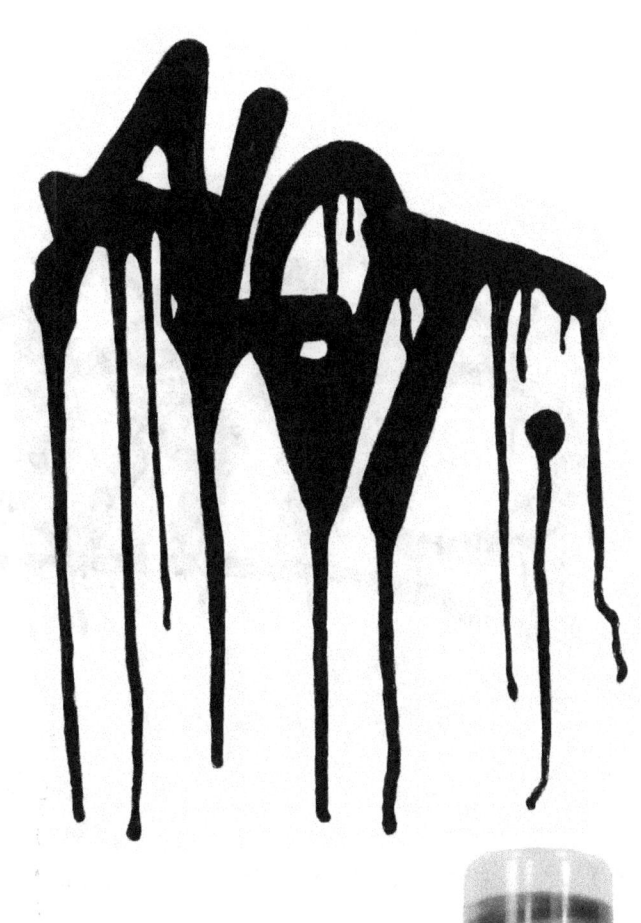

Just from an artists' perspective, these tools are really fun to experiment with on paper or cardboard. You can get really interesting effects, especially if you mix these tools with paints and other types of mediums. Remember this is just for art.

When graffiti tagging first began there were no such things as professionally made paint markers and mops, so writers invented their own. Nowadays markers and mops can be purchased in an art store or on the Internet. If you need really big paper to draw on, a pad of 18" x 24" drawing paper or cheap newsprint paper works great. As we said before, you should never use these tools on anything but paper and only use them where you have permission.

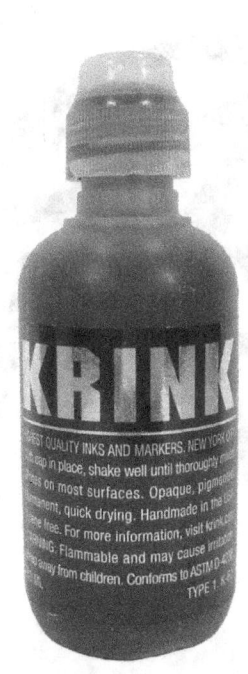

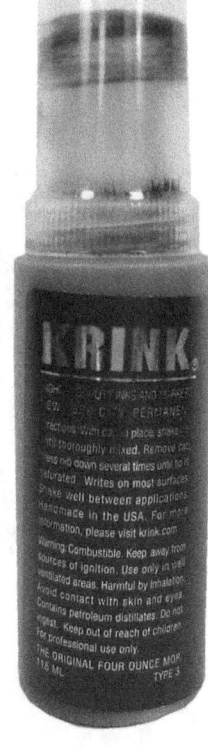

Krink k-60
Squeeze Marker
(round tip)

Krink Mop
4 ounce
(round tip)

More great drippy tags: "ANISO"

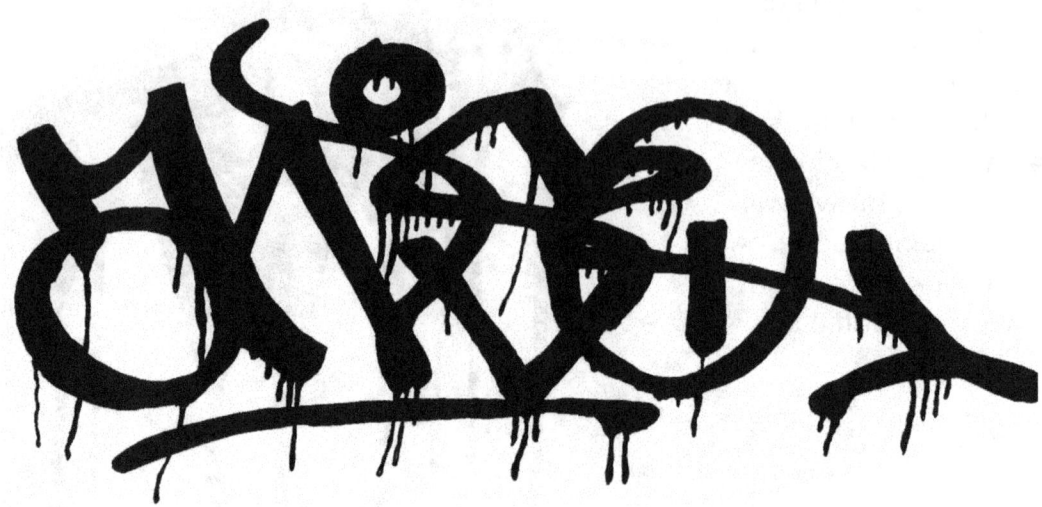

This one says says "INSANE". Can you read it?

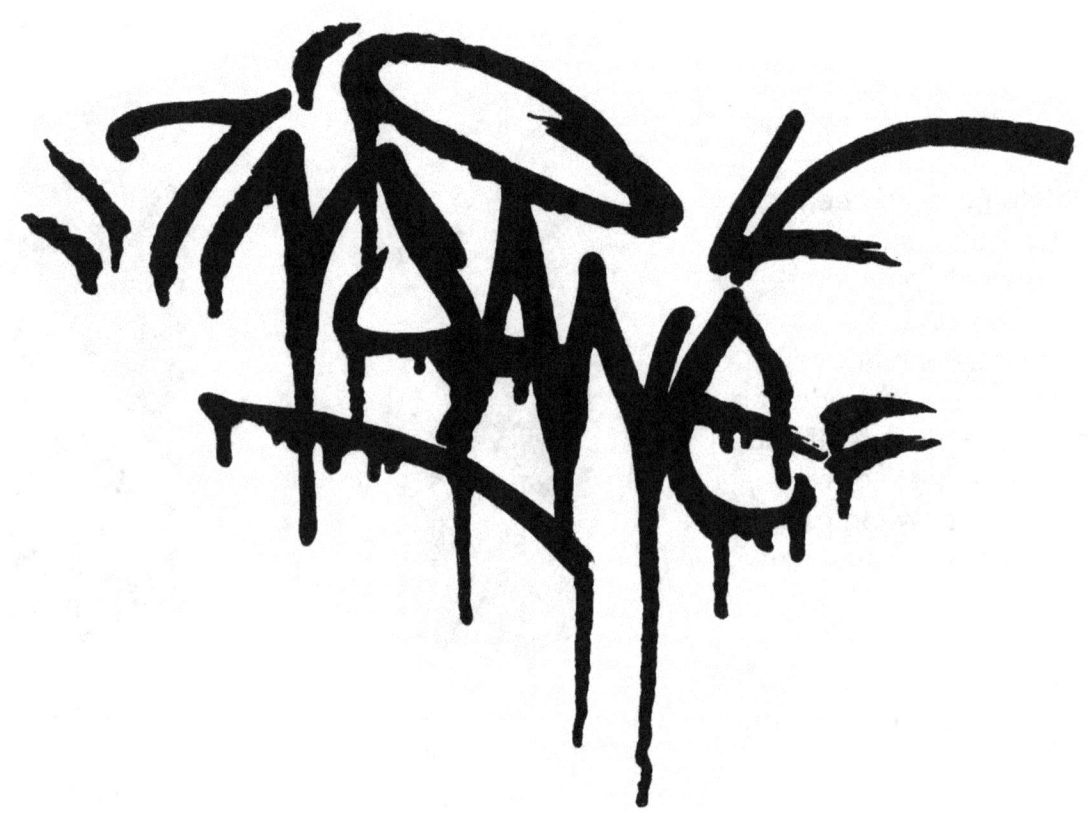

WHY WRITE WHEN YOU CAN TAG

Perhaps you can apply just enough pressure to get your marker or mop to make clean, crisp letters without drips, like in these three tags "JOKER", "SEF" and "MORE".

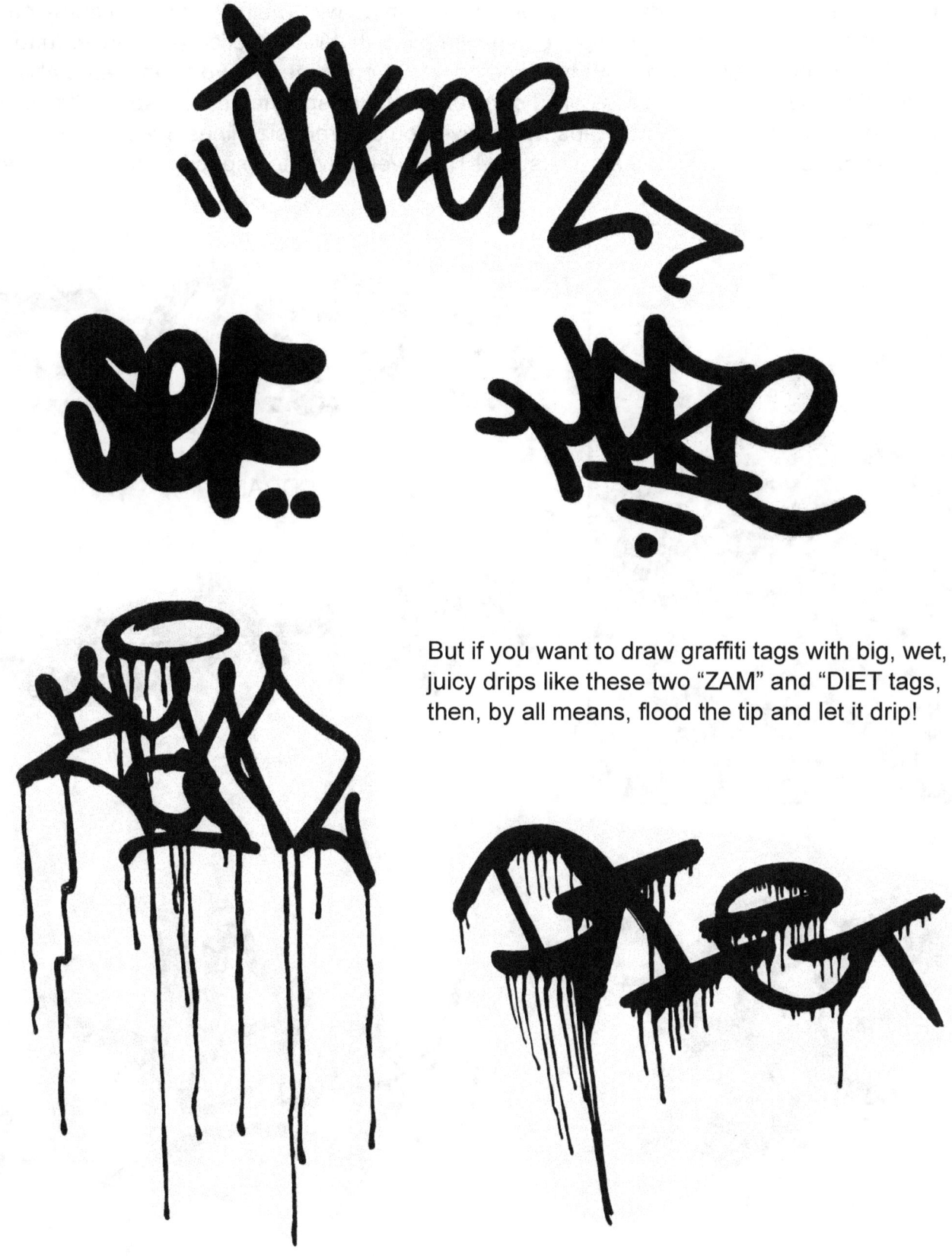

But if you want to draw graffiti tags with big, wet, juicy drips like these two "ZAM" and "DIET tags, then, by all means, flood the tip and let it drip!

Some of the tags pictured in this book were created with spray paint. Personally, we don't use spray paint, so we cannot give you any tips on how to use it. The fumes are dangerous and it's just not worth the risk. But the effects that a skilled writer can produce with spray paint are inspiring. A large graffiti piece on a wall painted with multiple colors of spray paint is a work of art rivaling any painting created with a brush. With practice you can learn to control how much paint is released from the nozzle at one time and you can create alternating thick and thin lines. This is called *can control*. Over-spraying in one spot will give you drips. You can buy different size caps which give you different size lines. Fatcaps are a specialized nozzle that widens the area of spray. They were invented specifically for graffiti art.

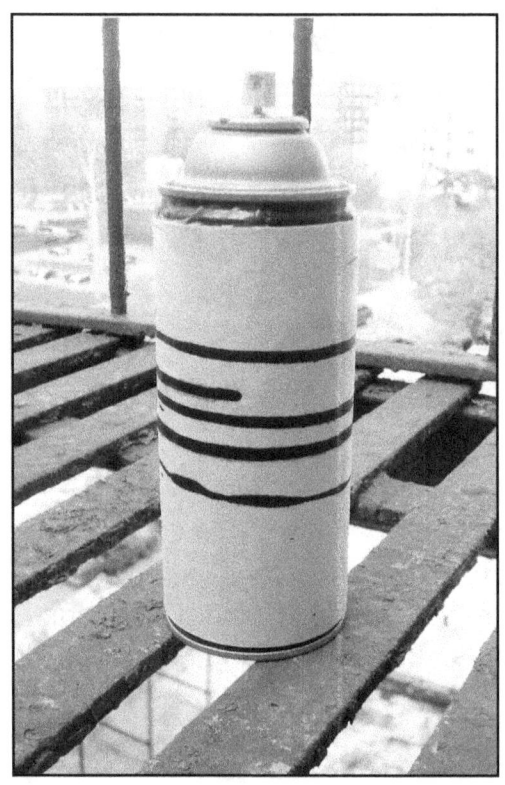

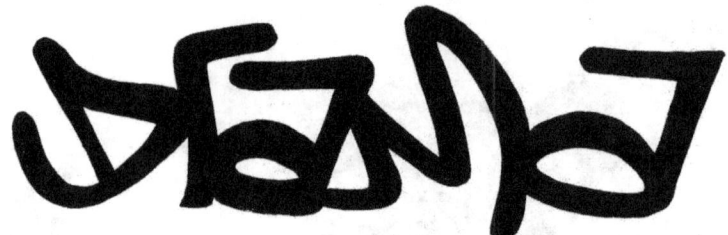

"DRAMA"

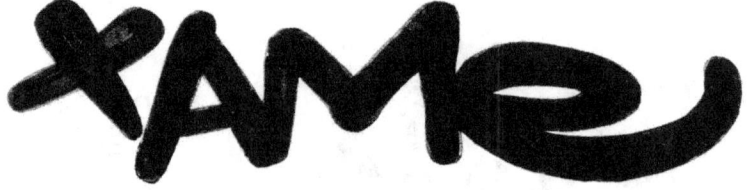

"TAME"

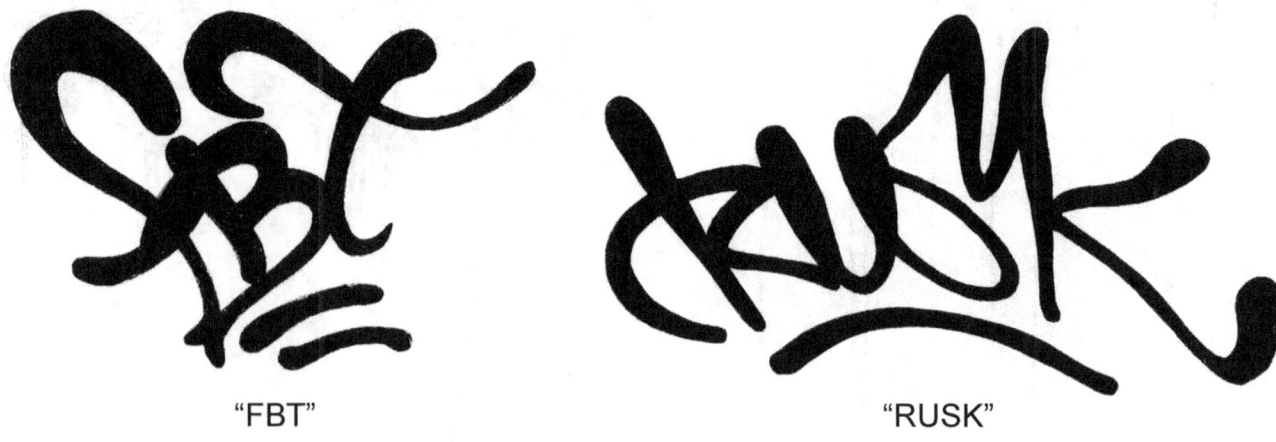

"FBT"   "RUSK"

The rules of tag letter construction are the same when tagging with spray paint as with any other tools. The structure of each individual letter must be maintained and the letters must work well together to form a rhythmic pattern and balanced tag design. Some people may think it's weird to talk about graffiti tags with terminology usually reserved for fine art. But we think it's totally appropriate because graffiti tags are art.

BE SAFE!

You don't need to use spray paint to become skilled at graffiti tagging. It's just another art tool to experiment with. But if you choose to use it, be sure to follow the safety directions indicated on the spray can to the letter. Wear latex gloves to keep your hands clean and change them often. Wear a legitimate gas mask to protect yourself from inhaling toxic fumes. A gas mask will also help keep your mouth and nose free of paint. Work in a well-ventilated area and protect your eyes.

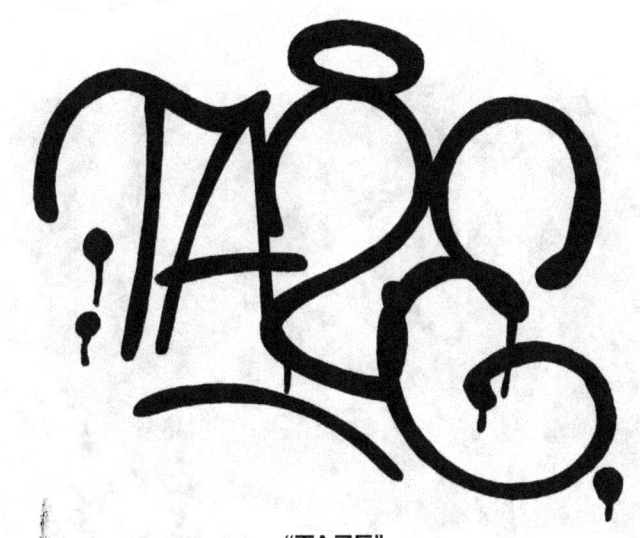

"SIN"

"TAZE"

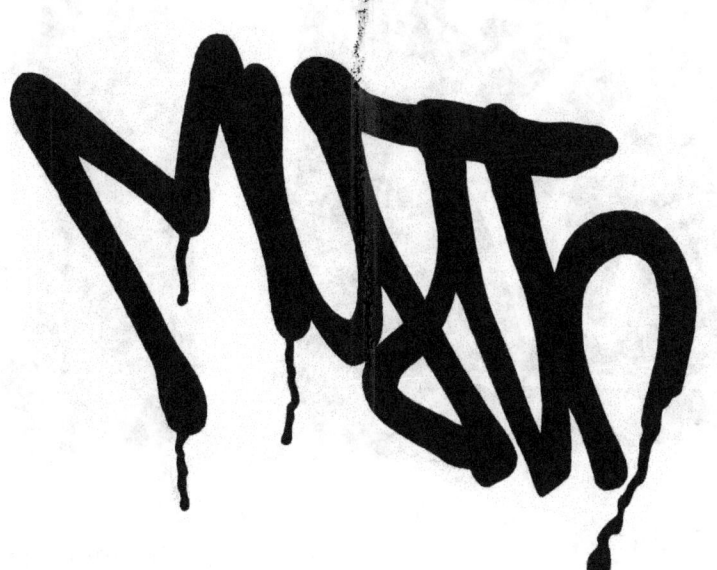

"MYTH"

For a change of pace, try white tags on black. White paint markers come in all shapes and sizes. You can even buy an empty paint marker and fill it up yourself with any color of acrylic paint made especially for paint markers. Just another art technique to experiment with.

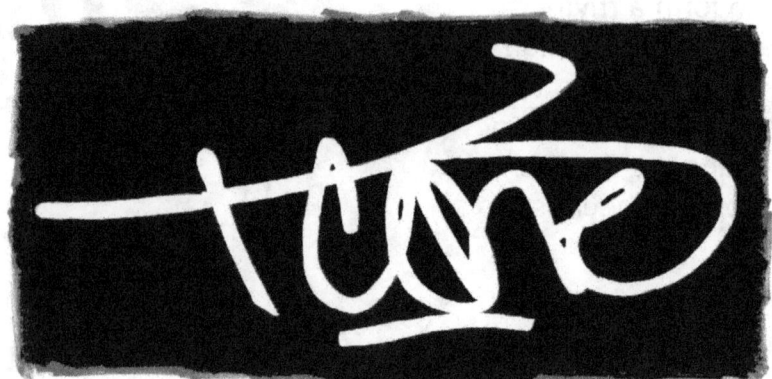

"TC ONE"

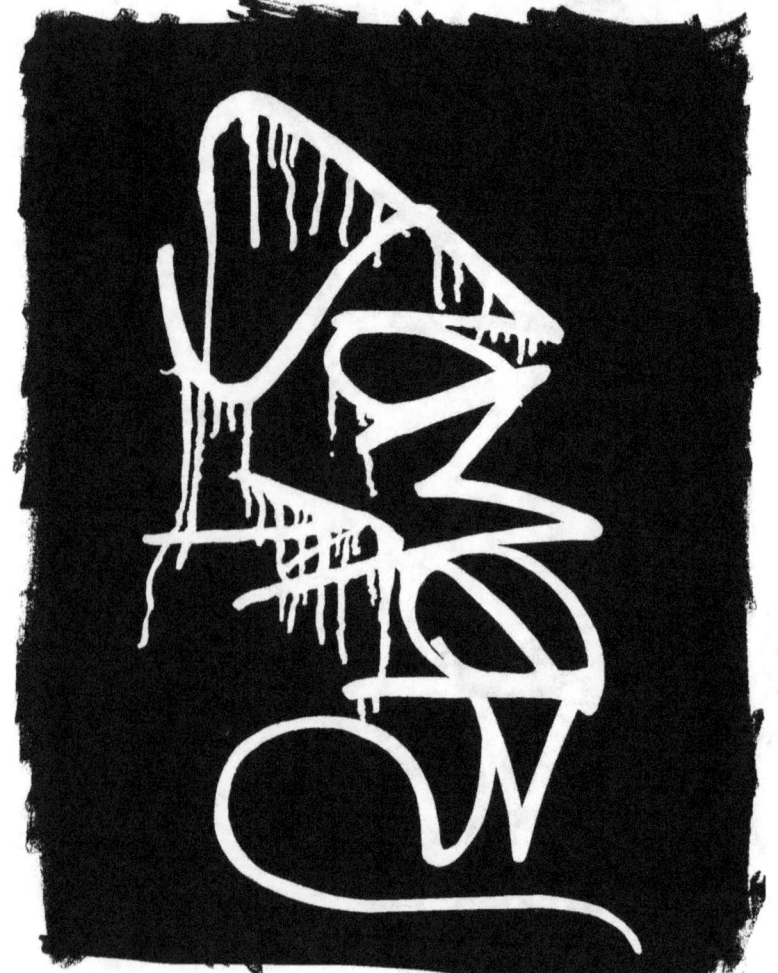

"JAMER"

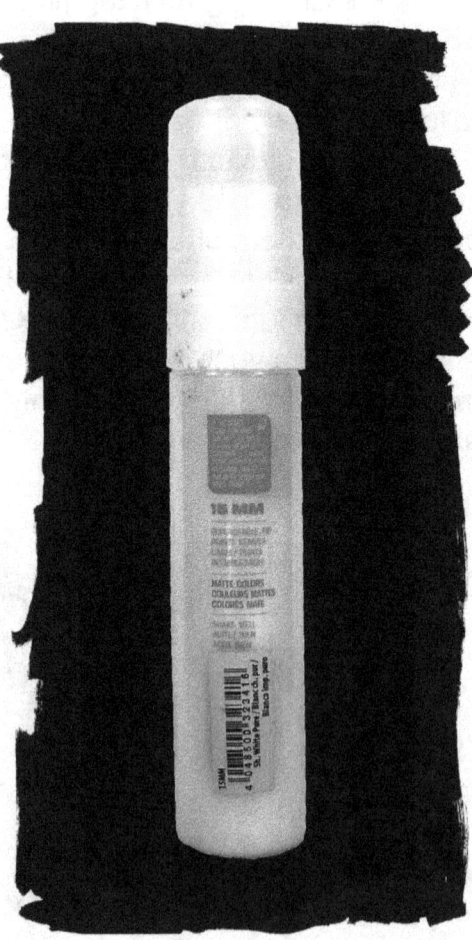

Paint Marker 15Mm White

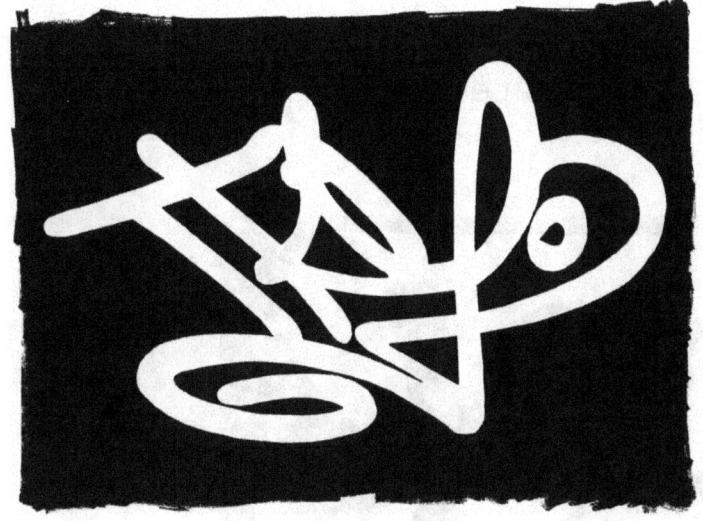

"TRY"

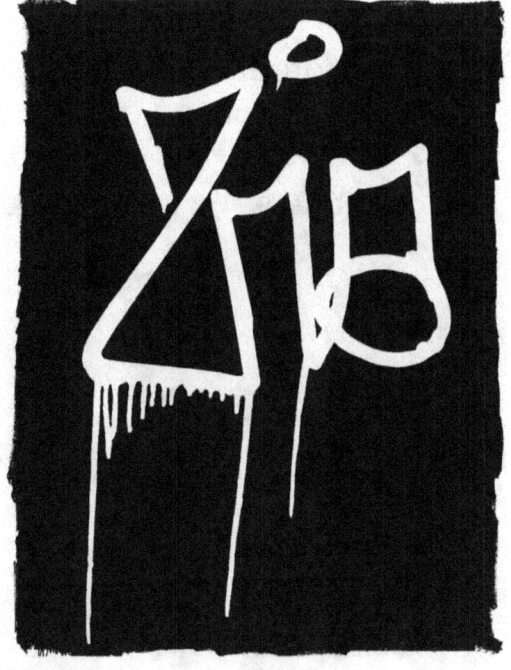

"REMO"

"ZIA"

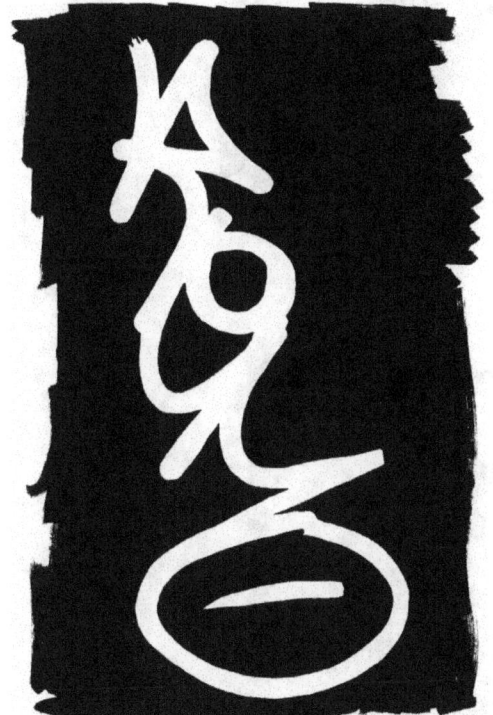

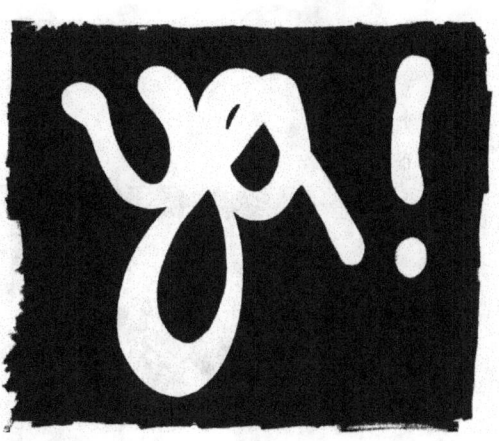

"YA"

"MINT"

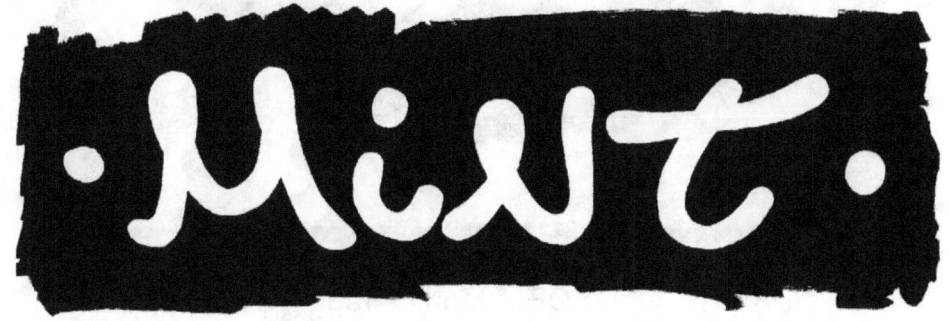

MARKER TAGS ON PAPER STICKERS

Stickers are a great alternative to drawing on paper. Order blank stickers on-line or buy some from an office supply store.

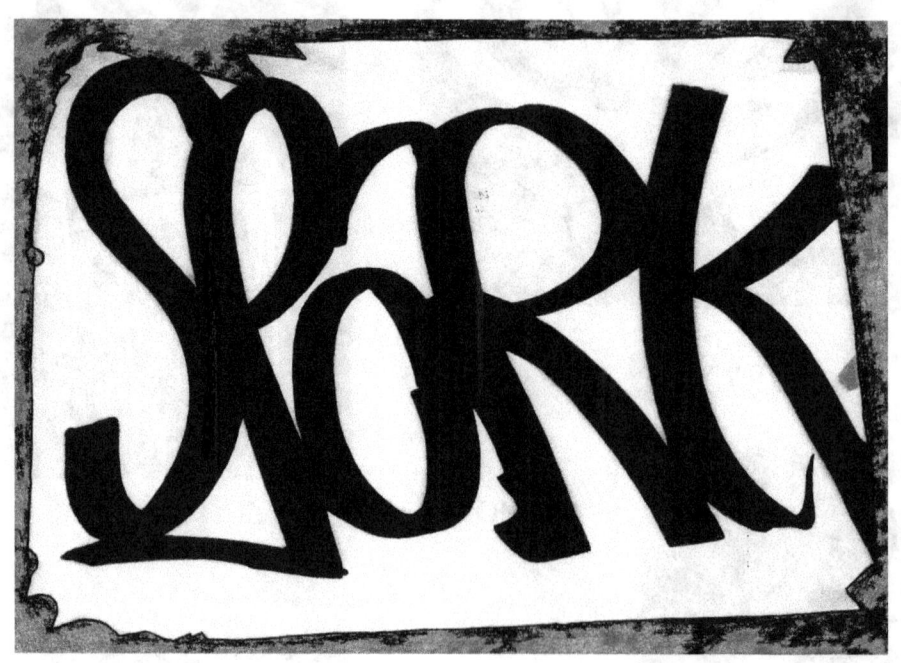

"SPARK" Marker Tag

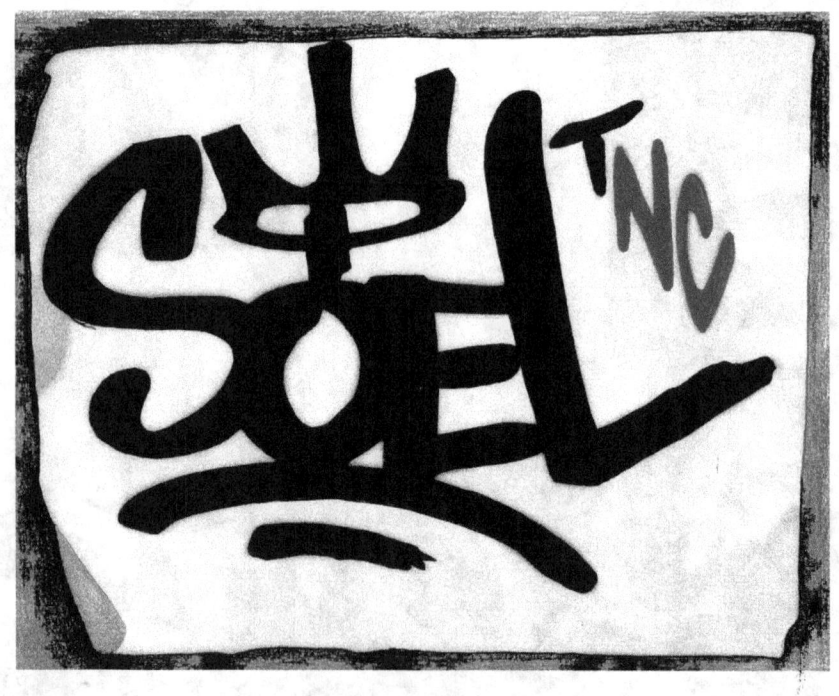

"SOEL" Marker Tag

You can also make your own stickers using double-stick tape and paper.

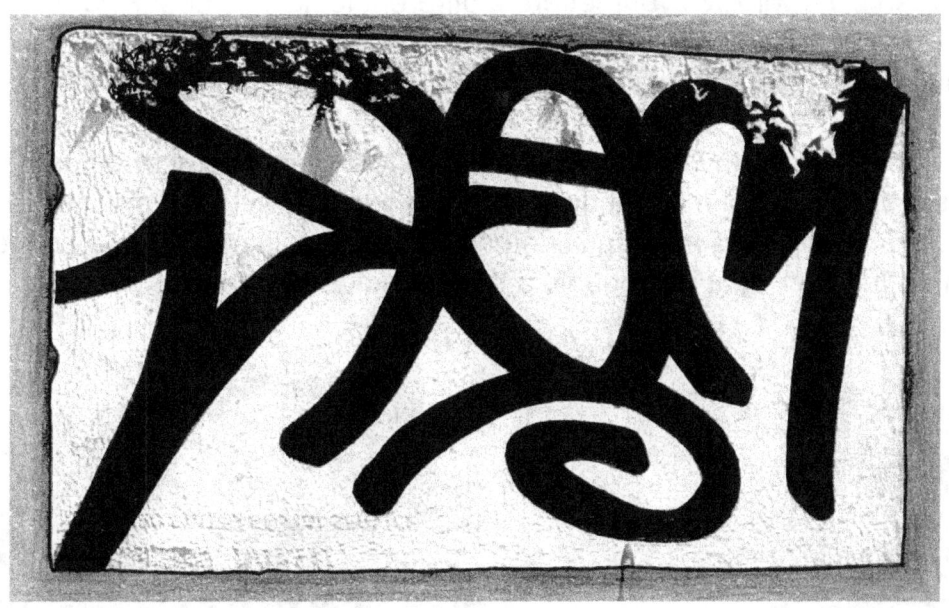

"MER" Marker Tag, drawn backwards

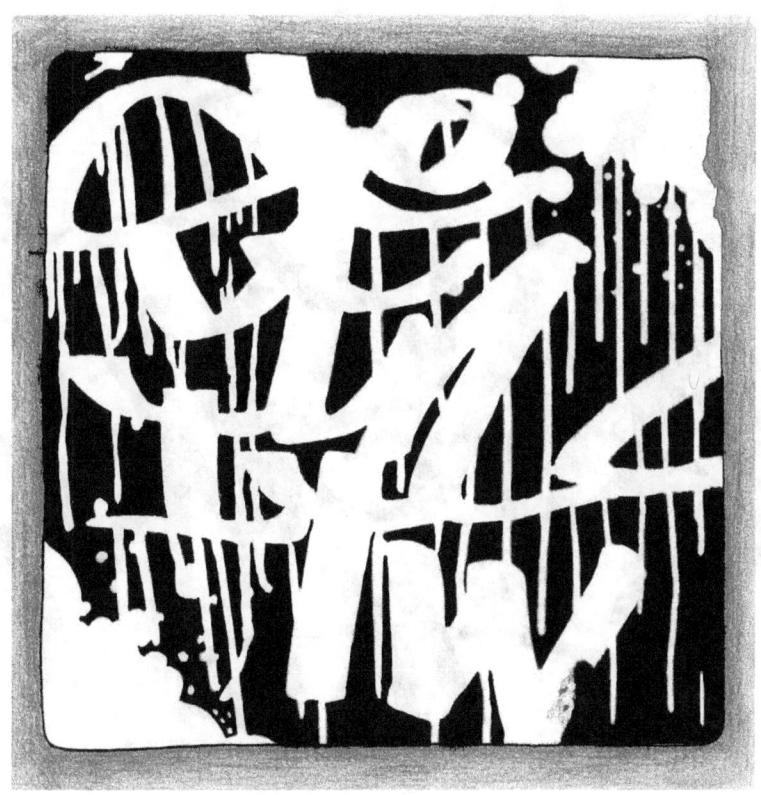

"SEN" ? Printed Tag on Sticker, white on black

Tagging with a brush and ink is a fun alternative to markers. There are several styles of brushes that are available in different sizes, several of which are pictured on the opposite page. Each brush style will give your letters a different look. The best kind of ink to use with a brush is water-soluble India ink or Sumi Ink. These inks can be used full strength to produce rich, dark lines, or can be diluted with water to create lighter gray washes.

You can also experiment with Chinese calligraphy tools called Sumi brushes and Ink sticks. An Ink stick is a solid cake of ink that dissolves into liquid form when dipped in water and rubbed over the smooth surface of an ink stone. Bottled ink is much more concentrated then ink from an Ink stick so it is probably a better choice for drawing bold tag letters.

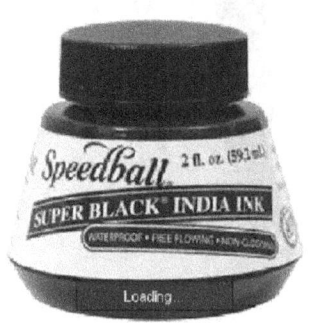

Black India Ink

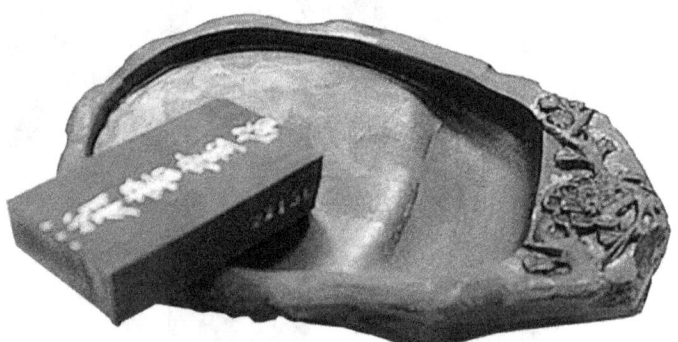

Sumi Ink Stick and Ink Stone

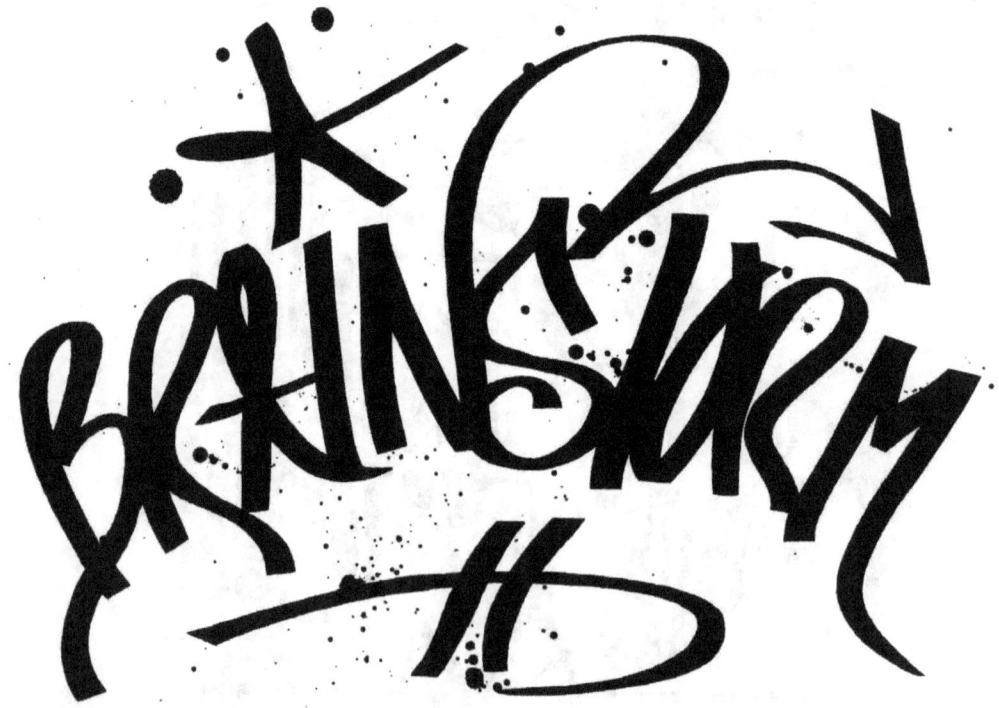

This tag "BRAINSTORM" was drawn with a flat acrylic brush and India ink. Then a fine-point marker was used to sharpen the edges and fill in any uneven spots.

ACRYLIC FLAT BRUSH

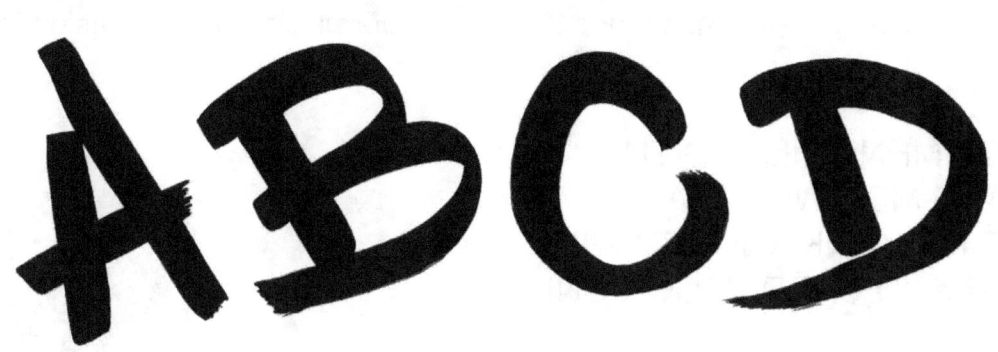

ROUND SABLE BRUSH

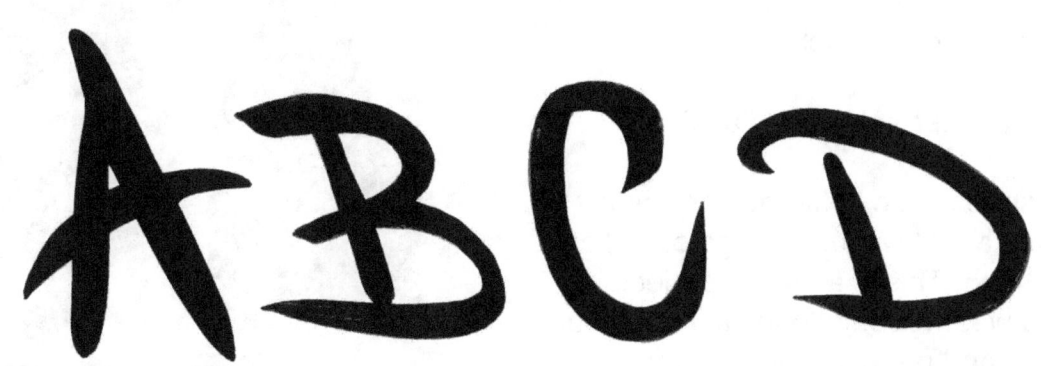

SUMI BAMBOO BRUSH

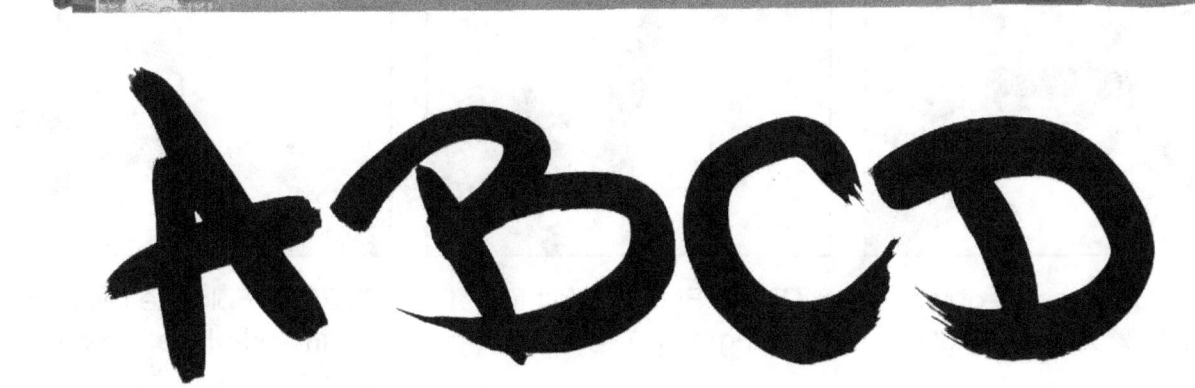

If you don't have access to a store bought mop, you can make one yourself. You just need thick felt and the other materials shown below. You should only fill this homemade graffiti mop with water-soluble India ink and use it to tag on paper or card stock. Think of a graffiti mop as just another art supply that you keep in your toolbox and use for specific types of drawing. Only make this homemade mop if you have permission or supervision from an adult.

WE RECOMMEND FILLING THIS HOMEMADE MOP WITH WATER-SOLUBLE INDIA INK AND DRAWING ON PAPER AND CARD STOCK ONLY!

WHAT YOU WILL NEED

1) an empty shoe polish bottle

2) a piece of thick felt

3) a small rectangle of kitchen sponge

4) a bottle of water-soluble India ink

Wash the shoe polish bottle out thoroughly before you start. Have lots of rags or paper towels on hand. This is a messy project. You should wear rubber gloves to keep your hands clean and protect your skin from un-necessary exposure to chemicals.

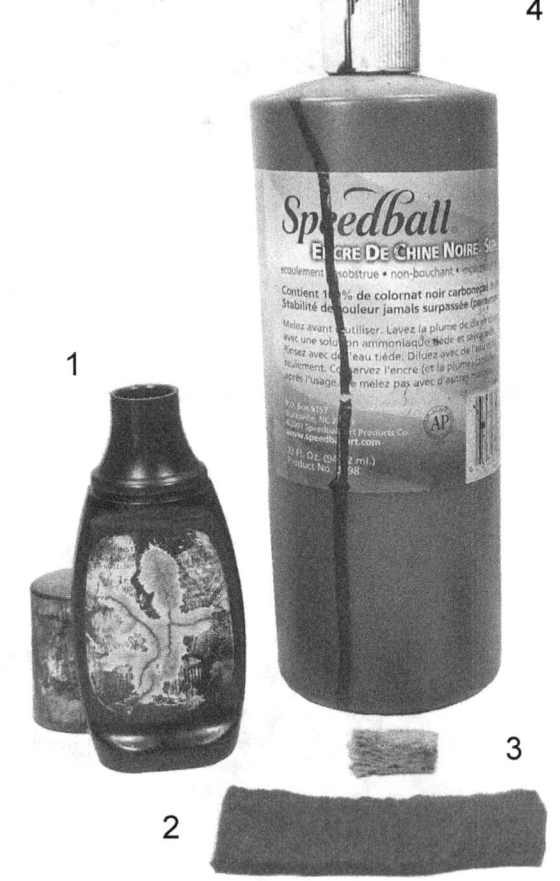

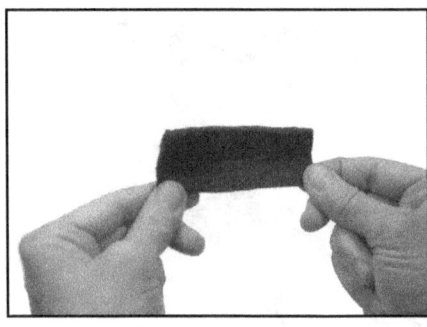

STEP 1. Cut a piece of felt into a 1.5" x 3.5" rectangle.

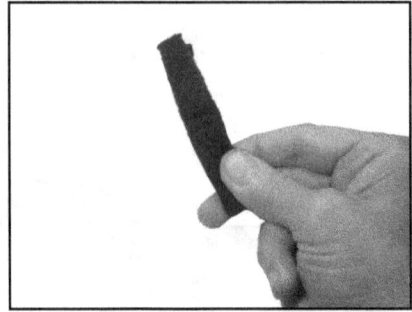

STEP 2. Fold the felt in half the long way.

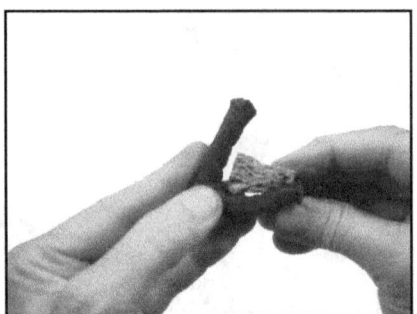

STEP 3. Fold the felt in half again and place the piece of sponge into the center.

WHY WRITE WHEN YOU CAN TAG

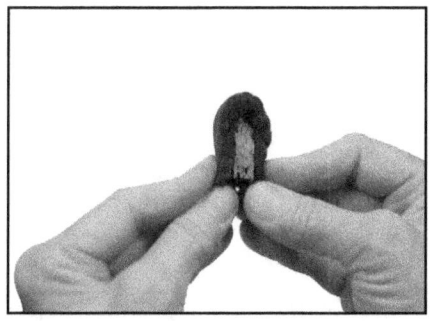

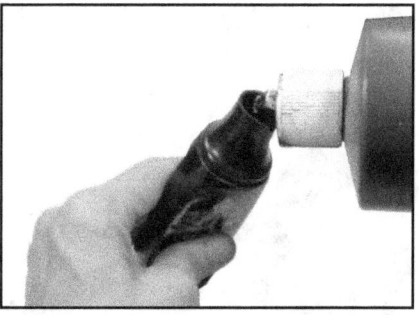

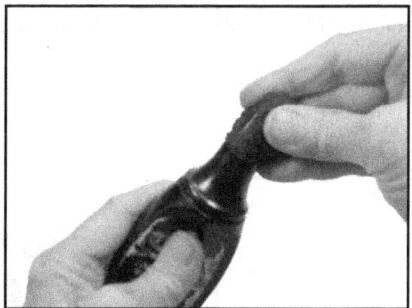

STEP 4. You now have a felt/sponge sandwich. The sponge helps to soak up ink and creates tension in the felt tip. You can sew it together if you like, but you don't have to.

STEP 5. Fill the bottle with ink about half way.

STEP 6. Push the end of the felt/sponge sandwich into the opening of the bottle. It should be a little tight.

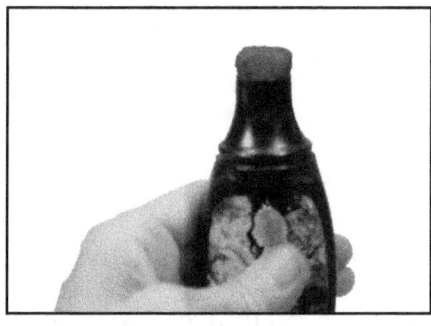

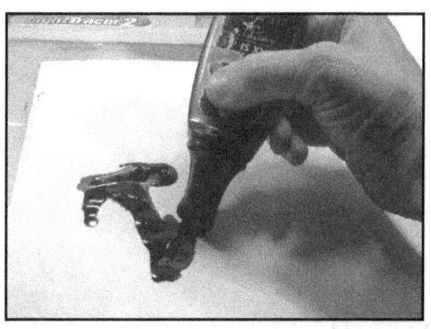

STEP 7. Force it in by twisting it gently. Leave about half an inch sticking out.

STEP 8. Turn the bottle over, firmly (but gently) press the tip against a piece of paper and squeeze the bottle to flood the tip with ink.

STEP 9.
Use your new homemade mop to draw great, drippy graffiti tags like this terrific "JAG" tag drawn by a local graffiti writer.

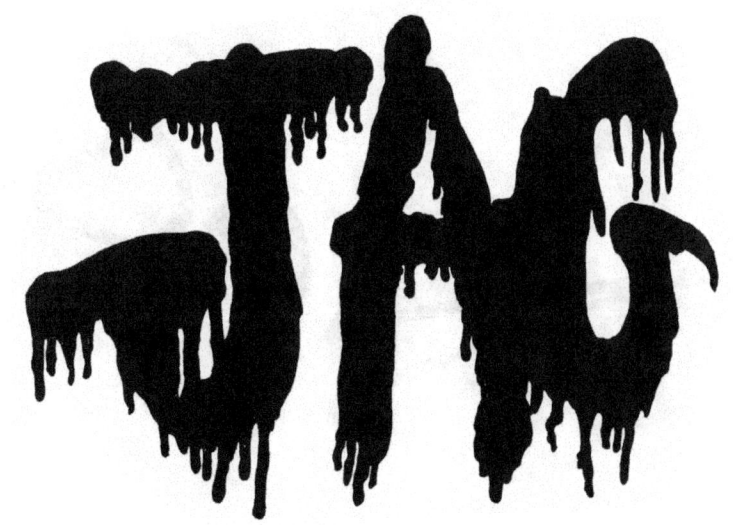

TAG READING CHALLENGE - CAN YOU READ THIS TAG?

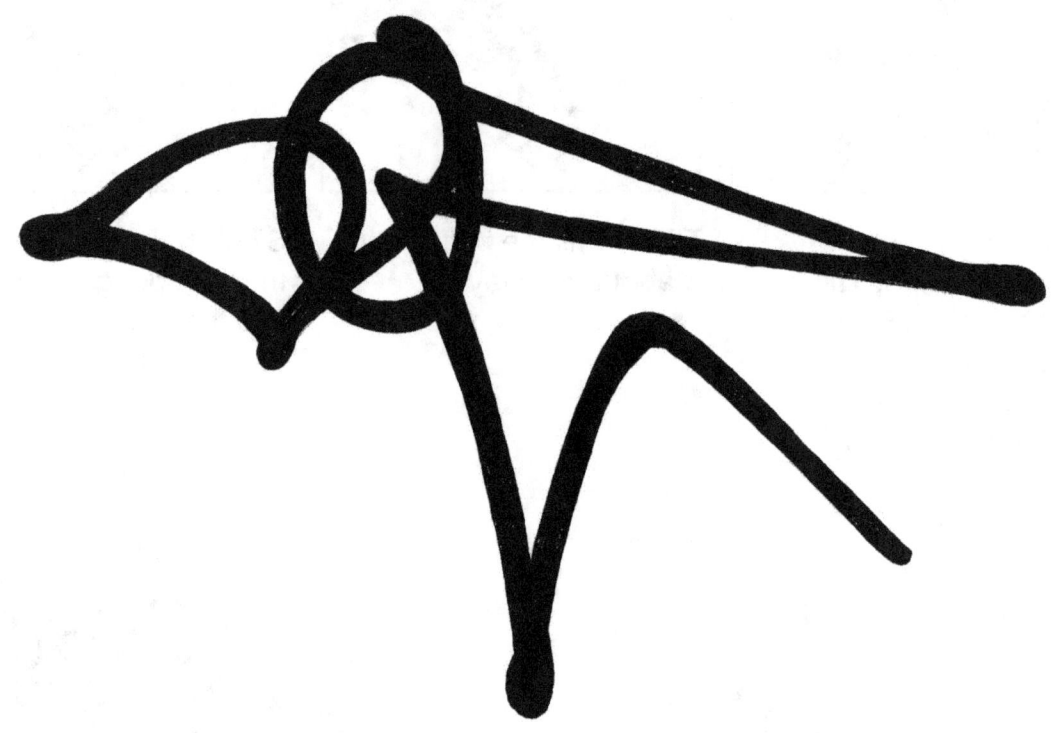

SEPARATE THE LETTERS AND TRY TO READ THIS TAG. THEN TURN THE BOOK UP-
SIDE DOWN TO READ OUR ANSWER BELOW.

„ZOD„

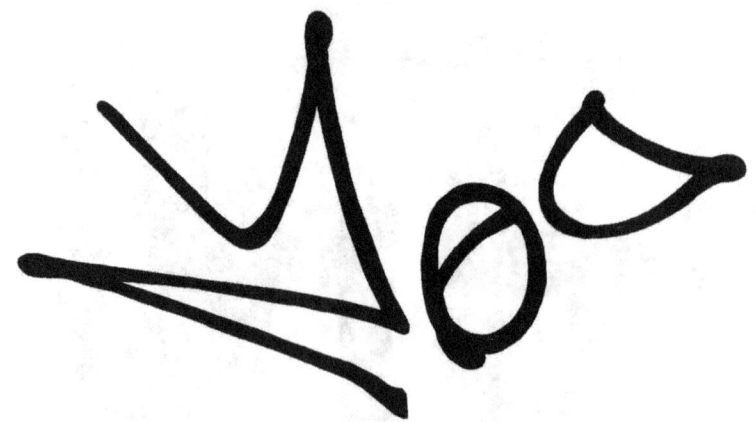

THIS TAG IS VERY DIFFICULT TO READ. WHAT DO YOU THINK IT SAYS?

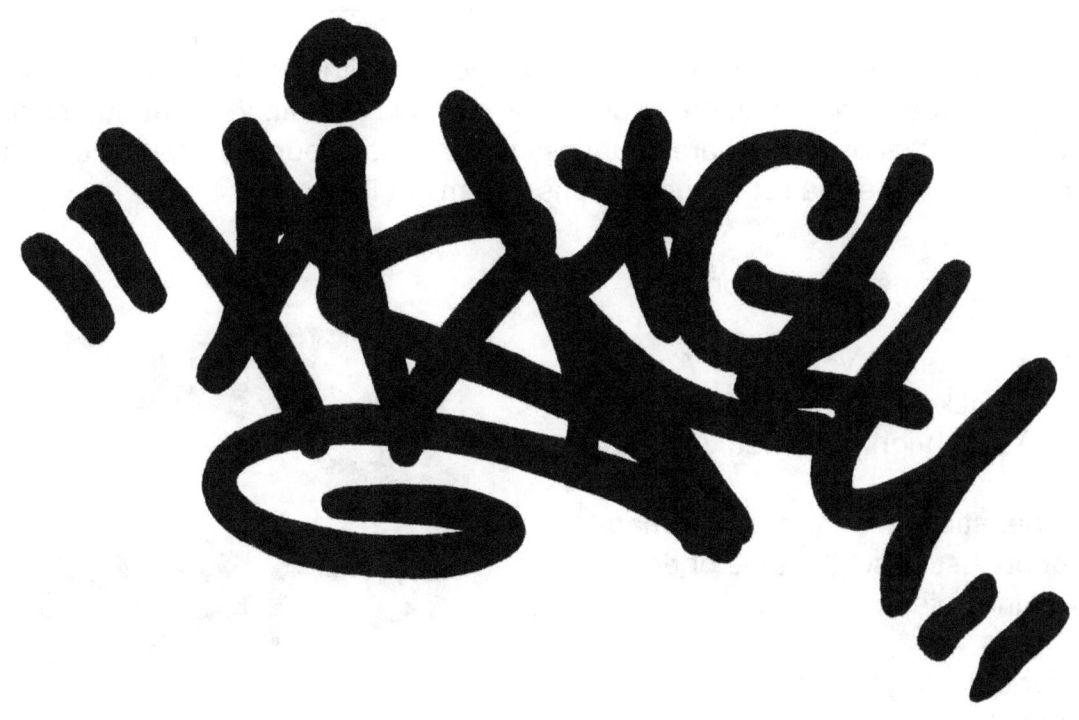

SEPARATE THE LETTERS AND TRY TO READ THIS TAG. SOME OF THE LETTERS ARE CONNECTED OR OVERLAP. TURN THIS BOOK UPSIDE DOWN TO READ OUR BEST GUESS AS TO WHAT THIS TAG SAYS BELOW.

¿ „∩ꓵ⅁∗SIꓘ„

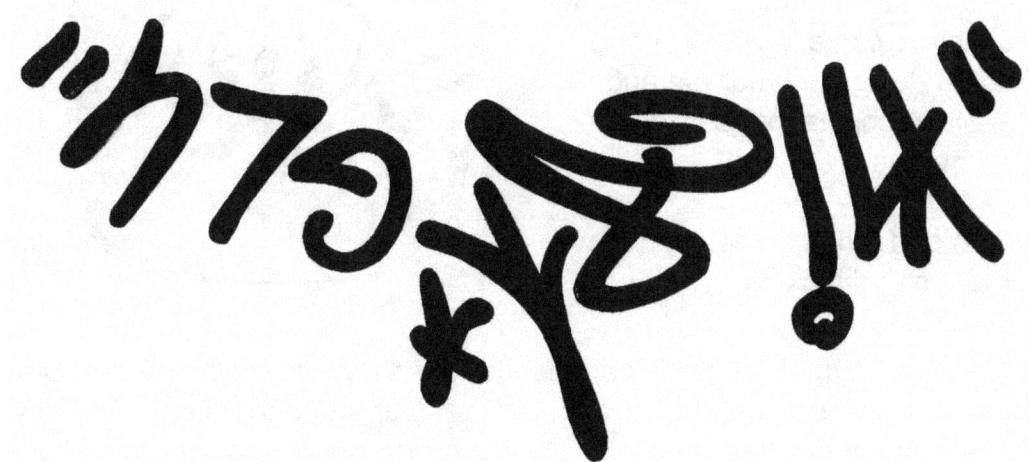

CHAPTER TEN
HOW TO PUT YOUR TAG TO WORK

So now that you have designed your tag what can you do with it? Well, quite a lot actually. You can use your tag as an ornament to decorate all kinds of stuff. What about making gifts for your family and friends? There are countless ways to use your tag designs to bring yourself and others joy. Here is a list of suggestions you might like to try:

1) Make greeting cards or invitations.

2) Make a tag poster for your room. Add glitter, puff paint, stickers, even wiggly eyes, and pom-poms. Add a brightly colored yarn fringe.

3) Make paper stickers or refrigerator magnets with double-stick scotch tape or double-stick magnetic tape.

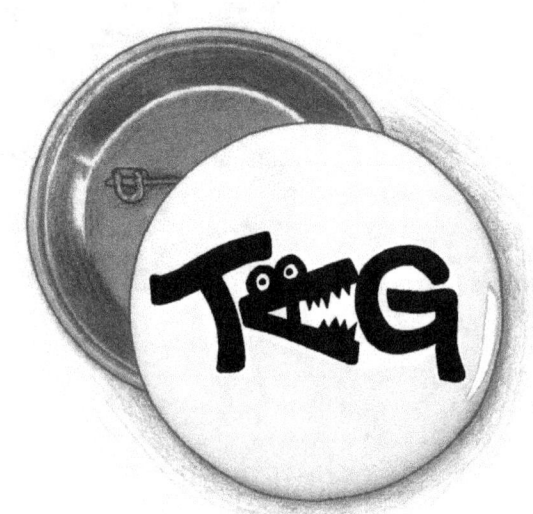

4) Scan your tag into your computer to make personalized stationary, letterhead or even your own business cards.

5) Scan your tag into your computer and go to websites like Cafe Press or Zazzle where you can download your file and put your tag on any of a zillion different products, like t-shirts, coffee mugs, buttons, aprons, or tote bags.

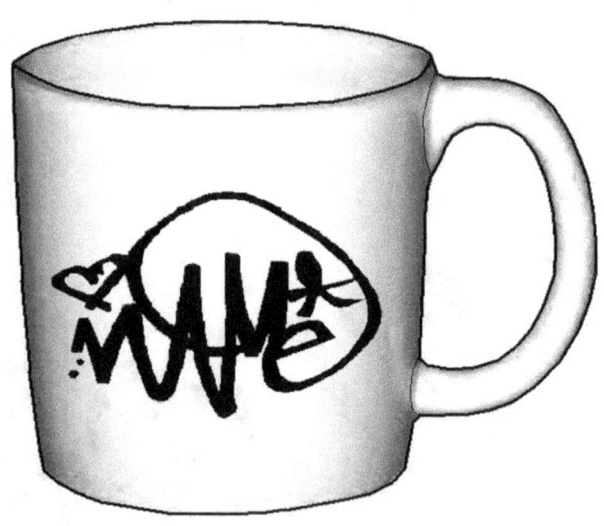

6) Here's where all those numbered sketches from earlier chapters come in handy. Write a little book about designing your tag and self-publish it. Make copies for your friends, families or classmates.

7) Paint your tag on fabric patches and sew them on your jeans and jackets.

Your finished tag is a work of art. But it can also be used as a springboard to create a more complex graffiti piece, which is short for masterpiece. Our first book "Learn To Draw a Graffiti Master-Piece" covers this topic in depth. We have included it here because, as Paul 107 says in his book 'ALL CITY', "Sometimes a tag just doesn't say enough".

TURNING A TAG INTO A PIECE

Turn a beginner's tag into a piece.

STEP 1. Draw the letters of your tag. Leave space around the letters so you have room to fatten them up.

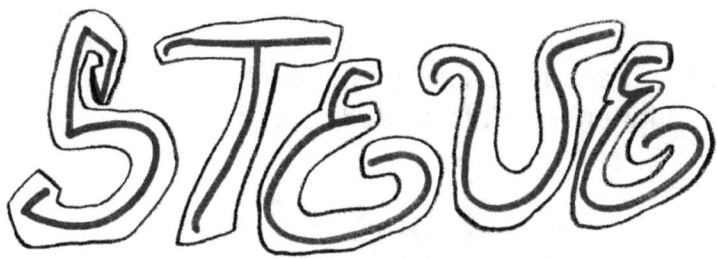

STEP 2. Draw a line all around the outside edge of each letter to fatten it up into an outline letter.

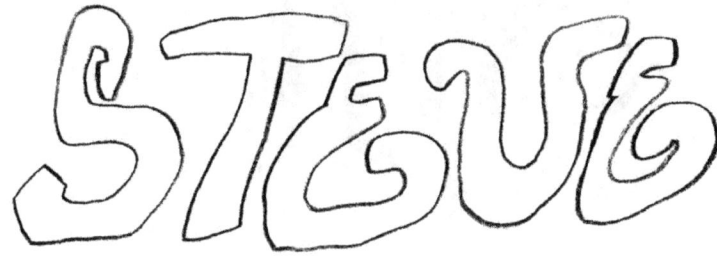

STEP 3. Erase the inside lines. These are your finished outline letters.

STEP 4. Add a force-field, a pattern inside the letters, a background cloud, some drips and a crown to complete the piece. (The pattern inside the letters is called the fill).

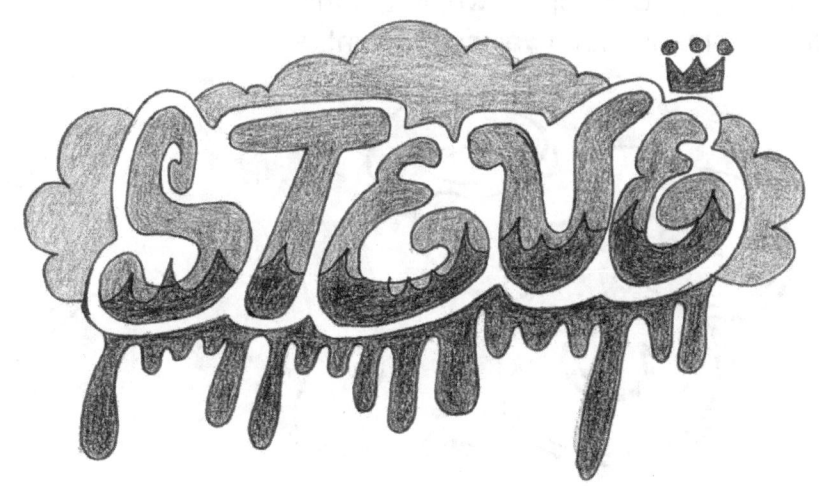

Here's an example of a more advanced tag turned into a piece. The process is the same.

STEP 1. Design a tag.

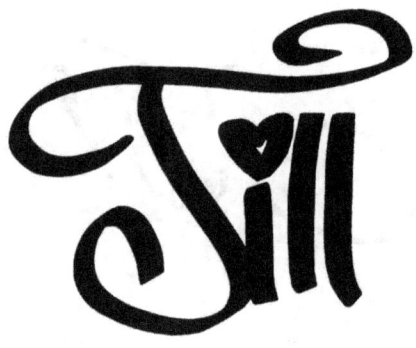

STEP 2. Move the letters apart so you have room to work on them.

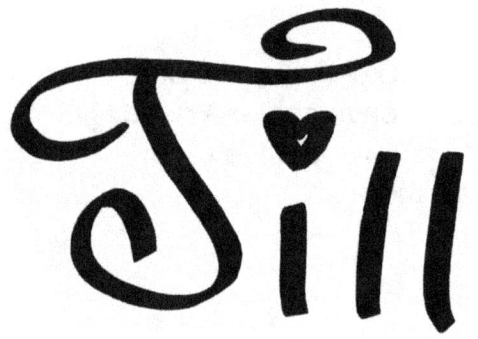

STEP 3. Draw an outline around each letter to fatten it up into an outline letter.

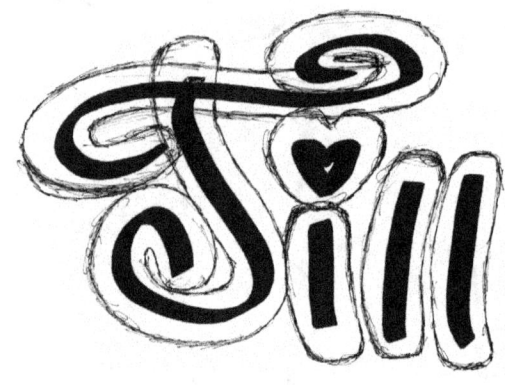

STEP 4. Erase the inside lines. At this stage you can move the letters closer together and overlap the edges a little.

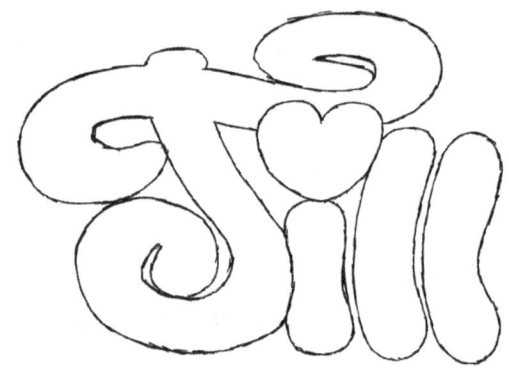

STEP 5. Add 3-D to the letters. You can make the 3-D go up, down, left, right, thick, thin, or with a vanishing point, etc...

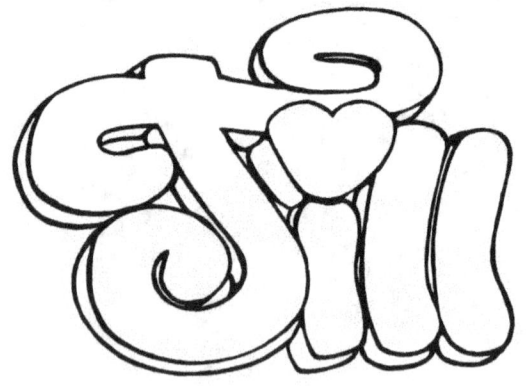

STEP 6. Add a force-field around the letters.

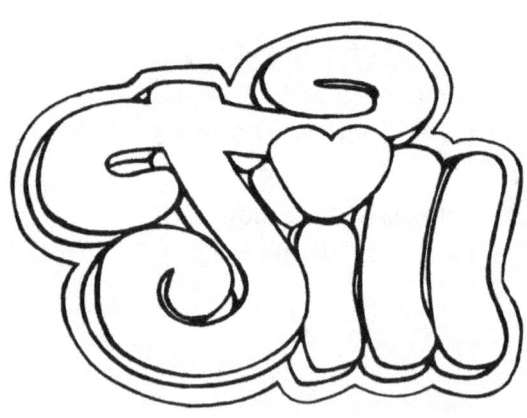

WHY WRITE WHEN YOU CAN TAG

STEP 7. Draw a pattern or fill inside the letters to decorate them and make them interesting.

STEP 8. Draw a background cloud surrounding the name.

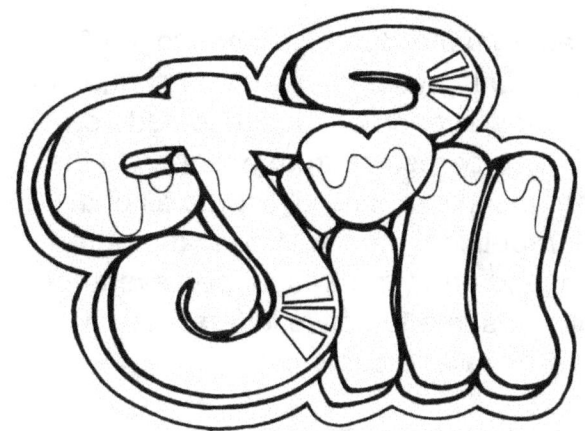

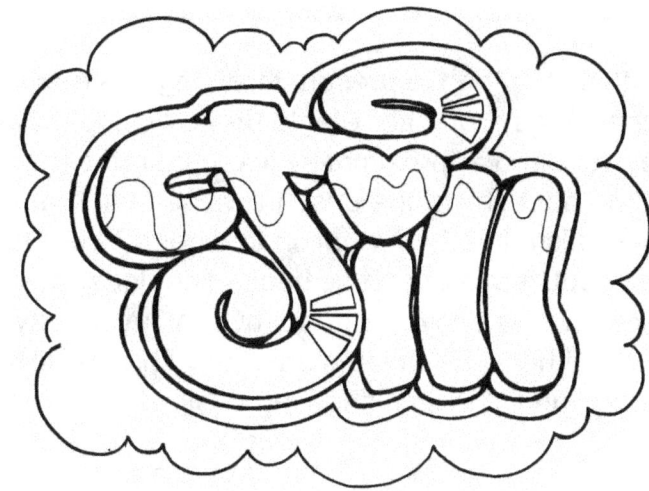

STEP 9. Add some small elements to fill up space and complete the piece. A chocolate kiss, a music note, some little bubbles and the letters XOXO, stars, hearts, drips and arrows are some options. It's those little extras that make a piece an eye-catching reflection of you.

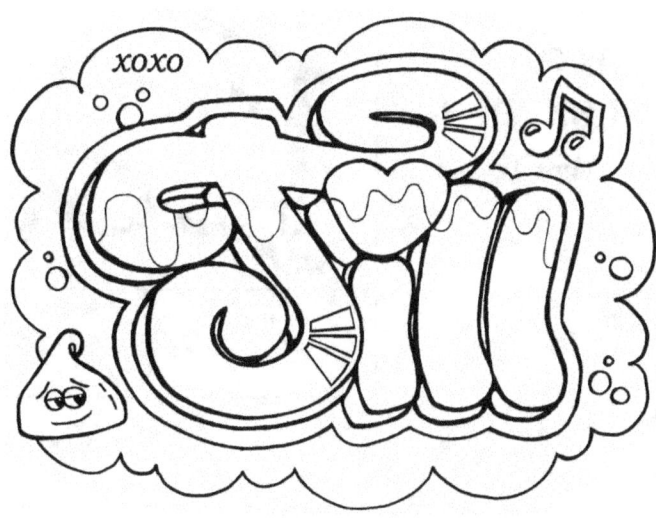

Alternate finish: You can finish your piece any way that you want. The possibilities and variations are endless.

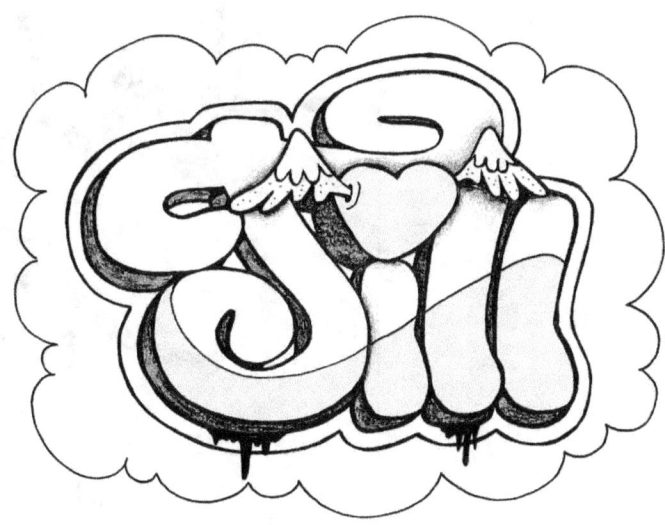

In this chapter, we present three tag designs modified from the Starting Points to the Finished Tags. You can refer to these examples when designing your own tags. Although each tag required approximately two hundred sketches to create, each one is presented here with about fifty of the best drawings to demonstrate the progression from one step to the next. It's a lot of information to digest. Taken together these examples illustrate all of the concepts covered in this book - line, letter structure, repetition, modification and progression, consistency, contrast, rhythm, layout, style, trial and error, frustration, perseverance - it's all here. Each tag starts out with a basic layout and some tag style letters, then proceeds until it is a finished tag design. Each took several days to complete.

TAG
DESIGN
NUMBER
ONE

"EASY"

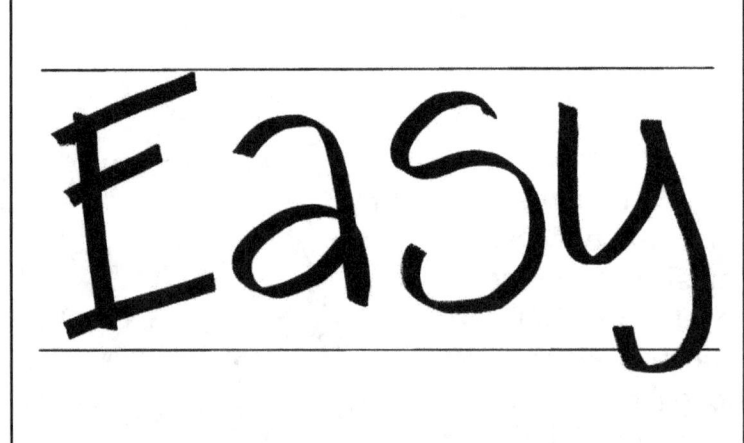

STARTING POINT

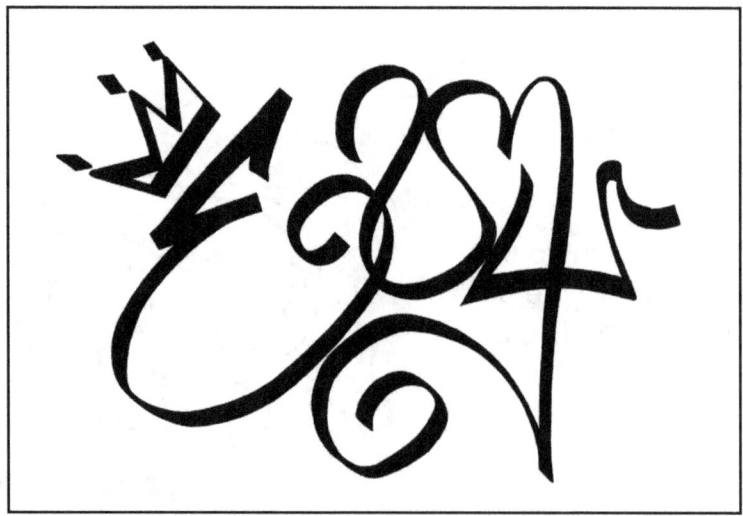

FINISHED TAG

TAG MODIFICATION AND PROGRESSION
STARTING POINT

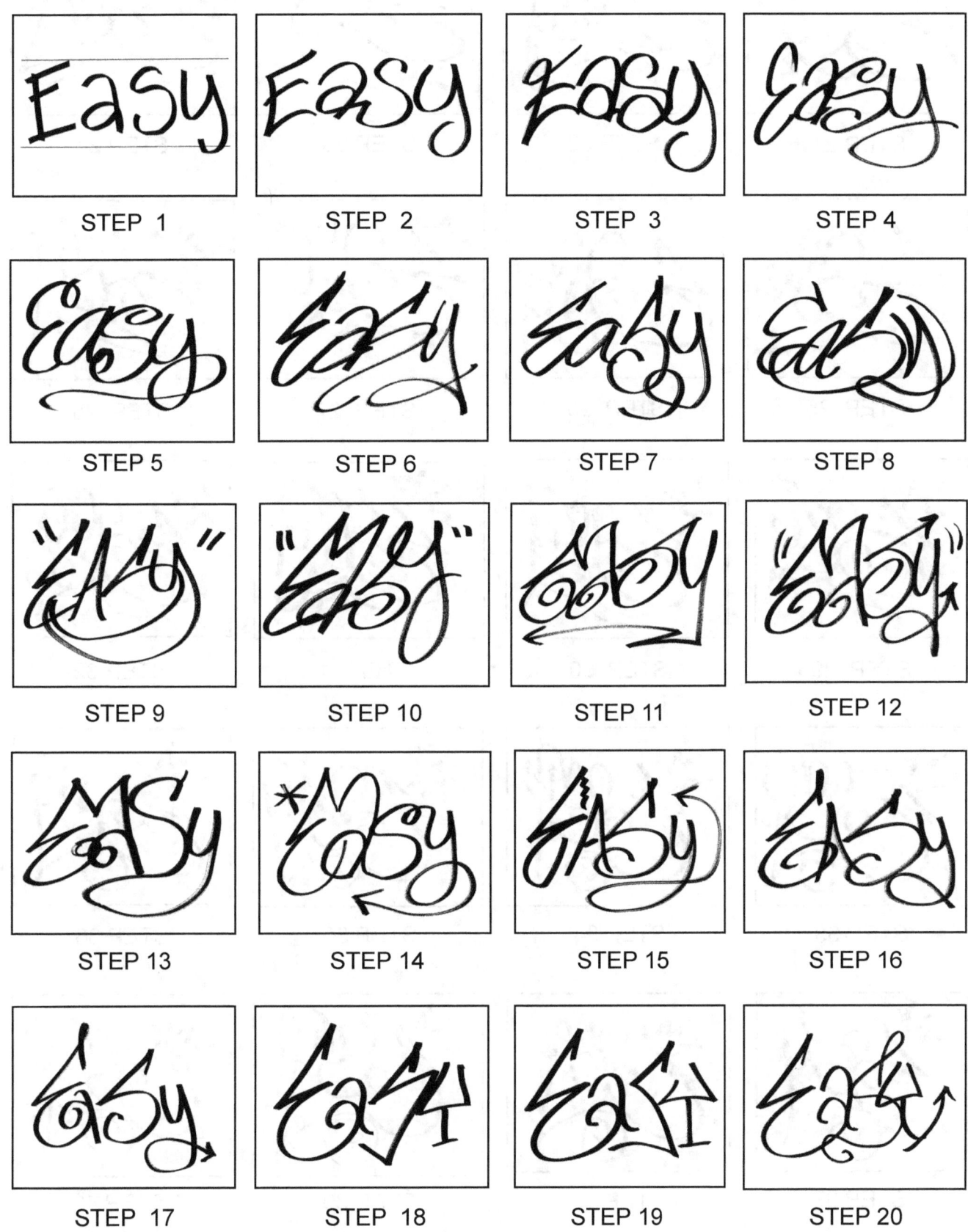

STEP 1 STEP 2 STEP 3 STEP 4

STEP 5 STEP 6 STEP 7 STEP 8

STEP 9 STEP 10 STEP 11 STEP 12

STEP 13 STEP 14 STEP 15 STEP 16

STEP 17 STEP 18 STEP 19 STEP 20

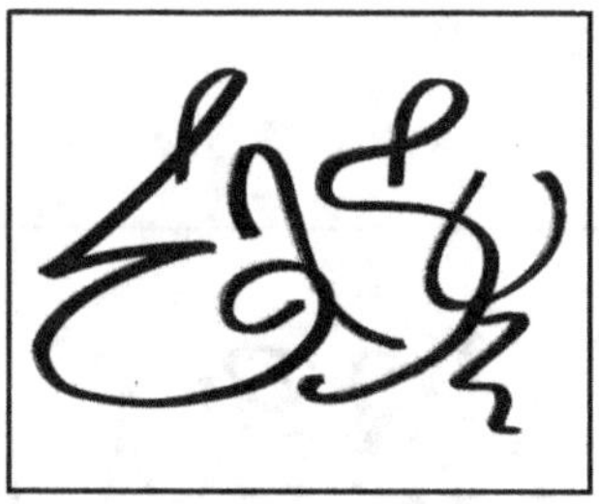

STEP 21	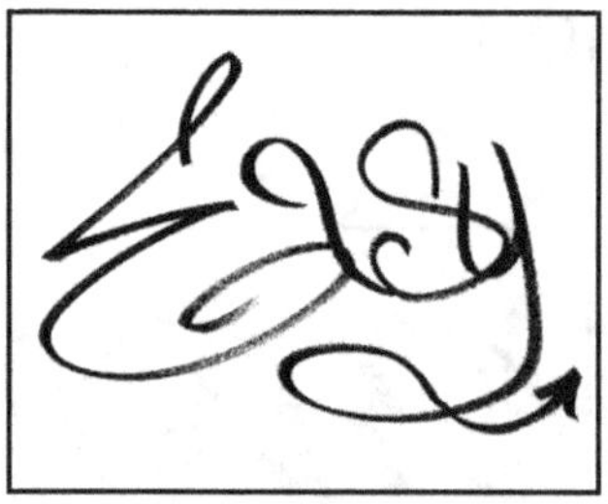 STEP 22	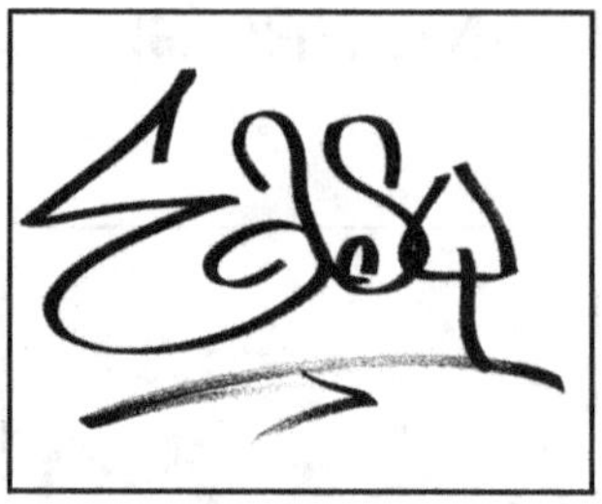 STEP 23	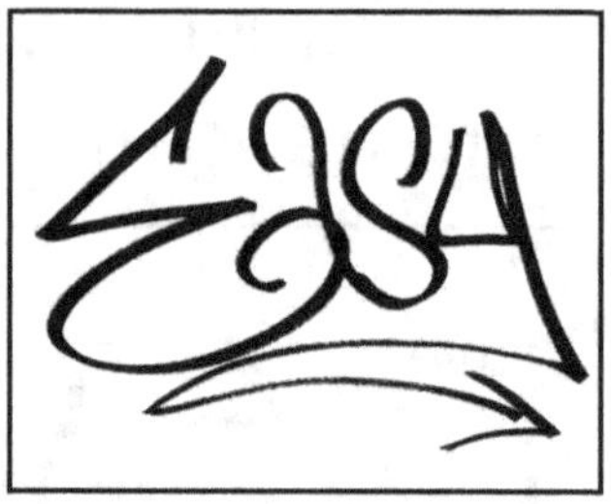 STEP 24
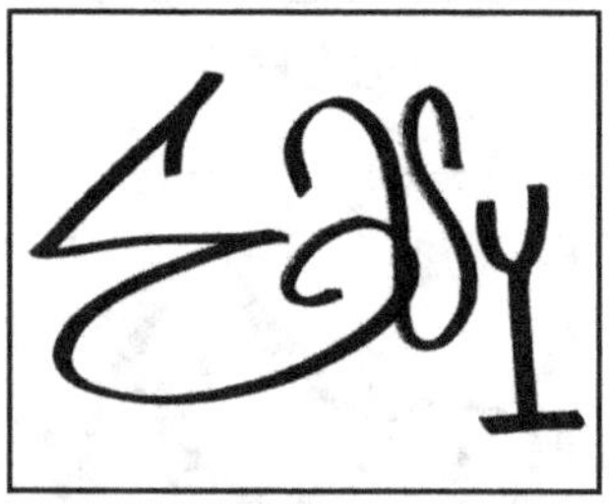 STEP 25	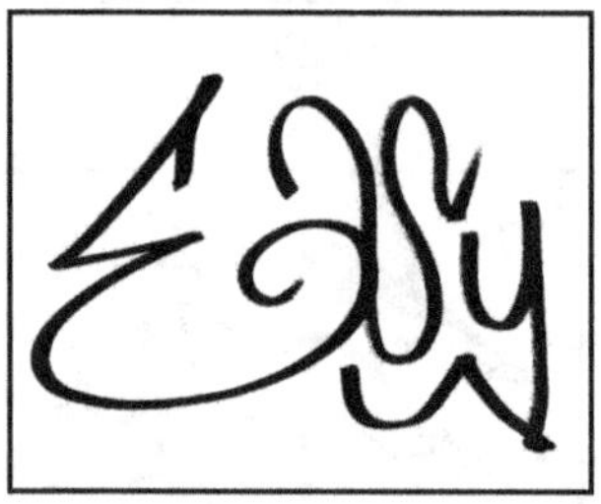 STEP 26	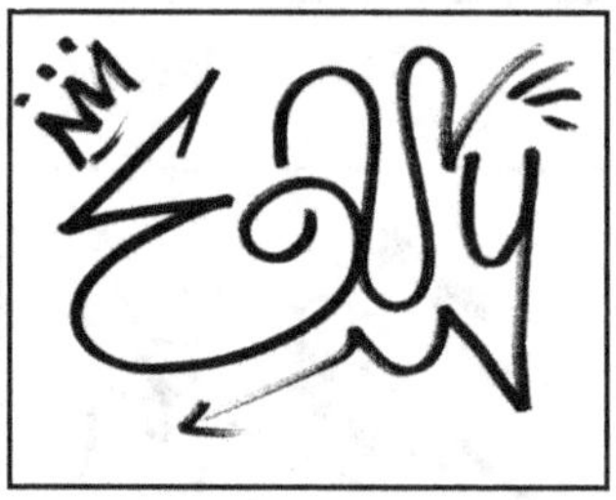 STEP 27	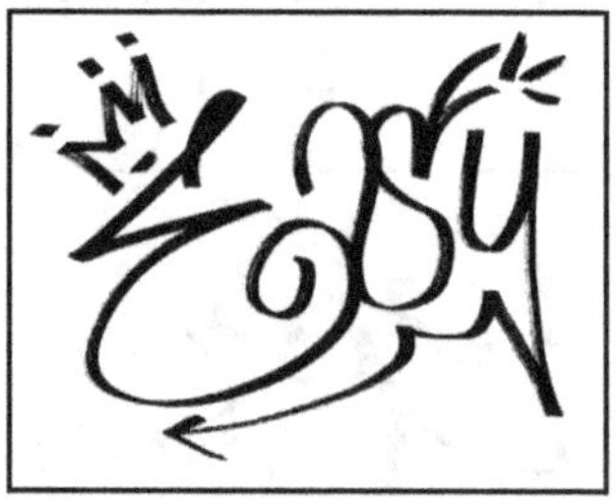 STEP 28
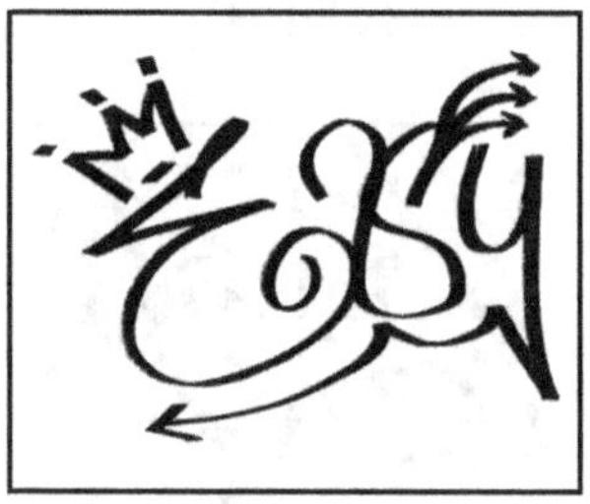 STEP 29	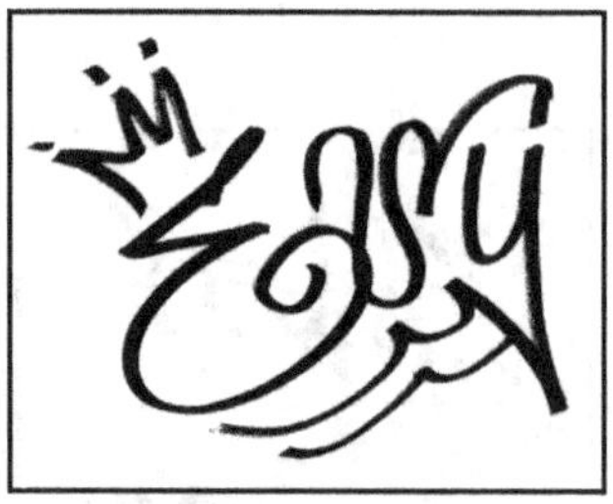 STEP 30	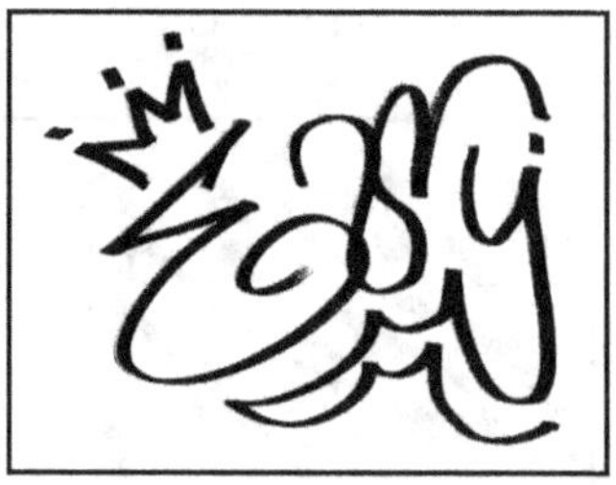 STEP 31	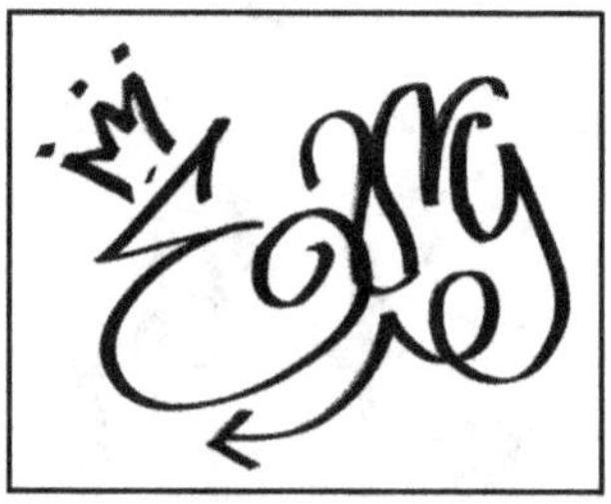 STEP 32
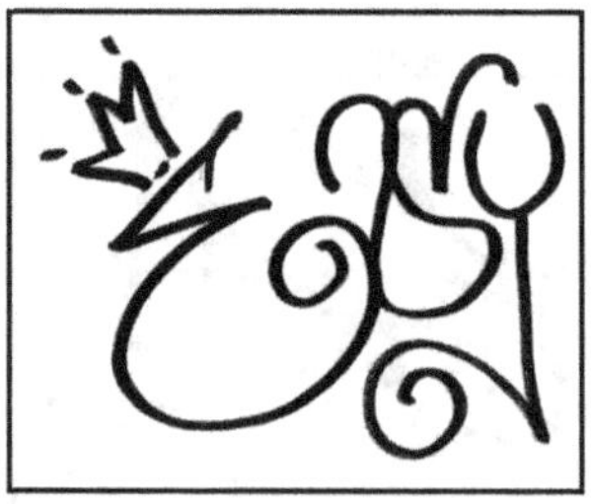 STEP 33	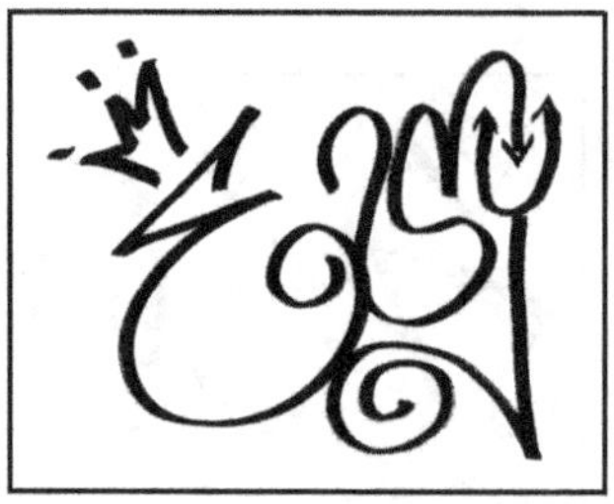 STEP 34	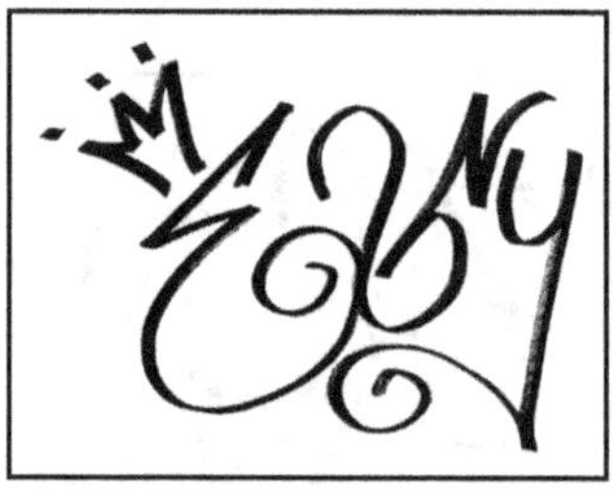 STEP 35	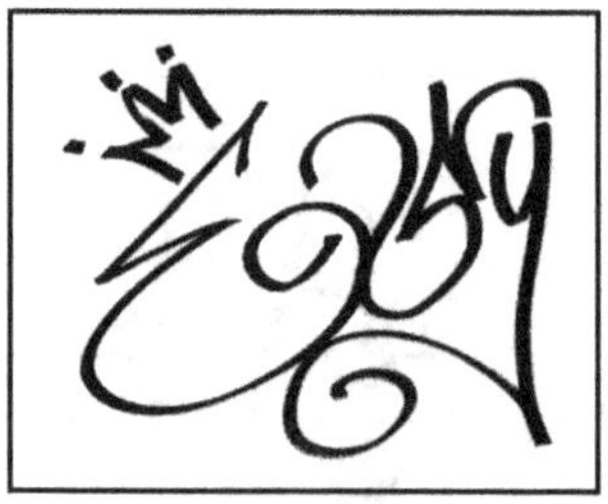 STEP 36
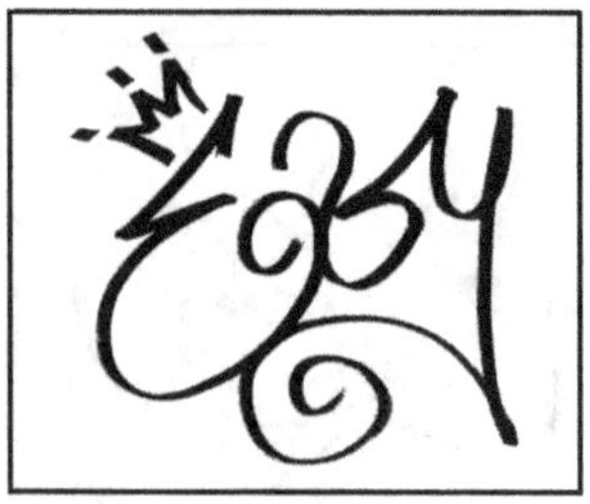 STEP 37	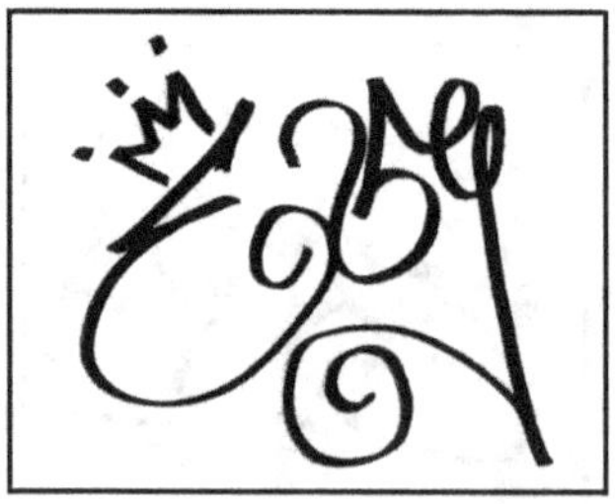 STEP 38	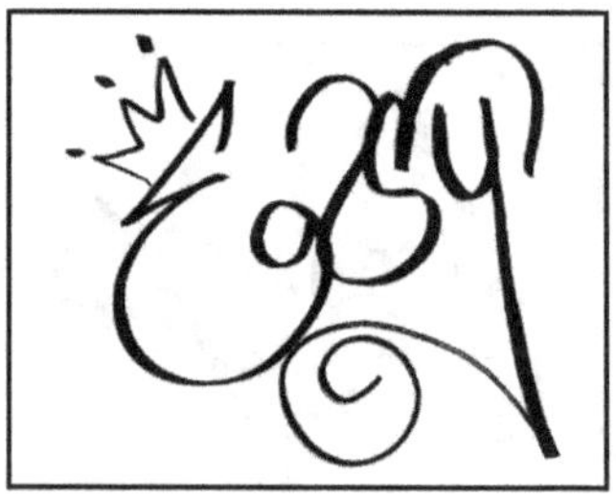 STEP 39	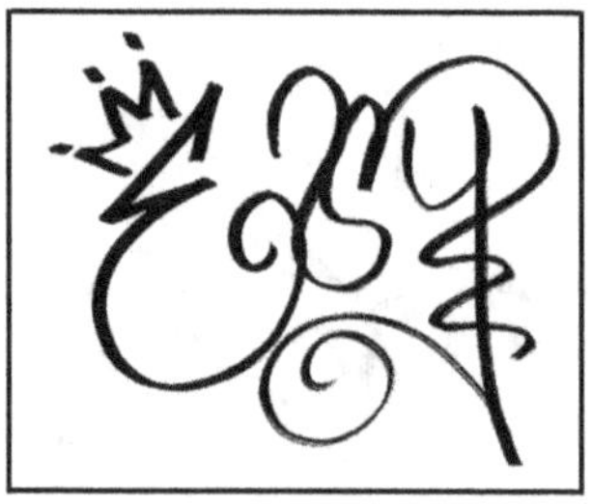 STEP 40

WHY WRITE WHEN YOU CAN TAG

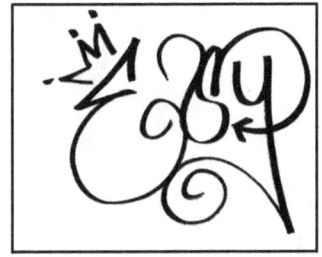

STEP 41

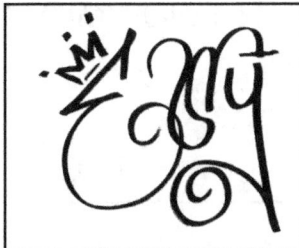

STEP 42

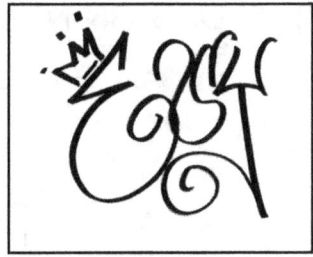

STEP 43

STEP 44

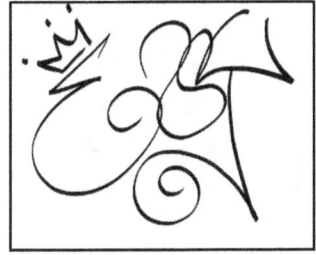

STEP 45

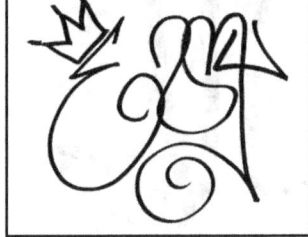

STEP 46

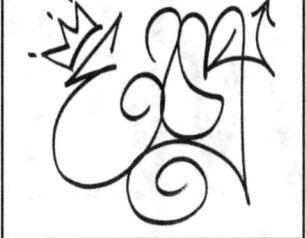

STEP 47

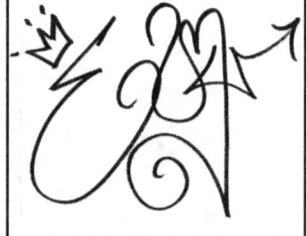

STEP 48

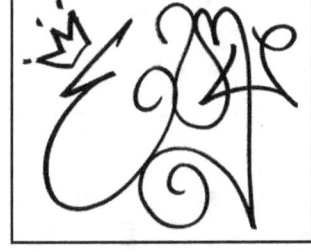

STEP 49

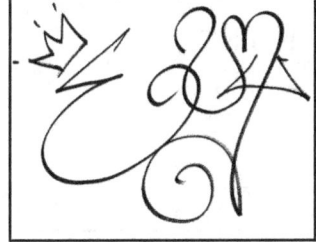

STEP 50

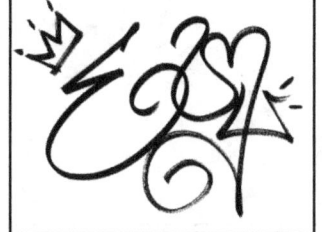

STEP 51

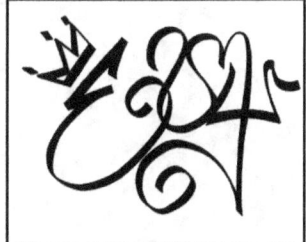

STEP 52

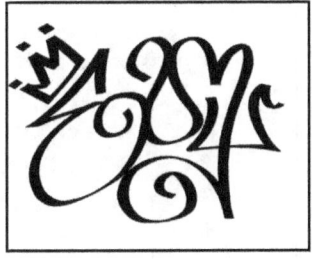

STEP 53

FINISHED TAG

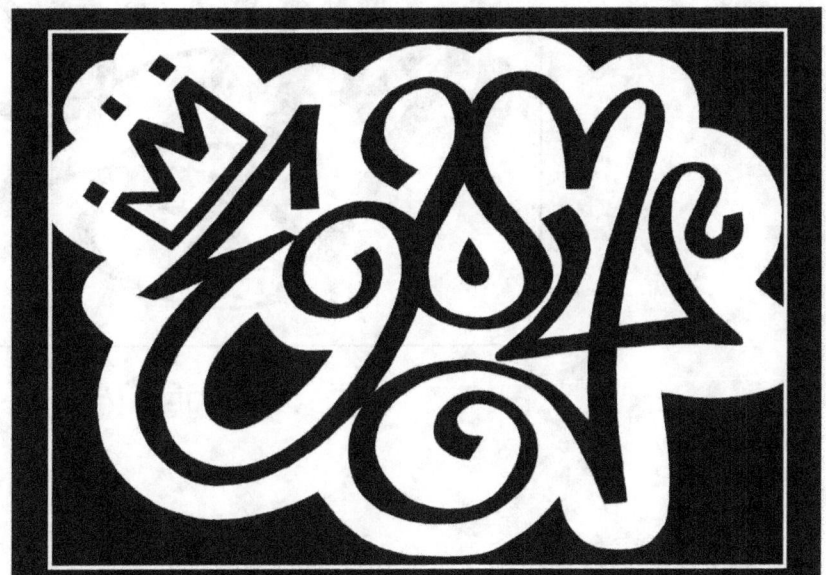

"EASY"
FINISHED TAG
This finished tag was scanned
into a computer, shrunk, and
printed on a paper sticker.

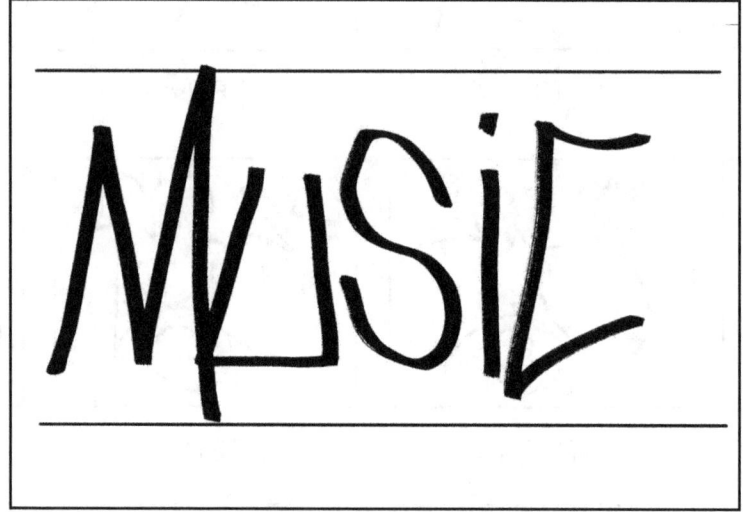

STARTING POINT

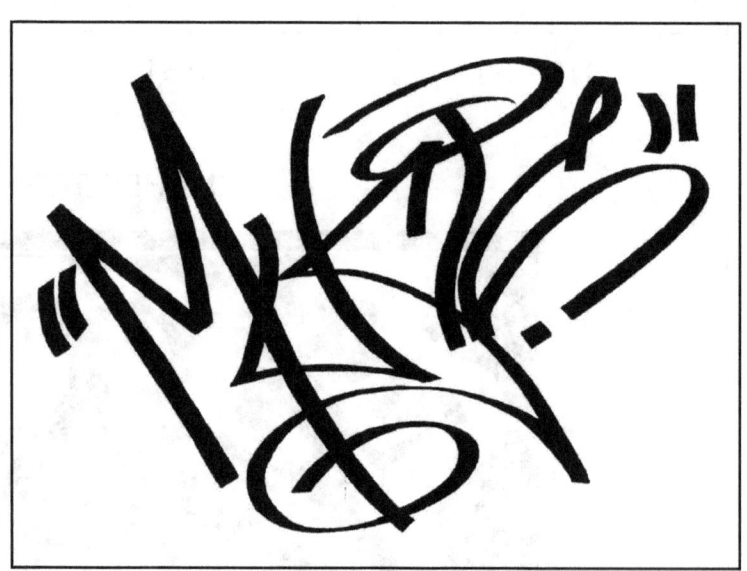

FINISHED TAG

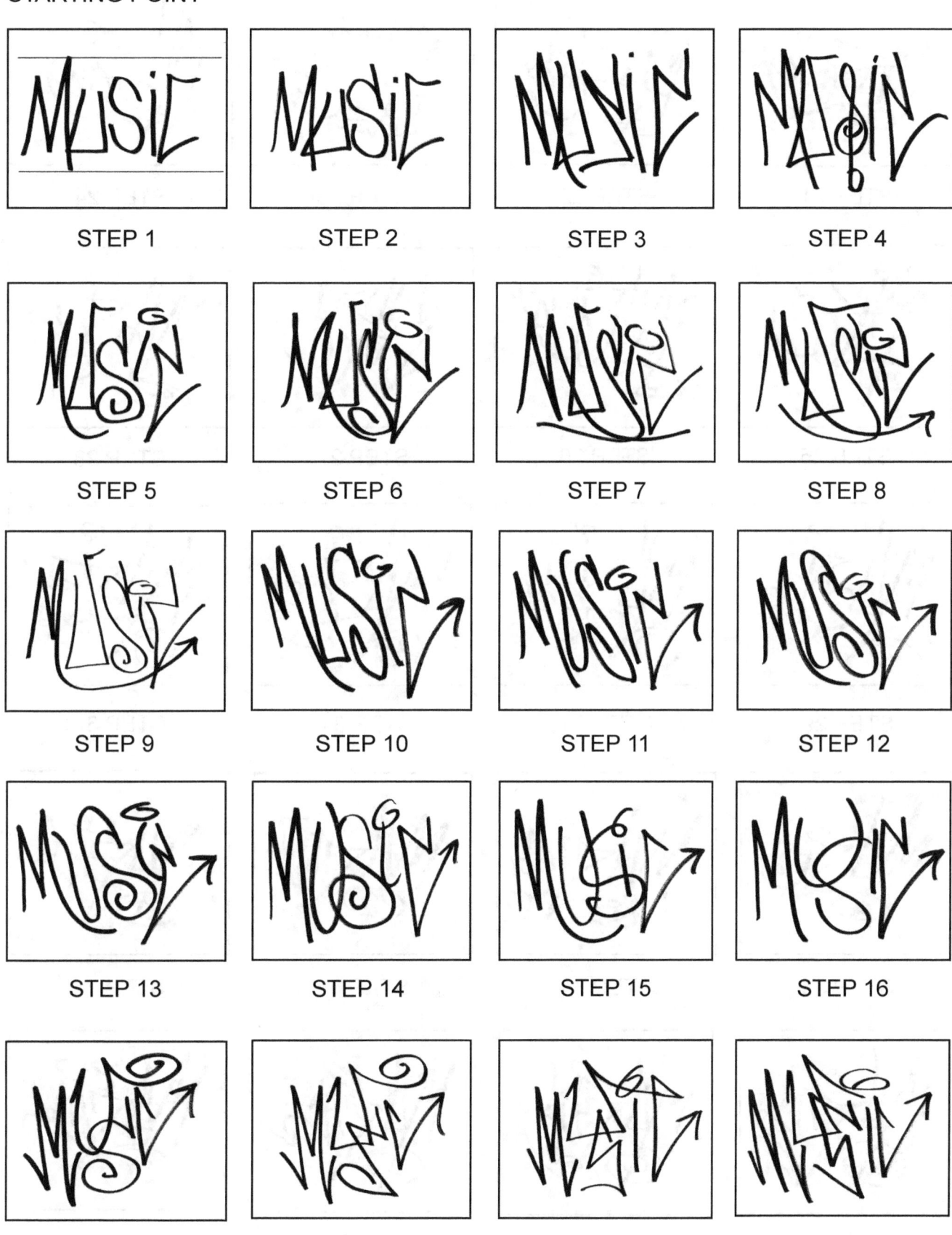

STEP 1 STEP 2 STEP 3 STEP 4

STEP 5 STEP 6 STEP 7 STEP 8

STEP 9 STEP 10 STEP 11 STEP 12

STEP 13 STEP 14 STEP 15 STEP 16

STEP 17 STEP 18 STEP 19 STEP 20

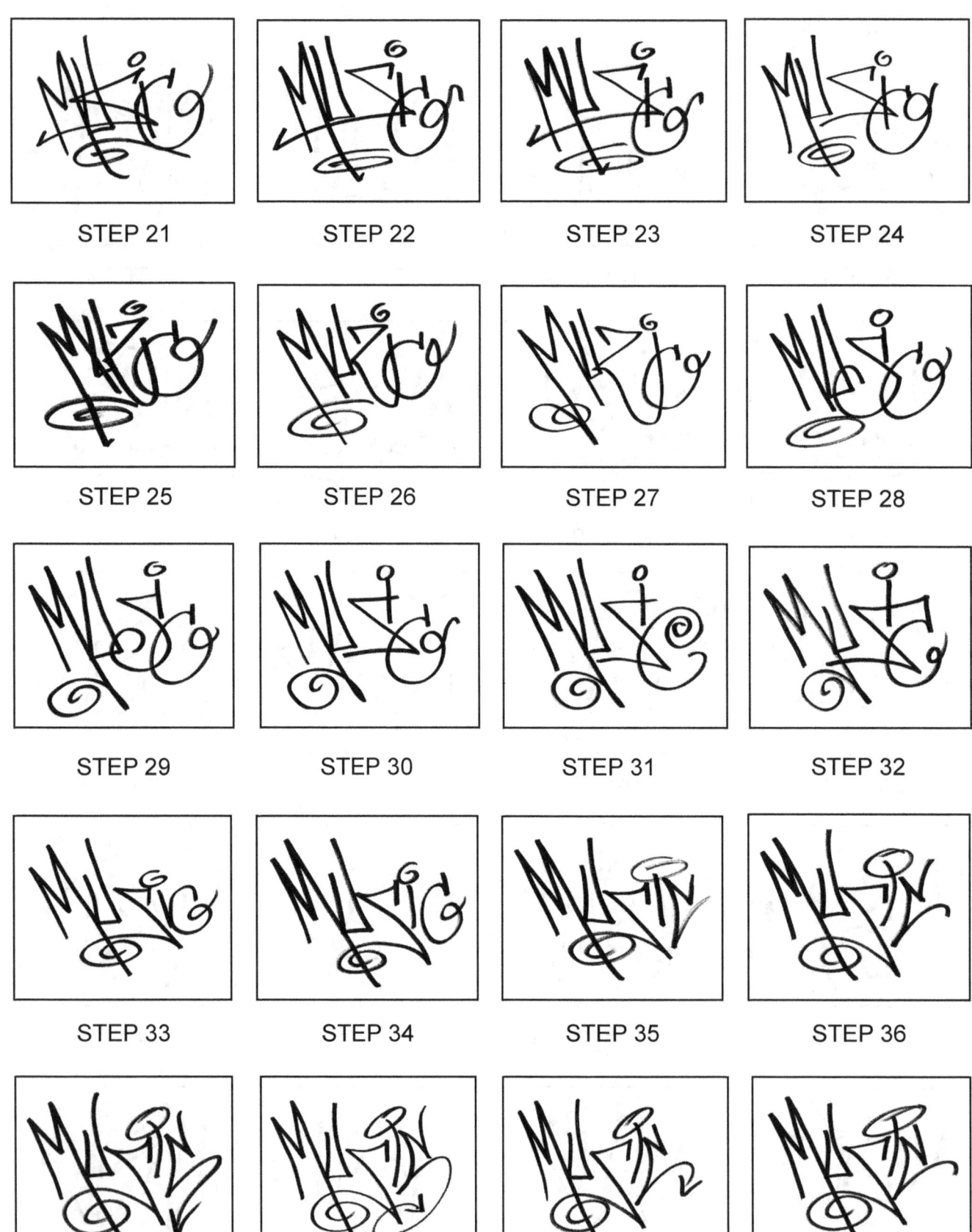

STEP 21   STEP 22   STEP 23   STEP 24

STEP 25   STEP 26   STEP 27   STEP 28

STEP 29   STEP 30   STEP 31   STEP 32

STEP 33   STEP 34   STEP 35   STEP 36

STEP 37   STEP 38   STEP 39   STEP 40

WHY WRITE WHEN YOU CAN TAG

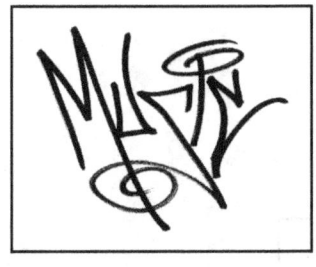

STEP 41

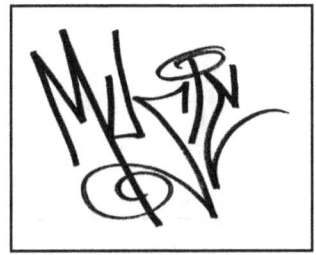

STEP 42

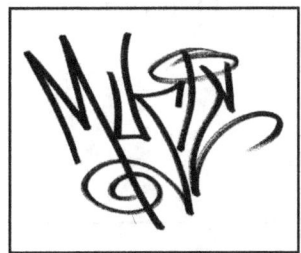

STEP 43

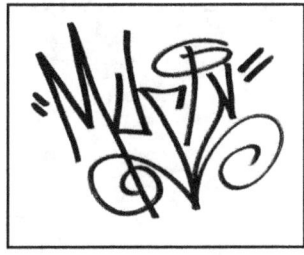

STEP 44

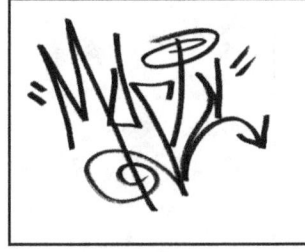

STEP 45

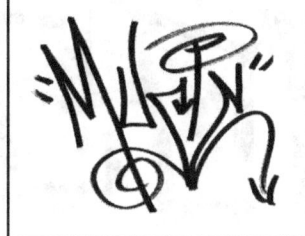

STEP 46

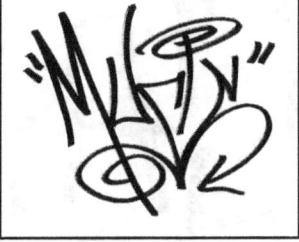

STEP 47

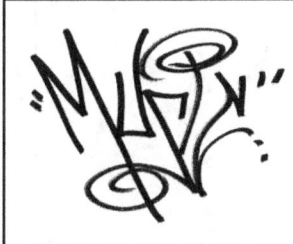

STEP 48

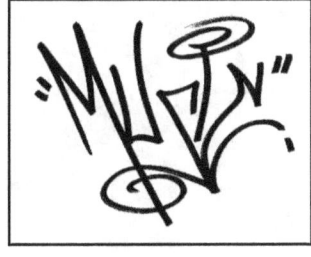

STEP 49

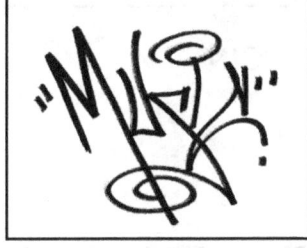

STEP 50

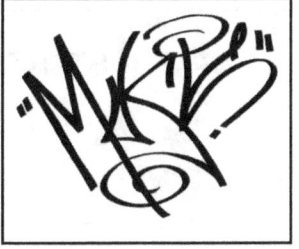

STEP 51

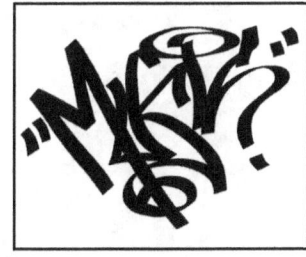

STEP 52

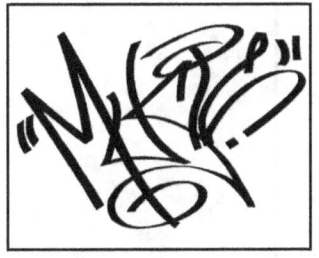

STEP 53

FINISHED TAG

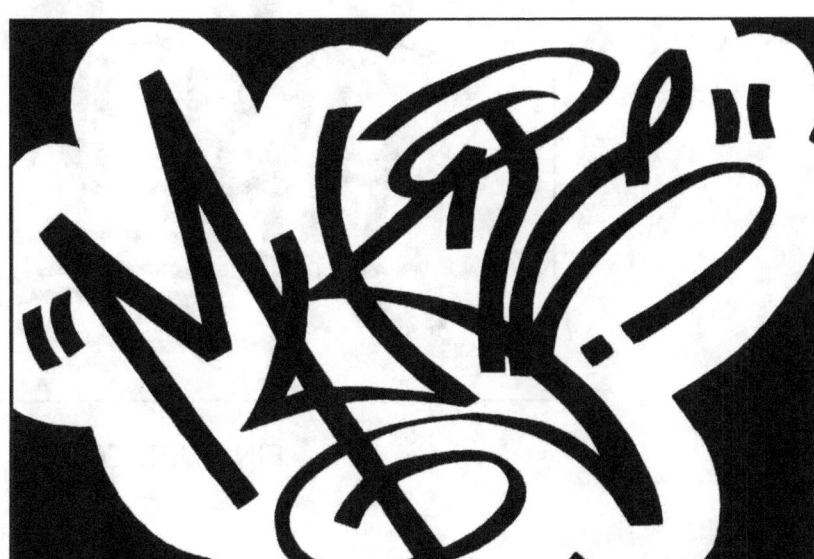

"MUSIC"
FINISHED TAG
This finished tag was scanned
into a computer, shrunk, and
printed on a paper sticker.

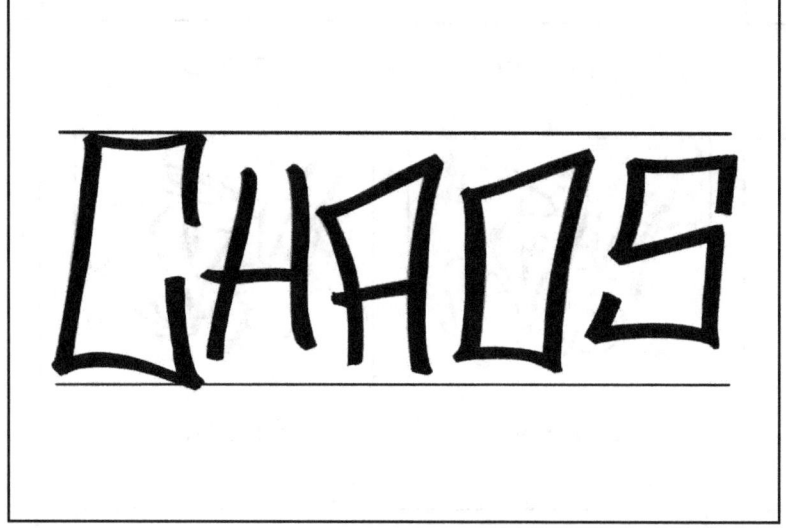

STARTING POINT

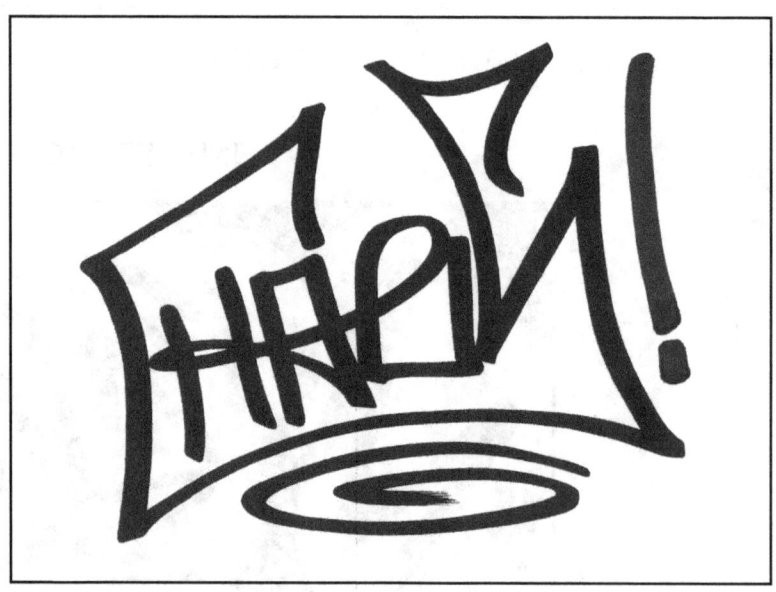

FINISHED TAG

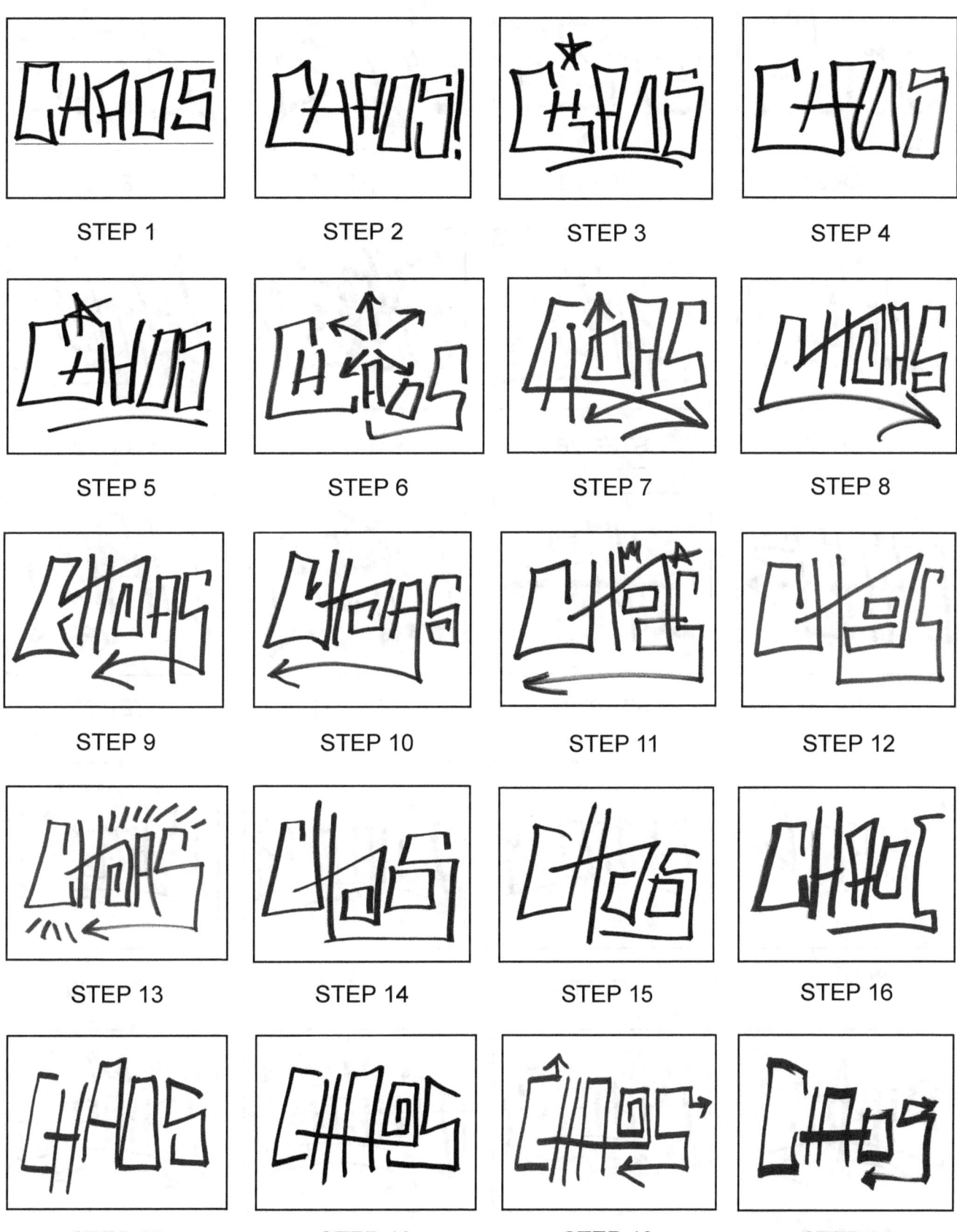

STEP 1 STEP 2 STEP 3 STEP 4

STEP 5 STEP 6 STEP 7 STEP 8

STEP 9 STEP 10 STEP 11 STEP 12

STEP 13 STEP 14 STEP 15 STEP 16

STEP 17 STEP 18 STEP 19 STEP 20

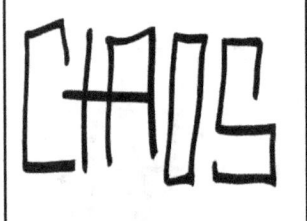

STEP 21

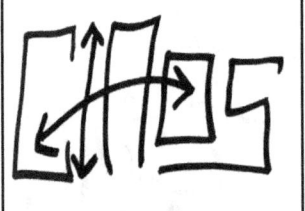

STEP 22

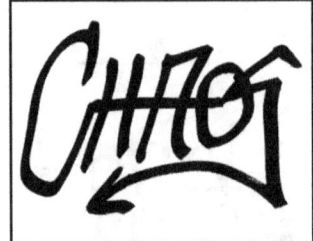

STEP 23

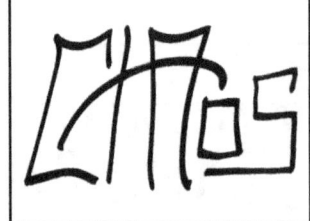

STEP 24

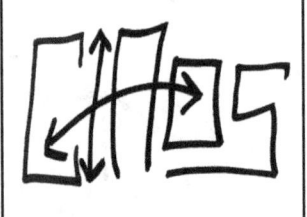

STEP 25

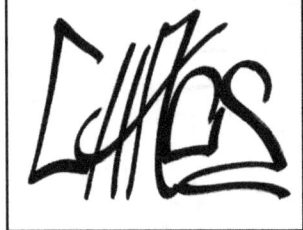

STEP 26

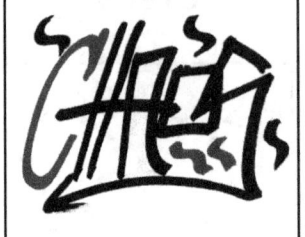

STEP 27

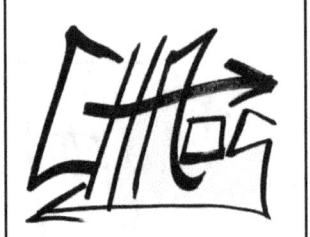

STEP 28

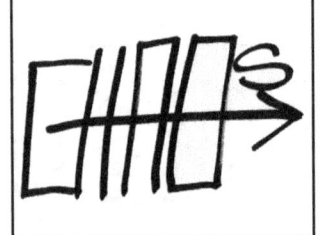

STEP 29

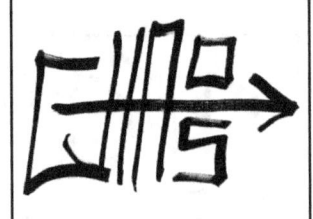

STEP 30

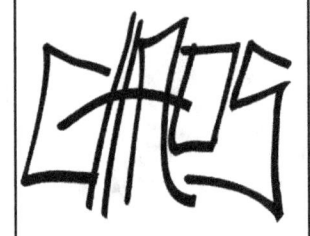

STEP 31

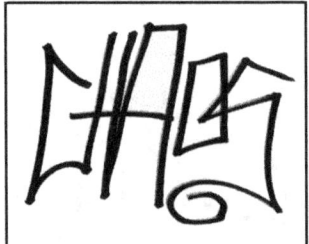

STEP 32

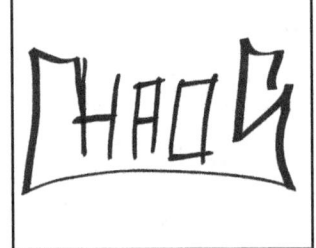

STEP 33

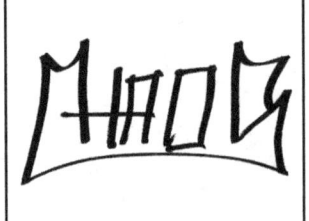

STEP 34

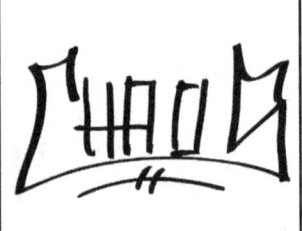

STEP 35

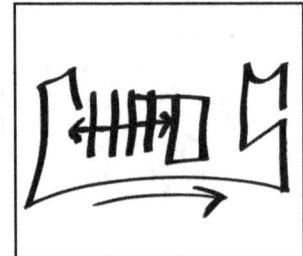

STEP 36

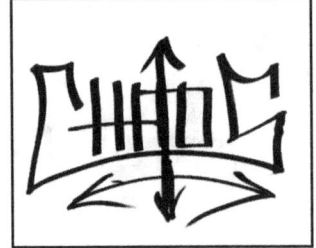

STEP 37

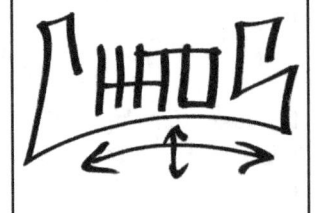

STEP 38

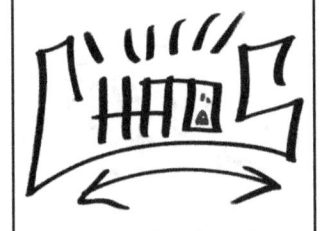

STEP 39

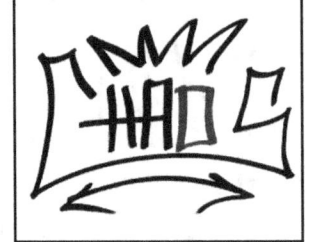

STEP 40

WHY WRITE WHEN YOU CAN TAG

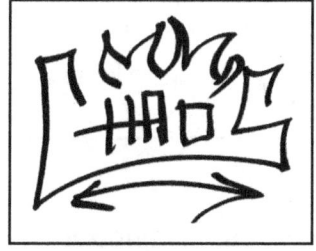

STEP 41

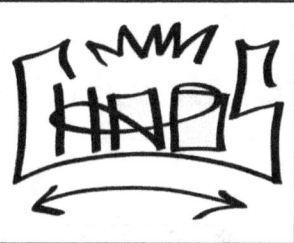

STEP 42

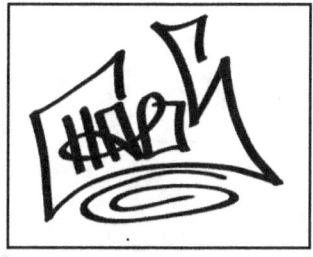

STEP 43

STEP 44

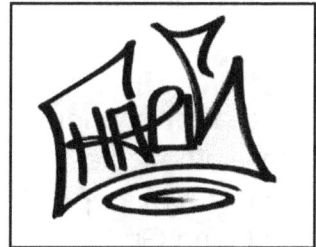

STEP 45

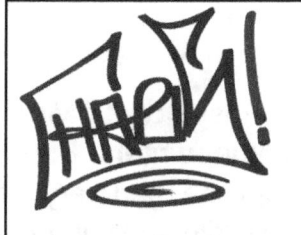

STEP 46

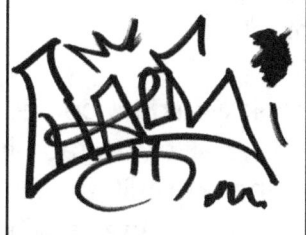

STEP 47

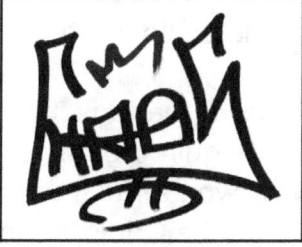

STEP 48

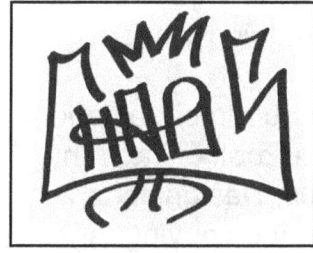

STEP 49

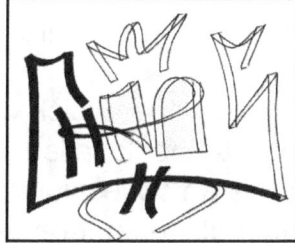

STEP 50

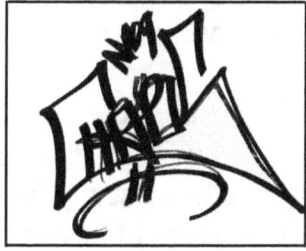

STEP 51

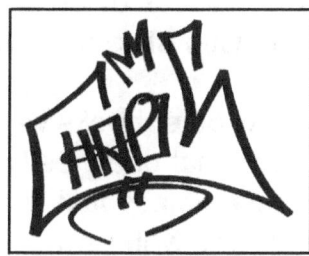

STEP 52

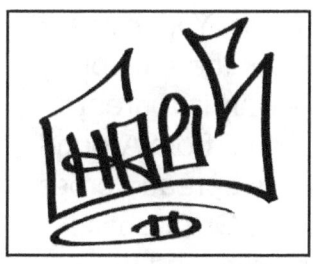

STEP 53

FINISHED TAG

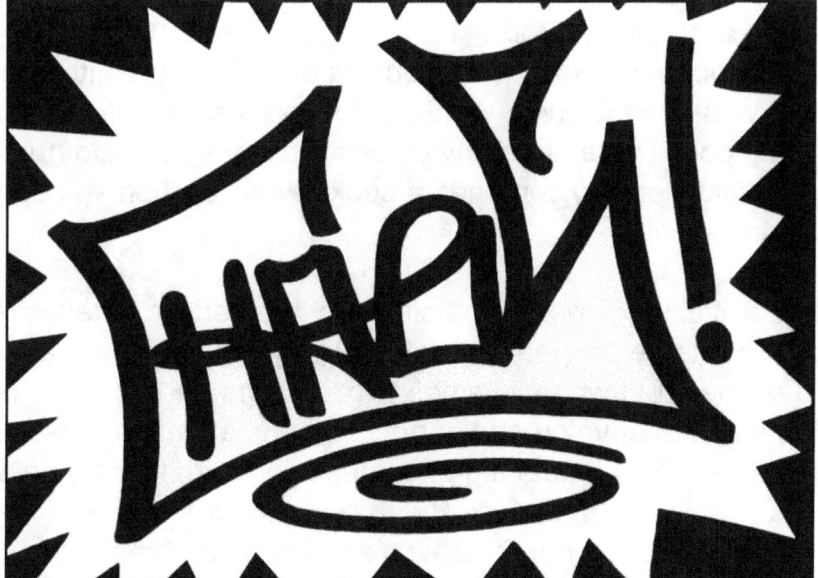

"CHAOS"
FINISHED TAG
This finished tag was scanned
into a computer, shrunk, and
printed on a paper sticker.

CHAPTER TWELVE
CONCLUSION AND BIBLIOGRAPHY

It turns out that writing a book on graffiti tagging and lettering design requires reading lots of other books on graffiti tagging and/or lettering design. We highly recommend you check out the Bibliography for recommended reading to help you with your graffiti tag training. Some of the best books we have read on tagging and lettering design were recommended in the bibliographies of other books.

Most of the tags in this book would be considered East Coast style, because that is where we acquired or photographed all of the tags from other writers. But there are other cities with wonderful traditions where graffiti tagging is approached very differently. An example would be Cholo writing from Los Angeles. The book "Cholo Writing: Latino Gang Graffiti in Los Angeles" by Francois Chastanet & Howard Gribble is a great resource and will provide you with an amazing education on Cholo graffiti. Also there are some excellent tattoo lettering books by artists such as BJ Betts. "Flip The Script" by Christian Acker explains Philly Gangster style and Wickeds/Wickets as well as everything else graffiti tagging related.

A few other books we like are "Tag Town" by Martha Cooper which was our first book about tags. That book really inspired us. And there's this little book called "The Book of Tags" by Hassan Massoudy that is totally amazing. Tagging is an obsession for us. Designing tags, studying writer's tag styles, trying out new tagging tools, photographing and copying tags, learning about tag history and techniques - it's all good. We also love tags in other languages. Arabic tags are fascinating as are Japanese and Chinese kanji tags.

"The Birth of Graffiti" by John Naar is full of atmospheric photographs of New York city and amazing tagging history. The air was a different color in New York City back then. If you were around then you'll know what we mean. "Graffiti Kings" by Jack Stewart is a great educational book about the origins of graffiti. "Graffiti Alphabets: Street Fonts from Around the World" by Claudia Walde gives you a sense of how far this art form has spread across the globe. There are many other excellent books too numerous to mention. Our website "graffitidiplomacy.com" has a book review section you can explore for reviews and more information.

All graffiti tagging has one similar characteristic. It takes discipline and repetition to develop a tag with great handstyle. Many tags have the appearance of having been hastily designed, but when it comes to great tags, the opposite is true. A great tag takes time and patience to develop and perfect. Careful attention must be paid to letter spacing, layout and balance. Over time a tag becomes a logo, an identifying symbol, a brand. Designing a good tag is actually hard work. But it all begins with the basics we have presented to you in this book. Pick a tag name, draw a starting point, then redraw and practice. That's the way you get it done. That's the magic, the secret sauce, the Zen of tagging. This book was made to share our passion for this amazing art form and to teach what we know about designing graffiti tags to anyone who wants to learn. Like we said in the beginning, a well designed graffiti tag is just that special. Yup!

SELECTED BIBLIOGRAPHY

These are some books that we refer to often for assistance. Not all of these books are right for everyone, so please research these titles yourself before investing in any of these books.

Books About Graffiti, Tags, or Tagging

"Cholo Writing: Latino Gang Graffiti in Los Angeles" by Francois Chastanet & Howard Gribble
"Calligraffiti: The Graphic Art of Niels Shoe" by Niels 'Shoe' Meulman & Adam Eeuwens
"Flip The Script" by Christian P. Acker
"Gates Of Graffiti" by Torkel Sjostrand and Malcolm Jacobson
"Getting Up: Subway Graffiti in New York" by Craig Castleman
"GRAFF: The Art & Technique of Graffiti" by Scape Martinez
"Graffiti Alphabets: Street Fonts from Around the World" by Claudia Walde
"Graffiti Kings: New York City Mass Transit Art of the 1970's" by Jack Stewart
"Graff 2: Next Level Graffiti Techniques" by Scape Martinez
"Graffiti School: A Student Guide and Teacher Manual" by Christoph Ganter
"Parallel Strokes" by Ian Lynam
"Piecebook: The Secret Drawings of Graffiti Writers" by Sacha Jenkins & David Villorente
"Subway Art" by Martha Cooper and Henry Chalfant
"Style: Writing from the UnderGround" by IGTimes & Phase 2
"Tag Town: The Evolution of New York Graffiti Writing" by Martha Cooper
"The Birth of Graffiti" by Jon Naar
"The Book Of Tags" by Hassan Massoudy & Barry Mcgee

Lettering Design and Calligraphy (these are not graffiti books)

"BJ Betts Tattoo Custom Lettering Guide No. 1- 4" by BJ Betts
"Calligraphy: Beginner's Guide" by Arthur Newhall
"How to Draw Lettering" by Carol Varley, Fiona Brown & Nigel Reece
"Italic Letters: Calligraphy and Handwriting" by Inga Dubay & Barbara Getty
"Lettering Art in Modern Use" by Raymond A. Ballinger
"Modern Lettering and Layout" by Cecil Wade
"Speedball Textbook for Pen and Brush Lettering" by Ross F. George

Learn To Draw A Graffiti Master-Piece: Your Essential Guide To Tags, Bubble Letters, Wildstyle, Layout And Piecing

#1 BEST SELLER ORDER YOUR COPY TODAY

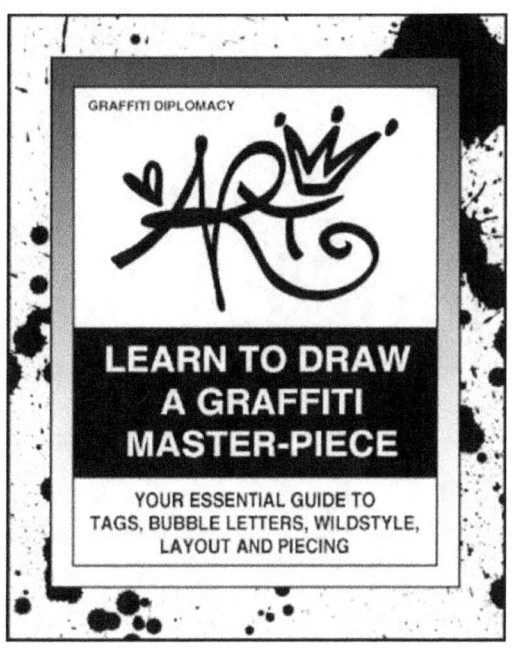

Starting with simple letters, you can learn to create an infinite variety of exciting graffiti word designs with this amazing book. It is jam packed with easy-to-follow, step-by-step, detailed instructions, in both pictures and text that will guide you through the process of creating a successful graffiti masterpiece. You will discover that the process of making graffiti is as satisfying as the end result. This book unlocks the secrets of this amazing art form and encourages creativity, experimentation, and fun.

WHO WE ARE

Graffiti Diplomacy is a Brooklyn based website, art studio and publisher that specializes in graffiti art, multicultural coloring books, how-to-draw books, and graffiti art workshops. We are dedicated to providing beginners and serious graffiti students of any age with graffiti-themed products and instructional materials that are both educational and fun. Now everyone can learn to draw graffiti! Seriously!!!

Find us on the web @ graffitidiplomacy.com